Instructor's Manual
And
Test Bank

to accompany

Global Business Today

Second Edition

Charles W. L. Hill
University of Washington

Instructor's Manual prepared by
Veronica Horton
University of Akron

Test Bank prepared by
Bruce Barringer
University of Central Florida

McGraw-Hill
Irwin

Boston   Burr Ridge, IL   Dubuque, IA   Madison, WI   New York   San Francisco   St. Louis
Bangkok   Bogotá   Caracas   Lisbon   London   Madrid
Mexico City   Milan   New Delhi   Seoul   Singapore   Sydney   Taipei   Toronto

Instructor's Manual and Test Bank to accompany
GLOBAL BUSINESS TODAY

Published by Irwin/McGraw-Hill, an imprint of the McGraw-Hill Companies, Inc.,
1221 Avenue of the Americas, New York, NY 10020.

1 2 3 4 5 6 7 8 9 0 QSR/QSR 0 9 8 7 6 5 4 3 2 1 0

ISBN 0-07-232056-7

www.mhhe.com

TABLE OF CONTENTS

		Instructor's Manual Page	Test Bank Page

INSTRUCTOR'S MANUAL

CHAPTER 1
GLOBALIZATION

<u>Chapter Outline</u>

OPENING CASE: The Emerging Global Telecommunications Industry

INTRODUCTION

WHAT IS GLOBALIZATION?

The Globalization of Markets
The Globalization of Production

DRIVERS OF GLOBALIZATION

Declining Trade and Investment Barriers
The Role of Technological Change
Management Focus: Global Yahoo!

THE CHANGING DEMOGRAPHICS OF THE GLOBAL ECONOMY

The Changing World Output and World Trade Picture
The Changing Foreign Direct Investment Picture
The Changing Nature of the Multinational Enterprise
Country Focus: South Korea's New Multinational
The Changing World Order
The Global Economy of the 21st Century

THE GLOBALIZATION DEBATE: PROSPERITY OR IMPOVERISHMENT?

Globalization, Jobs, and Incomes
Globalization, Labor Policies, and the Environment
Globalization and National Sovereignty

MANAGING IN THE GLOBAL MARKETPLACE

Management Focus: Proctor & Gamble in Japan

CHAPTER SUMMARY

DISCUSSION QUESTIONS

INTERNET EXERCISES

CLOSING CASE: Citigroup - Building A Global Financial Services Giant

1. Understand what is meant by the term globalization.

2. Be familiar with the main causes of globalization.

3. Understand why globalization is now proceeding at a rapid rate.

4. Appreciate how changing international trade patterns, foreign direct investment flows, differences in economic growth rates among countries, and the rise of new multinational corporations are all changing the nature of the world economy.

5. Have a good grasp of the main arguments in the debate over the impact of globalization on job security, income levels, labor and environmental policies, and national sovereignty,

6. Appreciate that globalization is giving rise to numerous opportunities and challenges that business managers must confront.

Chapter Summary

This opening chapter introduces the reader to the concepts of globalization and international trade, and provides an introduction to the major issues that underlie these topics. The components of globalization are discussed, along with the drivers of globalization and the role of the General Agreement on Tariffs and Trade (GATT) in lowering trade barriers. The role of technological change in facilitating globalization is also discussed, along with the role of multinational firms in international business.

The chapter also describes the changing demographics of the global economy, with a special emphasis on the increasingly important role of developing countries in world trade. This discussion is complemented by a description of the changing world order, which was brought on by the collapse of communism in Eastern Europe and republics of the former Soviet Union. The chapter ends with a candid overview of the pros and cons of the trend towards globalization.

OPENING CASE: The Emerging Global Telecommunications Industry

Summary

The opening case describes changes in the global telecommunications industry over the past twenty years. The effects of deregulation, technological change, and globalization are particularly noticeable in this industry. What has taken place in the telecommunications industry is not unlike that in many other industries, although the rate and degree of change is perhaps greater here than in many other industries. Discussion of this case can revolve around the following questions:

QUESTION 1: What have been the major changes in the global telecommunications industry over the past twenty years?

ANSWER 1: The telecommunication industry has changed from being primarily a series of individual domestic telecommunication industries controlled by a single firm in each country, to a much more interconnected international industry. Nations have deregulated and privatized domestic industries, allowing new competitors from both within the country and overseas to compete for local telecom business. New technologies, including wireless and digital communications, have decreased entry barriers and caused prices to fall significantly. Under the auspices of the World Trade Organization, most of the world's largest telecommunications markets are now open to foreign competition. The net effect has been a significant decrease in the cost of placing a call.

QUESTION 2: Why have the costs of placing a domestic or international call fallen in most countries?

ANSWER 2: There are three major reasons for the decrease in telecommunication prices. Firstly, improvement in technology has significantly decreased the costs of providing telecommunications services. Decreased satellite costs, fiber optic technology, digital switching (the computer), and digital transmission have significantly decreased the per call costs for providing the telecommunications infrastructure. Secondly, the huge increase in voice and data traffic has resulted in greater economies of scale for telecommunications providers, which also leads to lower costs. While technology and economies of scale made lower prices possible, competition has been key to lowering prices. As countries deregulated their domestic markets and allowed new domestic and foreign firms to compete for customers, the threat of competition in addition to actual competition has placed a great deal of downward pressure on prices.

Chapter Outline With Lecture Notes and Teaching Tips

INTRODUCTION

A) **Globalization** refers to the trend towards a more integrated global economic system.

Teaching Tip: The trend towards globalization has not gone unnoticed at many premier universities around the world. An organization called the Network of International Business Schools {http://www.bibsnet.org} provides a forum for schools with international business programs to discuss their curriculums. Consider visiting this web site, and providing your students some examples of how colleges and universities are integrating the realities of globalization into their business curriculums.

Lecture Note: The top ten trading partners for the United States, in terms of total exports, are: (1) Canada, (2) Japan, (3) Mexico, (4) China, (5) Germany, (6) United Kingdom, (7) South Korea, (8) Taiwan, (9) Singapore, and (10) France.

B) The rapidly emerging global economy raises a multitude of issues for businesses including all sorts of new opportunities for business to expand their revenues, drive down their costs, and boost their profits. It also gives rise to challenges and threats such as how best to expand into a foreign market, whether and how to customize their product offerings, marketing policies, human resources practices, and business strategies in order to deal with national differences in culture and how best to deal with the threat posed by efficient foreign competitors entering their home market place.

C) The opening case on the telecommunications industry illustrates how globalization is coming to firms that previously operated in a nice, easy, protected national market. It also illustrates the increasing importance of global strategic alliances. Discussion of the case, even if it involves handing out copies in

3

class and giving students a few minutes to read, provides a natural lead-in to the next topic - the globalization of the world economy

WHAT IS GLOBALIZATION?

A) Globalization involves to a shift towards a more integrated and interdependent economy.

The Globalization of Markets

B) The **globalization of markets** refers to the fact that in many industries historically distinct and separate national markets are merging into one huge global marketplace in which the tastes and preferences of consumers in different nations are beginning to converge upon some global norm. The global acceptance of Coca-Cola, Levi's jeans, Sony Walkmans, and McDonald's hamburgers are all examples. Yet there are still significant differences - German's still lead in per capita beer consumption, French in wine consumption, and Italians in pasta eaten, and these differences are unlikely to be eliminated any time soon. Hence often there is still a need for marketing strategies and product features be customized to local conditions.

Teaching Tip: The globalization of markets has provided many opportunities and challenges for business organizations. To gain some additional insight into the types of challenges that global firms confront, visit Danfoss Corporation's {http://www.danfoss.com/get_into/c12chan.htm} web site. At this location, the company highlights some of the challenges involved with globalization in an article entitled "Globalization and Change."

The Globalization of Production

C) The **globalization of production** refers to the tendency among many firms to source goods and services from different locations around the globe in an attempt to take advantage of national differences in the cost and quality of factors of production, thereby allowing them to compete more effectively against their rivals. . The examples of Boeing and Swan Optical illustrate how production is dispersed. While part of the rationale is based on costs and finding the best suppliers in the world, there are also other factors. In Boeing's case, if it wishes to sell airliners to countries like China, these countries often demand that domestic firms be contracted to supply portions of the plane - otherwise they will find another supplier (Airbus) who is willing to support local industry.

Teaching Tip: For more in-depth information and insight about globalization, an Internet site sponsored by Seattle University provides a comprehensive list of sites dedicated to all aspects of globalization. This site {http://www.seattleu.edu/~parker/homepage.html#Business} is well worth a visit.

DRIVERS OF GLOBALIZATION

A) Two macro factors seem to underlie the trend toward greater globalization. The decline in barriers to the free flow of goods and services, and the capital that has occurred since the end of World War II and technological change.

Declining Trade and Investment Barriers

4

B) After WWII, the industrialized countries of the West started a process of removing barriers to the free flow of goods, services, and capital between nations. Under GATT, over 100 nations negotiated even further decreases in tariffs and made significant progress on a number of non-tariff issues (e.g. intellectual property, trade in services). With the establishment of the WTO, a mechanism now exists for dispute resolution and the enforcement of trade laws.

Teaching Tip: A comprehensive overview of GATT is available at {http://itl.irv.uit.no/trade_law/documents/freetrade/wta-94/nav/toc.html}.

Teaching Tip: The World Trade Organization maintains an excellent web site at {http://www.wto.org/}. This site provides information about recent trade disputes and "hot" areas of international trade.

Lecture Note: According to the WTO, the volume of world merchandise trade increased by 4 percent in 1996. A modest increase in world trade is expected in 1997. In value terms, world merchandise exports exceeded the $5,000 billion mark for the first time

C) This removal of barriers to trade has taken place in conjunction with increased **trade** (the export of goods or services to consumers in another country), world output, and foreign direct investment.

D) The **growth of foreign direct investment** (the investing of resources and business activities outside a firm's home country) is a direct result of nations liberalizing their regulations to allow foreign firms to invest in facilities and acquire local companies. With their investments, these foreign firms often also bring expertise and global connections that allow local operations to have a much broader reach than would have been possible for a purely domestic company.

The Role of Technological Change

E) While the lowering of trade barriers made globalization of markets and production a theoretical possibility, technological change made it a tangible reality.

Microprocessors and Telecommunications

F) Since the end of World War II, there have been major advances in communications and information processing.

G) Moore's Law predicts the power of microprocessor technology doubles and its cost of production falls in half every 18 months. As this happens, the cost of global communication plummets, which lowers the cost of coordinating and controlling a global organization.

The Internet and the World Wide Web

H) The Internet and the World Wide Web, which have experienced explosive growth worldwide, promise to develop into the information backbone of tomorrow's global economy.

I) Included in this expanding volume of web based electronic commerce- or – e-commerce as it is commonly called is to facilitate the creation of the global electronic marketplace many of the main online commerce and media companies are already moving into the global arena.

Transportation Technology

J) In addition to these developments, several major innovations in transportation technology have occurred since World War II. In economic terms, the most important are probably development of commercial jet aircraft and super freighters and the introduction of containerization, which greatly simplifies trans-shipment from one mode of transport to another.

Implications for the Globalization of Production

K) Improvements in transportation technology, including jet transport, temperature controlled containerized shipping, and coordinated ship-rail-truck systems have made firms better able to respond to international customer demands

Implications for the Globalization of Markets

L) As a consequence of these trends, a manager in today's firm operates in an environment that offers more opportunities, but is also more complex and competitive than that faced a generation ago. People now work with individuals and companies from many countries, and while communications technology the universality of English as the language of business has decreased the absolute level of cultural difficulties individuals face, the frequency with which they face inter-cultural and international challenges has increased.

THE CHANGING DEMOGRAPHICS OF THE GLOBAL ECONOMY

As late as the 1960's four stylized facts described the facts of the demographics economy. The first was the U.S. dominance in the world economy and the world trade picture. The third fact was the dominance of large, multinational U.S. firms on the international business scene. The fourth was that roughly half of the globe- the centrally planned economies of the communist world, was off limits to Western international business.

The Changing World Output and the Changing World Trade Picture

B) In the early 1960s, the U.S. was still by far the world's dominant industrial power. In 1963, for example, the U.S. accounted for 40.3 percent of world manufacturing output. By 1996 the United States accounted for only 21.9 percent. This decline in the U.S. position was not an absolute decline, since the U.S. economy grew at a relatively robust average annual rate of 2.8 percent in the 1963-1995 period. Rather, it was a relative decline, reflecting the faster economic growth of several other economies, most notably that of Japan.

C) Given the rapid economic growth now being experienced by countries such as China, Thailand, and Indonesia, further relative decline in the U.S. share of world output and world exports seems likely.

D) If we look 20 years into the future, most forecasts now predict a rapid rise in the share of world output accounted for by developing nations such as China, India, Indonesia, Thailand, and South Korea, and a commensurate decline in the share enjoyed by rich industrialized countries such as Britain, Japan, and the United States

The Changing Foreign Investment Picture

E) Rising Importance of Developing Countries - As shown in Figure 1.3 in the textbook, the share of world output generated by developing countries has been on a steady increase since the 1960s, while the **stock** (total cumulative value of foreign investments) generated by rich industrial countries has been on a steady decline. This trend is expected to continue.

F) Similarly as shown in Fig. 1.4, the **flow of foreign direct investment** (amounts invested across national borders each year) has been directed at developing nations especially China.

The Changing Nature of Multinational Enterprise

G) A multinational enterprise is any business that has productive activities in two or more countries.

Non-U.S. Multinationals

H) The globalization of the world economy, together with Japan's rise to the top rank of economic power, has resulted in a relative decline in the dominance of U.S. (and, to a lesser extent, British) firms in the global marketplace. Looking to the future, we can reasonably expect the growth of new multinational enterprises (any business that has productive activities in two or more countries) from the world's developing nations.

The Rise of Mini-Multinationals

I) Another trend in international business has been the growth of medium-sized and small multinationals. These businesses are referred to as mini-multinationals.

The Changing World Order

J) The economic development of China presents huge opportunities and risks, in spite of its continued Communist control.

K) The economic development of China presents huge opportunities and risks, in spite of its continued Communist control.

L) For North American firms, the growth and market reforms in Mexico and Latin America also present tremendous new opportunities both as markets and sources of materials and production

The Global Economy of the 21st Century

M) The path to full economic liberalization and open markets is not without obstruction. Economic crises in Latin America, South East Asia, and Russia all caused difficulties in 1997 and 1998. In response much trade was curtailed, and some countries imposed new controls. Malaysia, for example, suspended foreigners from trading in its equity and currency markets to "prevent destabilizing influences." While firms must be prepared to take advantage of an ever more integrated global economy, they must also prepare for political and economic disruptions that may throw their plans into disarray.

THE GLOBALIZATION DEBATE: PROSPERITY OR IMPOVERISHMENT?

A) Is the shift toward a more integrated and interdependent global economy a good thing? While many economists, politicians and business leaders seem to think so, globalization is not without its critics. Globalization stimulates economic growth, raises the incomes of consumers, and helps to create jobs in all countries that choose to participate in the global economy. Some of this growth, however, creates "sweatshop" jobs, increases pollution, and draws people from the countryside into ever more crowded cities and slums. (On some college campuses there have been student protests that the clothing sold in the bookstore is made in overseas sweatshops. In response, some college bookstores have altered their procurement decisions.)

Globalization, Jobs, and Incomes

B) In developed countries, labor leaders lament the loss of good paying jobs to low wage countries.

Globalization, Labor Policies, and the Environment

C) A second source of concern is that free trade encourages firms from advanced nations to move manufacturing facilities offshore to less developed countries that lack adequate regulations to protect labor and the environment from abuse by the unscrupulous. Supporters of free trade and greater globalization express serious doubts about this scenario. They point out that tougher environmental regulation and stricter labor standards go hand in hand with economic progress. In general, as countries get richer, they enact tougher environmental and labor regulations.

D) Lower labor costs are only one of the reasons why a firm may seek to expand in developing countries. These countries may also have lower standards on environmental controls and workplace safety. Nevertheless, since investment typically leads to higher living standards, there is often pressure to increase safety regulations to international levels. No country wants to be known for its poor record on health and human safety. Thus supporters of globalization argue that foreign investment often helps a country to raise its standards.

Globalization and National Sovereignty

E) A final concern voiced by critics of globalization is that in today's increasingly interdependent global economy, economic power is shifting away from national governments and toward supranational organizations such as the World Trade Organization (WTO), the European Union (EU), and the United Nations. As perceived by critics, the problem is that unelected bureaucrats are now sometimes able to impose policies on the democratically elected governments of nation-states, thereby undermining the sovereignty of those states.

F) With the development of the WTO and other multilateral organizations such as the EU and NAFTA, countries and localities necessarily cede some authority over their actions.

Teaching Tip: There is a fascinating web site dealing with global business ethics at {http://www.globalethics.org/}. One of the ongoing features of the site is a set of "ethical dilemmas" that companies face in conducting business overseas. The current ethical dilemma deals with the ethics of paying "bribes" to get lifesaving medicine into remote areas of Bosnia. The ethical dilemmas are set up as short case studies and end with the question, "What would you do?"

MANAGING THE GLOBAL MARKETPLACE

A) An **international business** is any firm that engages in international trade or investment.

B) As their organizations increasingly engage in cross-border trade and investment, it means managers need to recognize that the task of managing an international business (any firm that engages in international trade or investment) differs from that of managing a purely domestic business in many ways. Countries differ in their cultures, political systems, economic systems, legal systems, and levels of economic development.

C) These differences require that business people vary their practices country by country, recognizing what changes are required to operate effectively. It is necessary to strike a balance between adaptation and maintaining global consistency, however.

D) As a result of making local adaptations, the complexity of international business is clearly greater than that of a purely domestic firm. Firms need to decide which countries to enter, what mode of entry to use, and which countries to avoid. Rules and regulations also differ, as do currencies and languages.

E) Managing an international business is different from managing a purely domestic business for at least four reasons: 1) countries differ, 2) the range of problems and manager faces is greater and more complex, 3) an international business must find ways to work within the limits imposed by governmental intervention and the global trading system, and 4) international transactions require converting funds and being susceptible to exchange rate changes.

Critical Thinking And Discussion Questions

1. Describe the shifts in the world economy over the last 30 years. What are the implications of these shifts for international business in
- Britain?
- North America?
- Hong Kong?

Answer: The world economy has shifted dramatically over the past 30 years. As late as the 1960s four stylized facts described the demographics of the global economy. The first was U.S. dominance in the world economy and world trade. The second was U.S. dominance in the world foreign direct investment picture. Related to this, the third fact was the dominance of large, multinational U.S. firms in the international business scene. The fourth was that roughly half of the globe - the centrally planned economies of the Communist world - was off-limits to Western international businesses.

All of these demographic facts have changed. Although the U.S. remains the world's dominant economic power, it's share of world output and world exports have declined significantly since the 1960s. This trend does not reflect trouble in the U.S. economy, but rather reflects the growing industrialization of developing countries such as China, India, Indonesia, and South Korea. This trend is also reflected in the world foreign direct investment picture. As depicted in Figure 1.3 in the textbook, the share of world output (or the stock of foreign direct investment) generated by developing countries has been on a steady increase since the 1960s, while the share of world output generated by rich industrial countries has been on a steady decline.

Shifts in the world economy can also be seen through the shifting power of multinational enterprises. Since the 1960s, there have been two notable trends in the demographics of the multinational enterprise. The first has been the rise of non-U.S. multinationals, particularly Japanese multinationals. The second has been the emergence of a growing number of small and medium-sized multinationals, called mini-multinationals. The fall of Communism in Eastern Europe and the republics of the former Soviet Union have brought about the final shift in the world economy. Many of the former Communist nations of Europe and Asia seem to share a commitment to democratic politics and free market economies. Similar developments are being observed in Latin America. If these trends continue, the opportunities for international business may be enormous. The implications of these shifts are similar for North America and Britain. The United States and Britain once had the luxury of being the dominant players in the world arena, with little substantive competition from the developing nations of the world. That has changed. Today, U.S. and British manufacturers must compete with competitors from across the world to win orders. The changing demographics of the world economy favor a city like Hong Kong. Hong Kong (which is now under Chinese rule) is well located with easy access to markets in Japan, South Korea, Indonesia, and other Asian markets. Hong Kong has a vibrant labor force that can compete on par with the industrialized nations of the world. The decline in the influence of the U.S. and Britain on the global economy provides opportunities for companies in Hong Kong to aggressively pursue export markets.

2. "The study of international business is fine if you are going to work in a large multinational enterprise, but it has no relevance for individuals who are going to work in smaller firms." Critically evaluate this statement.

Answer: Persons who believe in this view, and the firms that they work for, may find that they do not achieve their full potential (at best) and may ultimately fail because of their myopia. As barriers to trade decrease and state of the art technological developments take place throughout the world, new opportunities and threats exist on a worldwide basis. The rise of the mini-multinationals suggests there are global opportunities for even small firms. But staying attuned to international markets isn't only important from the perspective of seeking profitable opportunities for small firms; it can also be critical for long-term competitive survival. Firms from other countries may be developing products that, if sold internationally, may wipe out small domestic competitors. Scanning international markets for the best suppliers is also important for small firms, for if a domestic competitor is able to tap into a superior supplier from a foreign country, it may be able to seriously erode a small firm's competitive position before the small firm understands the source of its competitor's competitive advantage and can take appropriate counter actions.

3. How have changes in technology contributed to the globalization of markets and of production? Would the globalization of production and markets have been possible without these technological changes?

Answer: Changes in technology have contributed to the globalization of markets and of production in a very substantive manner. For instance, improvements in transportation technology have paved the way for companies like Coca-Cola, Levi Strauss, Sony and McDonalds to make their products available worldwide. Similarly, improvements in communications technology have had a major impact. The ability to negotiate across continents has been facilitated by improved communications technology, and the rapidly decreasing cost of communications has lowered the expense of coordinating and controlling a global corporation. Finally, the impact of information technology has been far reaching. Companies can now gain worldwide exposure simply by setting up a front-page on the World Wide Web. This technology was not available just a few short years ago. The globalization of production and markets may have been possible without improvements in technology, but the pace of globalization would have been much slower. The falling cost of technology has made it affordable for many developing nations, which has been instrumental in helping these nations improve their share of world output and world exports. The inclusion of these nations, such as China, India, Thailand, and South Korea, has been instrumental in the globalization of markets and production. In addition, improvements in global transportation and communication have made it relatively easy for business executives from different countries to converse with one another. If these forms of technology, such as air-travel, fax capability, e-mail, and overnight delivery of packages were not available, it would be much more difficult for businesses to conduct international trade.

4. How might the Internet and the associated World Wide Web impact international business activity and the globalization of the world economy?

Answer: According to the text, the Internet and World Wide Web (WWW) promise to develop into the information background of tomorrow's global economy. By the year 2000, it is likely that not only will voice, data, and real time video communication such as videoconferencing will be transmitted through the WWW, but also a vast array of commercial transactions. This improved technology will not only make it easier for individuals and companies in different countries to conduct business with one another, but will also further decrease the cost of communications. These improvements will undoubtedly hasten the already rapid pace of globalization.

Another distinct attribute of the Internet and the WWW is that they act as an equalizer between large (resource rich) and small (resource poor) firms. For instance, it does not cost any more for a small software firm to gain visibility via the WWW than it does for a large software company like Microsoft. As a result, the WWW helps small companies reach the size of audience that was previously only within the reach of large, resource rich firms.

5. If current trends continue, China may emerge as the world's largest economy by 2020. Discuss the possible implications of such a development for:
• The world trading system.
• The world monetary system.
• The business strategy of today's European and U.S. based global corporations.

Answer: The world trading system would clearly be affected by such a development. Currently China enjoys a somewhat privileged status within the World Trade Organization as a "developing" country. Such a rise to eminence, however, would clearly force it to become a full and equal member, with all the rights and responsibilities. China would also be in a position to actively affect the terms of trade between many countries. On the monetary front, one would expect that China would have to have fully convertible and trading currency, and it could become one of the "benchmark" currencies of the world. From the perspective of Western global firms, China would represent both a huge market, and potentially the home base of some very capable competitors.

6. "Ultimately, the study of international business is no different from the study of domestic business. Thus, there is no point in having a separate course on international business." Evaluate this statement.

Answer: This statement reflects a poor understanding of the unique challenges involved in international business. Managing an international business is different from managing a purely domestic business for at least four reasons. These are: (1) countries are different; (2) the range of problems confronted by a manager in an international business is wider and the problems themselves more complex than those confronted by a manager in a domestic business; (3) an international business must find ways to work within the limits imposed by government intervention in the international trade and investment system; and (4) international transactions involve converting money into different currencies.

As a result of these differences, there are ample reasons for studying international business as a specific field of study or discipline.

Internet Exercises

TEXT EXERCISE 1

Overview

This exercise raises the issue of whether the Internet and e-commerce are drivers of globalization. The exercise is aimed at getting students to consider the impact e-commerce is having on the global marketplace.

Suggested Use in the Classroom

Students are asked to make several online "purchases" and while doing so, note where they found the products, how long it took to buy them, and what information the sellers requested. Students are then asked to compare their online shopping experience to a more traditional shopping expedition. Most students will quickly identify that their online shopping process could be completed in a fairly short amount of time, that price comparisons were easier, and that their choices were greater. Consequently, students will probably recognize the increased competition that the Internet has brought to both the consumer products industry as well as the industrial products industry. Moreover, students should identify that the competition is global in nature, and that the Internet has the potential to bring markets even closer.

TEXT EXERCISE 2

Overview

This exercise considers the key issues raised at a recent international trade conference. As might be expected, a focal point in the conference was foreign expansion. The exercise is designed to explore how companies can take advantage of the Internet both as a marketing tool and also as a source of information to facilitate their international strategies.

Suggested Use in the Classroom

Issues such as the quality of the information, its timeliness, and its credibility will probably be identified as positive aspects of conducting online searches versus more traditional information seeking efforts. Many students will also note the numerous government-sponsored sites that have also facilitated both the marketing process and the information seeking process. Some students may also suggest that because governments have easy access to company information, they are in a more powerful bargaining position when it comes to foreign investments and incentives, while other students may feel the power lies in the hands of the companies because they know the governments' hand prior to making investments.

WEB EXERCISE 1

Overview

This exercise extends the second text Internet exercise and further explores the topics raised at an international trade conference. The exercise is designed to introduce students to the notion and process of "going international" and how companies can initiate their international strategies.

Suggested Use in the Classroom

This exercise asks students to consider the role of the small firm, and the process of entering foreign markets. Students are asked to develop a strategic plan indicating how they would begin the export process. Most students will probably be able to outline a fairly detailed plan thanks to the wealth of information available on the Internet. Students should recognize that their task has been greatly simplified when compared to pre-Internet days.

WEB EXERCISE 2

Overview

This exercise attempts to clarify the various terms that are currently in use in the press, among academics, and within the business world to describe the commerce activities that are taking place via the Internet. The exercise is aimed at developing pedagogy to describe e-commerce, online retailing, and so forth.

Suggested Use in the Classroom

Many of the terms that have been used to refer to the business activities currently taking place electronically are probably familiar to most students. However, the question of whether they all refer to the same idea will probably spark some debate. Similarly, the question of where global e-commerce will be in the future should result in varying opinions. Most students will probably agree that cross-border e-commerce will grow dramatically, but they may differ as to whether the growth will come mainly in business-to-business areas or business-to-consumer markets, whether there will be increased regulation or not, and whether security issues will continue to be of concern.

CLOSING CASE: Citigroup – Building a Global Financial Services Giant

Summary

The closing case describes the economic rationale behind the merger of Citicorp and Travelers. The opening of trade in financial services, the complementary capabilities of the firms, the ability to leverage capabilities internationally, and to "source" services from efficient locations worldwide all play a role in understanding the acquisition. Discussion of this case can revolve around the following questions:

QUESTION 1: What is the rationale for the merger between Travelers and Citicorp? How will this merger create value for (a) the stockholders of Citigroup and (b) the customers of Citigroup's global retail bank?

ANSWER 1: The rationale behind the merger is that the two firms have complementary assets. Citicorp has an international presence in the banking industry, and a recognized brand name. Travelers has a wide range of insurance and other financial products, but little international presence. By combining, Travelers has a much broader distribution channel for its services, and Citicorp can offer a much wider range of services to its clients. The stockholders of Citigroup should receive superior value, as the complementary assets of the merged firm should allow them to earn higher returns than would have been possible in either of the original firms individually. The customers of Citigroup's global retail bank now have a much broader range of products they can purchase at their Citigroup branch.

QUESTION 2: In 1997 the World Trade Organization brokered an agreement to liberalize cross-border trade and investment in global financial services. What will be the impact of this deal on competition in national markets? What would you expect to see occur?

ANSWER 2: Competition in national markets should increase, as competitors from other national markets can now enter each other's markets. This should lead to downward pressure on prices, and new options available to consumers. It will also likely lead to international mergers and acquisitions, as in the case of Travelers, it can be more efficient to "purchase" access to an existing distribution system in a country than to attempt to enter and build brand recognition and branch facilities.

QUESTION 3: Does the 1997 WTO agreement represent an opportunity for Citigroup or a threat?

ANSWER 3: The 1997 WTO agreement represents both an opportunity and a threat for Citigroup. By allowing Citigroup to sell insurance and other financial services in countries where it was previously prohibited, it clearly creates new market opportunities. The agreement also opens the door for financial services firms that had previously operated in only one country to expand internationally. Thus, Citigroup may face new competition in its international banking sector.

QUESTION 4: How is Citigroup trying to build a global retail brand in financial services? What assumptions is this strategy based on? Do you think the assumptions and strategy make sense?

ANSWER 4: Via expansion, standardization of product offerings, and advertising, Citigroup is trying to build a global retail brand in financial services. A basic assumption is that the financial services needs of individuals are similar world wide, and that most middle class individuals follow a fairly predictable lifecycle of financial services products. The basic Citigroup branch office and product offerings can be essentially standardized across many countries, with only minor differences to respond to local needs. This is not unlike McDonald's strategy, where the basic menu and infrastructure are similar world wide, although some adaptations are a made for local preferences. These assumptions are not unreasonable.

Management Focus: Global Yahoo!

Summary

This feature describes the process by which two graduate engineering students, Jerry Yang and David Filo developed the popular web directory known as Yahoo. Today, Yahoo remains one of the most visited sites on the Internet and can be accessed in 16 languages, thus making it a popular gateway to the web for users from around the globe. Yang and Filo, of course, are now billionaires.

Suggested Discussion Questions

1. Yahoo, although an American company, is considered a global company, and a global brand. Indeed, the company felt that establishing a presence in foreign markets was a necessary part of its strategy to become one of the most useful and well-known sites on the web. Discuss the process by which Yahoo was able to extend its reach to foreign markets. Did the fact that it was an Internet service provider rather than a traditional bricks and mortar enterprise facilitate the process?
2. Yahoo is currently available in some 16 languages. In your opinion, should Yahoo continue to develop additional language options? If so, why?
3. Yahoo's Homepage: {http://www.yahoo.com}.

Country Focus: South Korea's New Multinationals

Summary

This feature discusses the historical and present status of South Korean chaebols. A chaebol is a diversified business group. Historically, South Korea's chaebols took advantage of low labor costs to export a wide range of goods to industrialized countries. In recent years, however, the costs of both land and labor in South Korea have risen sharply, nullifying important sources of the chaebols' competitive advantage in the global economy. The chaebols have responded to rising costs at home by expanding overseas, establishing factories in countries where direct labor costs are lower and employee productivity is higher than in South Korea.

Suggested Discussion Questions

1. The South Korean chaebols have responded to rising costs at home by expanding overseas into countries where direct labor costs are lower and employee productivity is higher than in South Korea. In your opinion is this a good strategy? Why or why not?
2. Speculate on how globalization has affected the competitiveness of South Korean chaebols? What should the chaebols do to take advantage of the trend towards globalization?
3. Examples of South Korean chaebols: Samsung Homepage: {http://www.samsung.com/}; Hyundai Homepage: {http://www.hmc.co.kr/}.

Management Focus: Procter & Gamble in Japan

Summary

This feature depicts Procter & Gamble's (P&G) experiences in the Japanese market. P&G entered Japan in 1972, and had some early successes. For example, P&G introduced disposable diapers in Japan, and at one point commanded an 80 percent share of the market. P&G's success in Japan soon waned, however, largely as a result of the company's failure to customize its products to suite the tastes of Japanese consumers. Today, P&G is attempting to correct that problem and has started to appoint local nations to key management positions in its Japanese subsidiaries.

Suggested Discussion Questions

1. When is it appropriate to "standardize" products and when is it appropriate to "customize" products when selling in a foreign market? Earlier, Citibank's efforts to establish a global bank by "standardizing" its products and services worldwide were discussed. Why wouldn't this approach work for P&G in Japan, and other parts of the world?

2. What lessons can be learned from P&G's experiences in Japan? If you were a manager for P&G and you were entering the South Korean market for the first time, briefly explain how you would approach that market.

3. Think of examples of foreign companies that sell products in the United States. Do any of these companies adapt their products or services to better suit the tastes of American consumers? How do the adaptations fit into the overall strategies of these companies?

4. Procter & Gamble Homepage: {http://www.pg.com/}.

Additional Readings and Sources of Information

Uber Bank: {http://businessweek.com/2000/00_12/b3673017.htm}

The Global 1000: {http://www.bwarchive.businessweek.com/search.cgi?id=160192215x78&m=}

Globalization & Human Rights: {http://www.pbs.org/globalization/home.html}

Globalization: Focus on the International Monetary Fund & the World Bank: {http://www.ifg.org}

Trade and Globalization: {http://epinet.org/subjectpages/trade.html}

Attractiveness
Ethical Issues

CHAPTER SUMMARY

DISCUSSION QUESTIONS

INTERNET EXERCISES

CLOSING CASE: General Electric in Hungary

Learning Objectives

1. Understand how the political systems of countries differ.

2. Understand how the economic systems of countries differ.

3. Understand how the legal systems of countries differ.

4. Understand how political, economic, and legal systems collectively influence a country's ability to achieve meaningful economic progress.

5. Be familiar with the main changes that are currently reshaping the political, economic, and legal systems of many nation-states.

6. Appreciate how a country's political, economic, and legal systems influence the benefits, costs, and risks associated with doing business in that country.

7. Be conversant with the ethical issues that can arise when doing business in a nation in which the political and legal systems do not support basic human rights.

Chapter Summary

This chapter focuses on how political, economic, and legal systems collectively influence a country's ability to achieve meaningful economic progress. The first half of the chapter focuses on the different political, economic, and legal systems that are influential in the world. It is made clear to the reader that these differences are significant, and must be clearly understood by the managers of international firms. The section that focuses on legal systems includes a discussion of intellectual property, including patents, copyrights, and trademarks. Protecting intellectual property is a particularly problematic issue in international trade. The second half of the chapter focuses on the determinants of economic development. The author makes the point that a country's political, economic, and legal systems have a direct impact on it's economic potential. The importance of innovation, along with the types of systems that facilitate innovation, is discussed. Next, the author discusses the parts of the world that are transition from one political-economic ideology to another. Finally, the chapter ends with a brief discussion of ethical issues.

OPENING CASE: Brazilian Privatization

Summary

The opening case describes changes in Brazil's state ownership of business enterprises in the past decade. Along with many other Latin American governments, Brazil nationalized many industries during the 1960s so that firms could be "run for the benefit of the state and its citizens, rather than the enrichment of a small capitalist elite." The result, however, was the development of bloated enterprises run for the benefit of a bureaucratic elite. Most lost money, were not competitive internationally, and produced substandard products. In the 1990s, Brazil privatized many of these enterprises. Necessary next steps were large layoffs and the scaling back of operations. After the inevitable shakeout, many of these enterprises are returning to profitability, and attracting considerable foreign investment. A discussion of the case can revolve around the following questions:

QUESTION 1: What was the rationale for nationalizing enterprises?

ANSWER 1: Nationalization of industries was done to ensure that business enterprises were run for the benefit of the entire country. It was felt that capitalists (the elite in a country, or sometimes foreigners) were more interested in their own wealth than the development of a country. By having industries run by the state, products could be made that were needed by consumers, and any profits could be reinvested in the business for the good of consumers, workers, and the country as a whole.

QUESTION 2: Why did nationalized firms seem to perform so poorly?

ANSWER 2: Without a profit motive, many nationalized firms did not perform efficiently. The bureaucrats running the firms were often compensated based on the level of employment, and sought to create bigger (rather than better) enterprises. In addition to nationalization, countries often also enacted trade barriers to prevent foreign competition from undercutting the firms. Thus, these firms were also not challenged by competition, leading to the production of inferior products at high prices. Nationalization reduced incentives to improve production, and provide high quality goods to consumers.

QUESTION 3: What have been the primary benefits of privatization in Brazil?

ANSWER 3: The first benefit of privatization was that it forced many firms to consider economic efficiency in decision-making. In order to operate profitably, they had to fire excess employees and focus production on only those products that could be produced profitably. In the process of privatization, many foreign firms were attracted to invest in the former state-owned enterprises. This investment has helped these firms invest in more efficient equipment. The privatization has also encouraged other foreign firms to invest in new subsidiaries in these industries in Brazil. Thus, privatization has also spurred significant foreign direct investment.

Chapter Outline With Lecture Notes and Teaching Tips

INTRODUCTION

A) Different countries have different political systems, economic systems, and legal systems. Cultural practices can vary dramatically from country to country, as can the education and skill level of the population. All of these differences have major implications for the practice of international business.

B) This chapter explores how the political, economic, and legal systems of countries differ. Together these systems are known as the political economy of a country.

C) The opening case on privatization in Brazil shows how changing political views on the ownership of business enterprises can have dramatic effects on economic efficiency and foreign investment

POLITICAL SYSTEMS

A) By **political system** we mean the system of government in a nation. Political systems can be assessed according to two related dimensions. The first is the degree to which they emphasize collectivism as opposed to individualism. The second dimension is the degree to which they are democratic or totalitarian.

Collectivism and Individualism

Collectivism

A) Collectivism refers to a system that stresses the primacy of collective goals over individual goals. The modern day roots of collectivism can be traced to Marx, yet the foundations can be found in Plato's *Republic*. The general premise of collectivism is that the state must manage enterprises if they are to benefit society as a whole rather than individual capitalists. **Communists** generally believed that this could only be achieved though revolution and totalitarian dictatorship, while **social democrats** worked to achieve the same goals by democratic means.

B) While state owned firms might have been intended to promote the public interest, experience suggests that this isn't always the case. In many countries the performance of state owned companies has been poor. Protected from significant competition by their monopoly position, and guaranteed governmental financial assistance, many state owned enterprises have become increasingly inefficient. Thus both in former communist and Western European countries previously state owned enterprises are being privatized.

Individualism

D) **Individualism refers** to a political philosophy that an individual should have freedom over his or her economic and political pursuits. In contrast to collectivism, individualism stresses that the interests of the individual should take precedence over the interests of the state.

E) Individualism, while advocated by Aristotle, in modern days was encouraged by David Hume, Adam Smith, John Stuart Mill, and most recently, Hayek and Milton Friedman. Individualism focuses on i) guaranteeing individual freedom and self-expression, and ii) letting people pursue their own self-interest in order to achieve the best overall good for society. The US Declaration of Independence and the Bill of Rights embody the spirit of individualism.

F) While collectivism asserts the primacy of the collective over the individual, individualism asserts the opposite. This ideological difference shapes much of recent history and the Cold War.

Democracy and Totalitarianism

G) **Democracy** and **totalitarianism** are at different ends of a political dimension. Democracy refers to a political system in which government is by the people, exercised either directly or through elected representatives. Totalitarianism is a form of government in which one person or political party exercises absolute control over all spheres of human life, and opposing political parties are prohibited. There are four major forms of totalitarianism in the world today.

Democracy

H) Democracy in its pure state, with each individual voting on every issue, has generally been replaced by representative democracy, where elected representatives vote on behalf of constituents.

Totalitarianism

I) Under totalitarianism, a single political party, individual, or group of individuals monopolize the political power and do not permit opposition. There are four major forms of totalitarianism: **communist totalitarianism,** (form of totalitarianism that advocates achieving socialism through totalitarian dictatorship), **theocratic totalitarianism,** (form of totalitarianism in which political power is monopolized by a party, group, or individual that governs according to religious principles), **tribal totalitarianism** (form of totalitarianism found mainly in Africa in which a political party that represents the interests of a particular tribe monopolizes power), **right wing totalitarianism** (form of totalitarianism in which individual economic freedom is allowed but individual political freedom is restricted in the belief that it could lead to communism). There has been a general trend away from communist and right wing totalitarianism and towards democracy in the 1980s and 1990s. Issues relating to theocratic and tribal totalitarianism are presently at the root of some unrest in Asia and Africa.

J) The political environment of a country matters because 1) when economic freedoms are restricted, so may be the ability of an international business to operate in the most efficient manner, and 2) when political freedoms are restricted there are both ethical and risks concerns that have to be considered

ECONOMIC SYSTEMS

Economic Systems

A) There are four broad types of economic systems: market, command, mixed, and state-directed. In reality almost all are mixed to some extent, for even the most market oriented have some governmental controls on business and even the most command based either explicitly allow some free markets to exist or have black markets for some goods and services. Yet all countries can be considered to be at some point on a continuum between pure market and pure command.

Market Economy

B) In a pure **market economy** the goods and services that a country produces, and the quantity in which they are produced, is not planned by anyone. Rather price and quantity are determined by supply and demand. For a market economy to work, there must be no restrictions on either supply or demand - no monopolistic sellers or buyers.

Command Economy

C) In a pure **command economy** the goods and services that a country produces, the quantity in which they are produced, and the price at which they are sold are all planned by the government. Resources are allocated "for the good of society". The government owns most, if not all, businesses.

Mixed Economy

D) A **mixed economy** includes some elements of each. In Canada, for example, while most business is privately owned and operated under market principles, health care, electrical power, and liquor distribution are run by state owned enterprises in most provinces. Over the past few decades France has chosen to inefficiently operate many business enterprises "for the good of workers and the country," and complains vigorously to the EU when more efficient private firms from other EU countries seek to encroach on the markets these enterprises poorly serve.

State Directed Economy

E) In a **state-directed economy**, the government plays a significant role in directing the investment activities of private enterprises through "industrial policy." Both Japan and South Korea are often cited as examples of state-directed economies. In both situations the government has played a significant role in directing investment. This direction has helped in the creation of some leading international firms. For a state-directed economy to work well, state bureaucrats must make better decisions on the allocation of resources than capital markets. While state bureaucrats may be able to take a longer-term perspective than capital markets, they may also prove to be intransigent and resistant to making necessary changes. The difficulties many South East Asian countries faced in 1997-98 highlight some of the limitations of a state-directed economy. Resisting whims of the market has both its good and bad points.

LEGAL SYSTEMS

A) The **legal system** of a country refers to the rules, or laws, that regulate behavior, along with the processes by which the laws of a country are enforced and through which redress for grievances is obtained.

B) The legal environment of a country is of immense importance to international business because a country's laws regulate business practice, define the manner in which business transactions are to be executed, and set down the rights and obligations of those involved in business transactions. Differences in the structure of law can have an important impact upon the attractiveness of a country as an investment site and/or market.

Teaching Tip: The Seamless Website is the name of a site that contains a broad base of information about international law and the legal systems of the countries of the world. This site is available at {http://msm.byu.edu/c&i/cim/ibd/Dir.htm}.

Property Rights

C) Control over property rights (the bundle of legal rights over the use to which a resource is put and over the use made of any income that may be derived from that source) are very important for the functioning of business. Property rights can be violated by either private action (theft, piracy, blackmail, Mafia) or public action (governmental bribery and corruption, nationalization).

The Protection of Intellectual property

D) **Intellectual property** refers to property, such as computer software, a screenplay, or the chemical formula for a new drug that is the product of intellectual activity. Intellectual Property rights include **patents** (documents giving the inventor of a new product or process exclusive rights to the manufacture, use, or sale of that invention); **copyrights** (exclusive legal rights of authors, composers, playwrights, artists, and publishers to publish and dispose of their work as they see fit); and **trademarks** (designs and names, often officially registered, by which merchants or manufacturers designate and differentiate their products).

E) The protection of intellectual property rights differs greatly from country to country. While many countries have stringent intellectual property regulations on their books, the enforcement of these regulations has often been lax. In addition to lobbying their governments, firms may want to stay out of countries where intellectual property laws are lax rather than risk having their ideas stolen by local entrepreneurs (such reasons partly underlay decisions by Coca-Cola and IBM to pull out of India in the early 1970s).

Lecture Note: In 1947, Intellectual Property comprised just fewer than 10% of all U.S. exports. In 1986, the last year the government compiled statistics in this area, the figure had grown to more than 37% (U.S. Dept. of Commerce). Today, some estimates place the figure at over 50% of all exports.

Teaching Tip: A summary of U.S. Trademark law, which may be interesting to your students, can be found at {http://www.law.cornell.edu/topics/trademark.html}.

F) An International agreement signed by 96 countries to protect intellectual property rights is known as the **Paris Convention for the Protection of Industrial Property.**

Teaching Tip: An excellent article on the protection of intellectual property is available on the Internet at {http://www.journal.law.ufl.edu/~techlaw/1/gikkas.html}. This site contains a copy of an article entitled "International Licensing of Intellectual Property: The Promise and the Peril." The article, written by Nicholas S. Gikkas and published in the Journal of Technology Law and Policy (Vol. 6, 1996), examines the history, rationale, benefits, and dangers of international trademark licensing with consideration given to the hazards involved.

Product Safety and Product Liability

G) Different countries have different product safety and liability laws (safety standards to which a product must adhere). In some cases US businesses must customize products to adhere to local standards if they are to do business in a country, whether these standards are higher or just different.

H) When product standards are lower in other countries, firms face an important ethical dilemma. Should they produce products only of the highest standards even if this puts them at a competitive disadvantage relative other producers and results in not maximizing value to shareholders? Or should they produce products that respond to local differences, even if that means that consumers may not be assured of the same levels of safety in different countries?

Contract Law

I) Differences in contract law (the body of law that governs contract enforcement) force firms to use different approaches when negotiating contracts. In countries with common law traditions (legal systems based on tradition, precedent and custom), contracts tend to be much more detail oriented and need to specify what will happen under a variety of contingencies. Under civil law systems (legal systems based on a detailed set of laws, organized into codes), contracts tend to be much shorter and less specific since many of the issues relating to contracts are covered in the civil code of the country.

THE DETERMINANTS OF ECONOMIC DEVELOPMENT

A) One reason for looking at the different political, economic, and legal systems in the world is that collectively these different systems can have a profound impact on the level of a country's economic development, and hence on the attractiveness of a country as a possible market and/or production location for a firm.

Differences in Economic Development

B) Different countries have dramatically different levels of economic development.

C) The **Human Development Index** (a United Nations developed index based on life expectancy, literacy rates, and whether average incomes are sufficient to meet the basic needs of life in a country) was developed to gauge a country's economic development and likely future growth rate.

Political Economy and Economic Progress

D) What is the relationship between political economy and economic progress? This question has been the subject of a vigorous debate among academics and policy makers for some time.

Innovation Is the Engine of Growth

E) Innovation is the process through which people create new products, new processes, new organizations, new management practices, and new strategies. There is broad agreement that innovation is the engine of long-run economic growth.

Innovation Requires a Market Economy

F) It has also been argued that the economic freedom associated with a market economy creates greater incentives for innovation than either a planned or mixed economy.

Innovation Requires Strong Property Rights

G) Strong legal protection of property rights is another requirement for a business environment conducive to innovation and economic growth.

The Required Political System

H) In the West, it is often argued that democracy is good for economic growth. However, there are examples of totalitarian regimes that have fostered a market economy and strong property rights protection and experienced rapid economic growth. However, given all the facts, it seems likely that democratic regimes are far more conducive to long-term economic growth than a dictatorship, even one of the benevolent kind.

Economic Progress Begets Democracy

I) While it is possible to argue that democracy is not a necessary precondition for the establishment of a free market economy in which property rights are protected, it seems evident that subsequent economic growth leads to establishment of democratic regimes.

J) Geography can also affect economic development. A landlocked country with an inhospitable climate, poor soil, few natural resources, and terrible diseases is unlikely to develop economically as fast as country with the opposite characteristics on each of these attributes.

K) While it can be hard to do much about unfavorable geography, education is something that governments can affect. Numerous studies suggest that countries that invest more in the education of their young people develop faster economically.

STATES IN TRANSITION

The Spread of Democracy

A) Since the late 1980s there have been two major changes in the political economy of many of the world's nations. First, a wave of democratic revolutions swept the world, and many of the previous totalitarian regimes collapsed. Secondly, there has been a more away from centrally planned and mixed economies towards free markets.

Universal Civilization or a Clash in Civilizations

B) The revolutions in the USSR and Eastern Europe have (in general) moved these countries towards democracy (away from totalitarianism), towards individualism (away from collectivism), and towards mixed economies (away from command). The transitions have been difficult, however, and economic progress has not been easy. Recent elections have brought "reformed" communists back into power in some countries, and the economic problems facing the people are significant.

The Spread of Market-Based Systems

C) There are three main reasons for the spread of democracy. First, many totalitarian regimes failed to deliver economic progress to the vast bulk of their populations. Secondly, improved information technology limited the ability of the government to control citizens' access to information. Thirdly, increases in wealth and the standard of living have encouraged citizens to push for democratic reforms.

D) In Western Europe there has been a general trend towards privatization of state owned companies and deregulation of industry.

E) During the 1980s and early 1990s significant changes were also occurring in Asia. A shift toward greater political democracy occurred in the Philippines, Thailand, Taiwan, and South Korea. Latin America, too, shifted toward greater democracy and a greater commitment to free market economies during the late 1980s and early 1990s. The largest shift occurred in 1989 when Mexico, then run by the civilian government of President Salinas, moved toward a more free market economy. Similarly Africa is also moving toward more democratic modes of government and free market economies.

Teaching Tip: A number of countries and regions maintain an international "Chamber of Commerce" to disseminate current information about their respective country or regional of the world. These Chambers of Commerce are an excellent "first stop" when conducting research on the market potential of a particular country or area. An index of the Chambers of Commerce available on the Internet can be accessed at {http://www.serraintl.com//morelink2.html#cofc}.

Teaching Tip: The U.S. State Department produces a series of annual "Country Reports" to acquaint American businesses with other countries. Each report contains nine sections: (1) Key Economic Indicators; (2) General Policy Framework; (3) Exchange Rate Policies; (4) Structural Policies; (5) Debt Management Practices; (6) Significant Barriers to US Exports and Investments; (7) Export Subsidies Policies; (8) Protection of US Intellectual Property; and (9) Worker Rights. Information about obtaining these reports is available through the United States Stated Dept. at {http://www.state.gov/www/issues/economic/trade_reports/96_toc.html}.

The Nature of Economic Transformation

E) The shift toward a market-based economic system typically involves at least three distinct activities: deregulation, privatization, and legal enforcement of property rights.

Deregulation

F) **Deregulation** involves removing restrictions on the free operation of markets.

Privatization

G) **Privatization** transfers the ownership of state property into the hands of private investors. In order to attract investment and protect the interests of the private enterprise encouraged by the first two activities, changes typically need to be made to legal systems to protect the property rights of investors and entrepreneurs.

Legal Systems

H) Laws protecting private property rights and providing mechanisms for contract enforcement are required for a well functioning market economy. Without a **legal system** that protects property rights, and without the machinery to enforce that system, the incentive to engage in economic activity can be reduced substantially by private and public entities that expropriate the profits generated by the efforts of private sector entrepreneurs.

IMPLICATIONS FOR BUSINESS

<u>Attractiveness</u>

A) The overall attractiveness of a country as a market and/or investment site depends on balancing the likely long-term benefits of doing business in that country against the likely costs and risks. Next, the text covers the determinants of benefits, costs, and risks.

Benefits

B) The long run monetary benefits of doing business in a country are a function of the size of the market, the present wealth (purchasing power) of consumers, and the likely future wealth of consumers. By identifying and investing early in a potential future economic star, firms may be able to gain **first mover advantages** (advantages that accrue to early entrants into a market) and establish loyalty and experience in a country. Two factors that are reasonably good predictors of a country's future economic prospects are its economic system and property rights regime.

Costs

C) The costs of doing business in a country are determined by a number of political, economic, and legal factors. Political costs can involve the cost of paying bribes or lobbying for favorable or fair treatment. Economic costs relate primarily to the sophistication of the economic system, including the infrastructure and supporting businesses. Regarding legal factors, it can be more costly to do business in countries with dramatically different product, workplace, and pollution standards, or where there is poor legal protection for property rights.

Risks

D) As with costs, the risks of doing business in a country are determined by a number of political, economic, and legal factors. **Political risk** is the likelihood that political forces will cause drastic changes in a country's business environment that adversely affects the profit and other goals of a business enterprise. **Economic risk** is the likelihood that economic mismanagement will cause drastic changes in a country's business environment that adversely affects the profit and other goals of a business enterprise. **Legal risk** is the likelihood that a trading partner will opportunistically break a contract or expropriate property rights.

Overall Attractiveness

E) The overall attractiveness of a country as a potential market and/or investment site for an international business depends on balancing the benefits, costs, and risks associated with doing business in that country.

<u>Ethical Issues</u>

Ethics and Human Rights

F) One ethical concern regards whether firms should invest in countries where the government represses its citizens in political and/or economic freedom. While some argue that investing in these countries is implicitly supporting the repression, others argue that the best way to encourage change is from within, and that increasing economic development of the country will lead to greater political and economic freedoms.

Ethics and Regulations

G) A second ethical concern regards whether an international firm should adopt consistent and high levels of product safety, worker safety, and environmental protection worldwide, or whether they should focus only on meeting local regulations. If they adopt high standards, and subsequently lose business to other competitors with lower standards, was this an ethically correct position for it to take in light its requirements to act in the best interest of shareholders and provide advancement opportunities for its personnel?

Ethics and Corruption

H) Another ethical concern regards whether firms should pay bribes to governmental officials or business partners in exchange for business access. Should paying bribes be completely avoided, or are bribes just another cost of doing business that "grease the wheels" and lead to benefits for both the firm and consumers. If bribes are an integral part of business transactions in a country, is a firm being culturally insensitive and elitist if it finds bribes repulsive and refuses to pay them? Are large campaign contributions in the USA any different than bribes in reality?

Teaching Tip: The Carnegie Council on Ethics and International Affairs maintains a very substantive and thought-provoking website at {http://www.cceia.org/}. This site contains publications that comments on many of the ethical issues that surround globalization and international business.

Critical Thinking and Discussion Questions

1. Free market economies stimulate greater economic growth, whereas command economies stifle growth. Discuss.

Answer: In a market economy, private individuals and corporations are allowed to own property and other assets. This right of ownership provides a powerful incentive for people to work hard, introduce new products, develop better advertising campaigns, invent new products, etc., all in the hopes of accumulating additional personal capital and wealth. In turn, the constant search on the part of individuals and corporation to accumulate wealth enriches the entire economy and creates economic growth. In contrast, in a command economy, private individuals and corporations are not allowed to own substantial quantities of property and other assets. The objective of a command economy is for everyone to work for "the good of the society." Although this sounds like a noble ideal, a system that asks individuals to work for the good of society rather than allowing individuals to build personal wealth does not provide a great incentive for people to invent new products, develop better advertising campaigns, find ways to be more efficient, etc. As a result, command economies typically generate less innovation and are less efficient than market economies.

2. A democratic political system is an essential condition for sustained economic progress. Discuss.

Answer: This question has no clear-cut answer. In the West, we tend to argue that democracy is good for economic progress. This argument is largely predicted upon the idea that innovation is the engine of economic growth, and a democratic political system encourages rather than stifles innovation. However, there are examples of totalitarian regimes that have fostered a market economy and strong property rights protection and experienced rapid economic growth. The examples include four of the fastest growing economies of the past 30 years – South Korea, Taiwan, Singapore, and Hong Kong – all of which have grown faster than Western economies. However, while it is possible to argue that democracy is not a necessary precondition for the establishment of a free market economy, it seems evident that subsequent economic growth leads to establishment of democratic regimes. Several of the fastest-growing Asian economies have recently adopted more democratic governments.

3. During the late 1980s and early 1990s China was routinely cited by various international organizations such as Amnesty International and Freedom Watch for major human rights violations, including torture, beatings, imprisonment and executions of political dissidents. Despite this, in the mid-1990s China received record levels of foreign direct investment, mainly from firms based in democratic societies such as the United States, Japan, and Germany. Evaluate this trend from an ethical perspective. If you were the CEO of a firm that had the option of making a potentially very profitable investment in China, what would you do?

Answer: While there are those who argue that investing in totalitarian countries provides comfort to dictators and can help prop-up repressive regimes, in the case of China these arguments appear to have been ineffective. Western firms have continued to invest in spite of these concerns, either out of opportunism or a belief in a different ethical perspective. The alternate ethical perspective suggests that investment by a Western firm, by raising the level of economic development of a totalitarian country, can help change it from within. Since economic well-being and political freedoms often go hand in hand, and investment can create jobs and provide needed goods for individuals, an investment may be good for the people both in the short and the long run. Perhaps it was based on this rationale that the Bush administration claimed that US. firms should continue to be allowed to invest in Mainland China even after the 1989 crackdown on the democracy movement. As the CEO of a firm that had the option of making a potentially very profitable investment in China, not only should this ethical tradeoff be considered, but also so should the importance of the opportunity and the ethical responsibility one has to shareholders. If there are opportunities in China, passing these up may simply be allowing a competitor to gain a first mover advantage that will be difficult to overcome. Unless all potential competitors from all countries have the same ethical principles, it is likely that some firm will decide to undertake the investment in spite of the ethical concerns. (Investment withholding, like any other form of collusion or sanction adherence, requires compliance by all parties if it is to be effective.) Hence the CEO must consider the ethical responsibility to shareholders to maximize the value of the firm. In the end the decision must rest on both ethical concerns about doing business in China and ethical concerns about what is in the best interest of shareholders. There is no right or wrong decision, as each involves different tradeoffs.

4. You are the CEO of a company that has to choose between making a $100 million investment in either Russia or the Czech Republic. Both investments promise the same long-run return, so your choice of which investment to make is driven by considerations of risk. Assess the various risks of doing business in each of these nations. Which investment would you favor and why?

Answer: When assessing the risks of investment, one should consider the political, economic, and legal risks of doing business in either Russia or the Czech Republic. At this time (Spring 1999), the political risk in Russia is high as it is undergoing continual governmental changes. Yeltsin is on trial for impeachment and he has fired his fourth Prime Minister in the past year. Yeltsin's health is also uncertain. In addition, there are significant divisions in the country both ideologically and ethnically. Relatively, the Czech Republic is more stable. On the economic front, both countries have inflation and high economic turmoil as unproductive factories are still struggling. From the legal perspective, the Czech Republic is making clear progress, while the situation in Russia is in flux. Thus at this time, the risk in Russia would clearly be higher. Depending upon when you are using the book, this situation could be different. (You also may want to substitute other countries into this question depending on current events and the countries with which you feel your students will be most familiar.)

Internet Exercises

TEXT EXERCISE 1

Overview

This exercise explores the process of globalization, and in particular, the role of cross-border transfers of intellectual property in stimulating a more global marketplace. The exercise points out that such transfers may now be facilitated thanks to the Internet.

Suggested Use in the Classroom

Students are to visit Amazon's foreign sites and compare them to each other. In particular, students should look for similarities among the sites, and then discuss the implications of their findings in terms of the globalization of the world economy, and the transfer of intellectual property. Most students will recognize the advent of the Internet allows people in different countries, perhaps in a way never before possible, to gain detailed knowledge of "what's happening" in other countries. Many students will probably suggest that this will advance the process of both globalization and the transfer of intellectual ideas across borders.

TEXT EXERCISE 2

Overview

This exercise extends the previous one, and raises the issue of whether the English language is playing a role in the globalization of markets. The exercise suggests that online booksellers, with their worldwide reach, are limiting the role of government in restricting the free flow of ideas.

Suggested Use in the Classroom

In this exercise students are asked to visit barnesandnoble.com's foreign sites and examine in particular the politically oriented books and those related to pop culture. In addition, students are asked to note what language is being used in the various publications and consider the role of the English language in bringing markets closer together. Many students will probably argue that as English is becoming something of a common language, it will naturally advance the process of globalization. Similarly, many students will probably suggest that as books become available in an electronic format, it will make it virtually impossible for governments to restrict the free flow of ideas.

WEB EXERCISE 1

Overview

This exercise extends the discussion raised in the two text-based Internet exercises and further explores the role of the government and the Internet. In particular, the exercise examines the role of government regulation and e-commerce.

Suggested Use in the Classroom

The issue of whether the Internet should be regulated, and if so how, is a hotly debated issue, and will probably make for a good classroom discussion. Some students will strongly favor government intervention, particularly by the U.S., while others will probably argue that the Internet should be left to its own devices. Those in the former camp should be queried as to how government actions should be implemented and coordinated, while those in the latter group should be questioned as to whether firms necessarily have the consumer's best interests at heart.

WEB EXERCISE 2

Overview

This exercise explores market opportunities in China for telecommunications firms. At the present time, several large multinational companies are hoping to cash in on the potential in the Chinese marketplace, but are finding that because of government regulations, it may not be an easy task.

Suggested Use in the Classroom

China is a uniquely interesting market—on the one hand, its political predisposition makes it a risky option, while on the other hand, its vast market potential makes it enormously attractive. Depending on the status of China and Taiwan, students may respond to this exercise in very different ways. If China is continuing to threaten Taiwan (as it is at press time), many students may recommend that companies move very cautiously in the market. However, if the political situation has cooled, students will probably focus on the tremendous opportunities in the market, and suggest that companies try to capitalize on the potential.

CLOSING CASE: General Electric in Hungary

Summary

The closing case describes the challenges faced by General Electric in its investment in the Tungsram factory in Hungary. Discussion of this case can revolve around the following questions:

QUESTION 1: What does GE's experience in Hungary tell you about the relationship among economic systems, political systems, and national culture?

ANSWER 1: The economic system, political system, and national culture all played a role in describing both how Tungsram operated prior to GE's investment and how employees reacted to GE's initiatives. These are all intertwined, and changing only one of these variables is impractical. The challenges GE faced in working with employees had to do with deep seeded attitudes that reflected all three variables.

QUESTION 2: Given the problems GE experienced with Tungsram, in retrospect might it have chosen a better strategy to attack the Western European lighting products market?

ANSWER 2: It certainly may have been easier to open a new facility, but it is less clear that this would have had a better payoff. Tungsram is a well-known European brand, and building up GE's brand would have also entailed expenses. For a firm like GE, the learning it developed from the Tungsram venture was likely valuable in other ventures in Eastern Europe. Thus, even if there had been a more efficient way to attack the European lighting market, knowledge it gained at Tungsram could have helped GE's other Eastern Europe ventures to anticipate and deal with similar problems. (It may have even discouraged GE from making other, more costly, investments. Thus it may have saved money for GE in other areas.)

QUESTION 3: How important to the economic development of Hungary are investments such as GE's? What are the benefits that GE brings to Hungary?

ANSWER 3: Foreign direct investment, like GE's, has been critical to economic development in Eastern Europe. Not only did GE invest capital, it helped spread Western business practices critical to the development of other Hungarian firms. And by GE deciding to invest in Hungary, it sent a signal to many other smaller firms that investment in Eastern Europe was worth the risk. Thus this investment encouraged many other firms to invest in Hungary, providing a significant multiplier effect.

QUESTION 4: If Tungsram had continued under local ownership, what do you think would have been its fate?

ANSWER 4: This question requires pure speculation. On argument would be that Tungsram would have continued inefficient operation for some time without needing to make major changes. After all, relative to many other Eastern firms, it was a "gem." Its cost structures would likely still have allowed it to maintain sales in markets in Eastern Europe. Indifference to customers would however, limit its ability to compete in Western markets. Following many Eastern firms that have sought "rich" markets in the West, it may have eventually developed marketing skills and products that meet Western needs. Thus, under one scenario it might have done fine in the long run, but not made changes as quickly as those made by GE. An alternative speculation would be that its managers thought it such a "gem" that they would fail to take any significant action. Eventually competition would have put Tungsram out of business.

Management Focus: Microsoft Battles Software Piracy in China

Summary

This feature focuses on Microsoft's entry into the Chinese software market and, in particular, Microsoft's frustrations with software piracy in China. In 1995, over 90 percent of the software used in China was pirated. Microsoft is a prime target of this activity. Most Microsoft products used in China are illegal copies made and then sold with no payment to Microsoft. Incredibly, one of the biggest offenders is the Chinese government itself. Not only does the government use pirated software in its offices, but also has been reluctant until recently to enforce its own intellectual property rights laws. Fortunately, for Microsoft, the situation may be improving. The United States government has gone to bat for Microsoft and has made inroads in pressuring the Chinese government to create a more equitable environment for Microsoft in China.

Suggested Discussion Questions

1. What is "intellectual property?" What can companies do to help protect the intellectual property of their products and services in foreign markets?

2. Discuss Microsoft's efforts to deal with software piracy in China. Has Microsoft done all that it can do? Do you believe that Microsoft's recent initiative to work with the Chinese Ministry of Electronics to create a Chinese version of the Windows 95 operating system is a good move? Why or why not?

3. In your opinion, will Microsoft's frustrations with software piracy in China be satisfactorily resolved in the near future? Explain your answer.

4. Microsoft Homepage: {http://www.microsoft.com/}

Country Focus: The Changing Political Economy of India

Summary

This features focuses on the evolution of India's economic system from 1947 to today. After gaining independence from Britain in 1947, India adopted a democratic system of government. However, the economic system that developed in India was a mixed economy characterized by a heavy dose of state enterprise and planning. The feature discusses many of the attributes of India's mixed economy, such as high tariffs, limited foreign direct investment, and an oppressive bureaucracy. Under this system, the Indian people did poorly. Fortunately, in 1991 the government of Prime Minister P.V. Narasimha Rao embarked on an ambitious economic reform program. The results have been impressive. India's economy is now expanding, and much of the bureaucratic red tape that inhibited business growth is gone.

Suggested Discussion Questions

1. Explain what is meant by the term "mixed economy." Does a mixed economy inhibit business growth? Explain your answer.

2. How long do you believe that it will take for India to have a market economy that resembles those found in Western Europe and North America? Describe the benefits of a market economy. Will India's movement towards a market economy help or hurt its globalization efforts?

3. When India does establish a genuine market economy, do you believe that the companies that have had bad experiences in India (e.g. IBA, Coca-Cola, and Mobile) will come back? Why or why not?

4. Additional Information About India: The following web sites provide additional information about India's economic progress: Links to Sites Focused On India's Economy: {http://webhead.com/WWWVL/India/india205.html}; b)   The Indian Economy Overview:

{http://www.m-web.com/ieoindex.html}; All About India: {http://www.indiaintl.com/about.html}.

Additional Readings and Sources of Information

Fair Trade Watch: {http://www.fairtradewatch.org/contents.htm}

Microsoft's Long March: {http://www.businessweek.com/search.htm}

Business Central Europe: {http://www.bcemag.com}

A Hard Sell for Microsoft in China: {http://www.businessweek.com/search.htm}

World Economic Forum: {http://www.weforum.org}

Move Over Microsoft: {http://businessweek.com/search.htm}

CHAPTER 3
DIFFERENCES IN CULTURE

Chapter Outline

OPENING CASE: A Scotsman at Mazda

INTRODUCTION

WHAT IS CULTURE?

    Values and Norms
    Culture, Society, and the Nation-State
    The Determinants of Culture

SOCIAL STRUCTURE

    Individuals and Groups
    Social Stratification

RELIGIOUS AND ETHICAL SYSTEMS

    Christianity
    Islam
    Country Focus: Islamic Dissent in Saudi Arabia
    Hinduism
    Buddhism
    Confucianism

LANGUAGE

    Spoken Language
    Unspoken Language

EDUCATION

CULTURE AND THE WORKPLACE

    Hofstede's Model
    Evaluating Hofstede's Model

CULTURAL CHANGE

    Management Focus: Hitachi and Japan's Changing Culture

IMPLICATIONS FOR BUSINESS

    Cross-Cultural Literacy

Culture and Competitive Advantage

CHAPTER SUMMARY

INTERNET EXERCISES

CRITICAL DISCUSSION QUESTIONS

CLOSING CASE: Disney in France

Learning Objectives

1. Understand that substantial differences among societies arise from cultural differences.

2. Know what is meant by the term culture.

3. Appreciate that culture is different because of differences in social structure, religion, language, education, economic philosophy, and political philosophy.

4. Understand the relationship between culture and the values found in the workplace.

5. Appreciate that culture is not a constant, but changes over time.

6. Appreciate that much of the change in contemporary social culture is being driven by economic advancement, technological change, and globalization.

7. Understand the implications for international business management of differences in culture.

Chapter Summary

This chapter begins by introducing the concept of culture. The determinants of culture are identified, which include religion, political philosophy, economic philosophy, education, language, and social structure. The first half of the chapter focuses on the influence of social structure, religion, language, and education on culture. The section on religion is very thorough, and explains the economic implications of Christianity, Islam, Hinduism, Buddhism, and Confucianism. In addition, Geert Hofstede's model of how a society's culture impacts the values found in the workplace is presented. According to Hofstede, cultures vary along the lines of power distance, individualism versus collectivism, uncertainty avoidance, and masculinity versus femininity. The concept of ethnocentric behavior is introduced. Finally, the author reiterates the point that the value systems and norms of a country influence the costs of doing business in that country.

OPENING CASE: A Scotsman at Mazda

Summary

The opening case describes the anticipated cultural differences that would face Henry Wallace, a Scotsman, when he took over the presidency of Mazda. Many aspects of Japanese work practices and business culture are described which differ from common Western practices. It would appear that Mr. Wallace has been able to make remarkable progress at Mazda, without making too many waves. A discussion of the case can revolve around the following questions:

QUESTION 1: What were the primary cultural work values that Japanese employees were concerned about when Henry Wallace took over as president of Mazda?

ANSWER 1: Because of Mazda's poor financial performance and declining revenues, workers were clearly concerned about layoffs. Under Japan's system of lifetime employment, workers were not laid off during down periods. Internal promotions were made based on seniority rather than ability. Decision-making was consensus based, and there was an emphasis on harmony and a reluctance to create discord within the management group. Communication was often indirect, rather than direct, and silence in the discussion of a particular issue could mean as much as talking. Long standing relations extended not only to employees, but also to suppliers, many of which had worked with Mazda for decades.

QUESTION 2: What has changed at Mazda since Wallace took over? What has remained the same?

ANSWER 2: Wallace helped Mazda to articulate a clear strategy, and was able to reduce the workforce through attrition. Several unprofitable models were discontinued, and more attention was focused on marketing. Bigger changes took place in the internal management structure and decision making process, with merit playing a more important role in promotions and spirited debate becoming more common in meetings. The lifetime employment system has remained intact, and Mazda's traditional supplier network is still in place - albeit with some shift to more overseas suppliers.

Chapter Outline With Lecture Notes and Teaching Tips

INTRODUCTION

A) The focus of this chapter is on culture, and what some of the underlying characteristics of a country are that help define the values and norms of a society. This affects not only how an individual from one country must adapt to work in another country, as described in the opening case, but how organizations much must recognize the how cultural difference affect the way they work with other organizations.

B) Two themes run through this chapter. The first theme is that operating a successful international business requires cross-cultural literacy. By cross cultural literacy, we mean an understanding of how cultural differences across and within nations can affect the way in which business is practiced. The second theme is that a relationship may exist between culture and the costs of doing business in a country or region.

WHAT IS CULTURE?

A) The fundamental building blocks of culture are **values** and **norms**.

Value and Norms

B) Values are abstract ideas about what a group believes to be good, right, and desirable, and form the bedrock of a culture. They provide the context within which a society's norms are established and justified. Norms are the social rules that govern the actions of people toward one another. Norms can be subdivided further into Folkways (the routine conventions of everyday life) and Mores (norms that are seen as central to the functioning of a society and to its social life).

Culture, Society, and the Nation-State

C) A society can be defined as a group of people that share a common set of values and norms; that is, a group bound together by a common culture. But there is not a strict one-to-one correspondence between a society and a nation-state. Nation-states are political creations. They may contain a single culture or several distinct cultures.

The Determinants of Culture

D) The values and norms of a culture do not emerge from nowhere fully formed. They are the evolutionary product of a number of factors at work in a society.

SOCIAL STRUCTURE

A) A society's social structure refers to its basic social organization. Two dimensions stand out when explaining differences between cultures. The first is the degree to which the basic unit of social organization is the individual, as opposed to the group. The second dimension is the degree to which a society is stratified into classes or castes.

Individuals and Groups

The Individual

B) A focus on the individual, and individual achievement is common in many Western societies. In Chapter 2 the implications of this for political and economic systems was discussed. An emphasis on individual achievement has positive and negative implications. On the positive side, the dynamism of the US economy owes much to people like Sam Walton, Steve Jobs, and Ross Perot - people who took chances, tried new things, succeeded, and encouraged others to do likewise. On the other hand, individualism can lead to a lack of company loyalty and failure to gain company specific knowledge, competition between individuals in a company rather than team building, and limit people's ability to develop a strong network of contacts within a firm.

The Group

C) In sharp contrast to the Western emphasis on the individual, in many Asian societies the group is the primary unit of social organization. While in earlier times the group was usually the family or the village, today the group may be a work team or business organization. When meeting someone she may say she works for Sony rather than say she is an engineer that designs disk drives. The worth of an individual is more linked to the success of the group than individual achievement. This emphasis on the group may discourage job switching between firms, encourage lifetime employment systems, and lead to cooperation in solving business problems. On the other hand, individual creativity and initiative is suppressed.

Social Stratification

D) All societies are stratified on a hierarchical basis into social categories, or **social strata**.

Social Mobility

E) **Social mobility** refers to the extent to which individuals can move out of the strata into which they are born. A **caste system** is a form closed system of stratification in which social position is determined by the family into which a person is born, and change in that position is usually not possible during an individual's lifetime whereas a **class system** is a form of open social stratification in which the position a person has by birth can be changed through his or her achievement or luck.

Significance

F) The significance of the social strata can have important implications for the management and organization of businesses. In cultures where there is a great deal of consciousness over the class of others, the way individuals from different classes work together (i.e. management and labor) may be very prescribed and strained in some cultures (i.e. Britain), or have almost no significance in others (i.e. Japan). The class of a person may be very important in some hiring and promotion decisions, particularly in sales organizations where the person will be dealing with customers that may also come from a particular class.

RELIGIOUS AND ETHICAL SYSTEMS

A) **Religion** can be defined as a system of shared beliefs and rituals that are concerned with the realm of the sacred. **Ethical systems** refer to a set of moral principles, or values, that are used to guide and shape behavior. The ethical practices of individuals within a culture are often closely intertwined with their religion. While there are literally thousands of religions worldwide, four that have the largest following will be discussed: Christianity, Islam, Hinduism, and Buddhism. Confucianism, while not a religion, influences behavior and shapes culture in many parts of Asia. Map 3.1 shows dominant religions across the world.

<u>Christianity</u>

B) Christianity is the largest religion and is common throughout Europe, the Americas, and other countries settled by Europeans. Within Christianity there are three major branches: Protestant, Roman Catholic, and Eastern Orthodox.

Economic Implications of Christianity: The Protestant Work Ethic

C) At the turn of the century Weber suggested that is was the "Protestant work ethic" that was the driving force of capitalism. This focus on hard work, wealth creation, and frugality encouraged capitalism while the Catholic promise of salvation in the next world did not foster the same kind of work ethic. The Protestant emphasis on individual religious freedom, in contrast to the hierarchical Catholic Church, was also consistent with the individualist economic and political philosophy discussed in Chapter 2.

<u>Islam</u>

D) Islam has the same underlying roots of Christianity (Christ is viewed as a prophet), and suggests many of the same underlying societal mores. Islam, however, extends this to more of an all-embracing way of life that governs one's being. It also prescribes many more "laws" on how people should act and live that are entirely counter the US "separation of church and state."

Economic Implications of Islam

E) The past two decades have witnessed a surge in what is often referred to as "Islamic fundamentalism". The rise of fundamentalism has no one cause. In part it is a response to the social pressures created in traditional Islamic societies by the move towards modernization, and by the influence of western ideas, such as liberal democracy, materialism, equal rights for women, and by Western attitudes towards sex, marriage, and alcohol.

F) In Islam people do not own property, but only act as stewards for God and thus must take care of that which they have been entrusted with. They must use property in a righteous, socially beneficial, and prudent manner; not exploit others for their own benefit; and have obligations to help the disadvantaged. Thus while Islam is supportive of business, the way business is practiced is prescribed.

Hinduism

G) Hinduism, practiced primarily on the Indian sub-continent, focuses on the importance of achieving spiritual growth and development, which may require material and physical self-denial.

Economic Implications of Hinduism

H) Since Hindus are valued by their spiritual rather than material achievements, there is not the same work ethic or focus on entrepreneurship found in some other religions. Likewise, promotion and adding new responsibilities may not be the goal of an employee, or may be infeasible due to the employee's caste.

Buddhism

I) Buddhists also stress spiritual growth and the afterlife, rather than achievement while in this world. Buddhism, practiced mainly in South East Asia, does not support the caste system, however, so individuals do have some mobility not found in Hinduism and can work with individuals from different classes.

Confucianism

J) Confucianism, practiced mainly in China, teaches the importance of attaining personal salvation through right action. Unlike religions, Confucianism is not concerned with the supernatural and has little to say about the concept of a supreme being or an afterlife. The need for high moral and ethical conduct and loyalty to others is central in Confucianism.

Economic Implications of Confucianism

K) Three key teachings of Confucianism - loyalty, reciprocal obligations, and honesty - may all lead to a lowering of the cost of doing business in Confucian societies. The close ties between Japanese auto companies and their suppliers, which has been an important ingredient in the Japanese success in the auto industry, are facilitated by loyalty, reciprocal obligations, and honesty. In countries where these relationships are more adversarial and not bound by these same values, the costs of doing business are probably higher.

Teaching Tip: Duke University's Department of Religion sponsors a web site that offers links to and brief descriptions of four of the most comprehensive sites for religion on the Internet. These are excellent sites that provide a broad array of information to augment the information about religion provided in the textbook. The site is available at {http://www.duke.edu/web/CIS/}

LANGUAGE

A) One obvious way in which countries differ is language. By language, we mean both the spoken and the unspoken means of communication. Language is one of the defining characteristics of culture. It not only allows a society to communicate, but also directs the attention of people towards certain features of the world and human interactions.

Teaching Tip: There are a number of resources available on the Internet to help international executives overcome "language" barriers in doing business in other countries. An entire menu of these resources is available at {http://www.csuchico.edu/cedp/export/global/protocol.htm}.

Teaching Tip: For individuals with a particular interest in Language, the Human-Languages Page {http://www.june29.com/HLP/} is a comprehensive catalog of language-related Internet resources. The over 1600 links available at this site include links to other Internet sites that focus on online language lessons, translating dictionaries, native literature, translation services, software, and language schools.

Spoken Language

B) While English is clearly the language of international business, knowing at least some of the local language can greatly help when working in another country. In some situations knowing the local language can be critical for business success.

Unspoken Language

Non-verbal Communication

C) Unspoken language can be just as important for communication. Using a few facial expressions and hand gestures to the class can illustrate the point. The fact that these can have different interpretations in different cultures, and that many of these actions may be automatic or reflexive, obviously complicates international communication. Not only may the person you are dealing with be unintentionally sending non-verbal signals that you are not understanding or misunderstanding, you may be unconsciously sending your own signals.

EDUCATION

A) Formal education plays a key role in a society. Formal education is the medium through which individuals learn many of the language, conceptual, and mathematical skills that are indispensable in a modern society.

B) The knowledge base, training, and educational opportunities available to a country's citizens can also give it a competitive advantage in the market and make it a more or less attractive place for expanding business. In nations that have a ready trained workforce for particular types of jobs, it is easier to start operations than in nations where an investor will also have to undertake time-consuming and costly training.

CULTURE AND THE WORKPLACE

A) For an international business with operations in different countries, a question of considerable importance is how does a society's culture impact on the values found in the workplace? The question points to the need to vary management process and practices to take different culturally determined work-related values into account.

Hofstede's Model

B) The most famous study of how culture relates to values in the workplace was undertaken by Geert Hofstede. Hofstede isolated four dimensions that he claimed summarized different cultures. These were: power distance, individualism versus collectivism, uncertainty avoidance, and masculinity versus femininity where

Power Distance is focused on how a society deals with the fact that people are unequal in physical and intellectual capabilities,

Individualism Versus Collectivism is focused on the relationship between the individual and his or her fellows,

Uncertainty Avoidance measures the extent to which different cultures socialize their members into accepting ambiguous situations and tolerating ambiguity, and

Masculinity Versus Femininity looks at the relationship between gender and work roles.

Evaluating Hofstede's Model

C) Hofstede's results are interesting for what they tell us in a general way about differences between cultures. However, because of methodological issues, one should be careful about reading too much into Hofstede's research.

CULTURAL CHANGE

A) Culture evolves over time, although changes in value systems can be slow and painful for a society. Social turmoil is an inevitable outcome of culture change. The text provides several examples of cultural change and its impact on the society.

B) As countries become economically stronger and increase in the globalization of products bought and sold, cultural change is particularly common

IMPLICATIONS FOR BUSINESS

Cross-Cultural Literacy

A) Individuals and firms must develop cross-cultural literacy. International businesses that are ill informed about the practices of another culture are unlikely to succeed in that culture. One way to develop cross-cultural literacy is to regularly rotate and transfer people internationally.

B) One must also beware of ethnocentric behavior, or a belief in the superiority of one's own culture. Individuals who are ethnocentric frequently demonstrate disregard for other cultures.

Culture and Competitive Advantage

C) For the international business, the connection between culture and competitive advantage is important for two reasons. First, the connection suggests which countries are likely to produce the most viable competitors. Second, the connection between culture and competitive advantage has important implications for the choice of countries in which to locate production facilities and do business.

Critical Thinking and Discussion Questions

1. Outline why the culture of a country influences the costs of doing business in that country. Illustrate your answer with examples.

Answer: Since in a sense the entire chapter is about this question, there can be numerous reasons and examples of how culture influences the costs of doing business. Several are highlighted in the following sentences, but there could be numerous others. When there are simply different norms between how individuals from different countries interact, the costs of doing business rise as people grapple with unfamiliar ways of doing business. For example, while in the US we may get down to business first, and then get to know each other socially later, in many South American countries it is important develop a good social relationship before trying to discuss business issues. Different class structures and social mobility also raise the costs of doing business, for if there are inhibitions against working with people from different classes, then the efficiency with which information can flow may be limited and the cost of running a business increased. A country's religion can also affect the costs of business, as religious values can affect attitudes towards work, entrepreneurship, honesty, fairness, and social responsibility. In Hindu societies where the pursuit of material well-being can be viewed as making spiritual well being less likely, worker productivity may be lower than in nations with other religious beliefs. Finally, a country's education system can have important implications for the costs of business. In countries where workers receive excellent training and are highly literate, the need for specific worker training programs are decreased and the hiring of additional employees is facilitated.

2. Do you think business practices in an Islamic country are likely to differ from business practices in the United States and if so, how?

Answer: A number of aspects of the cultural differences between an Islamic country and the USA will cause business practices to differ. The role women can take, appropriate etiquette (including simple things like not passing papers with the left hand), holidays, and wining and dining all differ from in the USA. But beyond these, the underlying philosophy and role of business differs from in the USA. Since Muslims are stewards of property for God, rather than owners, they are more likely to use their resources carefully and may be less likely to give up or sell something to a person who may not practice the same stewardship. The importance of fairness to all parties in relations means that over-aggressiveness in self-interest may not be well received, and breaking an agreement, even if technically/legally permissible may be viewed as very inappropriate. Finally, the prohibitions on interest payments in some Islamic countries means that the wording of the terms of an agreement must be done carefully so that "fair profits" are not construed as being "interest payments."

3. What are the implications for international business of differences in the dominant religion of a country?

Answer: Differences in the dominant religion of a country affect relationships, attitudes toward business, and overall economic development. Firstly, differences in religion require inter-cultural sensitivity. This sensitivity requires things like simply knowing the religious holidays, accepting that some unexpected things may happen "because of Allah's will," or understanding how interpersonal relationships may be different between "believers" and "non-believers." (Hence non-believers may be treated differently.) Secondly, religious beliefs can significantly affect a countries attitude toward business, work, and entrepreneurship. In one country successfully beating a competitor may be considered a great achievement while in another it may be thought of as showing a lack of compassion and disruptive to the society and persons involved, both attitudes that may be derived from underlying religious beliefs. Likewise, hard work may be either rewarded positively or viewed as something of secondary importance to spiritual peace and harmony. Thirdly, different dominant religions may affect the overall competitiveness and potential for economic growth of a nation, and hence attractiveness of a country for international business.

4. Choose two countries that appear to be culturally diverse. Compare the culture of those countries and then indicate how cultural differences influence (i) the costs of doing business in each country, (ii) the likely future economic development of that country, (iii) business practices.

Answer: The answers will obviously vary based on the countries chosen by the students, and their knowledge of the countries. Hopefully the student can present some information on along the dimensions of values, norms, social structure, religion, language, and education of the countries and also describe the key differences and similarities of the countries along these dimensions. Relating the differences between the countries along these dimensions to differences in the costs of doing business, the potential for economic development, and business practices would fully answer the question. (While it may be more difficult for students to come up with really good examples relative to business practices, the costs and prospects for economic development should be quite feasible.)

Internet Exercises

TEXT EXERCISE 1

Overview

This exercise explores how Nestle, the global food giant, has chosen a strategy of adapting its product line to meet local cultural preferences in different markets. In many cases, Nestle has chosen to use local product names rather than develop the Nestle name on a worldwide basis, and but at the same time, the company sells the other products the same way across globe.

Suggested Use in the Classroom

The exercise asks students to examine Nestle's web sites in a number of locations around the world and identify how, and indeed if, Nestle is responding to local market preferences. Students should be able to identify those products that seem to have a global appeal, and also those products that do not. Based upon their findings, students should then draw conclusions about the local cultures in the various countries in which Nestle maintains a presence.

The exercise also asks students whether it is necessary for companies to develop a web site for each market, or whether a one-size-fits-all strategy is appropriate. Some students will probably indicate that given the global nature of the Internet and its easy accessibility, companies cannot possibly maintain a culturally correct site for everyone, and that therefore maintaining a standardized site makes sense. Others however, will probably suggest that companies that fail to make an attempt at meeting local needs will lose out in the long run to those companies that do make the effort.

TEXT EXERCISE 2

Overview

This exercise extends the discussion raised in the previous exercise and examines eBay's European strategy. Ebay, the American online auction house, apparently believing that its concept could be taken to other countries in a standardized format, found that it may have lost out on a key market opportunity. In Europe at least, the company should have developed a web site that met market preferences.

Students are asked to explore eBay's American and British sites, and also the site of its big British rival QXL.com. Students should examine differences between the sites and draw conclusions regarding the strategies of each company. Students are also asked whether eBay's cookie-cutter approach can work in new markets, or whether the company has to take local cultures into consideration. As with the previous exercise, some students will probably suggest that the Internet has its own culture and that the user must do the adapting, while other students will maintain that companies must take responsibility for responding to local market conditions.

WEB EXERCISE 1

Overview

This exercise further extends the issues discussed in the two text exercises, and explores how companies, in the age of the Internet and corporate web sites, can still maintain local market responsiveness.

Suggested Use in the Classroom

In this exercise, students must consider how global business is changing, thanks to the Internet. Is it possible to develop market-specific web sites, or the global nature of the Internet change the traditional rules of the game. Some students will probably recognize that the Internet has the potential to contribute to the homogenization of markets and that consequently it could provide companies with huge savings. Other students however, will take the opposite position arguing that now, more than ever, it is important for companies to be conscious of local market perceptions.

WEB EXERCISE 2

Overview

This exercise explores MTV's role in creating a cultural convergence among its target audience around the globe. MTV, while adapting its position in some ways, has maintained a fairly uniform appearance around the world.

Suggested Use in the Classroom

Students are asked to visit MTV's web sites around the world, and in particular explore the interactive components. Students should then comment on what they observe, looking for similarities and patterns across markets. Depending on when this exercise is used, students may conclude that topics are very localized in nature, or may have more common global elements. For example, when an internationally recognized music group announces a new tour, it may be possible to find discussion groups popping up around the world.

CLOSING CASE: Disney in France

Summary

The closing case describes the challenges faced Disney in its EuroDisney theme park in France. A short video segment is available to augment this case. Discussion of this case can revolve around the following questions:

QUESTION 1: What assumptions did Disney make about the tastes and preferences of French consumers? Which of these assumptions were correct? Which were not?

ANSWER 1: Disney assumed that the French would enjoy the park, but to many French it was just another example of an American assault on their ever-eroding national culture. Disney also assumed that breakfast would not be a big thing, that a French-style breakfast would be preferred, and that visitors would be willing to stagger their lunch times. All of these turned out to be incorrect. Visitors also received the initial lack of alcohol poorly. Disney assumed that Friday would be a more popular day than Monday, and staffed appropriately, when just the reverse occurred. The demographics of visitors also differed from what was expected. Relatively few French visited the park, and most visitors came for single day trips. This resulted in a huge over supply of hotel facilities. Over time Disney has adjusted to meet the needs of its visitors, and attendance is gradually improving.

QUESTION 2: How might Disney have had a more favorable initial experience in France? What steps might it have taken to reduce the mistakes associated with EuroDisney?

ANSWER 2: The simple answer to this question is that Disney should have been more sensitive to French and European culture, and adapted appropriately. Yet this answer misses an important point. Visitors do not go to EuroDisney for a French experience; they go there for an American experience. They want American food and American style entertainment. Yet they also want their wine for lunch (unheard of in a Disney park in the USA). Thus, Disney was faced with a difficult situation of 1) balancing adaptation to the culture and 2) providing an American-style theme park. This is a tough trade-off to make, and it is really hard to know in advance what aspects should be more French and what aspects should be more American.

QUESTION 3: In retrospect, was France the best choice for the location of EuroDisney?

ANSWER 3: In theme parks, as in many other businesses, location is an extremely important variable. The favorable location of Paris within Europe, and that fact that Paris itself is a tourist destination, made the location seem quite logical. No matter where it located a park in Europe, it would likely run into some cultural challenges - these challenges would just be different in Germany or England than they were in France. Thus while everything has not gone well for Disney in France, it is unclear whether a different location would have been as favorable demographically or that another location would have been without its own (different) problems.

Country Focus: Islamic Dissent in Saudi Arabia

Summary

This feature focuses on the cultural of Saudi Arabia and on the Islamic dissent that exists in the country. The feature traces the Saudi government from the founding of Saudi Arabia in 1935 until the present time. In addition, the feature comments on the relationship between Saudi Arabia and the Western democracies of the world. Western governments have gone out of their way to curry the favor of Saudi Arabia, a cynic might say, because the country sits on top of more than a quarter of the world's oil reserves. As a result of this and the involvement of the West in the Gulf War, there is growing dissention in Saudi Arabia against the ruling family.

<u>Suggested Discussion Questions</u>

1. Describe the basic beliefs of Islamic fundamentalists. Would the relationship between Saudi Arabia and the West change if Saudi Arabia shifted more towards a culture of strict Islamic fundamentalism? Explain your answer.
2. In your opinion, will Saudi Arabia remain a stable trading partner of the West. Why or why not?

1) Saudi Arabia Website: {http://www.yahoo.com/Regional/Countries/Saudi_Arabia/}

Management Focus: Hitachi and Japan's Changing Culture

<u>Summary</u>

This feature focuses on the changes that have taken place over the years for the employees of Hitachi Corporation of Japan. Namihei Odaira founded Hitachi in 1911. By 1965 Hitachi was one of the giants of Japanese industry. For many years, Hitachi was a typical Japanese company. Managers and their workers worked under a system of consensus decision making, the employees of the company lived in company housing, and everyone ate their meals in a company cafeteria. Two forces changed all of this – prosperity and globalization. Today, the company dorms and cafeterias have given away to private homes for the company's employees. Consensus decision-making is no longer stressed to the extent that it once was. The top executives of Hitachi have encouraged these changes, recognizing that changing times require changes in work environments.

<u>Suggested Discussion Questions</u>

1. In your opinion, have the changes that have taken place in the lives of Hitachi's workers resulted more from prosperity and globalization at Hitachi, or changes in Japanese society itself? Explain your answer.

2. Has Hitachi done a good job of allowing the lives of its employees to change in accordance with the changes in its business environment? In your opinion, what would have happened if Hitachi had tried to maintain its old culture despite its growing prosperity and move towards globalization?

3. How has Hitachi's prosperity change the lives of its employees? What can other companies learn from how Hatchi has handled its prosperity?

4. Hitachi Homepage: {http://hitachi.co.jp/}

<u>Additional Readings and Sources of Information</u>

<u>The World Gets in Touch with Its Inner American:</u>
{http://www.mojones.com/mother_jones/JF99/Americanization....}

<u>We're Betting on Hong Kong:</u> {http://www.businessweek.com/search.htm}

<u>Disneyland Paris: 5th Anniversary!:</u> {http://www.geoocities.com/Enchanted Forest/Dell/4588/5years.html}

<u>Paris Disneyland Naysayers Eat Crow:</u> {http://www.seattle-pi.com/pi/getaways/041797/diz17.html}

<u>Is Culture the Key to Growth?:</u> {http://www.businessweek.com/search.htm}

CHAPTER 4
INTERNATIONAL TRADE THEORY

Chapter Outline

IMPLICATIONS FOR BUSINESS

    Location Implications
    First-Mover Implications
    Policy Implications

SUMMARY OF CHAPTER

CRITICAL THINKING AND DISCUSSION QUESTIONS

INTERNET EXERCISES

CLOSING CASE: The Rise of The Indian Software Industry

Learning Objectives

1. Understand why nations trade with each other.

2. Be conversant with the different theories that have been offered to explain trade flows between nations.

3. Understand why many economists believe that unrestricted (free) trade between nations will raise the economic welfare of all countries that participate in a free trade system.

4. Be familiar with the arguments of those who maintain that government can play a proactive role in promoting national competitive advantage in certain industries.

5. Understand the important implications that international trade theory holds for business practice.

Chapter Summary

This chapter focuses on the benefits of international trade and introduces several theories that help explain the patterns of international trade that are observed in practice. The discussion begins with an explanation of the theory of mercantilism, and then proceeds to discuss the theories of absolute advantage and comparative advantage. Four additional theories are discussed, including the Heckscher-Ohlin theory, the Product Life Cycle theory, the New Trade theory, and the theory of National Competitive Advantage. Each of these theories helps explain why certain goods are (or should be) made in certain countries. The chapter ends by discussing the link between the theories of international trade and (1) a firm's decision about where (in the world) to locate its various productive activities, (2) the importance of establishing first-mover advantages, and (3) government trade policies.

OPENING CASE: The Gains From Trade – Ghana and South Korea

Summary

The opening case provides a comparison of the economic development and trade policies of Ghana and South Korea during the latter half of the 20th century. Whereas Ghana implemented an import substitution policy, South Korea had a very outward oriented pro-trade policy. The net effect is that South Korea has developed economically much faster than Ghana. Discussion of the case can center on the following questions:

QUESTION 1: Many countries have followed an import substitution policy. Explain the rationale behind this policy.

ANSWER 1: Many countries felt that they were being left behind as the "developed" world built larger and more extensive industries. They were afraid that they would be stuck only producing commodity products (e.g., cocoa, bananas, rubber), and importing all advanced good from other countries. They wanted to be able to develop their own industries for advanced manufactured goods.

QUESTION 2: What were the main elements of an import substitution policy?

ANSWER 2: The key to an import substitution policy is being able to produce a good that can be heavily taxed upon export in order to fund the development of other industries. In the case of Ghana, this was cocoa. Government tax revenues from the export of cocoa were used to subsidize the development of other industries that would replace imported goods (e.g., radios, household items). It was felt that once these industries got going, not only would they be able to supply the domestic market and lead to self-sufficiency in manufactured goods, the country would be able to export these goods and develop the capability for making ever more sophisticated manufactured goods.

QUESTION 3: Why was the import substitution policy such a failure?

ANSWER 3: The import substitution policy caused Ghana to shift productive resources away from goods in which it had an absolute advantage (cocoa), and into goods where its costs of production were much higher than that of other nations. Consumers were forced to pay higher prices for generally inferior goods, and productive resources were used in relatively unproductive pursuits. These inefficiencies put a brake on economic development.

QUESTION 4: In contrast, why has South Korea performed so well?

ANSWER 4: Part of the explanation for South Korea's success lies in its much more open trade policies. South Korea's policies allowed its resources to be put to their best productive use, and it liberally imported and exported goods. Thus, consumers were able to get the most for their money, and workers were able to earn higher wages.

Chapter Outline With Lecture Notes and Teaching Tips

INTRODUCTION

A) This chapter has two goals. The first goal is to review a number of theories that explain why it is beneficial for a country to engage in international trade. The second goal is to explain the pattern of international trade that is observed in the world economy.

Teaching Tip: It is often worth asking students before discussing the theories why countries trade the products they do. They will frequently – with a little prompting hit upon many of the ideas presented in this chapter and consequently relate better to the various theories that are discussed.

AN OVERVIEW OF TRADE THEORY

A) Free trade refers to a situation where a government does not attempt to influence through quotas or duties what its citizens can buy from another country or what they can produce and sell to another country. Having completely free trade is certain to hurt some domestic industries that are not competitive on a worldwide basis.

The Benefits Of Trade

B) While it is easy to see why it makes sense to trade for goods that a country cannot easily produce, it is sometimes harder to understand why a country should not make goods that it can easily produce. There is little reason why the USA should not be able to produce all the sneakers and jeans demanded by its citizens. All of the raw materials required for these goods are available in the USA, as is labor. Nevertheless, the USA imports most of the sneakers and jeans consumed. This is because production is fairly labor intensive, and American labor is much more costly than labor in other parts of the world. American consumers would have to pay a great deal more for these goods if they were only made domestically. Thus it is beneficial for consumers to purchase goods from their least expensive source, and better that labor produce goods that take advantage of the educational level of most American workers

The Pattern of International Trade

C) Some patterns of trade are fairly easy to explain - it is obvious why Saudi Arabia exports oil, the US exports agricultural products, and Mexico exports labor intensive goods. Yet others are not so obvious or easily explained. The US ships Jeep Cherokees to Scandinavia, and Scandinavia ships Volvo station wagons to the US. Clearly it would be technically possible for Scandinavian firms to produce Jeeps and American firms to produce high quality station wagons.

Trade Theory and Government Policy

D) While all of the trade theories discussed in the text agree that international trade is beneficial to a country, they lack agreement in their recommendations for government policy. Mercantilism discussed below makes a crude case for government involvement in promoting exports and limiting imports. While, the theories of Smith, Ricardo, and Heckscher-Ohlin discussed below form a part of the case for unrestricted free trade the argument for unrestricted free trade is that both import controls and export incentives (such as subsidies) are self defeating and result in wasted resources. Yet both the new trade theory and Porter's theory of national competitive advantage discussed below can be interpreted as justifying some limited and selective government intervention to support the development of certain export-oriented industries.

MERCANTILISM

A) The first theory of international trade emerged in England in the mid-16th century. Referred to as **mercantilism**, its principle assertion was that it is in a country's best interest to maintain a trade surplus, to export more than it imports. Consistent with this belief, the mercantilist doctrine advocated government intervention to achieve a surplus in the balance of trade.

Teaching Note: A historical perspective of Mercantilism is available at the following site sponsored by the University of California at Davis {http://ps.ucdavis.edu/classes/pol129/SWE/mercan.htm}.

B) The flaw of mercantilism was that it viewed trade as one in which a gain by one country results in a loss by another. It was left to Adam Smith and David Ricardo to show the shortsightedness of this approach and to demonstrate that trade is a positive-sum game.

As an economic philosophy, mercantilism is problematic and not valid. Yet many political views today have the goal of boosting exports while limiting imports by seeking only selective liberalization of trade.

ABSOLUTE ADVANTAGE

A) In his 1776 landmark book The Wealth of Nations, Adam Smith attacked the mercantilist assumption that trade is a zero-sum game. Smith argued that countries differ in their ability to produce goods efficiently, and that a country has an **absolute advantage** in the production of a product when it is more efficient than any other country in producing it. According to Smith, countries should specialize in the production of goods for which they have an absolute advantage and then trade these goods for the goods produced by other countries. The text provides a numerical example of Smith's theory.

B) When each country has an absolute advantage in one of the products, it is clear that trade is beneficial. But what if one country has an absolute advantage in both products?

COMPARATIVE ADVANTAGE

A) David Ricardo took Adam Smith's theory one step further by exploring what might happen when one country has an absolute advantage in the production of all goods. Smith's theory of absolute advantage suggests that such a country might derive no benefits from international trade. In his 1817 book Principles of Political Economy, Ricardo showed that this was not the case. According to Ricardo's theory of **comparative advantage**, it makes sense for a country to specialize in the production of those goods that it produces most efficiently and to buy the goods that it produces less efficiently from other countries, even if this means buying goods from other countries that it could produce more efficiently itself. The textbook provides a detailed example to explain the rationale of this theory. This simple example of comparative advantage presented in the text makes a number of assumptions: only two countries and two goods; zero transportation costs; similar prices and values; resources are mobile between goods within countries, but not across countries; constant returns to scale; fixed stocks of resources; and no effects on income distribution within countries. While these are all unrealistic, the general proposition that countries will produce and export those goods that they are the most efficient at producing has been shown to be quite valid.

Teaching Tip: An overview of the ideas and philosophies of David Ricardo, from which his theory of comparative advantage emerged, is available at {http://www.stg.brown.edu/projects/hypertext/landow/victorian/economics/ric.html}.

Teaching Tip: A more complete description of Ricardo's theory of international trade can be accessed at {http://dylee.keel.econ.ship.edu/intntl/ecn321/lecture/Ricardo.htm}. Lecture Note: An excellent source of material on Ricardo's theory of comparative advantage is available at a site sponsored by the University of California at Davis. The site contains the transcripts of lectures on this topic. The web site address is: {http://ps.ucdavis.edu/classes/pol129/SWE/compadv.htm}.

The Gains from Trade

B) The theory of comparative advantage argues that trade is a positive sum gain in which all gain. It provides a strong rationale for encouraging free trade.

Qualifications and Assumptions

C) The simple example of comparative advantage presented in the text makes a number of assumptions: only two countries and two goods; zero transportation costs; similar prices and values; resources are mobile between goods within countries, but not across countries; constant returns to scale; fixed stocks of resources; and no effects on income distribution within countries. While these are all unrealistic, the general proposition that countries will produce and export those goods that they are the most efficient at producing has been shown to be quite valid.

Trade and Economic Growth

D) Opening an economy to trade is likely to generate dynamic gains of two types. First, trade might increase a country's stock of resources as increased supplies become available from abroad. Secondly, free trade might increase the efficiency of resource utilization, and free up resources for other uses.

HECKSCHER-OHLIN THEORY

A) Hecksher and Ohlin argued that comparative advantage arises from differences in national factor endowments. As a result, the Heckscher-Ohlin theory predicts that countries will export goods that make intensive use of those factors that are locally abundant, while importing goods that make intensive use of factors that are locally scarce.

Teaching Tip: A more complete description of the Heckscher-Ohlin theory is available at {http://dylee.keel.econ.ship.edu/intntl/ecn321/lecture/hotheory.htm}.

The Leontief Paradox

B) Using the Heckscher-Ohlin theory, Leontief, in 1953 postulated that since the U.S. was relatively abundant in capital compared to other nations, the U.S. would be an exporter of capital intensive goods and an importer of labor-intensive goods. To his surprise, however, he found that U.S. exports were less capital intensive than U.S. imports. Since this result was at variance with the predictions of the theory, it has become know as the Leontief Paradox.

Teaching Tip: A more complete description of the Leontief Paradox is available at {http://dylee.keel.econ.ship.edu/intntl/ecn321/lecture/leont.htm}.

THE PRODUCT LIFE CYCLE THEORY

A) Raymond Vernon initially proposed the product life-cycle theory in the mid 1960s. According to the theory as products mature both the location of sales and the optimal production location will change affecting the flow and direction of trade.

B) Early in the life cycle of a typical new product, while demand is starting to grow in the U.S., demand in other advanced countries is limited to high-income groups. The limited initial demand in other advanced countries does not make it worthwhile for firms in those countries to start producing the new product, but it does necessitate some exports from the U.S. to those countries. Over time, however, demand for the new product starts to grow in other advanced countries. As it does, it becomes worthwhile for foreign producers to being producing for their home markets. In addition, U.S. firms might set up production facilities in those advanced countries where demand is growing. Consequently, production within other advanced countries begins to limit the potential for exports from the U.S.

C) As the market in the U.S. and other advanced nations matures, the product becomes more standardized, and price becomes the main competitive weapon. One result is that producers based in advanced countries where labor costs are lower than the United States might now be able to export to the U.S.

D) If cost pressures become intense, the process might not stop there. The cycle by which the U.S. lost its advantage to other advanced countries might be repeated once more as developing countries begin to acquire a production advantage over advanced countries.

E) The consequences of these trends for the pattern of world trade is that the United States switches from being an exporter of the product to an importer of the product as production becomes more concentrated in lower-cost foreign locations.

F) While the product life cycle theory accurately explains what has happened for products like photocopiers and a number of other high technology products developed in the US in the 1960s and 1970s, the increasing globalization and integration of the world economy has made this theory less valid in today's world.

THE NEW TRADE THEORY

A) New trade theory suggests that because of economies of scale and increasing returns to specialization, in some industries there are likely to be only a few profitable firms. Thus firms with first mover advantages (the economic and strategic advantages that accrue to many entrants into an industry) will develop economies of scale and create barriers to entry for other firms. The commercial aircraft industry is an excellent example.

B) Productive efficiency may not be the result of factor endowments or specific national characteristics, but instead be a result a firm's first mover advantages.

C) New trade theory does not contradict the theory of comparative advantage, but instead identifies a source of comparative advantage.

D) An obvious and controversial extension of new trade theory is the implication that governments should consider strategic trade policies. Strategic trade policies would suggest that governments should nurture and protect firms and industries where first mover advantages and economies of scale are likely to be important, as doing so can make it more likely that a firm will build economies of scale and eventually end up a winner in the global competitive race.

NATIONAL COMPETITIVE ADVANTAGE: PORTER'S DIAMOND

A) Porter's 1990 study tried to explain why a nation achieves international success in a particular industry. This study found 4 broad attributes that promote or impede the creation of competitive advantage. These are shown in Figure 4.6.

Factor Endowments

B) A nation's position in factors of production such as skilled labor or infrastructure necessary to compete in a given industry can be critical. These factors can be either basic (natural resources, climate, location) or advanced (skilled labor, infrastructure, technological know-how). While either can be important, advanced factors are more likely to lead to competitive advantage.

Demand Conditions

C) The nature of home demand for the industries product or service influences the development of capabilities. Sophisticated and demanding customers pressure firms to be competitive.

Relating and Supporting Industries

D) The presence in a nation of supplier industries and related industries that are internationally competitive can spill over and contribute to other industries. Successful industries tend to be grouped in clusters in countries - having world class manufacturers of semi-conductor processing equipment can lead to (and be a result of having) a competitive semi-conductor industry.

Firm Strategy, Structure, and Rivalry

E) The conditions in the nation governing how companies are created, organized, and managed, and the nature of domestic rivalry impacts firms' competitiveness. Firms that face strong domestic competition will be better able to face competitors from other firms.

F) In addition to these four main attributes, government policies and chance can impact any of the four. Government policy can affect demand through product standards, influence rivalry through regulation and antitrust laws, and impact the availability of highly educated workers and advanced transportation infrastructure.

G) The four attributes of the diamond, government policy, and chance work as a reinforcing system, complementing each other and in combination creating the conditions appropriate for competitive advantage. The Management Focus on Nokia provides a good example of how this Finnish firm built its competitive advantage as a result of factors in Porter's diamond.

IMPLICATIONS FOR BUSINESS

A) There are at least three main implications of the material discussed in this chapter for international businesses: location implications, first-mover implications, and policy implications.

Location Implications

B) One way in which the material discussed in this chapter matters to an international business concerns the link between the theories of international trade and a firm's decision about where to locate its various productive activities. Underlying most of the theories is the notion that different countries have particular advantages in different productive activities. Thus, from a profit perspective, it makes sense for a firm to disperse its various productive activities to those countries where, according to the theory of international trade, they can be performed most efficiently. Being a first mover can have important competitive implications, especially if there are economies of scale and the global industry will only support a few competitors. Firms need to be prepared to undertake huge investments and suffer losses for several years in order to reap the eventual rewards.

First Mover Implications

C) Being a first mover can have important competitive implications, especially if there are economies of scale and the global industry will only support a few competitors. Firms need to be prepared to undertake huge investments and suffer losses for several years in order to reap the eventual rewards.

Policy Implications

D) The theories of international trade also matter to international businesses because business firms are major players on the international trade scene. Because of their pivotal role in international trade, business firms can and do exert a strong influence on government trade policy. Government policies with respect to free trade or protecting domestic industries can significantly impact global competitiveness.

E) One of the most important implications for business is that they should work to encourage governmental policies that support free trade. If a business is able to get its goods from the best sources worldwide, and compete in the sale of products into the most competitive markets, it has a good chance to survive and prosper. If such openness is restricted, a business's long-term survival will be in greater question.

Teaching Tip: For information about foreign governments and their approaches to international trade, visit the Electronic Embassy at {http://www.embassy.org/}. This site provides links to all of the foreign embassies located in Washington D.C.

Critical Thinking and Discussion Questions

1. "Mercantilism is a bankrupt theory that has no place in the modern world." Discuss.

Answer: Mercantilism, in its purest sense, is a bankrupt theory that has no place in the modern world. The principle tenant of mercantilism is that a country should maintain a trade surplus, even if that means that imports are limited by government intervention. This policy is bankrupt for at least two reasons. First, it is inconsistent with the general notion of globalization, which is becoming more and more prevalent in the world. A policy of mercantilism will anger potential trade partners because it will exclude their goods from free access to the mercantilist country's markets. Eventually, a country will find it difficult to export if it imposes oppressive quotas and tariffs on its imports. Second, mercantilism is bankrupt because it hurts the consumers in the mercantilist country. By denying its consumers access to either "cheaper" goods from other countries or more "sophisticated" goods from other countries, the mercantilist country's ordinary consumers suffer.

2. The "Country Focus" reviews the arguments of those who suggest that Japan is a neo-mercantilist nation. Do you agree with this assessment? Can you think of cases in which your country has taken a neo-mercantilist stance to foreign competition?

Answer: This question is designed to stimulate class discussion and/or to force your students to "think" about this complex issue in answering the question in a written format. By the examples provided in the country focus feature, it is easy to jump to the conclusion that Japan is a neo-mercantilist nation. However, encourage students to think deeper, and argue both sides of this issue. Virtually every country supports some protectionist measures for some industries.

3. Using the theory of comparative advantage to support your arguments, outline the case for free trade.

Answer: If each country specializes in the production of goods in which it has a comparative advantage relative to its trading partners, and then trades these goods for those produced by trading partners that have a comparative advantage in other goods, all countries can end up increasing their utility and consuming higher quantities (or at least the same) of all goods than if they only consumed what they produced.

4. Using the new trade theory and Porter's theory of national competitive advantage outline the case for government policies that would build national competitive advantage in a particular industry. What kind of policies would you recommend that the government adopt? Are these policies at variance with the basic free trade philosophy?

Answer: Porter's theory of national competitive advantage argues that four broad attributes of a nation shape the environment in which local firms compete, and that these attributes promote or impede the creation of competitive advantage. These attributes are: factor endowments, demand conditions, related and supporting industries, and firm strategy, structure, and rivalry. Porter goes on to argue that firms are most likely to succeed in industries in which the diamond (which are the four attributes collectively) is favorable. Porter adds two factors to the list of attributes described above: chance and government policy. The New Trade theory addresses a separate issue. This theory argues that due to the presence of substantial scale economies, world demand will support only a few firms in many industries. Underpinning this argument is the notion of first-mover advantages, which are the economic and strategic advantages that accrue to early entrants into an industry. One could argue that when the attributes of a nation are conductive to the production of a product, and when the manufacturers of that product have experienced some "chance" events that have provided them first-mover advantages, the governmental policies of that nation should promote the building of national competitive advantage in that particular area. This could be accomplished through government R&D grants, policies that favor the industry in capital markets, policies towards education, the creation of a favorable regulatory atmosphere, tax abatements, and the like. Ask your students whether they think this policy is at variance with the basic free trade philosophy. One could argue that it is, because the government intervention is creating the basis for comparative advantage. Conversely, one could argue that if a country establishes a comparative advantage in a particular area that is based on a unique set of attributes (such as Swiss production of watches), world output will be favorably impacted by letting that country pursue its area of comparative advantage.

5. You are the CEO of a textile firm that designs and manufacturers mass-market clothing products in the United States. Your manufacturing process is labor-intensive and does not require highly skilled employees. Currently you have design facilities in Paris and New York and manufacturing facilities in North Carolina. Drawing on the theory of international trade, decide whether these are optimal locations for these activities.

Answer: Underlying the theories of international trade is the notion that different countries (or areas within a country), have particular advantages in different productive activities. Thus, from a profit perspective, it makes sense for a firm to disperse its various productive activities to those specific locations where they can be produced the most efficiently. If design activities can be produced most efficiently in Paris and New York, then these activities should remain in those locations. Similarly, if the manufacturing of the textile products can be conducted most efficiently in North Carolina, then the manufacturing operations should remain there. If the firm has better alternatives in other geographic locations (all other things being equal), then appropriate changes should be considered.

6. "Policies designed to limit competition from low-cost foreign competitors do not help a country to achieve greater economic growth." Discuss this statement.

Answer: This is an excellent question that will help you as a teacher determine whether your students understand the material in this chapter. Free trade, even if it results in low-cost foreign competitors to compete in a domestic market, can generate dynamic economic gains. These dynamic gains are of two sorts. First, free trade might increase a country's stock of resources as increased supplies of labor and capital from abroad become available for use within the country. Second, free trade might also increase the efficiency with which a country utilizes its resources. By not having to produce low cost goods, for example, a country could dedicate its efforts towards the production of higher-cost, higher-quality products.

Internet Exercises

TEXT EXERCISE 1

Overview

This exercise explores the question of national competitiveness through the eyes of Michael Porter and his Diamond of Competitive Advantage theory. According to Porter, governments may play a very real role in determining both a nation's overall competitiveness, and industry competitiveness.

Suggested Use in the Classroom

Students are asked to explore the notion of competitiveness, and in particular, competitiveness in an interconnected world using Porter's framework. Many students may use Microsoft as an example of how the government can play a role in determining industry competitiveness. Other students may explore how the Chinese government is restricting investment in its Internet companies, and consequently limiting the ability of the firms to grow and become competitive.

TEXT EXERCISE 2

Overview

Many of the traditional theories of trade such as Smith's Theory of Absolute Advantage, and Ricardo's Theory of Competitive Advantage are linked to the bricks and mortar world. This exercise raises the question of how well these theories can explain cross-border electronic trade.

Suggested Use in the Classroom

In this exercise, students are asked to evaluate how well each of the theories presented in the text explain international e-commerce. While many students may argue that the theories maintain their power and rigor, others may suggest that some theories are weakened because many of the players in international electronic trade are virtual companies, and as such are not necessarily linked to any single country.

WEB EXERCISE 1

Overview

The notion of the invisible hand, a central tenant in Adam's Smith's theory of trade, is discussed in this exercise. More specifically, the question of whether the invisible hand should be allowed to work in international e-commerce is raised.

Suggested Use in the Classroom

This exercise provides a good forum for debate as to whether, and if so, how, the government should be involved in e-commerce. The topic has been well covered in the business press, and many students will be familiar with issues related to security and taxes, but may be less informed about the WTO's efforts with regard to government intervention in the e-market. The discussion that evolves from this exercise may also be linked to the first text Internet exercise in this chapter.

WEB EXERCISE 2

Overview

This exercise examines the virtual corporation, and all that it entails within the framework of Hecksher and Ohlin's work in explaining international trade. Hecksher and Ohlin used the country as the basis for their explanation of why a country should produce and export certain products. The question of whether their theory holds in a virtual marketplace is raised.

Suggested Use in the Classroom

Students will probably take very different approaches to this exercise. Some may break the value-added chain into parts, and argue that taken in that form, where the virtual corporation is merely a linking mechanism, Hecksher and Ohlin's work still holds. Others, however, will probably consider the value-added chain as a whole, and suggest that Hecksher and Ohlin's explanation of trade is limited when taken in this capacity.

CLOSING CASE: The Rise of the Indian Software Industry

Summary

The closing case describes the thriving software in India. It outlines a number of factors that have allowed India to develop a world-class software industry. Discussion of the case can be based around the following questions:

QUESTION 1: To what extent does the theory of comparative advantage explain the rise of the Indian software industry?

ANSWER 1: The theory of comparative advantage gives a fairly straightforward explanation, as it states that a country should specialize in producing goods that it can produce most efficiently. Given that software can be produced very efficiently in India, it makes sense that India produces and exports software.

QUESTION 2: To what extent does the Hecksher-Ohlin theory explain the rise of the Indian software industry?

ANSWER 2: The Hecksher-Ohlin theory gives a more complete explanation than that of simple comparative advantage. It specifies the factor of production that India has in abundance, and which leads to the fact that India is an efficient producer of software. This factor of production is abundant software engineers. Given India's abundant supply of software engineers, it makes sense that India produces and exports a product that makes intensive use of this factor of production.

QUESTION 3: Use Michael Porter's diamond to analyze the rise of the Indian software industry. Does this analysis help explain the rise of this industry?

ANSWER 3: The Hecksher-Ohlin theory leaves us wondering why India has such an abundant supply of software engineers. Porter's theory helps explain why India was able to develop a software industry. India has a growing middle class that is well educated, has good skills in English, and is attracted to engineering due to the relatively high wages. The Indian government has assisted by providing both the educational system and interconnections to the global information network. Within the Indian software industry, there is competition for both local engineers and contracts from abroad. Other aspects of the Porter model, however, are not well supported - domestic demand conditions play no role, and that of related or supporting industries is minimal.

QUESTION 4: Which of the above theories - comparative advantage, Hecksher-Ohlin, or Porter's - gives the best explanation of the rise of the Indian software industry? Why?

ANSWER 4: The three theories each build upon each other. Comparative advantage identifies software as a product where India is an efficient producer, Hecksher-Ohlin shows that a particular factor of production is responsible for this efficiency, and the Porter model identifies several variables that have contributed the development of this factor of production. While the Porter model gives the most complete explanation, it is perhaps a more complex model than required, and aspects of the model would have appeared to play little role in the development of the industry. If parsimony were taken into consideration, the Hecksher-Ohlin theory would seem to provide the best explanation

Management Focus: Crawfish Wars

<u>Summary</u>

This feature explores the battle over crawfish prices in Louisiana. Louisiana, with its thriving Cajun culture, relies on crawfish for many of its culinary delights. While the crawfish is a natural inhabitant in the local bayous, in the early 1990's, Louisiana importers began importing the fish from the Chinese. Chinese crawfish were available at a considerably lower price than local fish. By 1996, however, as the Louisiana crawfish industry continued to lose jobs at an alarming rate, charges of dumping were levied against the Chinese. Eventually, the International Trade Commission sided with Louisiana fishers and a tariff was implemented on all imports of Chinese crawfish.

1. Who are the winners and who are the losers in the crawfish battle? Discuss the decision of the International Trade Commission and its assessment that China was dumping in the U.S. market.

2. Using the trade theories presented in this chapter, explain the case of the Louisiana crawfish wars.

Country Focus: Is Japan a Neo-Mercantilist Nation?

<u>Summary</u>

This feature explains the basis for the allegation that Japan is a neo-mercantilist nation. Several examples are provided which furnish evidence that the Japanese government works hard to ensure that Japan has a positive balance of trade, even if it has to resort to formal and informal trade barriers to achieve this objective.

<u>Suggested Discussion Questions</u>

1. In your opinion, is Japan a neo-mercantilist nation? Support you answer.

2. Today, the trade imbalance between the United States and Japan is $60 billion (meaning that the United States imported $60 billion more in goods from Japan than it exported to Japan). Does this fact alone suggest that Japan is a neo-mercantilist nation? What other reasons could have created such a large trade imbalance between the two countries?

3. Should the United States government fight back by imposing stricter import quotas on Japanese good coming into America? Discuss the wisdom of this suggestion.

Management Focus: The Rise of Finland's Nokia

Summary

This feature is about the growth of the cellular telephone equipment industry, and more specifically, about the rise in competitiveness of Nokia, a Finnish cellular telephone company. The feature explains the reasons that Nokia was particularly well positioned to take advantage of the growth of the global cellular telephone industry.

Suggested Discussion Questions

1. Using the New Trade Theory and Porter's theory of National Competitive Advantage, describe why Nokia emerged as a leading competitor in the global cellular telephone equipment industry.

2. Explain why the cellular telephone industry caught on in Finland and the other Scandinavian countries faster than the rest of the world.

3. Why didn't the development of the cellular telephone equipment industry take place in Mexico or another Central or South American country rather than Finland, Sweden, and the United States? Base your answer of the international trade theories described in Chapter 4.

4. Nokia's Homepage: {http://www.nokia.com/}

Additional Readings and Sources of Information

Biography of Adam Smith: {http://grid.let.rug.nl/~usa/B/asmith/adamsl.htm}

Playing the Cellular Boom: Nokia vs. Ericsson: {http://www.businessweek.com/1998/32/b3590014.htm}

Nokia is Shopping for a New Number: {http://www.businessweek.com/1999/99_14/b3623173.htm}

The Best Wireless Phone on the Market: {http://www.businessweek.com/1998/32/b3590010.htm}

America's Indian Ambassador: {http://www.businessweek.com/dnflash/feb2000/nf00209b.htm}

CHAPTER 5
THE POLITICAL ECONOMY OF INTERNATIONAL TRADE

Chapter Outline

OPENING CASE: Trade in Hormone-Treated Beef

INTRODUCTION

INSTRUMENTS OF TRADE POLICY

Tariffs
Subsides
Country Focus: The Costs of Protectionism in the United States
Import Quotas and Voluntary Export Restraints
Local Content Requirements
Administrative Polices

THE CASE FOR GOVERNMENT INTERVENTION

Political Arguments for Intervention
Economic Arguments for Intervention

THE REVISED CASE FOR FREE TRADE

Retaliation and Trade War
Domestic Politics

DEVELOPMENT OF THE GLOBAL TRADING SYSTEM

From Smith to the Great Depression
1947-1979: GATT, Trade Liberalization, and Economic Growth
1980-1993: Disturbing Trends
The Uruguay Round and the World Trade Organization
WTO: Early Experience
The Future: Unresolved Issues
Management Focus: Toyota's Response to Rising Protectionist Pressure in Europe and the United States

IMPLICATIONS FOR BUSINESS

Trade Barriers and Firm Strategy
Policy Implications

CRITICAL THINKING AND DISCUSSION QUESTIONS

INTERNET EXERCISES

CLOSING CASE: Shrimps, Turtles, and the WTO

Learning Objectives

1. Discuss the various policy instruments that governments use to restrict imports and promote exports.

2. Understand why some governments intervene in international trade to restrict imports and promote exports.

3. Appreciate the position of those who argue that government intervention in international trade can be self-defeating and typically fail to produce the gains that advocates of intervention claim.

4. Be familiar with the evolution, purpose, current status, and future prospects of the global trading system as embodied in the General Agreement on Tariffs and Trade and the World Trade Organization.

5. Understand the important implications for business practice of government intervention in international trade and of the current global trading system.

Chapter Summary

This chapter begins with a discussion of the six main instruments of trade policy, including tariffs, subsidies, import quotas, voluntary export restraints, local content requirements, and administrative policies. This section is followed by a discussion of the merits of government intervention into international trade. The author provides a balanced view of this difficult issue.
The second half of the chapter focuses on the development of the global trading system. A historical context is provided, along with a view of the global trading system as it exists today. The author acquaints the reader with the General Agreement on Trade and Tariffs (GATT) and the World Trade Organization.

OPENING CASE: Trade in Hormone-Treated Beef

Summary

The opening case describes the trade battle between the USA and EU over beef from cattle that have been given growth hormones. It outlines the basic issues that led to the dispute, and shows how the World Trade Organization has treated the case. A discussion of the case can revolve around the following questions:

QUESTION 1: Why is the EU so concerned about beef from cattle that have been given growth hormones?

ANSWER 1: There are multiple reasons, some of which have changed over time. One concern is that the hormones, while naturally occurring in cattle, should not be given to cattle above the level produced naturally. There are concerns over the potential health effects on humans from eating such beef. (Many consumers who choose to purchase only organically grown vegetables use a similar argument.) Even if there is no scientific evidence suggesting such beef is dangerous for human consumption, if consumers are concerned about it and skeptical, some argue that the beef should be banned to support the preferences of consumers. A third argument, not articulated in the article, was that the ban was promoted by the domestic cattle industry. Given the EU's comparative disadvantage in beef production, if they could effectively block imports from more efficient producers, it would allow them to raise prices and expand production of beef within the EU.

QUESTION 2: Why did the WTO rule against the EU?

ANSWER 2: Scientific evidence, the UN, and the World Health Organization all indicated that beef was beef, regardless of the use of growth hormones in the production of the beef. Thus the EU's ban had no scientific basis of support.

QUESTION 3: What would you recommend as the next step for the USA, New Zealand, and Australia? Should they enter a negotiated settlement with the EU that would continue the ban?

ANSWER 3: There is no one answer to this question, but it could be used to set up a brief debate. While beef is the item of trade, it may be less important than some others. If the winning countries could use this to gain concessions on other items, it may be rational to allow temporary continuation of the ban while trying to educate EU consumers on the prevalence of similar practices in the production of many of the other products they consume. On the other hand, this dispute clearly has implications for other products. Given the competitive advantage of the USA in developing many new technologies that promote agricultural efficiency, it may be dangerous to allow the EU to start banning such products.

Chapter Outline With Lecture Notes and Teaching Tips

INTRODUCTION

A) This chapter explores the political and economic reasons that governments have for intervening in international trade.

B) The major objective of this chapter is to describe how political realities have shaped, and continue to shape, the international trading system.

INSTRUMENTS OF TRADE POLICY

A) In this section, the text reviews seven main instruments of trade policy. These are: tariffs, subsidies, import quotas, voluntary export restraints, local content requirements, antidumping policies and administrative policies.

Teaching Tip: An excellent site on tariffs and quotas, containing case studies and a role-playing example, is available at {http://ps.ucdavis.edu/classes/pol129/SWE/tariffs.htm}. The role-playing example in particular may stimulate good classroom interaction.

B) A **tariff** is a tax levied on imports that effectively raises the cost of imported products relative to domestic products. **Specific tariffs** are levied as a fixed charge for each unit of a good imported, while **ad valorem tariffs** are levied as a proportion of the value of the imported good. The important thing to understand about a tariff is who suffers and who gains. The government gains, because the tariff increases government revenues. Domestic producers gain, because the tariff affords them some protection against foreign competitors by increasing the cost of imported foreign goods. Consumers lose since they must pay more for certain imports.

C) Thus, tariffs are unambiguously pro-producer and anti-consumer, and tariffs reduce the overall efficiency of the world economy.

Subsidies

D) A **subsidy** is a government payment to a domestic producer. By lowering costs, subsidies help domestic producers in two ways: they help them compete against low-cost foreign imports and they help them gain export markets. However, many subsidies are not that successful at increasing the international competitiveness of domestic producers. Moreover, consumers typically absorb the costs of subsidies.

Import Quotas And Voluntary Export Restraints

E) An **import quota** is a direct restriction on the quantity of some good that may be imported into a country. A **voluntary export restraint** is a quota on trade imposed by the exporting country, typically at the request of the importing country's government.

F) While import quotas and voluntary export restraints benefit domestic producers by limiting import competition, they raise the prices of imported goods.

Teaching Tip: A review of the role of voluntary export restraints in world trade is available at {http://ps.ucdavis.edu/classes/pol129/SWE/restrain.htm}. This site is well worth a visit if you plan to emphasize this topic in your lecture.

Local Content Requirements

G) A **local content requirement** demands that some specific fraction of a good be produced domestically. As with import quotas, local content requirements benefit domestic producers, but consumer face higher prices.

Antidumping Policies

H) **Dumping** is variously defined as selling goods in a foreign market below their costs of production, or as selling goods in a foreign market at below their "fair" market value. Dumping is viewed as a method by which firms unload excess production in foreign markets. Alternatively, some dumping may be the result of predatory behavior, with producers using substantial profits from their home markets to subsidize prices in a foreign market with a view to driving indigenous competitors out of that market. Once this has been achieved the predatory firm can raise prices and earn substantial profits.

I) **Antidumping polices** are policies designed to punish foreign firms that engage in dumping. The ultimate objective is to protect domestic producers from "unfair" foreign competition.

Administrative Policies

J) **Administrative trade policies** are bureaucratic rules that are designed to make it difficult for imports to enter a country. As with all instruments of trade policy, administrative instruments benefit producers and hurt consumers, who are denied access to possibly superior foreign products.

THE CASE FOR GOVERNMENT INTERVENTION

A) In general, there are two types of arguments for government intervention, political and economic. Political arguments for intervention are concerned with protecting the interests of certain groups within a nation (normally producers), often at the expense of other groups (normally consumers). Economic arguments for intervention are typically concerned with boosting the overall wealth of a nation (to the benefit of all, both producers and consumers).

Political Arguments for Intervention

B) Political arguments for government intervention cover a range of issues including protecting jobs, protecting industries deemed important for national security, retaliating to unfair foreign competition, protecting consumers from "dangerous" products, furthering the goals of foreign policy, and protecting the human rights of individuals in exporting countries.

Protecting Jobs and Industries

C) The most common political reason for trade restrictions is "protecting jobs and industries." Usually this results from political pressures by unions or industries that are "threatened" by more efficient foreign producers, and have more political clout than the consumers that will eventually pay the costs.

National Security

D) Keeping industries "vital for national security" viable is an oft used argument for trade restrictions. While this is reasonable for industries like steel, aerospace, and electronics, in the US the shoe industry has regularly lobbied that soldiers need boots, and thus the US needs to have a viable shoe industry in order to be able to provide shoes during a time of war.

Lecture Note: In the United States, the Bureau of Export Administration enhances the nation's security and its economic prosperity by controlling exports for national security, foreign security, foreign policy, and short supply reasons. The Bureau of Export Administration maintains a web site at {http://www.bxa.doc.gov/}.

Retaliation

E) Government intervention in trade can be used as part of a "get tough" policy to open foreign markets. By taking, or threatening to take, specific actions, other countries may remove trade barriers. But when threatened governments don't back down, tensions can escalate and new trade barriers may be enacted.

Protecting Consumers

F) Consumer protection can also be an argument for restricting imports. The opening case suggests that the EU's concern over beef was, in part, due to an interest in protecting consumers. Since different countries do have different health and safety standards, what may be acceptable in one country may be unacceptable in others.

Furthering Foreign Policy Objectives

G) On occasion, governments will use trade policy to support their foreign policy objectives. One aspect of this is to grant preferential trade terms to countries that a government wants to build strong relations with. Trade policy has also been used several times as an instrument for pressuring punishing "rogue states" that do not abide by international laws or norms. A serious problem with using trade as an instrument of foreign policy is that other countries can undermine any unilateral trade sanctions.

Protecting Human Rights

H) Concern over human rights in other countries plays an important role in foreign policy. Governments sometimes use trade policy to improve the human rights policies of trading partners. Governments also use trade policies to put pressure on governments to make other changes. In recent years the USA has had trade restrictions against Libya, Iran, Iraq, North Korea, Cuba, and other countries whose governments were pursuing policies that were not viewed favorably by the US government. Unless a large number of countries choose to take such action, however, it is unlikely to prove successful.

Economic Arguments for Intervention

The Infant Industry Argument

I) The "infant industry" argument suggests that an industry should be protected until it can develop and be viable and competitive internationally. Unless an industry is allowed to develop and achieve minimal economies of scale, foreign competitors may undercut prices and prevent a domestic industry from developing. The infant industry argument has been accepted as a justification for temporary trade restrictions under the WTO.

J) A problem with the infant industry argument is determining when an industry "grows up." Some industries that are just plain inefficient and uncompetitive have argued they are still infants after 50 years. The other problem is that given the existence of global capital markets, if the country has the potential to develop a viable competitive position its firms should be capable of raising the necessary funds without additional support from the government.

Strategic Trade Policy

K) Strategic trade policy suggests that in cases where there may be important first mover advantages, governments can help firms from their countries attain these advantages. Strategic trade policy also suggests that governments can help firms overcome barriers to entry into industries where foreign firms have an initial advantage.

THE REVISED CASE FOR FREE TRADE

A) While strategic trade policy identifies conditions where restrictions on trade may provide economic benefits, there are two problems that may make restrictions inappropriate: retaliation and politics.

Retaliation and Trade War

B) Krugman argues that strategic trade policies aimed at establishing domestic firms in a dominant position in a global industry are beggar-thy-neighbor policies that boost national income at the expense of other countries. A country that attempts to use such policies will probably provoke retaliation.

Domestic Politics

C) Governments do not always act in the national interest when they intervene in the economy. Instead special interest groups may influence governments. Thus, a further reason for not embracing strategic trade policy, according to Krugman, is that such a policy is almost certain to be captured by special interest groups within an economy, who will distort it to their own ends.

DEVELOPMENT OF THE GLOBAL TRADING SYSTEM

From Smith to the Great Depression

A) Up until the Great Depression of the 1930s, most countries had some degree of protectionism. Great Britain, as a major trading nation, was one of the strongest supporters of free trade.

B) Although the world was already in a depression, in 1930 the US enacted the Smoot-Hawley tariff, which created significant import tariffs on foreign goods. As other nations took similar steps and the depression deepened, world trade fell further.

Teaching Tip: A review of the causes of the great depression, including a discussion of the role of tariffs, is available at {http://ps.ucdavis.edu/classes/pol129/SWE/depress.htm}.

1947-79: GATT, Trade Liberalization, and Economic Growth

C) After WWII, the US and other nations realized the value of freer trade, and established the General Agreement on Tariffs and Trade (GATT).

D) The approach of GATT (a multilateral agreement to liberalize trade) was to gradually eliminate barriers to trade. Over 100 countries became members of GATT, and worked together to further liberalize trade.

Teaching Tip: A full review of GATT, containing an actual copy of the agreement, is available at {http://itl.irv.uit.no/trade_law/documents/freetrade/wta-94/nav/toc.html}.

1980-1993: Disturbing Trends

E) During the 1980s and early 1990s the world trading system as "managed" by GATT underwent strains. First, Japan's economic strength and huge trade surplus stressed what had been more equal trading patterns, and Japan's perceived protectionist (neo-mercantilist) policies created intense political pressures in other countries. Second, the persistent trade deficits by the US, the world's largest economy, caused significant economic problems for some industries and political problems for the government. Thirdly, many countries found that although limited by GATT from utilizing tariffs, there were many other more subtle forms of intervention that had the same effects and did not technically violate GATT (e.g. VERs).

F) Against the background of rising protectionist pressures, in 1986 GATT members embarked on their eighth round of negotiations to reduce tariffs (called the Uruguay Round). This was the most ambitious round to date.

Services and Intellectual Property

G) The goal was to expand beyond the regulation of manufactured goods and address trade issues related to services and intellectual property, agriculture, and enforcement mechanism.

The World Trade Organization

H) When the WTO was established, its creators hoped the WTO's enforcement mechanisms would make it a more effective policeman of the global trade rules than the GATT had been.

Implications of the Uruguay Round

I) On balance, the world is better off with a GATT deal than without it. Without the deal, there was a very real possibility that the world might have slipped into increasingly dangerous trade wars, which might have triggered off a recession. With a GATT deal concluded the current world trading system looks secure, and there is a good possibility that the world economy will now grow faster than would otherwise have been the case.

WTO: Early Experience

J) At the time of its establishment, the great hope was that the WTO might emerge as an effective advocate and facilitator of future trade deals, particularly in such areas as services. In general, the experience so far has been encouraging.

WTO as a Global Policeman

K) The WTO has handed down a number of rulings that have led to changes in governmental policies that restricted trade, and in other cases governments have made changes in advance of WTO rulings.

WTO Telecommunications Agreement

L) Under the WTO, 68 countries that account for more than 90% of world telecommunications revenues pledged to open their markets to foreign competition and to abide by common rules for fair competition in telecommunications.

WTO Financial Services Agreement

M) The WTO has also made headway in liberalizing trade in financial services, although the current agreement still includes a number of exceptions.

The Future: Unresolved Issues

N) Substantial work still remains to be done on the international trade front. Environmental policies are one area of concern, as are regulations regarding foreign direct investment.

IMPLICATIONS FOR BUSINESS

Trade Barriers and Firm Strategy

O) Trade barriers are a constraint upon a firm's ability to disperse its productive activities. First, trade barriers raise the cost of exporting products to a country. Second, voluntary export restraints (VERs) may limit a firm's ability to serve a country from locations outside that country. Third, to conform to local content requirements, a firm may have to locate more production activities in a given market than it would otherwise. All of the above effects are likely to raise the firm's costs above the level that could be achieved in a world without trade barriers.

Policy Implications

P) In general, international firms have an incentive to lobby for free trade, and keep protectionist pressures from causing them to have to change strategies. While there may be short benefits to having governmental protection in some situations, in the long run these can backfire and other governments can retaliate.

Critical Thinking and Discussion Questions

1. Do you think the US government should take human rights considerations into account when granting most favored nation trading status to China? What are the arguments for and against taking such a position?

Answer: The answer to the first question clearly is a matter of personal opinion. In stating their opinions, students should consider the following points. Trade with the US is very important to China, as China views the US as an important market. The US is also an important source of certain products. Thus, the US has some leverage with trade when trying to influence China's human rights policies. For this policy to have much effect, however, other nations important to China must adopt similar policies. Otherwise China will simply choose to work with other countries, and US consumers and producers may be more negatively impact than the Chinese. Another concern with tying MFN status to human rights is that denying MFN may make the human rights situation worse rather than better. By engaging in trade, the income levels in China will increase, and with greater wealth the people will be able to demand and receive better treatment.

2. Whose interests should be the paramount concern of government trade policy - the interests of producers (businesses and their employees) or of consumers?

Answer: The long run interests of consumers should be the primary concern of governments. Unfortunately consumers, each of whom may be negatively impacted by only a few dollars, are less motivated and effective lobbyists than a few producers that have a great deal at stake. While in some instances it could be argued that domestic consumers will be better off if world-class domestic producers are nurtured and allowed to gain first mover advantages in international markets, it is doubtful that the government will be better than international capital markets at "picking winners", and will more likely pick the firms with the greatest political clout. While employees may well lose jobs if there are more efficient foreign competitors, some would argue that this is just the nature of competition, and that the role of government should be to help these employees get jobs where they can be efficiently employed rather than to protect them from reality in inefficient firms.

3. Given the arguments relating to the new trade theory and strategic trade policy, what kind of trade policy should business be pressuring government to adopt?

Answer: According to the textbook, businesses should urge governments to target technologies that may be important in the future and use subsidies to support development work aimed at commercializing those technologies. Government should provide export subsidies until the domestic firms have established first mover advantages in the world market. Government support may also be justified if it can help domestic firms overcome the first-mover advantages enjoyed by foreign competitors and emerge as viable competitors in the world market. In this case, a combination of home market protection and export-promoting subsidies may be called for.

4. 4. You are an employee of an US firm that produces personal computers in Thailand and then exports them to the US and other countries for sale. The personal computers were originally produced in Thailand to take advantage of relatively low labor costs and a skilled workforce. Other possible locations considered at that time were Malaysia and Hong Kong. The US government decides to impose punitive 100% ad valorem tariffs on imports of computers from Thailand to punish the country for administrative trade barriers that restrict US exports to Thailand. How should your firm respond? What does this tell you about the use of targeted trade barriers?

Answer: As long as the manufacturing requirements haven't changed significantly, looking at Malaysia or Hong Kong again for production would appear obvious. By the US government introducing a specific ad valorem tariff on Thai computer imports, it would be easy to get around these by looking at other locations. Hence such targeted trade barriers can often be easily circumvented without having to locate production facilities in an expensive country like the US

Internet Exercises

TEXT EXERCISE 1

Overview

This exercise explores the World Trade Organization's position towards e-commerce. The WTO has indicated that it wants to ensure that trade barriers that could limit the free flow of electronic trade will not be erected.

Suggested Use in the Classroom

Students are asked whether a separate set of rules should be established for international e-commerce, or whether a common set of rules should be applied across the board, regardless of how the goods are actually traded. Many students will probably suggest that all goods should be treated the same, that the actual form of commerce should not influence the decision. Others however, may argue that by establishing and maintaining a new set of rules—rules that allow for the free flow of international e-trade, the WTO can actually take great strides in making its mission of free trade a reality.

TEXT EXERCISE 2

Overview

American media companies are flocking to China. As this exercise points out, the market is not only huge, but also seemingly welcoming to new entrants. Many firms are finding that by collaborating with the government, they can improve their chances for success in the market.

Suggested Use in the Classroom

This exercise asks students to identify the best way to enter the Chinese market. Many students will follow the suggestion in the exercise, and recommend that companies form alliances with the Chinese government, arguing that by doing so, their path will be greatly facilitated. Others however, may suggest that the Chinese government is not always easy to predict, and that by maintaining a distance from the government, firms may actually bring themselves some degree of protection.

WEB EXERCISE 1

Overview

There are few regulations limiting the so-called "junk mail" that every American finds in their mailbox just about everyday. In contrast, as this exercise points out, sending junk mail in Germany can be very difficult thanks to a strict set of regulations imposed by the German government.

Suggested Use in the Classroom

This exercise asks students to consider the implications of Germany's junk mail regulations, and what impact they may have on a firm that relies on direct mail campaigns. Most students will probably suggest that Germany is unfairly limiting certain market activities, and in doing so, are establishing a barrier to trade. Others however, will probably point out that since the rules apply across the board, German firms are also affected, and that firms doing business in Germany must play by the German rules.

WEB EXERCISE 2

Overview

This exercise explores the current situation in Iran. The country, after decades of repression, is beginning to rebel, demanding more rights both politically and socially.

Suggested Use in the Classroom

Students are asked to consider the changes that are currently taking place in Iran, and the role of the Internet in facilitating those changes. Most students will quickly recognize that the Internet has probably opened many doors to the West for Iranians, and in doing so, may have influenced the reform that is presently taking place. Most students will probably agree that it will be difficult for the government to continue to impose restrictions similar to those in the past.

CLOSING CASE: Shrimps, Turtles, and the WTO

Summary

The closing case describes a conflict between US regulations to help save sea turtles, and foreign governments' views that these regulations restrict free trade in shrimp. Discussion of this case can revolve around the following questions:

QUESTION 1: Do you think the United States is correct to try to use its law and trade policy to force other countries to adopt environmental policies that it perceives to be sound?

ANSWER 1: This is clearly a question of personal opinion. Supporting the affirmative position is a view that issues should not be viewed in isolation, and it is completely appropriate for a government to have consistent policies regarding natural resources, trade, and foreign affairs. Similarly, it would be unfair to US shrimp harvesters to force them to use a more expensive production technology than is required of foreign producers that wish to sell their goods in the US. Supporting the other position is the argument that the US really has no business telling producers in other countries how to run their businesses. Another argument is that environmental regulation should be negotiated multilaterally through environmental organizations, and trade regulations through their own body.

QUESTION 2: Does the WTO decision have implications for US national sovereignty? If so, what?

ANSWER 2: The decision has a couple of implications for US national sovereignty. One is that national sovereignty is limited to the borders of the US, and that US law cannot be used to impose US regulations on other countries. Another implication is that as a member of the WTO, the US must either change its law, or agree to compensate other countries affected by its laws.

QUESTION 3: Do you think that it is correct for the WTO to decouple trade policy from environmental policy? Why?

ANSWER 3: While as stated this question clearly allows for personal interpretation, the organization is called the World TRADE Organization, not the World ENVIRONMENT and Trade Organization. For the joining nations to have also reached an agreement on environmental matters would have clearly led to a much different agreement.

QUESTION 4: Do you think that other countries are correct to accuse the United States of hypocrisy on the environmental issue?

ANSWER 4: Again, this is open to personal opinion. Given the general record of the US on environmental matters, accusations of hypocrisy are not unwarranted.

QUESTION 5: How should the United States react to the WTO decision in this case?

ANSWER 5: The US would appear to have three options. One would be to change US law to not limit imports of shrimp based on the turtle excluder equipment. Another would be to compensate the litigants for their lost sales to the US. A third option would be to reach some multilateral agreement with these nations that represented a compromise acceptable to all. Students could propose and support any of these options.

Country Focus: The Costs of Protectionism in the United States

Summary

This feature illustrates that although American trade negotiators are quick to suggest that the U.S. economy is an open one with few import tariffs, import tariffs imposed by the U.S. government still exist. The feature illustrates the adverse impact of these tariffs on the U.S. economy. A study conducted by the Institute for International Economics looked at the effect of import tariffs on economic activity in 21 industries that the U.S. protected most heavily from foreign competition. The study found that while the import tariffs saved about 200,000 jobs in the protected industries that would otherwise have been lost to foreign competition, they also cost American consumers about $32 billion per year in the form of higher prices, or over $50,000 per job saved.

Suggested Discussion Questions

1. The case illustrates the downside of subsidies. Looking at this situation from a different perspective, who benefits from subsidies? Are there occasions when subsidies are appropriate? Explain your answer.

2. Draw upon the material presented in Chapter 5 to describe the destructive nature of tariffs. Does the information provided in the case support or hinder your arguments?

Management Focus: Toyota's Response to Rising Protectionist Pressures in Europe and the United States

Summary

This feature describes the emergence of Toyota on the world stage as an auto producer. Until the 1960s, Toyota was viewed as little more than an obscure Japanese automobile company. As a result of its world-class design and manufacturing skills, Toyota grew dramatically during the 1970s and 1980s, and is now one of the most productive auto companies in the world. The feature also focuses on the challenges that Toyota has experienced in its export operations. For most of its history Toyota has exported cars from its plants in Japan. However, by the early 1980s political pressure and talk of local requirements in the United States and Europe forced an initially reluctant Toyota to rethink its trade policy. The trade policy that Toyota has adopted is to produce an increasingly number of cars in its major export markets. The feature reviews that challenges that Toyota has faced in implementing this strategy.

Suggested Discussion Questions

1. In your option, would the United States government have imposed increasingly stringent tariffs and import quotas on Toyota if the company had not decided to build manufacturing facilities in the U.S.? From Toyota's perspective, what was the advantage of acting proactively rather than waiting for tariffs and quotas to be imposed?

2. Explain the concept of "voluntary" export restraints. What role have voluntary export restraints played in Toyota's trade policy with the United States?

3. Based on the information provided in the case, do you think that Toyota has been a good trade partner with the United States? Explain your answer.

4. Toyota Homepage: {http://www.toyota.com/}.

Additional Readings and Sources of Information

China Builds a Wall—But Will It Hold: {http://www.businessweek.com/1998/41/b3599008.htm}

What is the World Trade Organization: {http://www.wto.org/wto/about/facts0.htm}

A Rising Tide of Protectionism Threatens to Swamp Clinton: {http://www.businessweek.com/search.htm}

Global Growing Pains: {http://www.businessweek.com/1999/99_50/b3659074.htm}

Free Trade Needs a Nod From Labor: {http://www.businessweek.com/search}

It's A Big Black Hole For Foreign Investors: {http://www.businessweek.com/search}

CHAPTER 6
FOREIGN DIRECT INVESTMENT

Government Policy

SUMMARY OF CHAPTER

CRITICAL THINKING AND DISCUSSION QUESTIONS

INTERNET EXERCISES

CLOSING CASE: FDI in Russia

Learning Objectives

1. Be familiar with the forces underpinning the rising tide of foreign direct investment in the world economy.

2. Understand why firms often prefer direct investment as a strategy for entering a foreign market over alternatives such as exporting and granting foreign entities the right to produce the firm's product under license.

3. Appreciate why firms based in the same industry often undertake foreign direct investment at the same time.

4. Understand why certain locations are favored as the target of foreign direct investment activity.

5. Appreciate how political ideology influences government policy toward foreign direct investment.

6. Be conversant with the costs and benefits of foreign direct investment to receiving and source countries.

7. Have a good grasp of the different policy instruments that governments can use to restrict and encourage foreign direct investment.

OPENING CASE: Electrolux's Global Inventory Strategy

Summary

The opening case describes the steps taken by Electrolux to expand its presence in Eastern Europe, Latin America, and Asia. Due to the slow growth in its traditional markets, and the fact that these markets had been largely penetrated so that most sales were for replacement purposes, the management knew that growth would have to come from countries where there was still a large portion of the population that did not have household appliances. Electrolux undertook a variety of approaches when investing in the new markets. A discussion of the case can revolve around the following questions:

QUESTION 1: Why did Electrolux decide to expand into Eastern Europe, Latin America, and Asia?

ANSWER 1: While Electrolux was already an international company, its primary markets were Europe and North America. In these countries the market was fully penetrated, limiting sales to replacement goods and population growth. Electrolux estimated this to be about 2-3%. In comparison, growth rates in Eastern Europe, Latin America, and Asia were estimated to be around 20%. In addition this much higher growth rate, Electrolux's main global competitors were also targeting these markets. Thus unless it wished to be left behind, it needed to expand into these higher growth markets.

QUESTION 2: Why did Electrolux undertake such a wide variety of investments? Would it not have been simpler to undertake one type of investment (e.g., greenfield or joint venture) in all countries?

ANSWER 2: Whereas it may seem that Electrolux did not have a single global strategy for expansion, Electrolux realized that different locations required different types of investments. Where it could purchase viable local firms, this was its preferred strategy. Yet in many countries the local firms may not have fit with Electrolux's needs, or been asking too high a price. Thus it entered into joint ventures, greenfield investments, and other forms of foreign direct investment depending upon the needs in the market and the opportunities it foresaw. Any single approach would have failed to take into consideration the country differences identified in Chapters 2 and 3.

QUESTION 3: Given that Electrolux had to lay off so many people and close so many facilities, didn't expand too much too fast?

ANSWER 3: This is certainly one explanation for the poor performance, although the economic crisis in Latin America and Asia certainly contributed. But inherent in the acquisition strategy was a need to rationalize production, and turn what had been relatively inefficient nationally based plants into efficient components in a global production system. Thus some restructuring within the industry was inevitable. This inevitability was accelerated by the fact that so many plants were now under the operation of one firm that could recognize the strengths and weaknesses of each, as well as by the economic downturn.

Chapter Summary

This chapter focuses on the topic of foreign direct investment (FDI). FDI occurs when a firm invests directly in new facilities to produce and/or market a product in a foreign country. At the outset, the chapter discusses the growth in FDI, particularly by medium-sized and small firms. The theoretical underpinnings of FDI are discussed, which describe under what circumstances it is advantageous for a firm to invest in production facilities in a foreign country. The chapter also addresses the different policies that governments have toward foreign direct investment. Some governments are opposed to FDI and some governments encourage it. Three specific ideologies of FDI are discussed, including the radical view, the free market view, and pragmatic nationalism. The chapter also provides a discussion of the costs and benefits of FDI from the perspective of both the home country and the host country involved. The chapter concludes with a review of the policy instruments that governments use to regulate FDI activity by international firms.

Chapter Outline With Lecture Notes and Teaching Tips

INTRODUCTION

A) This chapter is concerned with the phenomenon of foreign direct investment (FDI). **Foreign direct investment** occurs when a firm invests directly in new facilities to produce and/or market in a foreign country. Once a firm undertakes FDI it becomes a **multinational enterprise**.

Teaching Tip: Each year Fortune magazine publishes a list of the 500 largest global corporations in the world. Fortune calls its list the "Global 500." This list, along with the article that accompanies the 1997 list, can be accessed at {http://pathfinder.com/fortune/1997/specials/g500/intro.html}. The article contains an excellent discussion of the role of global firms in the world economy.

Teaching Tip: Another web site that provides an excellent discussion of the role of multinational corporations in the world economy is available at {http://ps.ucdavis.edu/classes/pol129/SWE/multinat.htm}.

FOREIGN DIRECT INVESTMENT IN THE WORLD ECONOMY

A) When discussing foreign direct investment, it is important to distinguish between the **flow** and the **stock** of foreign direct investment. The flow of FDI refers to the amount of FDI undertaken over a given time period (normally a year). The stock of FDI refers to the total accumulated value of foreign-owned assets at a given time. Outflows of FDI, meaning the flow of FDI out of a country, and inflows of FDI, meaning the flow of FDI into a country are also discussed.

Teaching Tip: An excellent web site, sponsored by the University of California at Davis, provides a full array of information about Foreign Direct Investment. The site is available at {http://ps.ucdavis.edu/classes/pol129/SWE/direct.htm}.

The Growth of Foreign Direct Investment

B) Over the past 20 years there has been a marked increase in both the flow and stock of FDI in the world economy. The significant growth in FDI has both to do with the political economy of trade as outlined in the previous chapter and the political and economic changes that have been taking place in developing countries.

The Direction of FDI

C) Another important trend is has been the rise of inflows into the US. The stock of foreign FDI in the US increased more rapidly than US FDI abroad.

D) The rapid increase in FDI growth into the US may be due to the attractiveness of the US market, the falling value of the dollar, and a belief by some foreign corporations that they could manage US assets and workers more efficiently than their American managers.

E) It is difficult to say whether the increase in the FDI into the US is good for the country or not. To the extent that foreigners are making more productive use of US assets and workers, it is probably good for the country.

The Source of Foreign Direct Investment

F) Not only has the flow of FDI been accelerating, but its composition has also been changing. For most of the period after World War II, the U.S. was by far the largest source country for FDI. By 1990, however, the U.S. share of FDI outflows had slumped to 10.3 percent, pushing the U.S. into second place behind Japan.

THE THEORY OF FOREIGN DIRECT INVESTMENT

A) In this section of the text, several theories of foreign direct investments are discussed. These theories attempt to explain the observed pattern of foreign direct investment flows.

Why Foreign Direct Investment

B) Why do so many firms apparently prefer FDI to either **exporting** (producing goods at home and then shipping them to the receiving country for sale) or **licensing** (granting a foreign entity the right to produce and sell the firm's product in return for a royalty fee on every unit that the foreign entity sells)? The answer lies in the limitations of these methods for exploiting foreign market opportunities producing goods at home and then shipping them to the receiving country for sale. Granting a foreign entity the right to produce and sell the firm's product in return for a royalty fee on every unit that the foreign entity sells.

Limitations of Exporting

C) The viability of an exporting strategy is often constrained by transportation costs and trade barriers. Much foreign direct investment is undertaken as a response to actual or threatened trade barriers such as import tariffs or quotas.

Limitations of Licensing

D) There is a branch of economic theory known as internalization theory that seeks to explain why firms often prefer foreign direct investment to licensing as a strategy for entering foreign markets. According to internationalization theory, licensing has three major drawbacks as a strategy for exploiting foreign market opportunities.

> (1) First, licensing may result in a firm's giving away valuable technological know-how to a potential foreign competitor.
> (2) Second, licensing does not give a firm the tight control over manufacturing, marketing, and strategy in a foreign country that may be required to maximize its profitability.
> (3) Third, a problem arises with licensing when the firm's competitive advantage is based not so much on its products as on the management, marketing, and manufacturing capabilities that produce those products. Such capabilities are often not amenable to licensing.

E) So, when one or more of the following conditions holds, markets fail as a mechanism for selling know-how and FDI is more profitable than licensing. (i) when the firm has valuable know-how that cannot be adequately protected by a licensing contract, (ii) when the firm needs tight control over a foreign entity to maximize its market share and earnings in that country, and (iii) when a firm's skills and know-how are not amenable to licensing.

Advantages of Foreign Direct Investment

F) It follows from the above discussion that a firm will favor FDI over exporting as an entry strategy when transportation costs or trade barriers make exporting unattractive. Furthermore, the firm will favor FDI over licensing when it wishes to maintain control over its technological know-how, or over its operations and business strategy, or when the firm's capabilities are simply not amenable to licensing.

Teaching Tip: An article entitled "Constructing a Market Economy: A Guide to Countries in Transition" by Raymond Vernon (the author of the Product Life Cycle theory), discusses, among other things, the role of foreign direct investment in building a strong economy. The site is available at {http://www.cipe.org/e20/ver_E20.html}.

The Pattern of Foreign Direct Investment

G) Observation suggests that firms in the same industry often undertake foreign direct investment around the same time and tend to direct their investment activities towards certain locations.

Following Competitors

H) One theory used to explain foreign direct investment patterns is based on the idea that firms follow their domestic competitors overseas. First expounded by F.T. Knickerbocker, this theory has been developed with regard to oligopolistic industries. An oligopoly is an industry composed of a limited number of large firms.

The Product Life Cycle

C) Vernon's view is that firms undertake FDI at particular stages in the life cycle of a product they have pioneered. They invest in other advanced countries when local demand in those countries grows large enough to support local production. They subsequently shift production to developing countries when product standardization and market saturation give rise to price competition and cost pressures. Investment in developing countries, where labor costs are lower, is seen as the best way to reduce costs.

D) What Vernon's theory fails to explain, however, is why it is profitable for a firm to undertake FDI at such times, rather than continuing to export from its home base, and rather than licensing a foreign firm to produce its product.

The Eclectic Paradigm

E) The eclectic paradigm has been championed by the British economist John Dunning. Dunning argues that in addition to the various factors discussed above, **location-specific advantages** (that arise from using resource endowments or assets that are tied to a particular location and that a firm finds valuable to combine with its own unique assets) and **externalities** (knowledge spillovers that occur when companies in the same industry locate in the same area) are also of considerable importance in explaining both the rationale for and the direction of foreign direct investment.

POLITICAL IDEOLOGY AND FOREIGN DIRECT INVESTMENT

A) Historically, ideology toward FDI has ranged from a radical stance that is hostile to all FDI to the non-interventionist principle of free market economies. Between these two extremes is an approach that might be called pragmatic nationalism.

The Radical View

B) The radical view tracts its roots to Marxist political and economic theory. Radical writers argue that the multinational enterprise is an instrument of imperialist domination. They see MNEs as a tool for exploiting host countries to the exclusive benefit of their capitalist-imperialist home countries. By the end of the 1980's, however, the radical position was in retreat almost everywhere. There seem to be three reasons for this. First, the collapse of communism in Eastern Europe. Second, the generally abysmal economic performance of those countries that embraced the radical position, and a growing belief by many of these countries that, contrary to the radical position, FDI can be an important source of technology and jobs and can stimulate economic growth. And third, the strong economic performance of developing countries that embraced capitalism rather than ideology.

The Free Market View

C) The free market view argues that international production should be distributed among countries according to the theory of comparative advantage. The free market view has been embraced by a number of advanced and developing nations, including the United States, Britain, Chile, and Hong Kong.

Pragmatic Nationalism

D) The pragmatic nationalist view is that FDI has both benefits, such as inflows of capital, technology, skills

81

and jobs, and costs, such as repatriation of profits to the home country and a negative balance of payments effect.

E) Recognizing this, countries adopting a pragmatic stance pursue policies designed to maximize the national benefits and minimize the national costs. According to this view, FDI should be allowed only if the benefits outweigh the costs.

Shifting Ideology

F) In recent years the center of gravity on the ideological spectrum has shifted strongly toward the free market stance.

COSTS AND BENEFITS OF FDI TO THE NATION

Host Country Effects: Benefits

A) There are three main benefits of inward FDI for a host country: the resource transfer effect, the employment effect and the balance of payments effect.

Resource-Transfer Effects

B) FDI can make a positive contribution to a host economy by supplying capital, technology, and management resources that would otherwise not be available.

Employment Effects

C) The beneficial employment effect claimed for FDI is that FDI brings jobs to a host country that would otherwise not be created there.

Balance-of-Payments Effect

D) The effect of FDI on a country's balance-of-payments accounts is an important policy issue for most host governments. A country's **balance-of-payments account** is a record of a country's payments to and receipts from other countries. The **current account** is a record of a country's export and import of goods and services.

E) Governments typically prefer to see a current account surplus than a deficit. There are two ways in which FDI can help a country to achieve this goal. First, if the FDI is a substitute for imports of goods and services, the effect can be to improve the current account of the host country's balance of payments. A second potential benefit arises when the MNE uses a foreign subsidiary to export goods and services to other countries.

Host Country Effects: Costs

F) Three main costs of inward FDI concern host countries; the possible adverse effects of FDI on competition within the host nation, adverse effects on the balance of payments, and the perceived loss of national sovereignty and autonomy.

Adverse Effects on Competition

G) Host governments sometimes worry that the subsidiaries of foreign MNEs operating in their country may have greater economic power than indigenous competitors because they may be part of a larger international organization.

Adverse Effects on the Balance of Payments

H) The possible adverse effects of FDI on a host country's balance-of-payments position are twofold. First, set against the initial capital inflows that come with FDI must be the subsequent outflow of capital as the foreign subsidiary repatriates earnings to its parent country. A second concern arises when a foreign subsidiary imports a substantial number of its inputs from abroad, which results in a debit on the current account of the host country's balance of payments.

National Sovereignty and Autonomy

I) Many host governments worry that FDI is accompanied by some loss of economic independence. The concern is that key decisions that can affect the host country's economy will be made by a foreign parent that has no real commitment to the host country, and over which the host country's government has no real control.

Home Country Effects: Benefits

J) The benefits of FDI to the home country arise from three sources. First, the capital account of the home country's balance of payments benefits from the inward flow of foreign earnings. Second, benefits to the home country from outward FDI arise from employment effects. Third, benefits arise when the home country MNE learns valuable skills from its exposure to foreign markets that can subsequently be transferred back to the home country.

Home Country Effects: Costs

K) The most important concerns center around the balance-of-payments and employment effects of outward FDI. With regard to employment effects, the most serious concerns arise when FDI is seen as a substitute for domestic production.

International Trade Theory and Offshore Production

L) When assessing the costs and benefits of FDI to the home country, keep in mind the lessons of international trade (Chapter 4). International trade theory tells us that home country concerns about the negative economic effects of "offshore production" may be misplaced.

GOVERNMENT POLICY INSTRUMENTS AND FDI

A) We have now reviewed the costs and benefits of the FDI from the perspective of both home country and host country. Before tackling the important issue of bargaining between the MNE and the host government, we need to discuss the policy instruments that governments use to regulate FDI activity by MNE's. Both home countries and host countries have a range of policy instruments that they can use to regulate FDI activity by MNE's. We will look at each in turn.

Home Country Policies

B) By their choice of policies, home countries can both encourage and restrict FDI by local firms.

Encouraging Outward FDI

C) Many investor nations now have government-backed insurance programs to cover major types of foreign investment risk.

Restricting Outward FDI

D) Virtually all investor countries, including the United States, have exercised some control over outward FDI from time to time.

Host Country Policies

E) Host countries adopt policies designed both to restrict and to encourage inward FDI.

Encouraging Inward FDI

F) It is increasingly common for governments to offer incentives to foreign firms to invest in their countries.

G) Incentives are motivated by a desire to gain from the resource-transfer and employment effects of FDI. They are also motivated by a desire to capture FDI away from other potential host countries.

Restricting Inward FDI

H) Host governments use a wide range of controls to restrict FDI. The two most common, however, are ownership restraints and performance requirements.

I) The rationale underlying ownership restraints seems to be twofold. First, foreign firms are often excluded from certain sectors on the grounds of national security or competition. Second, ownership restraints seem to be based on a belief that local owners can help to maximize the resource transfer and employment benefits of FDI for the host country.

International Institutions and the Liberalization of FDI

J) Until recently there has been no consistent involvement by multinational institutions in the governing of FDI. With the formation of the World Trade Organization in 1995, this is now changing rapidly.

IMPLICATIONS FOR BUSINESS

The Theory of FDI

A) The implications of the theories of FDI for business practice are straightforward. First, the location-specific advantages argument associated with John Dunning helps explain the direction of FDI. However, the location-specific advantages argument does not explain why firms prefer FDI to licensing or to exporting. In this regard, from both an explanatory and a business perspective, perhaps the most useful theories are those that focus on the limitations of exporting and licensing.

Government Policy

B) A host government's attitude toward FDI should be an important variable in decisions about where to locate foreign production facilities and where to make a foreign direct investment.

Teaching Tip: A site entitled Business Monitor has a section that provides information about the regulations involving foreign direct investment in almost every country in the world (you have to look for the information in each country's profile). The site can be accessed at {http://www.businessmonitor.co.uk/trading_blocks.shtml}.

Teaching Tip: A very extensive directory of country specific web sites is available at {http://msm.byu.edu/c&i/cim/ibd/Country.htm}. These sites cover a wide variety of international business issues in regard to international business.

Critical Thinking and Discussion Questions

1. In recent years Japanese FDI in the United States has grown far more rapidly than US FDI in Japan. Why do you think this is the case? What are the implications of this trend?

Answer: There are two primary explanations for the inequity in the growth of FDI between the US and Japan. Firstly, there has been a significant decrease in the US dollar relative to the Japanese Yen. This makes investment in the US more attractive to Japanese investors, and Japanese investments less attractive to US investors. Secondly, the nature of business in Japan, where long-term business relationships are important and investments can take a significant period of time to pay off, makes Japan a less attractive place to invest than the more open US economy. To the extent that the trend is simply a result of exchange rate changes, the trend will follow changes in exchange rates, and could reverse if the exchange rate change reverses direction. The implication of this is simply that the value of international investing between the US and Japan will be determined by the relative value of the currencies. To the extent that the trend is a result of structural differences in the economies of the US and Japan, it suggests that there will continue to be a disparity in the flows of FDI between the US and Japan. Hence Japanese companies will find it easier to compete in the US market against US competitors than US companies will be able to compete in Japan against Japanese competitors.

2. Compare these explanations of FDI: internalization theory, Vernon's product life cycle theory, and Knickerbocker's theory of FDI. Which theory do you think offers the best explanation of the historical pattern of FDI? Why?

Answer: Internalization theory seeks to explain why firms often prefer foreign direct investment to licensing as a strategy for entering foreign markets. According to internationalization theory, licensing has three major drawbacks as a strategy for exploiting foreign market opportunities: licensing may result in a firm giving away proprietary technology, licensing does not permit a firm to maintain tight control over its activities, and licensing is not appropriate when a firm's competitive advantage is based not so much on its products as on the management, marketing, and manufacturing capabilities that produce those products.
Vernon's product life cycle theory argues that firms undertake FDI at particular stages in the life cycle of a product they have pioneered. They invest in other advanced countries when local demand in those countries grows large enough to support local production. They subsequently shift production to developing countries when product standardization and market saturation give rise to price competition and cost pressures. Investment in developing countries, where labor costs are lower, is seen as the best way to reduce costs. Finally, Knickerbocker's theory of FDI suggests that firms follow their domestic competitors overseas. This theory had been developed with regard to oligopolistic industries. Imitative behavior can take many forms in an oligopoly, including FDI. .
The second part of this question is designed to stimulate classroom discussion and/or force students to think

through these theories and select the one that they feel provides the best explanation for the historic pattern of FDI.

3. You are the international manager of a US business that has just invented a revolutionary new personal computer that can perform the same functions as IBM and Apple computers and their clones, but costs only half as much to manufacture. Your CEO has asked you to decide how to expand into the Western European market. Your options are (i) export from the US, (ii) license a European firm to manufacture and market the computer in Europe, and (iii) set up a wholly owned subsidiary in Europe. Evaluate the pros and cons of each alternative and suggest a course of action to your CEO.

Answer: In considering expansion into Western Europe, three options will be considered: FDI, licensing, and export. With export, assuming there are no trade barriers, the key considerations would likely be transport costs and localization. While transport costs may be quite low for a relatively light and high value product like a computer, localization can present some difficulties. Power requirements, keyboards, and preferences in model all vary from country to country. It may be difficult to fully address these localization issues from the US, but not entirely infeasible. Since there are many computer manufacturers and distributors in Europe, there are likely to be a number of potential licensees. But by signing up licensees, valuable technological information may have to be disclosed, and the competitive advantage lost if the licensees use or disseminate this information. FDI (setting up a wholly owned subsidiary) is clearly the most costly and time consuming approach, but the one that best guarantees that critical knowledge will not be disseminated and that localization can be done effectively. Given the fast pace of change in the personal computer industry, it is difficult to say how long this revolutionary new computer will retain its competitive advantage. If the firm can protect its advantage for a period of time, FDI may pay off and help assure that no technological know-how is lost. If, however, other firms can copy or develop even superior products relatively easily, than licensing, while speeding up knowledge dissemination, may also allow the firm to get the quickest large scale entry into Europe and make as much as it can before the advantage is lost.

4. Explain how political ideology of a host government might influence the process of negotiating access between the host government and a foreign MNE.

Answer: If a host country subscribes to pure free market principles, then there is little to negotiate about. It may be possible, however, to negotiate with different regions of the country to obtain more favorable tax treatment or access to local resources. If a host country subscribes to pure radical views, there is also little to negotiate about since the government will likely prohibit any FDI. As a general rule, as the overall ideology of a country moves from the left (radical) to the right (free market), the foreign MNE will need to spend less time negotiating matters relating to access and control and more time on matters relating to incentives and most favorable locations.

5. "Firms should not be investing abroad when there is a need for investment to create jobs at home!" Discuss.

Answer: This question is designed to stimulate classroom discussion or force your students to "think" about this provocative issue. While there may be a need for investment and job creation at home, investors need to have the capability to adequately manage their investments. Hence some local firm may be much more able to exploit their technological advantages and invest internationally than they would be able benefit from domestic investment. If firm's primary goal is to maximize their shareholder's value, then they and probably the economy are better off if they invest where they can earn the best return. If firms from other countries have capabilities for which local workers and assets are most appropriate, then it is better that they make the investments locally and use these resources to their best use rather than having local firms use these resource sub-optimally.

Internet Exercises

TEXT EXERCISE 1

Overview

Disney is expanding its reach once again, this time by opening a theme park in Hong Kong. The company has struck a deal with the Hong Kong government that is providing Disney with a large monetary incentive package to help make the park a reality.

Suggested Use in the Classroom

Students are asked whether governments should be involved in sponsoring and attracting foreign investment by providing monetary incentives to corporations. This topic provides a good forum for debate. Many students will probably argue that foreign companies bring many benefits to a host country including capital, jobs, and technology, and that therefore, it is in the best interests of the country for the government to attract investments like the Disney one outlined in this case. Others however, may suggest the money could be better spent on a country's own firms—that by giving it to foreigners, local companies are actually hurt, and a country's overall national competitiveness is negatively affected.

TEXT EXERCISE 2

Overview

China is on the Internet! The very image of a country with such a vast market potential as China being in a position to buy and sell products electronically is creating a lot of excitement. However, the picture is not all positive. The Chinese government has been active in establishing various restrictions limiting the development of Internet firms, and consequently the development of e-commerce in China.

Suggested Use in the Classroom

This exercise asks students to consider the alternatives available in the Chinese marketplace. In particular, students are asked whether American Internet companies should make an effort to expand into the market immediately, or whether it might be more beneficial to wait. Students who suggest immediate action will probably cite first mover advantages and the speed of change in electronic commerce as reasons for expanding now. Those students who take a wait and see perspective may argue that the political situation is still too unclear, and that firms would be wiser to take a more cautious approach to the market.

WEB EXERCISE 1

Overview

Like the text-based exercises, this exercise explores foreign expansion by a corporation—this time a services firm. Fidelity Investments, the American financial services company, is currently focusing its sights on the European and Asian markets.

Suggested Use in the Classroom

Students are asked to consider how the challenges of foreign direct investment differ for services companies as compared to manufacturing firms. Many students will focus on the cultural challenges that may be faced, and indeed have challenged Fidelity Investments, by services firms as they expand into foreign markets. Many will probably agree that the Internet has the potential to facilitate the expansion process.

WEB EXERCISE 2

Overview

This exercise explores German media group, Bertelsmann, recent forays into foreign markets. The company has shifted its global book-publishing business to New York, and also taken over Random House, and American publishing concern.

Suggested Use in the Classroom

This exercise extends the discussion of foreign expansion that was presented in previous three exercises. Students are asked to consider the Bertelsmann company and discuss whether, given the firm's foreign activities it should still be consider a German company. Students will probably enjoy debating exactly what constitutes a local versus a foreign corporation, and the exercise should generate a lot of class discussion.

CLOSING CASE: FDI in Russia

Summary

The closing case provides background information on the state of investment in Russia, and particularly in the oil industry. While Russia has significant reserves, and could use Western investment in order to exploit these reserves and earn foreign exchange, existing laws and contract uncertainty have limited the attractiveness of such investments to Western firms. Discussion of the case can be based on the following questions:

QUESTION 1: What are the benefits to the Russian economy from foreign direct investment in general, and in the oil industry in particular?

ANSWER 1: Russia can benefit from inflows of capital and technology. In the oil industry both of these are very important, as Western technology can help Russia to access reserves that are hard to exploit with Russia's existing technology. FDI will also lead to jobs. In the oil industry, investment will allow Russia to not only have domestic petroleum more cheaply (which can help many industries), but will provide Russia with a valuable source of currency from oil exports. Inevitably some technology will also be transferred to domestic firms that will help them exploit other oil fields.

QUESTION 2: What are the risks that foreign companies must bear when making investments in Russia? What is the source of these risks? How substantial are they?

ANSWER 2: The risks to foreign firms is that they might not only lose their entire investment, but that their investment could be used against them if Russia were to use Western technology to flood markets with oil while not giving foreign firms any of the profits. These risks arise from the unstable nature of the government, and concerns that a future government could choose to seize Western assets without providing compensation. Given the current state of the Russian government, these risks are substantial.

QUESTION 3: How can foreign companies reduce these risks?

ANSWER 3: The best way to reduce these risks is to try and get as much money back out as quickly as possible. Of course it is the short-term needs of Russia that are most important to the government, and if it appear that Western firms were taking too much out too quickly, it would increase the likelihood of resentment. Thus rapid withdrawal of earnings from the investment has risks, and in what is necessarily a long-term venture (oil fields typically take years of investment before they are productive), this is infeasible. The primary thing investors can do is attempt to work the political landscape to their benefit, and by working with a number of influential local firms and politicians, increase the political support behind the investment. Investors must make certain that many groups stand to benefit from the long- term success of the investment.

Country Focus: Foreign Direct Investment in China

Summary

This feature explores investment opportunities in China. In the late 1970's, China opened its doors to foreign investors. By 1997, the country was the recipient of some $45.2 billion dollars in foreign direct investment. China's large population is a magnet for many companies and because high tariffs make it difficult to export to the Chinese market, firms frequently turn to foreign direct investment. However, many companies have found it difficult to conduct business in China, and in recent years investment rates have slowed. In response, the Chinese government, hoping to continue to attract foreign companies has established a number of incentives for would-be investors.

1. How do China's political preferences affect its ability to attract foreign direct investment?

2. Much of China's growth in foreign direct investment has come from neighboring countries. Discuss this trend, why it has occurred, and its implications.

Management Focus: Wal-Mart's International Expansion

Summary

This feature explores Wal-Mart's international expansion strategy. In the early 1990's, Wal-Mart, the American discount retailer, recognized that new growth was more likely to come form outside the U.S., than inside. Accordingly, Wal-Mart began to explore foreign opportunities. The company concluded its best option was to expand via wholly owned subsidiaries.

Suggested Discussion Questions

1. Wal-Mart decided to implement its foreign expansion plans by establishing wholly owned affiliates. The company felt that because its competitive advantage revolved around corporate world cultures and supporting information and logistics systems, maintaining control was important. Discuss the process of transferring proprietary assets such as Wal-Mart's to foreign markets.

2. Much of Wal-Mart's strength lies with its corporate culture. In your opinion, can the company duplicate its operating philosophy in foreign markets? Why or why not?

3. Wal-Mart's homepage: {www.walmart.com}

Country Focus: Foreign Direct Investment in Venezuela's Petroleum Industry

Summary

This feature focuses on Venezuela's plan to significantly upgrade its domestic petroleum industry. The plan assigns a key role to foreign investment in Venezuela's oil industry for the first time since the country nationalized all private oil companies in 1976. The feature focuses on Venezuela's reasons for wanting foreign companies to be involved in its initiative. First, the initiative will be very expensive, and Venezuela needs outside capital. However, in addition, the country lacks the technological resources and skills of many of the world's major oil companies. By letting foreign companies participate in its initiative to upgrade its own oil industry, Venezuela hopes to learn new technologies and oil refining techniques to use in the future.

Suggested Discussion Questions

1. Discuss how this feature illustrates the valuable role that foreign direct investment plays in the global trade picture?

2. Many protectionist minded people object to foreign direct investment, arguing that a company should provide jobs for its own citizens and not invest abroad. Similarly, people also argue that a government should keep foreign companies "out" in the interest of protecting local jobs. However, after reading this case, one could argue that foreign direct investment in Venezuela's oil initiative could be a "win-win" proposition for all the parties involved. Justify this argument.

Additional Readings and Sources of Information

Emerging markets: 'We're Fighting to Survive': {http://www.businessweek.com/1999/99_06/b3615007.htm}

China: WTO or Bust: {http://www.businessweek.com/search}

Europe: Ten Years After the Wall: {http://www.businessweek.com/1999/99_45/b3654002.htm}

Wal-Mart's Big Push South of the Border:
{http://www.businessweek.com/bwdaily/dnflash/june/nf70603c.htm}

BP Amoco: This Giant Sure Has a Big Appetite: {http://www.businessweek.com/1999/99_15/b3624173.htm}

Chapter Outline

OPENING CASE: Consolidation in the European Insurance Market

INTRODUCTION

LEVELS OF ECONOMIC INTEGRATION

Free Trade Area
Customs Union
Common Market
Economic Union
Political Union

THE CASE FOR REGIONAL INTEGRATION

The Economic Case for Integration
The Political Case for Integration
Impediments to Integration

THE CASE AGAINST ECONOMIC REGIONAL INTEGRATION

Country Focus: The Impact of NAFTA on the U.S Textile Industry

REGIONAL ECONOMIC INTEGRATION IN EUROPE

Evolution of the European Union
The Single European Act
The Euro
Enlargement of the European Union
Fortress Europe?

REGIONAL ECONOMIC INTEGRATION IN THE AMERICAS

The North American Free Trade Agreement
The Andean Pact
MERCOSUR
Central American Common Market and CARICOM
Free Trade Area of the Americas

REGIONAL ECONOMIC INTEGRATION ELSEWHERE

Association of South East Asian Nations
Asia Pacific Economic Cooperation

IMPLICATIONS FOR BUSINESS

    Opportunities
    Management Focus: Atag Holdings
    Threats

SUMMARY OF CHAPTER

CRITICAL THINKING AND DISCUSSION QUESTIONS

INTERNET EXERCISES

CLOSING CASE: Martin's Textiles

<u>Learning Objectives</u>

1. Appreciate the different levels of economic integration that are possible between nations.

2. Understand the economic and political arguments for regional economic integration.

3. Understand the economic and political arguments against regional economic integration.

4. Be familiar with the history, current scope, and future prospects of the world's most important regional economic agreements, including the European Union, the North American Free Trade Agreement, MERCOSUR, and the Asian Pacific Economic Cooperation.

5. Understand the implications for business that are inherent in regional economic integration agreements.

OPENING CASE: Consolidation in the European Insurance Market

<u>Summary</u>

The opening case describes how changes in regulations in insurance in Europe, resulting from the closer integration of EU countries, led to a consolidation in the insurance industry. Within nations companies have been merging in order to former a stronger firm against foreign entrants. Insurance companies have also been acquiring insurance firms in other nations and creating pan-European firms. Discussion of the case can be focused on the implications of regional economic integration for firms. The following questions can be helpful in directing the discussion.

QUESTION 1: Why did insurance firms within the same country merge in response to the liberalization of insurance across Europe (e.g., Axa/UAP in France, Royal Insurance/Sun Alliance in the UK)?

ANSWER 1: Firms within the same country were motivated to merge for several reasons. Firstly, they were concerned about large foreign firms entering their market, and felt that in order to defend against well-financed foreign rivals they needed to merge to form a stronger local firm. A second reason was to improve their ability to enter foreign markets. It might have been fairly difficult and expensive for smaller firms to simultaneously expand into other countries in Europe. By merging they would be able to "share" these expansion costs and be able to profitably enter more markets more quickly.

QUESTION 2: Why did insurance firms start acquiring insurance firms in other countries?

ANSWER 2: With the liberalized regulations, insurance firms were able to sell products across Europe. Yet it can be expensive to enter a market and build a customer base, as this generally means attracting people to switch from their current insurance company. It may well be cheaper to gain access to customers through buying an existing insurance company operating in a foreign country than trying to build the customer base from zero. There was also a sense of urgency among many firms in building a truly pan-European insurance company, and those that moved first in merging would have the greatest choice in selecting partners. If a firm were to wait too long, they may find that they were competing against global firms, and that most attractive merger partners were already taken. Behind all of this is the view that there are considerable economies of scale in insurance - bigger is better. Firms that choose to remain focused on their home markets may find themselves marginalized and unable to compete against their pan-European rivals.

Chapter Summary

In this chapter, the topic of regional economic integration is explored. The levels of regional economic integration discussed (from least integrate to most integrated) include: a free trade area, a customs union, a common market, an economic union, and a full political union. The arguments for and against regional economic integration are provided. Many students will remember some of these arguments from the debate of the ratification of the North American Free Trade Agreement (NAFTA). The chapter also provides information about the major trade blocks of the world, including the European Union, NAFTA, the Andean Group, MERCOSUR, and several other Latin American and Asian trade alliances. In addition, the implications for business of these trade agreements and others are fully discussed.

Chapter Outline With Lecture Notes and Teaching Tips

INTRODUCTION

A) One notable trend in the global economy in recent years has been the accelerated movement toward regional economic integration. **Regional economic integration** refers to agreements between countries in a geographic region to reduce tariff and nontariff barriers to the free flow of goods, services, and factors of production between each other.

B) Despite the rapid spread of regional trade agreements designed to promote free trade, there are those who fear that the world is moving toward a situation in which a number of regional trade blocks compete against each other. In this scenario of the future, free trade will exist within each bloc, but each bloc will protect its market from outside competition with high tariffs.

LEVELS OF ECONOMIC INTEGRATION

A) Several levels of economic integration are possible in theory (see Figure 7.2 in the textbook). From least integrated to most integrated, they are a free trade area, a customs union, a common market, an economic union, and, finally, a full potential union.

Free Trade Area

B) In a free trade area all barriers to the trade of goods and services among member countries are removed. In a theoretically ideal free trade area, no discriminatory tariffs, quotas, subsidies, or administrative impediments are allowed to distort trade between member nations. Each country, however, is allowed to determine its own trade policies with regard to nonmembers.

C) The most enduring free trade area in the world is the European Free Trade Association. EFTA currently joins four countries-Norway, Iceland, Liechtenstein, and Switzerland. Other free trade areas include the North American Free Trade Agreement (NAFTA).

Teaching Tip: An excellent description of the major free trade areas of the world is available at: {http://ps.ucdavis.edu/classes/pol129/SWE/SWEfta.htm}.

Customs Union

D) The customs union is one step further along the road to full economic and political integration. A customs union eliminates trade barriers between member countries and adopts a common external trade policy.

E) Customs Unions around the world include the current version of the Andean Pact (between Bolivia, Columbia, Ecuador and Peru).

Common Market

F) Like a customs union, the theoretically ideal common market has no barriers to trade between member countries and a common external trade policy. Unlike in a customs union, in a common market, factors of production also are allowed to move freely between members. Thus, labor and capital are free to move, as there are no restrictions on immigration, emigration, or cross-border flows of capital between markets.

G) Currently, MERCOSUR, the South America grouping that comprises Brazil. Argentina, Paraguay, and Uruguay, is aiming to eventually establish itself as a common market.

Economic Union

H) An economic union entails even closer economic integration and cooperation than a common market. Like the common market, an economic union involves the free flow of products and factors of production between members and the adoption of a common external trade policy. Unlike a common market, a full economic union also requires a common currency, harmonization of the member countries' tax rates, and a common monetary and fiscal policy.

I) There are no true economic unions in the world today, but the EU is clearly moving in this direction, particularly given the current attempt to create a single EU currency, the Euro, by January 1st 2002.

Political Union

J) In a political union, independent states are combined into a single union.

Teaching Tip: The International Trade Law Monitor is a site that provides a broad depth of information pertaining international trade law. This site is well worth a visit, and helps acquaint the reader with the legal ramifications of international trade agreements. The site is available at {http://ra.irv.uit.no/trade_law/itlp.html}.

THE CASE FOR REGIONAL INTEGRATION

A) The case for regional integration is both economic and political.

The Economic Case for Integration

B) Regional economic integration can be seen as an attempt to achieve additional gains from the free flow of trade and investment between countries beyond those attainable under international agreements such as the WTO.

The Political Case for Integration

C) The political case for integration has two main points: 1) by linking countries together, making them more dependent on each other, and forming a structure where they regularly have to interact, the likelihood of violent conflict and war will decrease, and 2) by linking countries together, they have greater clout and are politically much stronger in dealing with other nations

Impediments to Integration

D) There are two main impediments to integration. First, although economic integration benefits the majority, it has costs. Although a nation as a whole may benefit significantly from a regional free trade agreement, certain groups may lose. A second impediment to integration arises from concerns over national sovereignty.

THE CASE AGAINST REGIONAL INTEGRATION

A) Although the tide has been running strongly in favor of regional free trade agreements in recent years, some economists have expressed concern that the benefits of regional integration have been oversold, while the costs have often been ignored.

B) Whether regional integration is in the economic interests of the participants depends upon the extent of **trade creation** as opposed to **trade diversion**. Trade creation occurs when low cost producers within the free trade area replace high cost domestic producers. Trade diversion occurs when higher cost suppliers within the free trade area replace lower cost external suppliers. A regional free trade agreement will only make the world better off if the amount of trade it creates exceeds the amount it diverts.

REGIONAL ECONOMIC INTEGRATION IN EUROPE

A) There are two trade blocks in Europe: the European Union (EU) and the European Free Trade Association. Of the two, the EU is by far the more significant, not just in terms of membership, but also in terms of economic and political influence in the world economy.

Evolution of the European Union

B) The EU is the product of two political factors: first, the devastation of two world wars on Western Europe and the desire for a lasting peace, and second, the European nations' desire to hold their own on the world's political and economic stage.

Teaching Tip: The EU maintains an excellent web site at {http://europa.eu.int/index-en.htm}. The site is very substantive, and contains a broad array of information about the historical role and current activities of the EU in the global economy.

C) The forerunner of the EU was the European Coal and Steel Community, which had the goal of removing barriers to trade in coal, iron, steel, and scrap metal formed in 1951. The EEC was formed in 1957 at the Treaty of Rome. While the original goal was for a common market, progress was generally very slow. Over the years the EU expanded in spurts, as well as moved towards ever-greater integration.

The Single European Act

D) The Single European Act, adopted by the EU member nations in 1987, committed the EC countries to work toward establishment of a single market by December 31, 1992.

The Stimulus for the Single European Act

E) The Single European Act was born out of frustration among EC members that the community was not living up to its promise. In the early 1980s, many of the EC's prominent businesses people mounted an energetic campaign to end the EC's economic divisions. The result was the Single European Act, which was independently ratified by the parliaments of each member country and became EC law in 1987.

The Objectives of the Act

F) The purpose of the Single European Act was to have a single market in place by December 31, 1992. The changes the act proposed include the following:
>   (i) frontier controls to remove all frontier controls between EC countries,
>   (ii) mutual recognition of standards to apply the principle of "mutual recognition," which is that a standard developed in one EC country should be accepted in another, provided it meets basic requirements in such matters as health and safety,
>   (iii) public procurement to open procurement to non-national suppliers,
>   (iv) financial services to lift barriers to competition in the retail banking and insurance businesses,
>   (v) exchange controls to remove all restrictions on foreign exchange transactions between members by the end of 1992,
>   (vi) freight transport to abolish restrictions on sabotage, the right of foreign truckers to pick up and deliver goods within another member's borders, by the end of 1992, and
>   (vii) supply-side effects should lower the costs of doing business in the EC, but the single-market program is also expected to have more complicated supply-side effects.

Implications

G) The implications of the Single European Act are potentially enormous. If the EU is successful in establishing a single market, member countries can expect significant gains from the free flow of trade and investment.

H) On the other hand, as a result of the single European Act many EU firms are facing increased competitive pressure. Countries such as France and Italy long used administrative trade barriers and subsidies to protect their home markets from foreign competition. Removal of these barriers has increased competition and some firms may as well go out of business. Ultimately, however, both consumers and EU firms will benefit from this.

The Euro

I) The Treaty of Maastricht, signed in 1991, took the EU one step further, by specially spelling out the steps to economic union and partial political union. In addition to simply spelling out the steps needed, the Treaty also laid out the future outlines of a common foreign policy, economic policy, defense policy, citizenship, and currency, as well as strengthened the role of the European Parliament. The single currency will eliminate exchange costs and reduce risk, making EC firms more efficient.

J) Of immediate interest are the implications for business of the establishment of a single currency. By adopting the Euro, the EU has created the second largest currency zone in the world after that of the dollar in importance as the most important currency in the world.

K) Three EU countries, Britain, Denmark and Sweden are opting out of the euro-zone although there is speculation that Britain and Sweden may join before 2002.

L) Euro notes and coins will not actually be issued until January 1st, 2002. In the interim, national currencies will continue to circulate in each of the 11 countries. In each participating state, banks and businesses will now start to keep 2 sets of accounts, one in the local currency and one in euros.

Benefits of Euro

M) There are a number of reasons why the Europeans decided to establish a single currency in the EU. First they believe that business and individuals will realize significant savings from having to handle one currency, rather than many. Second, and perhaps most importantly, the adoption of a common currency will make it easier to compare prices across Europe. Third, faced with lower prices European producers will be forced to look for ways to reduce their production costs in order to maintain their profit margins. Fourth, the introduction of a common currency should give a strong boost to the development of highly liquid pan-European capital market. Finally, the development of a pan-European euro denominated capital market will increase the range of investment options open both to individuals and institutions.

Costs of Euro

N) The drawback of a single currency is that national authorities would lose control over the monetary policy. Thus it is crucial to ensure that the EU's monetary policy is well managed. The Maastricht treaty called for the establishment of an independent European central bank (ECB), similar in some respects to the US Federal Reserve, with a clear mandate to manage monetary policy so as to ensure price stability. The ECB has now been established and is based in Frankfurt. Like the US Federal reserve, the ECB is meant to be independent from political pressure – although critics question this. Among other things the ECB sets interest rates and determines monetary policy across the euro-zone. The implied loss of national sovereignty to the ECB underlies the decision by Britain, Denmark and Sweden to stay out of the euro-zone for the time being.

O) Another drawback of the Euro is that the EU is not what the economists would call an optimal currency area. An optimal currency area is an area where similarities in the underlying structure if economic activities make it feasible to adopt a single currency and use a single exchange rate as an instrument of macro-economic policy. Many of the European economies in the euro-zone, however, are very dissimilar.

Enlargement of the European Union

P) A number of countries have applied for membership in the EU, particularly from Eastern Europe. Given the profound differences in income, development, and systems, however, makes near term integration of these countries into the EU difficult.

Fortress Europe?

Q) Many firms and countries (including the EFTA countries) are concerned that the EU will result in a "fortress Europe," where insiders will be given preferential treatment over outsiders. This clearly already exists in agriculture, although whether it will be extended to other areas is a matter of debate.

REGIONAL ECONOMIC INTEGRATION IN THE AMERICAS

A) In 1988 the US and Canada agreed to form a free trade area, with the goal of gradually eliminating all barriers to the trade of goods and services between the countries. In 1991 an agreement was signed between the US, Canada, and Mexico aimed at forming a free trade area between all three countries. In all three countries the political and economic consequences of the agreement are still being felt, and politicians in all countries are able to strike a cord with workers who perceive that they lost their jobs as a result of the agreement.

The North American Free Trade Agreement (NAFTA)

The NAFTA Agreement

B) The free trade agreement between the United States, Canada, and Mexico became law January 1, 1994. It contains the following actions:

> Abolishes within 10 years tariffs on 99 percent of the goods traded between Mexico, Canada, and the United States, removes most barriers on the cross-border flow of services, protects intellectual property rights, removes most restrictions on FDI between the three member countries, allows each country to apply its own environmental standards, provided such standards have a scientific base, establishes two commissions with the poser to impose fines and remove trade privileges when environmental standards or legislation involving health and safety, minimum wages, or child labor are ignored.

Teaching Tip: The NAFTA Homepage can be accessed at {http://www.nafta.net/naftagre.htm}.

Arguments for NAFTA

C) Proponents of NAFTA argue that it will provide economic gains to all countries: Mexico will benefit from increased jobs as low cost production moves south, and will attain more rapid economic growth as a result. The US and Canada will benefit from the access to a large and increasingly prosperous market and from the lower prices for consumers from goods produced in Mexico. In addition, US and Canadian firms with production sites in Mexico will be more competitive on world markets

Teaching Tip: There are many organizations anxious to take advantage of the opportunities offered by NAFTA. As evidence of this, direct your students' attention towards a web site entitled The NAFTA Register {http://www.nafta.net/global/}. The NAFTA Register is a directory of export management companies, export service providers, and trading companies that want to profit from NAFTA by helping buyers and selling take advantage of NAFTA related opportunities.

Arguments Against NAFTA

D) Opponents of NAFTA argue that jobs will be lost and wage levels will decline in the US and Canada, Mexican workers will emigrate north, pollution will increase due to Mexico's more lax standards, and Mexico will lose its sovereignty.

Teaching Tip: A thoughtful article on the environmental impact of NAFTA is available at {http://lanic.utexas.edu/cswht/NAFTA-environ.html}.

The Early Experience

E) Since NAFTA is an ongoing process, and the implications are still unclear, it likely will be another decade before the true costs and benefits are known.

Enlargement

F) One big issue now confronting NAFTA is that of enlargement. Following approval of NAFTA by the US Congress a number of other Latin American countries indicated their desire to eventually join NAFTA. Currently the governments of both Canada and the US are adopting a wait and see attitude with regard to most countries.

The Andean Pact

G) The Andean Pact, originally formed in 1969, and reformed and renegotiated several times, has made little progress to due political and economic turmoil in most of the countries. The countries are making another strong attempt again, and their initial progress on removing trade barriers is promising. But the tremendous differences between the countries will make agreement on many issues difficult.

MERCOSUR

H) MERCOSUR originated in 1988 as a free trade pact between Brazil and Argentina. In 1990 it was expanded to include Paraguay and Uruguay. MERCOSUR has been making progress on reducing trade barriers between member states. Given some fairly high tariffs for goods from other countries, it would appear that in some industries MERCOSUR is trade diverting rather than trade creating, and local firms are investing in industries that are not competitive on a worldwide basis.

Teaching Tip: MERCOSUR's Homepage, which includes a broad array of useful information, can be accessed at {http://www.americasnet.com/mauritz/mercosur/english/}.
Lecture Note: A case study of the effects of MERCOSUR on Uruguay is available at {http://sunsite.scu.eun.eg/untpdc/incubator/ury/tpmon/mercosur.htm}.

Central American Common Market and CARICOM

I) There are two other trade pacts in the America, the Central American Trade Market and CARICOM, although neither has made much progress as yet.

Free Trade of The Americas

J) In April 1988, 34 heads of state traveled to Santiago, Chile for the second summit of the Americas where they formally inaugurate talks to establish a FTAA (Free Trade of The Americas) by 2005. The talks will continue for 7 years, and will address a wide range of economic, political and environmental issues, related to cross-border trade and investment.

REGIONAL ECONOMIC INTEGRATION ELSEWHERE

Association of Southeast Asian Nations

A) Formed in 1967, ASEAN currently includes Brunei, Indonesia, Malaysia, the Philippines, Singapore, Thailand, and, most recently, Vietnam. The basic objectives of ASEAN are to foster freer trade between member countries and to achieve some cooperation in their industrial policies. Progress has been limited, however.

Asian Pacific Economic Cooperation (APEC)

B) APEC currently has 18 members including such economic powerhouses as the United States, Japan, and China. The stated aim of APEC is to increase multilateral cooperation in view of the economic rise of the pacific nations and the growing interdependence within the region.

Teaching Tip: The Homepage of the APEC can be accessed at {http://www.apecsec.org.sg/}. A wealth of information about the APEC is available at this site.

IMPLICATIONS FOR BUSINESS

Opportunities

A) Creation of a single market offers significant opportunities because markets that were formerly protected from foreign competition are opened.

B) The greatest implication for MNEs is that the free movement of goods across borders, the harmonization of product standards, and the simplification of tax regimes, makes it possible for them to realize potentially enormous cost economies by centralizing production in those locations where the mix of factor costs and skills is optimal. By specialization and shipping of goods between locations, a much more efficient web of operations can be created.

C) On the other hand, even after the removal of barriers to trade and investment, enduring differences between nations in culture and competitive practices often limits the ability of companies to realize cost economies by centralizing production in key locations and producing a standardized product for a single multi-country market.

<u>Threats</u>

D) Just as the emergence of single markets in the EU and North America creates opportunities for business, so it also presents a number of threats. For one thing, the business environment within both groups will become more competitive.

E) A further threat to non-EU and/or non-North American firms arises from the likely long-term improvements in the competitive position of many European and North American companies.

F) A final threat to firms outside of trading blocks is the threat of being shut out of the single market by the creation of "Trade Fortress".

Critical Thinking and Discussion Questions

1. NAFTA is likely to produce net benefits for the U.S. economy. Discuss.

Answer: The proponents argue that NAFTA should be viewed as an opportunity to create an enlarged and a more productive base for the U.S., Canada, and Mexico. As low-income jobs move from Canada and the United States to Mexico, the Mexican economy should be strengthened giving Mexico the ability to purchase higher-cost American products. The net effect of the lower income jobs moving to Mexico and Mexico increasing its imports of high quality American goods should be positive for the American economy. In addition, the international competitiveness of United States and Canadian firms that move production to Mexico to take advantage of lower labor costs will be enhanced, enabling them to better compete with Asian and European rivals.

2. What are the economic and political arguments for regional economic integration? Given these arguments, why don't we see more integration in the world economy?

Answer: The economic case for regional integration is straightforward. As we saw in Chapter 4, unrestricted free trade allows countries to specialize in the production of goods and services that they can produce most efficiently. If this happens as the result of economic integration within a geographic region, the net effect is greater prosperity for the nations of the region. From a more philosophical perspective, regional economic integration can be seen as an attempt to achieve additional gains from the free flow of trade and investment between countries beyond those attainable under international agreements such as the WTO. The political case for integration is also compelling. Linking neighboring economies and making them increasingly dependent on each other creates incentives for political cooperation between neighboring states. Also, the potential for violent conflict between the states is reduced. In addition, by grouping their economies together, the countries can enhance their political weight in the world.
Despite the strong economic and political arguments for integration, it has never been easy to achieve (on a meaningful level). There are two main reasons for this. First, although economic integration benefits the majority, it has its costs. Although a nation as a whole may benefit significantly from a regional free trade agreement, certain groups may loose. These groups may block a potential form of economic integration is the garner sufficient political clout. The second impediment to integration arises from concerns over national sovereignty.

3. What is the likely effect of creation of a single market within the EU likely to be on competition within the EU? Why?

Answer: If the EU is successful in establishing a single market, member countries can expect significant gains from the free flow of trade and investment. This will result from the ability of the countries within the EU to specialize in the production of the product that they manufacture the most efficiently, and the have the freedom to trade those products with other EU countries without being encumbered by tariffs and other trade barriers. In terms of competition, the competition between European firms will increase. Some of the most inefficient firms may go out of business, because they will no longer be protected from other European companies by high tariffs, quotas, or administrative trade barriers.

4. How should a US business firm that currently only exports to Western Europe respond to the creation of a single market?

Answer: A US business firm that is currently only exporting to Western Europe should seriously consider opening a facility somewhere in Western Europe, as the economics of a common market suggest that outsiders can be at a disadvantage to insiders. The opening of borders within Western Europe also has the potential to increase the size of the market for the firm. Of course it is possible, after careful consideration, that exporting may still be the most appropriate means of serving the market in many situations.

5. How should a firm that has self-sufficient production facilities to in several EU countries respond to the creation of a single market? What are the constraints on its ability to respond in a manner that minimizes production costs?

Answer: The creation of the single market means that it may no longer be efficient to operate separate duplicative production facilities in each country. Instead, the facilities should either be linked so that each specializes in the production of only certain items (as it was described that 3M has done), or several sites should be closed down and production consolidated into the most efficient locations. Existing differences between countries as well as the need to be located near important customers may limit a firm's ability to fully consolidate or relocate production facilities for production cost reasons. Minimizing production costs are only one of many objectives of firms, as location of production near R&D facilities can be critical for new product development and future economic success. Thus what is most important in location decisions is long run economic success, not just cost minimization.

Internet Exercises

TEXT EXERCISE 1

Overview

This exercise explores move toward a single currency system in Europe, and the implications of the euro on consumer behavior. Some experts believe that monetary union will lead to more uniform buying behavior by consumers.

Suggested Use in the Classroom

Students are asked to consider how companies should prepare to do business in a state of monetary union. Some students will outline the more obvious aspects of the process, suggesting that companies adapt their computer and accounting systems to the euro, and adjust prices accordingly. Other students may explore some of the less obvious aspects of the impact of currency union and consider the cost savings and cost increases monetary union might impose. Most students will agree that despite how it is viewed, monetary union will force companies to make adjustments to their European strategies.

TEXT EXERCISE 2

Overview

This exercise examines economic integration, and particularly four well-known examples of cooperation between countries: NAFTA, the EU, MERCOSUR, and ASEAN.

Suggested Use in the Classroom

Students are asked to compare and contrast the four alliances noted above using the framework presented in the text. In addition, students are queried as to whether the alliances should take a stand on cross-border e-commerce. Most students will probably agree that the four organizations should indeed indicate their position towards e-commerce, however, students may not agree as exactly what those positions should be.

WEB EXERCISE 1

Overview

Wal-Mart, the American retailer, is currently expanding into Europe. However, the company is finding that despite the commonalities regional economic integration brings, it cannot use a cross-border formula in its expansion efforts.

Suggested Use in the Classroom

Students are asked to study Wal-Mart's European expansion efforts and comment on whether it can not only duplicate its American success story in Europe, but how, and if, the company can convince Europeans to shop like Americans. Most students will probably agree that Wal-Mart faces a strong challenge as it enters the European marketplace, noting that the firm has to contend with new regulations and ingrained shopping habits.

WEB EXERCISE 2

Overview

This exercise explores the recent European expansion of Land's End, the American catalogue company. The company has found that despite claims that economic integration will bring markets closer together, it is still necessary to treat markets individually. _

Suggested Use in the Classroom

Students are asked to consider how the Internet may affect corporations as they conduct cross-border activities. More specifically, the question is raised as to whether differences in a company's web sites across borders has the potential to irk consumers as they surf the web, and how companies can anticipate differences in consumer reactions. This exercise provides a good forum for debate among students.

CLOSING CASE: Martin's Textiles

Summary

The closing case describes the effects of NAFTA on one firm, Martin's Textiles. Martin's makes undergarments at several unionized plants in the Northeastern US. Since this is a labor-intensive industry, its costs are high and it is losing money. Martin's must decide if it can stay in business in the current location, or if it will have to open plants in Mexico in order to compete. Complicating this decision is the fact that this is a family run business, and many of the employees "are just like" family and will be in a difficult position if it were to close down its current factories. Discussion of the case can be assisted by the following questions:

QUESTION 1: What are the economic costs and benefits to Martin's Textiles of shifting production to Mexico?

ANSWER 1: The primary economic benefit might be the potential to stay in business. This is based on lower wages, and hence lower production costs. The economic costs involve the costs of potentially closing the current facilities and providing severance packages to workers, and the costs that could result from reduced product quality.

QUESTION 2: What are the social costs and benefits to Martin's Textiles of shifting production to Mexico?

ANSWER 2: There are few short-term social benefits, other than to Mexican workers and the Mexican economy. The social costs are also short term, in that goodwill and relations with existing employees are lost.

QUESTION 3: Are the economic and social costs and benefits of moving production to Mexico independent of each other?

ANSWER 3: No. If production is shifted to Mexico, current workers will be upset and impart a social cost on Martin's and the community. They may also choose to perform their duties poorly during the transition, thus creating economic costs. Likewise in Mexico, the social benefits and the economic benefits to Martin's are related. This is in fact one of the arguments for free trade.

QUESTION 4: What seems to be the most ethical action?

ANSWER 4: Neither Neither Neither John Martin nor his employees benefit if his firm goes out of business. Thus, some gradual transition that makes it easier on employees may be the most ethical approach. What is most ethical, however, will depend upon the values of the student.

QUESTION 5: What would you do if you were John Martin?

ANSWER: This question is left to the discretion of each student

Country Focus: The Impact of NAFTA on the U.S. Textile Industry

<u>Summary</u>

This feature explores the effect of NAFTA on the U.S. textile industry. Prior to the signing of the NAFTA agreement, many concerns were raised regarding the potential for a significant loss of jobs in the American textile industry. Indeed, four years after the establishment of NAFTA, the U.S. textile industry has lost some 15% of its jobs to Mexico. However, at the same time, U.S. consumers have enjoyed lower clothing prices and U.S. fabric and yarn makers have seen a boost in their exports to Mexico.

<u>Suggested Discussion Questions</u>

1.Ross Perot may always be remembered for his notion of the "giant sucking sound" that the U.S. would hear as jobs moved to Mexico if NAFTA came into being. Discuss Perot's idea within the context of the U.S. textile industry.

2. During the period since the establishment of NAFTA, U.S. consumers have watched prices fall on many imported clothing products. Explain the trade-offs involved with economic integration from the perspective of the consumer.

Management Focus: Atag Holdings

<u>Summary</u>

Atag Holdings, a Dutch kitchen appliance producer, has struggled with its European product line. Hoping to benefit from the single market, Atag Holdings planned to market just two varieties of stovetops throughout the European Union. The company found however, that differences in consumer preferences were so great that it needed 11 stove tops instead. Atag Holdings now maintains a wide product line in order to be successful within the Single Market.

<u>Suggested Discussion Questions</u>

1. Atag Holdings found the notion of the Euro-Consumer to be just a myth. Discuss the idea of economic integration creating commonalities in consumer demands.

2. Atag Holdings envisioned cost savings resulting from a narrower product line, yet, in order to be successful, found that it had to carry a wide range of products instead. Are there other areas where Atag Holdings could benefit from the Single Market?

<u>Additional Readings and Sources of Information</u>

<u>Laurent Piepszownik/France: 'We Are a Euroland Company'</u>: {http://www.businessweek.com/search}

<u>The Atlantic Century</u>: {http://www.businessweek.com/search}

<u>Europe's Continental Divide</u>: {http://www.businessweek.com/search}

<u>A Talk with Mack McLarty: Mexico, NAFTA, and Beyond</u>: {http://www.businessweek.com/search}

<u>Hurdles for a Mexican's New Business North of the Border</u>: {http://www.businessweek.com/search}

CHAPTER 8
THE FOREIGN EXCHANGE MARKET

Chapter Outline

OPENING CASE: Foreign Exchange Losses at JAL

INTRODUCTION

THE FUNCTIONS OF THE FOREIGN EXCHANGE MARKET

Currency conversion
Management Focus: George Soros – The Man Who Can Move Currency Markets
Insuring Against Foreign Exchange Risk

THE NATURE OF THE FOREIGN EXCHANGE MARKET

ECONOMIC THEORIES OF EXCHANGE RATE DETERMINATION

Prices and Exchange Rates
Interest Rates and Exchange Rates
Investor Psychology and Bandwagon Effects
Country Focus: Why Did the Korean Won Collapse?
Summary

EXCHANGE RATE FORECASTING

Efficient Market School
Inefficient Market School
Approaches to Forecasting

CURRENCY CONVERTIBILITY

Convertibility and Government Policy
Countertrade

IMPLICATIONS FOR BUSINESS

SUMMARY OF CHAPTER

CRITICAL THINKING AND DISCUSSION QUESTIONS

INTERNET EXERCISES

CLOSING CASE: The Collapse of the Thai Bhat

Learning Objectives

1. Be familiar with the form and function of the foreign exchange market.

2. Understand the different between spot and forward exchange rates.

3. Understand how currency exchange rates are determined.

4. Appreciate the role of the foreign exchange market in insuring against foreign exchange risk.

5. Be familiar with the merits of different approaches toward exchange rate forecasting.

6. Appreciate why some currencies cannot always be converted into other currencies.

7. Understand how countertrade is used to mitigate problems associated with an inability to convert currencies.

Chapter Summary

This chapter focuses on the foreign exchange market. At the outset, the chapter explains how the foreign exchange market works. Included in this discussion is an explanation of the difference between spot exchange rates and forward exchange rates. The nature of the foreign exchange market is discussed, including an examination of the forces that determine exchange rates. In addition, the author provides a discussion of the degree to which it is possible to predict exchange rate movements. Other topics discussed in the chapter include exchange rate forecasting, currency convertibility, and the implications of exchange rate movements on business. In regard to the later, a number of implications of exchange rates for businesses are contained in the chapter. For instance, it is absolutely critical that international businesses understand the influence of exchange rates on the profitability of trade and investment deals. Adverse changes in exchange rates can make apparently profitable deals unprofitable.

OPENING CASE: Foreign Exchange Losses at JAL

Summary

The feature focuses on the currency exchange rate implications of the manner in which Japan Air Lines (JAL) purchases commercial aircraft from Boeing. Because JAP is a Japanese company, the majority of the money that it earns is paid in Japanese yen. However, when JAL purchases aircraft from Boeing, it must covert its yen into dollars to make payment to Boeing. The problem is that JAL must place an order with Boeing approximately five years before the actual plane can be delivered. Along with the order, JAL must pay Boeing a 10 percent deposit. The aircraft that JAL purchase from Boeing involve substantial amounts of money, ranging from $35 million for a 737 to $160 million for a top-of-the line 747-400. Because of this, when purchasing an aircraft from Boeing, JAL uses forward exchange contracts to protect itself against adverse currency movements. The case relates the positive and negative consequences of this policy.

Chapter Outline With Lecture Notes and Teaching Tips

INTRODUCTION

A) This chapter has three main objectives. The first is to explain how the foreign exchange market works. The second is to examine the forces that determine exchange rates and to discuss the degree to which it is possible to predict exchange rate movements. The third objective is to map the implications for international business of exchange rate movements and the foreign exchange market.

Lecture Note: FX Week is an on-line newsletter for foreign exchange specialists. The newsletter provides current information and features about the foreign exchange market that might provide interesting lecture material. The site is available at {http://www.fxweek.com/}.

B) The foreign exchange market is a Market for converting the currency of one country into that of another country.

C) The exchange rate is the rate at which one currency is converted into another.

D) While dealing in multiple currencies is a requirement of doing business internationally, it also creates risks and significantly alters the attractiveness of different investments and deals over time. Firms can use the foreign exchange market to minimize the risk of adverse changes, but this can prevent them for benefiting from favorable changes.

THE FUNCTIONS OF THE FOREIGN EXCHANGE MARKET

A) The foreign exchange market serves two main functions. The first is to convert the currency of one country into the currency of another. The second is to provide some insurance against foreign exchange risk, by which we mean the adverse consequences of unpredictable changes in exchange rates.

Currency Conversion

B) The four main uses of foreign exchange markets to international businesses. First, the payments a company receives for its exports, the income it receives from foreign investments, or the income it receives from licensing agreements with foreign firms may be in foreign currencies. Second, international businesses use foreign exchange markets when they must pay a foreign company for its products or services in its country's currency. Third, international businesses use foreign exchange markets when they have spare cash that they wish to invest for short terms in money markets. Finally, currency speculation is another use of foreign exchange markets. Currency speculation typically involves the short-term movement of funds from one currency to another in the hopes of profiting from shifts in exchange rates.

Teaching Tip: There are several sites available on the Internet that are "currency converters." These sites provide on-line currency conversion information. An example of one of these sites can be found at {http://www.dna.lth.se/cgi-bin/kurt/rates}.

Insuring Against Foreign Exchange Risk

C) A second function of the foreign exchange market is to provide insurance to protect against the possible adverse consequences of unpredictable changes in exchange rates.

Spot Exchange Rate

D) The spot exchange rate is the rate at which a foreign exchange dealer converts one currency into another currency on a particular day.

Forward Exchange Rate

E) A forward exchange rate occurs when two parties agree to exchange currency and execute the deal at some specific date in the future.

Forward Exchange

F) Rates for currency exchange are typically quoted for 30, 90, or 180 days into the future.

THE NATURE OF THE FOREIGN EXCHANGE MARKET

A) The foreign exchange market is not located in any one place. Rather, it is a global network of banks, brokers, and foreign exchange dealers connected by electronic communications systems.

B) The exchange rates quoted worldwide are basically the same. If different US dollar/French Franc rates were being offered in New York and Paris, there would be an opportunity for arbitrage and the gap would close. An illustrative example can be done showing how someone could make money in arbitrage, (the process of buying a currency low and selling it high), and how this would affect the supply and demand for the currencies in both markets to close the gap.

Teaching Tip: There is a very entertaining and information "Foreign Currency Aptitude Test" available on-line at {http://www.cme.com/market/cfot/quiz}. The test, which is sponsored by the Chicago Mercantile Exchange, contains 16 multiple-choice questions that are scored on-line.

C) The US dollar frequently serves as a vehicle currency to ease the exchange of two other currencies.

ECONOMIC THEORIES OF EXCHANGE RATE DETERMINATION:

A) While at the most basic level, exchange rates are determined by the demand and supply for different currencies; what affects the supply and demand is the focus of this section. In competitive markets free of transportation costs and trade barriers, identical products sold in different countries must sell for the same price when their price is expressed in the same terms of currency. An example can be illustrative, like the one on jackets in the book. The Purchasing Power Parity (PPP) exchange rate shows what the exchange rate would be if the law of one price held. Every April the Economist magazine prints the implied PPP and the real exchange rate based on McDonald's Big Mac – a product that is virtually identical across a number of locations worldwide but priced in local currencies. The covers of some magazines, for example, *The Economist*, print their prices in multiple currencies.

Prices and Exchange Rates

B) The law of one price: The law of one price states that in competitive markets free of transportation costs and barriers to trade (such as tariffs), identical products sold in different countries must sell for the same price when their price is expressed in terms of the same currency.

Purchasing Power Parity

C) If the law of one price were true for all goods and services, the purchasing power parity (PPP) exchange rate could be found from any individual set of prices. A less extreme version of the PPP theory states that given relatively efficient markets – that is, markets in which few impediments to international trade and investment exist – the price of a "basket of goods" should be roughly equivalent in each country.

Money Supply and Price Inflation

D) There is a positive relationship between the inflation rate and the level of money supply. When the growth in the money supply is greater than the growth in output, inflation will occur. Table 9.4 illustrates the extreme case of this occurring in Bolivia.

E) Simply put, PPP suggests that changes in relative prices between countries will lead to exchange rate changes. The empirical tests suggest that this relationship does not hold in the long run, but not in the short run. While PPP assumes no transportation costs or barriers to trade and investment, it also assumes that governments do not intervene to affect their exchange rates – a topic for the next chapter.

Empirical Tests of PPP Theory

F) Extensive empirical testing of the PPP theory has not shown it to be completely accurate in estimating exchange rate changes.

Interest Rates and Exchange Rates

G) Interest rates also affect exchange rates. The fisher effect says that the real interest rates should be the same in each, while the nominal rate will include both this real rate and expected inflation. The International Fisher effect states that for any two countries the spot exchange rate should change in an equal amount but in the opposite direction to the difference in nominal interest rates between two countries. Stated more formally:

$$(S_1 - S_2) / S_2 \times 100 = i^{\$} - i^{DM}$$

where $i^{\$}$ and i^{DM} are the respective nominal interest rates in two countries (in this case the US and Germany), S_1 is the spot exchange rate at the beginning of the period and S_2 is the spot exchange rate at the end of the period.

H) While interest rate differentials suggest future exchange rates, this appears to hold in the long run but not necessarily in the short run.

Investor Psychology and Bandwagon Effects

I) Investor psychology and can also affect exchange rate movements. Expectations on the part of traders can turn into self-fulfilling prophecies, and traders can joint he bandwagon and move exchange rate based on group expectations. While such changes can be important in explaining some short-term exchange rate movements, they are very difficult to predict. At times governmental intervention can prevent the bandwagon from starting, but at other times it is ineffective and only encourages traders.

EXCHANGE RATE FORECASTING

A) A company's need to predict future exchange rate variations raises the issue of whether it is worthwhile for the company to invest in exchange rate forecasting services to aid decision-making. Two schools of thought address this issue. One school, the efficient market school, argues that forward exchange rate do the best possible job of forecasting future spot exchange rates, and, therefore, investing in forecasting services would be a waste of money. The other school of thought, the inefficient market school, argues that companies can improve the foreign exchange market's estimate of future exchange rates (as contained in the forward rate) by investing in forecasting services.

The Efficient Market School

B) Many economists believe the foreign exchange market is efficient at setting forward rates. An efficient market is one in which prices reflect all available information. There have been a large number of empirical tests of the efficient market hypothesis. Although most of the early work seems to confirm the hypothesis (suggesting that companies should not waste their money on forecasting services), more recent studies have challenged it.

The Inefficient Market School

C) An inefficient market is one in which prices do not reflect all available information. In an efficient market, forward exchange rates will not be the best possible predictors of future spot exchange rates. If this is true, it may be worthwhile for international businesses to invest in forecasting services (and many do).

Fundamental Analysis.

D) Forecasters that use fundamental analysis draw upon economic theories to predict future exchange rates, including factors like interest rates, monetary policy, inflation rates, or balance of payments information.

Technical Analysis

E) Forecasters that use technical analysis typically chart trends, and believe that past trends and waves are reasonable predictors of future trends and waves.

CURRENCY CONVERTIBILITY

Convertibility and Government Policy

A) A currency is said to be freely convertible when a government of a country allows both residents and non-residents to purchase unlimited amounts of foreign currency with the domestic currency. A currency is said to be externally convertible when non-residents can convert their holdings of domestic currency into a foreign currency, but when the ability of residents to convert currency is limited in some way. A currency is not convertible when both residents and non-residents are prohibited from converting their holdings of domestic currency into a foreign currency.

B) Free convertibility is the norm in the world today, although many countries impose some restrictions on the amount of money that can be converted. The main reason to limit convertibility is to preserve foreign exchange reserves and prevent capital flight.

Countertrade

C) Countertrade refers to a range of barter like agreements by which goods and services can be traded for other goods and services; used in international trade when a country's currency is nonconvertible.

Teaching Tip: A brief, yet informative, article about countertrade can be accessed at {http://www.iccwho.org/html/countertrade.thml}.

Lecture Note: According to the Department of Trade and Industry in the United Kingdom, countertrade is now thought to account for between 10 and 15% of trade worldwide.

IMPLICATIONS FOR BUSINESS

A) First, it is absolutely critical that international businesses understand the influence of exchange rates on the profitability of trade and investment deals.

B) It is important that international businesses understand the forces that determine exchange rates. If a company wants to know how the value of a particular currency will change over the long term in the foreign exchange market, it should take a close look at all those economic level fundamentals that appear to predict long run exchange rate movements- i.e. the growth in a country's money supply, its inflation rate, and nominal interest rates.

C) When governments restrict currency convertibility, firms must find ways to facilitate international trade and investment.

Critical Thinking and Discussion Questions

1. The interest rate on South Korean government securities with one-year maturity is 4% and the expected inflation rate for the coming year is 2%. The US interest rate on government securities with one-year maturity is 7% and the expected rate of inflation is 5%. The current spot exchange rate for Korea won is $1 = W1200. Forecast the spot exchange rate one year from today. Explain the logic of your answer.

Answer: From the Fisher effect, we know that the real interest rate in both the US and South Korea is 2%. The international Fisher effect suggests that the exchange rate will change in an equal amount but opposite direction to the difference in nominal interest rates. Hence since the nominal interest rate is 3% higher in the US than in South Korea, the dollar should depreciate by 3% relative to the South Korean Won. Using the formula from the book: $(S_1 - S_2)/S_2 \times 100 = i^\$ - i^{Won}$ and substituting 7 for $i^\$$, 4 for i^{Won}, and 1200 for S_1, yields a value for S_2 of $1=W1165.

2. Two countries, Britain and the US produce just one good - beef. Suppose that the price of beef in the US is $2.80 per pound, and in Britain it is £3.70 per pound.
(a) According to PPP theory, what should the $/£ spot exchange rate be?
(b) Suppose the price of beef is expected to rise to $3.10 in the US, and to £4.65 in Britain. What should be the one year forward $/£ exchange rate?
(c) Given your answers to parts (a) and (b), and given that the current interest rate in the US is 10%, what would you expect current interest rate to be in Britain?

Answer: (a) According to PPP, the $/£ rate should be 2.80/3.70, or .76$/£.
(b) According to PPP, the $/£ one year forward exchange rate should be 3.10/4.65, or .67$/£.
(c) Since the dollar is appreciating relative to the pound, and given the relationship of the international fisher effect, the British must have higher interest rates than the US. Using the formula $(S_1 - S_2)/S_2 \times 100 = i^£ - i^\$$ we can solve the equation for $i^£$, with $S_1=.76$, $S_2=.67$, $I^\$ = 10$, yielding a value of 23.4% for the British interest rates.

3. You manufacture wine goblets. In mid June you receive an order for 10,000 goblets from Japan. Payment of ¥400,000 is due in mid December. You expect the yen to rise from its present rate of $1=¥130 to $1=¥100 by December. You can borrow yen at 6% per annum. What should you do?

Answer: The simplest solution would be to just wait until December, take the ¥400,000 and convert it at the spot rate at that time, which you assume will be $1=¥100. In this case you would have $4,000 in mid-December. If the current 180 day forward rate is lower than 100¥/$, then it would be preferable since it both locks in the rate at a better level and reduces risk. If the rate is above ¥100/$, then whether you choose to lock in the forward rate or wait and see what the spot does will depend upon your risk aversion. There is a third possibility also. You could borrow money from a bank that you will pay back with the ¥400,000 you will receive (400,000/1.03 = ¥388,350 borrowed), convert this today to US$ (388,350/130 = $2,987), and then invest these dollars in a US account. For this to be preferable to the simplest solution, you would have to be able to make a lot of interest (4,000 - 2,987 = $1,013), which would turn out to be an annual rate of 51% ((1,013/4000) * 2). If, however, you could lock in these interest rates, then this method would also reduce any exchange rate risk. What you should do depends upon the interest rates available, the forward rates available, how large a risk you are willing to take, and how certain you feel that the spot rate in December will be ¥100 = $1.

Internet Exercises

TEXT EXERCISE 1

Overview

This exercise explores the notion of purchasing power parity within the European Union. Britons are currently facing significantly higher prices than their neighboring countries, and questions are being raised as to why this is the case.

Suggested Use in the Classroom

Students are asked to discuss why firms are charging higher prices in Britain. Student responses to this question may range from the more simplistic idea of matching competitors' prices, to a detailed discussion of how cost structures may be higher in Britain, therefore higher prices are justified. Most students will agree that the Internet has the potential to bring prices into line.

TEXT EXERCISE 2

Overview

This exercise extends the previous exercise by asking how the Internet is changing firms' pricing strategies. As British consumers make their concerns public, companies are being forced to either explain their higher British prices, or bring them into line with prices in neighboring markets.

Suggested Use in the Classroom

Students are asked to "go shopping" for various items in various countries and identify any price differences they encounter. Then, students are asked to comment on firm price strategy in foreign markets. Most students will probably agree that companies may have a very difficult time justifying the use of differing pricing scales in similar markets.

WEB EXERCISE 1

Overview

The euro, after a strong entry to the world marketplace, is presently in a slump. How Europe will respond to its weak currency is not yet clear, and some investors are finding the situation to be a nerve racking one.

Suggested Use in the Classroom

This exercise requires students to track the value of the euro relative to the British pound and the U.S. dollar for a period of time. Then, students are asked to use the framework presented in the text to discuss their findings, and make predictions for the future. Most students will recognize the difficulty in accurately predicting currency values, but should be able to make some guesses as to the euro's value by considering variables such as interest rate and inflation rates.

WEB EXERCISE 2

Overview

Japan, at the beginning of the new millennium, was struggling with the effects of a high yen to dollar ratio. With its economic recovery still tenuous, the Japanese government was asking the U.S. and Europe for assistance in stopping the yen's rise.

Suggested Use in the Classroom

In this exercise, students are asked to consider how the rising yen might affect various companies operating in the Japanese market. Students, after considering the situation of each company, should come to the conclusion that exchange rates are very much a global issue, and that no company can afford to ignore events occurring in the foreign exchange market.

CLOSING CASE: The Collapse of The Thai Baht

Summary

The closing case describes the events leading up to the collapse of the Thai baht in 1997. A number of economic events and conditions are portrayed, which present a complex and inter-related series of events that affected the baht's exchange rate. Discussion of the case can be assisted by the following questions:

QUESTION 1: Identify the main factors that led to the collapse of the Thai baht in 1997.

ANSWER 1: Inflation of prices in Thailand clearly played a role, particularly those of property. The current account deficit also was a factor in changing the fundamental supply and demand for baht. Speculation affected the size and timing of the fall of the baht, but not the inevitability of the decline.

QUESTION 2: Do you think the sudden collapse of the Thai baht can be explained by the purchasing power parity theorem?

ANSWER 2: Relative inflation rates indicated that the value of the baht should fall in comparison to the dollar. Because the value was fixed, however, a gradual adjustment of the exchange rate was not possible. The timing of the sudden collapse cannot be explained by PPP, but that some devaluation should occur could have been expected.

QUESTION 3: What role did speculators play in the fall of the Thai baht? Did they cause it to fall?

ANSWER 3: The speculators played a role in the timing and magnitude of the devaluation of the baht. Traders who acted accordingly recognized economic fundamentals, and mismanagement of funds by banks. These factors created the downward pressure on the baht that the speculators were happy to profit from.

QUESTION 4: What steps might the Thai government have taken to preempt the financial crisis that swept the nation in 1997?

ANSWER 4: One simple answer would be to have let the baht float much earlier. This would have allowed it to gradually adjust over time, preventing a crisis. This would have also limited the attractiveness of some of the lending practices that ultimately accelerated the need for a correction. Related to this last point, banking regulations could have been changed so that banks would not have been allowed to get into the situation that caused them to collapse. People with a more interventionist approach to government, and a belief in the ability of policies that allow economic micromanagement, may have other more detailed suggestions. Unless students have studied such policies in an economics or political science course, it is unlikely that they will be able to answer the question along these lines. The philosophy of this text is clearly free market based.

QUESTION 5: How will the collapse of the Thai baht affect businesses in Thailand, particularly those that purchase inputs from abroad or export finished products?

ANSWER 5: Those businesses that purchase inputs from abroad will likely find that their costs of business (inputs) have increased, unless purchased from one of the other Asian countries that also saw a significant currency depreciation. Those that export finished products to other countries that have also experienced an economic downturn will see a decrease in demand. Exports to countries with much stronger currencies (e.g., USA) will likely increase, as these goods will now seem much cheaper to consumers whose currency has remained higher. Thai businesses that primarily do business in Thailand will be negatively impacted by the decline in the local economy.

QUESTION 6: Do you notice any similarities between the collapse of the Thai baht in 1997 and the collapse of the Korean won around the same time (see the Country Focus in this chapter)? What are these similarities? Do you think these two events are related? How?

ANSWER 6: There are some significant similarities. Based on the interest rate information, it would seem that some gradual decline of won should have taken place. This did not occur, however, since the currency was pegged. This interest rate differential caused borrowers to reduce their preference for won and increase their preference for dollars. This put additional pressure on the won, as was the case with the baht. An additional similarity is that both countries were growing quickly, and governmental policies encouraged further investment that led to excess capacity (be that in housing and/or semiconductor factories).

Management Focus: George Soros – The Man Who Can Move Currency Markets

Summary

This feature focuses on George Soros, a 65-year old Hungarian-born financier, who is the principal partner of the Quantum Group, which controls a series of hedge funds with assets of around $12 billion. The Quantum Group, which holds a diversified portfolio of assets, is one of the world's largest currency "speculators." The case relates several incidences in which the Quantum Group took major positions in foreign currency exchange rates, and experienced substantial profits and losses. According to the feature, the Quantum Group takes positions that are so large and closely watched, that a major action by the Quantum Group can start a "bandwagon effect" that causes currency movements in the direction that the Quantum Group expects.

Suggested Discussion Questions

1. Describe what is meant by the term "bandwagon effect."

2. Describe how an investor can make money by "short selling" one currency against another.

3. In your opinion, does the Quantum Group serve a useful function or a disruptive function in regard to world currency markets? Why or why not?

4. Web Site: George Soros Biographical Information: {http://soros.org/gsbio.html}

Country Focus: Why Did the Korean Won Collapse?

Summary

This feature describes South Korea's 1997 financial crisis. In the space of a few months Korea saw its economy and currency move from   prosperity to critical lows. Much of the blame for Korea's financial collapse can be placed with the country's chaebol (large industrial conglomerates) that had built up massive debts as they invested in new factories. Speculators, concerned about Chaebol's ability to repay their debts, began to withdraw money from the Korean Stock And Bond markets fueling a depreciation in the Korean Won. Despite government efforts to halt the fall in the currency, the Won fell some 67% relative to the dollar.

1. Discuss investor psychology and bandwagon effects and their role in accelerating Korea's difficulties.

2. As a CEO of an American company, what or how does Korea's situation affect your operations?

3. In your opinion, did the Korean government take the right steps to ease the crisis? Explain your response.

Additional Readings and Sources of Information

Will the Yen's Surge Do Japan In?: {http://www.businessweek.com/search}

Brazil: Looks Like a Recovery Coming: {http://www.businessweek.com/search}

The Currency Game has Brand-New Rules: {http://www.businessweek.com/2000/00_08/b3669116.htm}

Japan's Central Banker is Right: There's No Quick Fix for the Yen: {http://www.businessweek.com/bwdaily/dnflash/oct1999/nf91005a.htm}

Don't Let the Forex Market Scare You—Simple Strategies for Small Biz: {http://www.businessweek.com/smallbiz/briefcase/1999/ib990823.htm}

Why the Euro is so Wimpy: {http://www.businessweek.com/1999/99_50/b3659101.htm}

CHAPTER 9
THE GLOBAL MONETARY SYSTEM

IMPLICATIONS FOR BUSINESS

    Currency Management
    Business Strategy
    Corporate - Government Relations

SUMMARY OF CHAPTER

INTERNET EXERCISES

CRITICAL THINKING AND DISCUSSION QUESTIONS

CLOSING CASE: Caterpillar Inc.

Learning Objectives

1. Understand the role played by the global monetary system in exchange rate determination.

2. Be familiar with the historical development of the modern global monetary system.

3. Appreciate the differences between a fixed and a floating exchange rate system.

4. Understand why the world's fixed exchange rate regime collapsed in the 1970s.

5. Understand the arguments for and against fixed and floating exchange rate systems.

6. Be familiar with the role played by the International Monetary Fund and the World Bank in the global monetary system.

Chapter Summary

The objective of this chapter is to explain how the international monetary system works to point out its implications for international business. The chapter begins by reviewing the historical evolution of the monetary system, starting with the gold standard and the Bretton Woods System. The chapter explains the role of the International Monetary Fund (IMF) and the World Bank, both of which were initiated by the Bretton Woods Conference. The fixed exchange rate system that was initiated by the Bretton Woods Conference collapsed in 1973. The majority of the chapter explains the workings of the international monetary system. The pluses and minuses of fixed exchange rates versus floating exchange rates are discussed. Scholars differ in regard to which system is best. The current role of the IMF and the World Bank is discussed, including the manner in which the IMF has helped nations restructure their debts.

OPENING CASE: The Tragedy of the Congo (Zaire)

Summary

The opening case describes the economic and political situation in Zaire. Economic mismanagement, political corruption, and the policies of the IMF and the World Bank all contributed to the dismal economic performance. The following questions can be helpful in directing the discussion:

QUESTION 1: Why did Zaire's economy perform so poorly between 1967 and 1997?

ANSWER 1: There are multiple factors behind the poor performance. Clearly there was economic mismanagement and corruption on the part of the government, as evidenced by the personal wealth of Mobutu Sese Seko. Money intended to help the country instead went to he and his cronies. Policies imposed by the IMF and the World Bank, it has been argued, also contributed to a downward spiral. By continuing to pour good money into a corrupt economy, these agencies helped dig Zaire even further into debt and kept it from needing to take difficult measures.

QUESTION 2: What are the implications of the situation in Zaire for future lending policies of the IMF and the World Bank?

ANSWER 2: As much as they would like, international institutions are not able to direct how money is actually used once dispersed. In the case of Zaire (as well as Russia in the 1990s), it seems as if political corruption and skimming by powerful individuals in business and government has meant that funds were not allocated as intended. Thus the country took on debt for which it is receiving no flow of funds that can be used to pay back the loans, and must take on additional loans simply to service the debt. This leads to a dangerous spiral of increased debt that does not help fix the fundamental problems. It makes little sense to throw more money into a bad situation.

Chapter Outline With Lecture Notes and Teaching Tips

INTRODUCTION

A) The objective of this chapter is to explain how the international monetary system works and to point out its implications for international business.

B) The exchange rates quoted worldwide are basically the same. If different US dollar/French Franc rates were being offered in New York and Paris, there would be an opportunity for arbitrage and the gap would close. An illustrative example can be done, showing how someone could make money in arbitrage, and how this would affect the supply and demand for the currencies in both markets to close the gap.

C) The US dollar frequently serves as a vehicle currency to ease the exchange of two other currencies.

THE GOLD STANDARD

A) The gold standard had its origin in the use of gold coins as a medium of exchange, unit of account, and store of value - a practice that stretches back to ancient times.

Lecture Note: A very informative and well-written explanation of the gold standard is available at {http://www.clev.frb.org/annual/essay.htm#gold}.

Nature of the Gold Standard

B) The practice of pegging currencies to gold and guaranteeing convertibility is known as the gold standard. For example, under the **gold standard** one U.S. dollar was defined as equivalent to 23.22 grains of "fine (pure) gold.

C) The exchange rate between currencies was determined based on how much gold a unit of each currency would buy.

The Strength of the Gold Standard

D) The great strength claimed for the gold standard was that it contained a powerful mechanism for simultaneously achieving balance-of-trade equilibrium by all countries.

The Period Between the Wars, 1918-39

E) The gold standard worked fairly well until the inter-war years and the great depression. Trying to spur exports and domestic employment, a number of countries started regularly devaluing their currencies, with the end result that people lost confidence in the system and started to demand gold for their currency. This put pressure on countries' gold reserves, and forced them to suspend gold convertibility.

THE BRETTON WOODS SYSTEM

A) In 1944, at the height of World War II, representatives from 44 countries met at Bretton Woods, New Hampshire, to design a new international monetary system. With the collapse of the gold standard and the Great Depression of the 1930s fresh in their minds, these statesmen were determined to build an enduring economic order that would facilitate postwar economic growth. The agreement reached at Bretton Woods established two multinational institutions - the International Monetary Fund (IMF) and the World Bank. The task of the IMF would be to maintain order in the international monetary system and that of the World Bank would be to promote general economic development.

B) The US dollar was to be pegged and convertible to gold, and other currencies would set their exchange rates relative to the dollar. Devaluations were not to be used for competitive purposes, and a country could not devalue the currency by more than 10% without IMF approval.

Teaching Tip: A well written, brief history of the rise and fall of the Bretton Woods is available at {http://ps.ucdavis.edu/classes/pol129/SWE/bw2.htm}.

The Role of the IMF

C) The aim of the Bretton Woods agreement, of which the IMF was the main custodian, was to try to avoid a repetition of the chaos that occurred between the wars through a combination of discipline and flexibility.

Teaching Tip: The homepage of the IMF is available at {http://www.imf.org}.

Discipline

D) A fixed exchange rate regime imposes discipline in two ways. First, the need to maintain a fixed exchange rate puts a brake on competitive devaluations and brings stability to the world trade environment. Second, a fixed exchange rate regime imposes monetary discipline on countries, thereby curtailing price inflation.

Flexibility

E) Although monetary discipline was a central objective of the Bretton Woods agreement, it was recognized that a rigid policy of fixed exchange rates would be too inflexible. The IMF stood ready to lend foreign currencies to members to tide them over during short periods of balance-of-payments deficit, when a rapid tightening of monetary or fiscal policy would hurt domestic employment.

The Role of the World Bank

F) The official name of the World Bank is the International Bank for Reconstruction and Development (IBRD). The bank lends money under two schemes. Under the IBRD scheme, money is raised through bond sales in the international capital market. Borrowers pay what the bank calls a market rate of interest - the bank's cost of funds plus a margin for expenses. A second scheme is overseen by the International Development Agency, an arm of the bank created in 1960. IDA loans go only to the poorest countries.

Teaching Tip: The Homepage of the World Bank can be accessed at {http://www.worldbank.org/}

THE COLLAPSE OF THE FIXED EXCHANGE RATE SYSTEM

A) The fixed exchange rate system established in Bretton Woods collapsed mainly due to the economic management of the USA. Under Johnson, the US financed huge increases in welfare programs and the Vietnam War by increasing its money supply.

B) Speculation that the dollar would have to be devalued relative to most other currencies, as well as underlying economics and some forceful threats by the US forced other countries to increase the value of their currency relative to the dollar

C) The key problem with the Bretton Woods system was that it relied on an economically well managed US, since the dollar was the base currency. When the US began to print money, run high trade deficits, and experience high inflation, the system was strained to the breaking point

THE FLOATING EXCHANGE RATE REGIME

A) The floating exchange rate regime that followed the collapse of the fixed exchange rate system was formalized in January 1976 when IMF members met in Jamaica and agreed to the rules for the international monetary system that are in place today.

The Jamaica Agreement

B) The purpose of the Jamaica meeting was to revise the IMF's Articles of Agreement to reflect the new reality of floating exchange rates. The three main elements of the Jamaican agreement include the following:
  i) Floating rates were declared acceptable.
  ii) Gold was abandoned as a reserve asset.
  iii) Total annual IMF quotas - the amount member countries contribute to the IMF - were increased to $41 billion.

Exchange Rates since 1973

C) Since March 1973 exchange rates have become much more volatile and far less predictable than they were between 1945 and 1973. The volatility has been partly due to a number of unexpected shocks to the world monetary system including:

i) The oil crisis in 1973.
ii) The loss of confidence in the dollar that followed the rise of U.S. inflation in 1977 and 1978.
iii) The oil crisis of 1979.
iv) The unexpected rise in the dollar between 1980 and 1985.
v) The rapid fall of the U.S. dollar against the Japanese yen and German deutsche mark between 1985 and 1987, and against the yen between 1993 and 1995.

FIXED VERSUS FLOATING EXCHANGE RATES

A) The breakdown of the Bretton Woods system has not stopped the debate about the relative merits of Fixed versus floating exchange rate regimes. Indeed, disappointment with the system of floating rates in recent years has led to renewed debate about the merits of a fixed exchange rate system.

The Case for Floating Exchange Rates

B) The case for floating exchange rates has two main elements: monetary policy autonomy and automatic trade balance adjustments.

Monetary Policy Autonomy

C) It is argued that a floating exchange rate regime gives countries monetary policy autonomy. Under a fixed system, a country's ability to expand or contract its money supply as it sees fit is limited by the need to maintain exchange rate parity. Advocates of a floating exchange rate regime argue that removal of the obligation to maintain exchange rate parity restores monetary control to a government.

Trade Balance Adjustments

D) Under the Bretton Woods system, if a country developed a permanent deficit in its balance of trade that could not be corrected by domestic policy, the IMF would agree to a currency devaluation. Critics of this system argue that the adjustment mechanism works much more smoothly under a floating exchange rate regime.

The Case for Fixed Exchange Rates

E) The case for fixed exchange rates rests on arguments about monetary discipline, uncertainty, and the lack of connection between the trade balance and exchange rates.

Monetary Discipline

F) The need to maintain a fixed exchange rate parity ensures that governments do not expand their money supplies at inflationary rates.

Speculation

G) Critics of a floating exchange rate regime also argue that speculation can cause fluctuations in exchange rates.

Uncertainty

H) Speculation also adds to the uncertainty surrounding future currency movements that characterizes floating exchange rate regimes.

Trade Balance Adjustments

I) Those in favor of floating exchange rates argue that floating rates help adjust trade imbalances.

Who is Right?

J) There is no real agreement as to which system is better. We do, however, know that a fixed exchange rate regime modeled along the lines of the Bretton Woods system will not work. It is telling that speculation ultimately broke the system - a phenomenon that advocates of fixed rate regimes claim is associated with floating exchange rates. Nevertheless, a different kind of fixed exchange rate system might be more enduring and might foster the kind of stability that would facilitate more rapid growth in international trade and investment.

Teaching Tip: A book entitled "International Monetary Cooperation Since Bretton Woods" by Harold James is a comprehensive account of the management of the international monetary system from the 1944 Bretton Woods conference to the present day. A review of the book is available at {http://www.oup-usa.org/docs.019510448X.html}.

EXCHANGE RATE REGIMES IN PRACTICE

A) Under a pegged exchange rate regime a country will peg the value of its currency to that of another major currency. Pegged exchange rates are popular among the world's smaller nations, as they peg their exchange rate to that of other currencies.

B) There is some evidence that adopting a pegged exchange rate regime does moderate inflationary pressures in a country.

C) A country that introduces a currency board commits itself to converting its domestic currency on demand into another currency at a fixed exchange rate. To make this commitment credible, the currency board holds reserves of foreign currency equal at the fixed exchange rate to at least 100% of the domestic currency issued.

RECENT ACTIVITIES AND THE FUTURE OF THE IMF

A) With the introduction of the floating rate system and the emergence of global capital markets, much of the original reason for the IMF's existence have disappeared. Financial difficulties have not disappeared however, and like any good bureaucracy, the IMF has found away to grow and redefine its mission

Financial Crisis in the Post Bretton Woods Era

B) A number of broad types of financial crisis have occurred over the last quarter of a century, many of which have required IMF involvement. A **currency crisis** occurs when a speculative attack on the exchange value of a currency results in a sharp depreciation in the value of the currency, or forces authorities to expend large volumes of international currency reserves and sharply increase interest rates in order to defend prevailing exchange rate.

C) A **banking crisis** refers to a situation in which a loss of confidence in the banking system leads to a run on the banks, as individuals and companies withdraw their deposits.

D) A **foreign debt crisis** is a situation in which a country cannot service its foreign debt obligations, whether private sector or government debt.

E) In terms of IMF involvement, four main crises have been of particular significance; the Third World debt crisis of the 1980s, the 1995 Mexican currency crisis, the crisis experienced by Russia as that country moved towards a market based economic system, the 1995 Mexican currency crisis, and the Asian financial crisis.

F) To a varying extent, all of these crises were the result of excessive foreign borrowings, a weak or poorly regulated banking system, and high inflation rates.

<u>1995 Mexican Currency Crisis</u>

G) The Mexican currency crisis of 1995 was a result of high Mexican debts, and a pegged exchange rate that did not allow for a natural adjustment of prices. In order to keep Mexico from defaulting on its debt, a $50 billion aid package was put together. The effect of the Mexican currency crisis on the US automobile industry is described in the Management Focus box.

<u>Russian Ruble Crisis</u>

H) Between 1992 and 1995, the value of the Russian ruble relative to the dollar fell from 125 to 5130. This fall occurred while Russia was implementing an economic reform program designed to transform the country's crumbling centrally planned economy into a dynamic market economy. This fall was directly related to the hyperinflation in Russia, in line with what would be expected by purchasing power parity.

<u>The Asian Crisis</u>

I) The financial crisis that erupted across Southeast Asia during the fall of 1997 were sown in the previous decade when these countries were experiencing unprecedented growth.

J) As the volume of investments ballooned during the 1990s, often at the bequest of national governments, so the quality of many of these investments declined significantly. Often the investments were made on the basis of projections about future demand conditions that were unrealistic. The result was the emergence of significant excess capacity.

The Investment Boom

K) Huge increases in exports, and hence the incoming funds, helped fuel a boom in commercial and residential property, industrial assets, and infrastructure. As the volume of investments grew, the quality of these investments declined, leading to significant excess capacity.

The Debt Bomb

L) These investments were often supported by dollar-based debts. When inflation and increasing imports put pressure on the currencies, the resulting devaluations led to default on dollar denominated debts

Expanding Imports

M) A final complicating factor was that by the mid 1990's although exports were still expanding across the region, so were imports.

The Crisis

N) The Asian meltdown began in mid 1997 in Thailand when it became clear that several key Thai financial institutions were on the verge of default. Seeing these developments, foreign exchange dealers and hedge funds started to speculate against the Baht, selling it short. The Thai government tried to defend the peg, but only succeeded in depleting its foreign exchange reserves. On July 2nd, 1997, the Thai government abandoned its defense and announced that they would allow the Baht to float freely against the dollar. Thee Baht started a slide that would bring the exchange rate down to $1 = BT55 by January1988.

O) With its foreign exchange rates depleted, Thailand lacked the foreign currency needed to finance its international trade and service debt commitments, and was in desperate need of the capital the IMF could provide.

P) Following the devaluation of the Thai Baht, wave after wave of speculation hit other Asian countries. One after another in a period of weeks the Malaysian Ringgit, Indonesian Rupaih and the Singapore Dollar were all marked sharply lower.

Q) With the exception of Singapore, whose economy is probably the most stable in the region, these devaluations were driven by similar factors to those that underlay the earlier devaluation of the Thai Baht. A combination of excess investment, high borrowings, much of it in dollar denominated debt, and a deteriorating balance of payments position.

R) The final domino to fall was South Korea. When the Korean Won started to decline in the fall of 1997 in sympathy with the problems elsewhere in Asia, Korean companies saw their debt obligations balloon. Several large companies were forced to default on their debt service obligations and file for bankruptcy.

Evaluating the IMF's Policy Prescription

S) In helping bail out countries under financial crisis, the IMF's policies have come under criticism. One criticism is that the IMF has a "one size fits all" policy that does not adequately deal with the differences across countries. Another is that the IMF creates a moral hazard - since people and governments believe that the IMF will bail them out, they undertake overly risky investments. While it may be that the IMF has become too big and does not have enough accountability for its actions, it has also been extremely helpful to many countries

Teaching Tip: The International Monetary Fund maintains a very substantive web site at {http://www.imf.org/external/}. It is very easy to access current information about the IMF at the web site. The site includes current press releases, new briefs, and research reports pertaining to IMF activities.

Lecture Note: The World Bank makes many loans to developing countries. To provide your students an understanding of the types of loans that the World Bank makes, the following is an example of a loan that the World Bank approved on November 20, 1997: Title: Brazil Rural Poverty Alleviation Projects – Paraiba and Maranhao; Loan Amount: $140 million (U.S. dollars). Project Description: These projects will help finance small projects in the States of Paraiba and Maranhao to finance improvements in rural water supply, electricity, roads and bridges, sanitation, community centers and daycare centers, and other farming projects (such as communal irrigation schemes, rearing farm animals). The project will also support training and consultant services and research (information taken from World Bank website at http://www.worldbank.com/}.

IMPLICATIONS FOR BUSINESS

Currency Management

A) An obvious implication with regard to currency management is that companies must recognize that the foreign exchange market does not work quite as depicted in Chapter 8. The current system is a managed float system in which government intervention can help drive the foreign exchange market. A second message contained in this chapter is that under the present system, speculative buying and selling of currencies can create volatile movements in exchange rates.

Business Strategy

B) The volatility of the present floating exchange rate regime presents a conundrum for international businesses. Exchange rate movements are difficult to predict, and yet their movement can have a major impact on the competitive position of businesses. One response to the uncertainty that arises from a floating exchange rate regime might be to build strategic flexibility.

Corporate-Government Relations

C) As major players in the international trade and investment environment, businesses can influence government policy towards the international monetary system.

Critical Thinking and Discussion Questions

1. What did the gold standard collapse? Is there a case for returning to some type of gold standard? What is it?

Answer: The gold standard worked reasonably well from the 1870s until the start of World War I in 1914, when it was abandoned. During the war several governments financed their massive military expenditures by printing money. This resulted in inflation, and by the war's end in 1918, price levels were higher everywhere. Several countries returned to the gold standard after World War I. However, the period that ensued saw so many countries devalue their currencies that it became impossible to be certain how much gold a currency could buy. Instead of holding onto another country's currency, people often tried to exchange it into gold immediately, least the country devalue its currency in the intervening period. This put pressure on the gold reserves of various countries, forcing them to suspend gold convertibility. As a result, by the start of World War II, the gold standard was dead.
The great strength of the gold standard was that it contained a powerful mechanism for simultaneously achieving balance-of-trade equilibrium by all countries, as explained in the example provided on pages 294-

295 of the textbook. This strength is the basis for reconsidering the gold standard as a basis for international monetary policy.

2. What opportunities might IMF lending policies to developing nations create for international businesses? What threats might they create?

Answer: The IMF lending policies require the recipient countries to implement governmental reforms to stabilize monetary policy and encourage economic growth. One of the principal ways for a developing nation to spur economic growth is to solicit foreign direct investment and to provide a hospitable environment for the foreign investors. These characteristics of IMF lending policies work to the advantage of international businesses that are looking for investment opportunities in developing countries.

3. Do you think it is in the best interest of Western international businesses to have the IMF lend money to the former Communist states of Eastern Europe to help them transform their economies? Why?

Answer: Yes. By helping these countries transform their centrally planned economies to market economies, the IMF will help create stronger potential trading partners for Western International Business to invest in.

4. Debate the relative merits of fixed and floating exchange rate regimes. From the perspective of an international business, what are the most important criteria in a choice between the systems? Which system is the more desirable for an international business?

Answer: The case for fixed exchange rates rests on arguments about monetary discipline, speculation, uncertainty, and the lack of connection between the trade balance and exchange rates. In terms of monetary discipline, the need to maintain fixed exchange rate parity ensures that governments do not expand their money supplies at inflationary rates. In terms of speculation, a fixed exchange rate regime precludes the possibility of speculation. In terms of uncertainty, a fixed rate regime introduces a degree of certainty in the international monetary system by reducing volatility in exchange rates. Finally, in terms of trade balance adjustments, critics question the closeness of the link between the exchange rate and the trade balance. The case for floating exchange rates has two main elements: monetary policy autonomy and automatic trade balance adjustments. In terms of the former, it is argued that a floating exchange rate regime gives countries monetary policy autonomy. Under a fixed rate system, a country's ability to expand or contract its money supply as it sees fit is limited by the need to maintain exchange rate parity. In terms of the later, under the Bretton Woods system, if a country developed a permanent deficit in its balance of trade that could not be corrected by domestic policy, the IMF would agree to a currency devaluation. Critics of this system argue that the adjustment mechanism works much more smoothly under a floating exchange rate regime. They argue that if a country is running a trade deficit, the imbalance between the supply and demand of that country's currency in the foreign exchange markets will lead to depreciation in its exchange rate. An exchange rate depreciation should correct the trade deficit by making the country's exports cheaper and its imports more expensive.

It is a matter of personal opinion in regard to which system is better for an international business. We do know, however, that a fixed exchange rate regime modeled along the lines of the Bretton Woods system will not work. Nevertheless, a different kind of fixed exchange rate system might be more enduring and might foster the kind of stability that would facilitate more rapid growth in international trade and investment.

Internet Exercises

TEXT EXERCISE 1

Overview

The Bretton Woods Agreement, signed in 1944, ushered in an era of fixed exchange rates. Today, as the U.S. dollar, the Japanese yen, and the European Union's euro approach parity, there is debate as to whether a fixed exchange rate system is better than a floating system.

Suggested Use in the Classroom

Students are asked to consider the benefits of a fixed versus floating system from the perspective of a company. Most students will point out the predictability that is associated with a fixed exchange rate system as being a clear benefit. Others however, may question the viability of fixed exchange rates in today's global economy.

TEXT EXERCISE 2

Overview

Brazil and Argentina, although neighbors, are hardly on friendly terms these days. After Brazil abruptly devalued its currency, Argentina has seen production move into the northern country, and is now facing a deep recession.

Suggested Use in the Classroom

Brazil's 35% depreciation of its currency raises numerous strategic issues for companies. Students are asked to consider the impact of such a devaluation from the perspective of several firms. Most will recognize that the devaluation significantly reduces the cost of doing business in Brazil, and that if the Latin American market is taken as a whole, companies will have a strong incentive to move their production to Brazil.

WEB EXERCISE 1

Overview

The majority of countries in the European Union have embraced the new currency, the euro. However, questions still remain as to the viability of monetary union, and particularly the loss of autonomy it implies. Countries belonging to the Mercosur Accord have also agreed to move toward a single currency, however they still have a long row to hoe before monetary union becomes a reality.

Suggested Use in the Classroom

Students are asked to compare and contrast the move toward monetary union in the European Union with the Mercosur Accord's effort. Many students may focus on a key difference between the two efforts—the fact that the European Union countries, and particularly Germany already had a powerful currency prior to monetary union, whereas none of the Mercosur countries can make a similar claim.

WEB EXERCISE 2

Overview

This exercise extends the second text-based exercise by furthering the discussion of the notion of parity between the dollar, the yen, and the euro.

Suggested Use in the Classroom

Students are asked to consider the implications of a single exchange rate among the three currencies—in terms of both prices and the global economy in general. Most students will probably agree that a single exchange rate would force greater parity in prices, and that such a situation could greatly simplify the strategies of companies doing business internationally.

CLOSING CASE: The Fall and Rise of Caterpillar Tractor

Summary

The closing case describes the effects of exchange rate changes and economic conditions worldwide on the Caterpillar Tractor company. Discussion of the case can be assisted by the following questions:

QUESTION 1: To what extent is the competitive position of Caterpillar against Komatsu dependent on the dollar/yen exchange rate? Between mid 1996 and early 1998, the dollar appreciated by over 40% against the yen. How do you think this would have affected the relative competitive position of Caterpillar?

ANSWER 1: Exchange rates clearly affect the relative competitiveness of Caterpillar and Komatsu. When the dollar appreciates relative to the yen, the cost of Caterpillar products on the world market seem expensive relative to Komatsu's. This is one factor directly affecting the profitability of the firms over which they have little control.

QUESTION 2: If you were the CEO of Caterpillar, what actions would you take now to make sure there is no repeat of the early 1980s experience?

ANSWER 2: One thing that could be done to reduce the effects of the dollar exchange rate on Caterpillar would be to disperse more production outside of the US to other locations - specifically those where the currencies are unlikely to move in concert with the dollar. Then production could be shifted to more competitive locations depending on relative exchange rates.

QUESTION 3: What potential impact can the actions of the IMF and World Bank have on Caterpillar's business? Is there anything Cat can do to influence the actions of the IMF and World Bank?

ANSWER 3: To the extent that the policies of the IMF and World Bank affect the ability of countries (and firms in those countries) to make investments in infrastructure, the demand for Cat's products are directly affected. While Cat is a large company, there is little it can do to influence the policies of the World Bank and the IMF.

QUESTION 4: As the CEO of Caterpillar, would you prefer a fixed exchange rate regime or a continuation of the current managed-float regime? Why?

ANSWER 4: Obviously a truly fixed exchange rate at very favorable levels for Cat would be the best. There are two practical problems with this, however. One is that it is unlikely that a fixed exchange rate would be one that was extremely favorable. It would most likely just be a fair rate. The second is that even fixed rates don't stay that way when governments pursue independent policies that lead to differing levels of inflation and interest rates. Thus most fixed rates have to change at some point in time, and when they do, the changes tend to be dramatic and disruptive. When these disruptions occur, it can be very difficult for businesses like Cat. Thus while the current managed float has its problems, there is no way to completely eliminate the challenges of dealing with changing currencies for international businesses.

Country Focus: Japan's Soaring Yen

Summary

What was widely referred to in Japan as "yen shock." in the mid 1990s Japanese firms saw prices and profit margins on exports squeezed relentlessly as the yen climbed against the dollar. This feature discusses the raise of the yen against the dollar, and also provides insightful background into the historic relationship between the Japanese yen and the U.S. dollar.

Suggested Discussion Questions

1. Describe the role that a country's inflation rate plays in the value of its currency.

2. What effect did the Japanese recession have on the yen/dollar relationship?

3. Does the large trade imbalance between the United States and Japan make it harder or easier for the two countries to maintain a relatively stable dollar/yen exchange rate? Explain your answer.

Management Focus: Mexican Peso Crisis and The Automobile Industry?

Summary

This feature explores the effect of Mexico's 1995 peso policy on the auto industry. Prior to Mexico's decision to allow the peso to float freely against the dollar, U.S. automakers were enjoying a strong export market in Mexico, and many were also establishing production operations in Mexico. After the decision, however, the peso fell some 40% and the demand for autos fell dramatically.

Suggested Discussion Questions

1. How can a company that exports to and/or operates within foreign markets protect itself from situations similar to the one that occurred in Mexico?

2. The feature notes that despite the negative short-term effect of the currency depreciation, companies may find a silver lining in the situation as exports from Mexico become more attractive. Discuss the strategic implications of the "silver lining" for firms operating both in Mexico and in the US.

3. Ford's homepage: {www.ford.com}; Nissan's homepage {www.Nissan.com}

Additional Readings and Sources of Information

Why a Weaker Yen May Be Just Fine with U.S. Policymakers: {http://www.businessweek.com/bwdaily/dnflash/july1999/nf90726f.htm}

Fixing the IMF: {http://www.buisnessweek.com/1999/99_40/b3649034.htm}

Did the IMF Drop the Ball in Ecuador?: {http://www.businessweek.com/2000/00_04/b3665160.htm}

The IMF: Doctor, Savior—or Wastrel?: {http://www.businessweek.com/1998/52/b3610100.htm}

Will the Yen's Surge Do Japan In?: {http://www.businessweek.com/1999/99_50/b3659099.htm}

CHAPTER 10
GLOBAL STRATEGY

CHAPTER SUMMARY

CRITICAL THINKING AND DISCUSSION QUESTIONS

INTERNET EXERCISES

CLOSING CASE: Sweden's IKEA

Learning Objectives

1. Be conversant with the concept of strategy.

2. Understand how firms can profit from expanding their activities globally.

3. Be familiar with the different strategies for competing globally.

4. Understand how cost pressures influence a firm's choice of global strategy.

5. Understand how country differences can influence a firm's choice of global strategy.

6. Understand how firms can use strategic alliances to support their global strategy.

Chapter Summary

This chapter focuses on the strategies that firms use to compete in foreign markets. At the outset, the chapter reviews the reasons that firms engage in international commerce, which range from earning a greater return from distinctive skills to realizing location economies by dispersing particular value creation activities to locations where they can be performed most efficiently. A major portion of the chapter is dedicated to the pressures that international firm's face for cost reductions and local responsiveness. These pressures place conflicting demands on firms. On the one hand, cost reductions are best achieved through product standardization and economies of scale. On the other hand, pressures for local responsiveness require firms to modify their products to suite local demands. The chapter also discusses the four basic strategies that firms utilize to compete in international markets. These strategies include an international strategy, a multidomestic strategy, a global strategy, and a transnational strategy. The advantages and disadvantages of each of these strategies are discussed. The chapter concludes with a discussion of international strategic alliances.

OPENING CASE: Global Strategy at General Motors

Summary

The opening case describes the history and current challenges facing GM in its global strategy. GM has always had to manage a trade-off between a centrally driven global strategy and a strategy that would allow each plant or national organization to design and build cars specifically tailored for its market. The best approach lies somewhere between pure centralization and pure decentralization, but finding the right mix is a challenge for GM and many other firms. The following questions can be helpful in directing the discussion.

QUESTION 1: Why did GM traditionally sell only cars with obsolete technology in the developing world? What is different with the new strategy for developing markets? Why?

ANSWER 1: Traditionally the developing world could only afford inexpensive cars, and demand was not particularly large given income levels. The most efficient way to provide cars for these markets was to use existing designs for extended periods of time, as it was not economically feasible to make model changes. Not only are income levels and the attractiveness of these markets increasing, but also new competition is forcing GM to bring new models to the market. It still must try and keep costs down, and to do this it is designing identical plants for different countries. These plants, however, will be building new models using the latest technology available.

QUESTION 2: Why did GM have a much more decentralized strategy in its European operations?

ANSWER 2: One part of the answer is that many of these operations were historically independent companies, so when acquiring interests in these firms, GM decided that they could retain their autonomy. Another aspect is that the needs of the markets differed. This decentralization is partly because of the desired product attributes differed (Germans emphasize performance, Swedes safety). Competition in the markets differed since most Western European countries had their own domestic auto firms. Thus a much more locally responsive strategy was essential.

QUESTION 3: Do you think GM now has the right mix between centralization (globalization) and decentralization (localization) in its strategy?

ANSWER 3: This question is clearly open to the airing of opinions. Proponents of the increasing globalization can argue that cost pressures and the need to bring state of the art products to developing markets make the current strategy appear appropriate. Opponents can argue that the world still has very different consumers with different needs (American buys seem to have an insatiable desire for cup holders that are deemed unnecessary clutter in Germany), and that while a global consumer may exist for jeans and Coke, this is not true with autos.

Chapter Outline With Lecture Notes and Teaching Tips

INTRODUCTION

A) The primary concern so far in this book has been with aspects of the larger environment in which international businesses compete. Now, our focus shifts from the environment to the firm itself and, in particular, to the actions managers can take to compete more effectively as an international business.

STRATEGY AND THE FIRM

A) Firms can increase their profits in two ways: by adding value to a product so that customers are willing to pay more for it and by lowering the costs. Thus there are two basic strategies for improving a firm's profitability- a differentiation strategy and a low cost strategy.

The Firm as a Value Chain

B) It is useful to think of the firm as a value chain composed of a series of distinct value creation activities, including production, marketing, materials management, R&D, human resources, information systems, and the firm infrastructure. We can categorize these value creation activities as primary activities and support activities.

Teaching Tip: An insightful article on the strategy, staffing, and structure of a multinational enterprise is available at {http://pacific.commerce.ubc.ca/keith/Lectures/sss.html}.

Primary Activities

C) The primary activities of a firm have to do with creating the product, marketing and delivering the product to buyers, and providing support and after-sale service to the buyers of the product.

Support Activities

D) Support activities provide the inputs that allow the primary activities of production and marketing to occur. The materials management function controls the transmission of physical materials through the value chain - from procurement through production and into distribution. The efficiency with which this is carried out can significantly reduce the cost of creating value.

The Role of Strategy

E) A firm's **strategy** can be defined as the actions that managers take to attain the goals of the firm.

F) Strategy is often concerned with identifying and taking actions that will lower the costs of value creation and/or will differentiate the firm's product offering through superior design, quality, functionality, service and the like.

PROFITING FROM GLOBAL EXPANSION

A) Firms that operate internationally are able to: (1) Earn a greater return from their distinctive skills, or core competencies. (2) Realize location economies by dispersing particular value creation activities to locations where they can be performed most efficiently. (3) Realize greater experience curve economies, which reduce the costs of value creation.

Transferring Core Competencies

B) The term **core competence** refers to skills within the firm that competitors cannot easily match or imitate. These skills may exist in any of the firm's value creation activities. For many firms, global expansion is a way of further exploiting the value creation potential of their skills and product offering by applying those skills and products in a larger market.

C) Trade barriers and transportation costs permitting, the firm will benefit by placing each value creation activity it performs at that location where economic, political, and cultural conditions, including relative factor costs, are more conducive to the performance of that activity.

Realizing Location Economies

D) **Location economies** are the economies that arise from performing a value creation activity in the optimal location for that activity, wherever in the world that might be.

E) Locating a value creation activity in the optimal location for that activity can have one or two effects. It can lower the costs of value creation and help the firm to achieve a low cost position, and/or it can enable a firm to differentiate its product offering from offerings of competitors.

Creating a Global Web

F) MNE's that take advantage of different locational economies around the world create a global web of activities. In the worldwide market does your local economy have some specific locational advantages?

Some Caveats

G) Introducing transportation costs and trade barriers complicates this picture. Due to favorable factor endowments, New Zealand may have a comparative advantage for automobile assembly operations, but high transportation costs would make it an uneconomical location for them. Another caveat concerns the importance of assessing political risks when making location decisions.

Realizing Experience Curve Economies

H) The experience curve refers to the systematic reductions in production costs that have been observed to occur over the life of a product. The experience curve relationship between production costs and output is illustrated in Figure 10.2.

Learning Effects

I) **Learning effects** refer to cost savings that come from learning by doing. In other words, labor productivity increases over time as individuals learn the most efficient ways to perform particular tasks and management typically learns how to manage the new operation more efficiently over time.

Economies of Scale

J) The term **economies of scale** refers to the reductions in unit cost achieved by producing a large volume of a product. Economies of scale have a number of sources, one of the most important of which seems to be the ability to spread fixed costs over a large volume. Another source of scale economies arises from the ability of large firms to employ increasingly specialized equipment or personnel.

Strategic Significance

K) The strategic significance of the experience curve is clear. Moving down the experience curve allows a firm to reduce its cost of creating value. Serving a global market from a single location is consistent with moving down the experience curve and establishing a low-cost position.

PRESSURES FOR COST REDUCTIONS AND LOCAL RESPONSIVENESS

Firms that compete in the global marketplace typically face two types of competitive pressures. They face pressures for cost reductions and pressures to be locally responsive. These pressures place conflicting demands on a firm.

Teaching Tip: An article entitled "Forging a Global Appliance" that appeared in CIO magazine (May 1, 1995) provides an excellent example of how Whirlpool is coping with the challenge of simultaneously managing cost reductions and local responsiveness. In a nutshell, what Whirlpool is trying to do is to have its engineers worldwide work together to crate several basic designs for its appliances, and then have each region customize the boilerplate designs to be compatible with local market demands. The full text of this article is available at {http://www.cio.com/archive/050195_group.html}.

Pressures for Cost Reductions

B) Responding to cost pressures requires that a firm try to lower the costs of value creation by mass-producing a standard product at the optimal locations worldwide. Pressures for cost reductions are greatest in industries producing commodity type products where price is the main competitive weapon. Pressures for cost reductions are also intense when major competitors are based in low cost locations, where there is persistent excess capacity, and where consumers are powerful and face low switching costs.

Pressures for Local Responsiveness

C) Pressures for local responsiveness arise from a number of sources including (i) differences in consumer tastes and preferences. (ii) differences in traditional practices and infrastructure, (iii) differences in distribution channels, and (iv) host government demands.

Differences in Consumer Tastes and Preferences

D) Strong pressures for local responsiveness emerge when consumer tastes and preferences differ significantly between countries.

Differences in Infrastructure and Traditional Practices

E) Pressures for local responsiveness emerge when there are differences in infrastructure and/or traditional practices between countries.

Differences in Distribution Channels

F) A firm's marketing strategies may have to be responsive to differences in distribution channels between countries.

Host Government Demands

G) Economic and political demands imposed by host country governments may necessitate a degree of local responsiveness.

Implications

H) Pressures for local responsiveness imply that it may not be possible for a firm to realize the full benefits from experience curve and location economies.

STRATEGIC CHOICE

A) Firms use four basic strategies to compete in the international environment: an international strategy, a multidomestic strategy, a global strategy, and a transnational strategy. The appropriateness of each strategy varies with the extent of pressures for cost reductions and local responsiveness. Figure 10.4 in the text illustrates when each of these strategies is most appropriate.

International Strategy

B) Firms pursuing an international strategy transfer the skills and products derived from core competencies to foreign markets, while undertaking some limited local customization. However, they may suffer from a lack of extensive local responsiveness and from an inability to exploit experience curve and location economies

Multidomestic Strategy

C) Firms pursuing a multidomestic strategy customize their product offering, marketing strategy, and business strategy to national conditions. However, they may suffer from an inability to transfer skills and products between countries, and from an inability to exploit experience curve and location economies.

Global Strategy

D) Firms pursuing a global strategy focus on reaping the cost reductions that come from experience curve and location economies. However, they may suffer from a lack of local responsiveness.

Transnational Strategy

E) In a transnational strategy firms must exploit experience curve cost economies and location economies, transfer distinctive competencies within the firm, and pay attention to pressures for localization. To do these there needs to be flows of knowledge from the parent to subsidiaries, flows from foreign subsidiary to home country, and from foreign subsidiary to foreign subsidiary - a process called **global learning.**

Summary

G) The advantages and disadvantages of each of the four strategies are summarized in Figure 10.6 in the textbook.

STRATEGIC ALLIANCES

A) The term **strategic alliances** refers to cooperative agreements between potential or actual competitors. In this textbook, we are concerned specifically with strategic alliances between firms from different countries.

The Advantages of Strategic Alliances:

B) Strategic alliances may facilitate entry into a foreign market. Alliances allow firms to share the fixed costs (and associated risks) of developing new products or processes. An alliance is a way to bring together complementary skills and assets that neither company could easily develop on its own. It can make sense to form an alliance that will help the firm establish technological standards for the industry that will benefit the firm.

The Disadvantages of Strategic Alliances

C) The can give competitors low-cost routes to new technology and markets. Unless a firm is careful, it can give away more than it receives.

Teaching Tip: An Internet site that provides information on joint ventures in an international context is available from the University of California at Davis at {http://ps.ucdavis.edu/classes/pol129/SWE/ventures.htm}.

MAKING ALLIANCES WORK

Partner Selection

A) The failure rate for international strategic alliances seems to be quite high. For example, one study of 49 international strategic alliances found that two-thirds run into serious managerial and financial troubles within two years of their formation and that although many of these problems are ultimately solved, 33% are ultimately rated as failures by the parties involved.

Alliance Structure

B) One of the keys to make strategic alliance work is to select the right kind of ally. A good ally or partner has three principal characteristics. First, a good partner helps the firm achieve its strategic goals- whether they are market access, sharing the costs and risks of new product development, or gaining access to critical core competencies. In other words, the partner must have capabilities that the firm lacks and that it values. Second, a good partner shares the firm's vision for the purpose of the alliance. Third, a good partner is unlikely to try to opportunistically exploit the alliance for its own ends: that it, to expropriate the firm's technological know-how while giving away little in return.

C) The alliance should be structures such that the firm's risks of giving too much away to the partner are reduced to an acceptable level. Figure 10.7 depicts the four safeguards against opportunism by alliance partners. First, alliances can be designed to make it difficult (if not impossible) to transfer technology not meant to be transferred. Second, contractual safeguards can be written into an alliance agreement to guard against the risk of opportunism by a partner. Third, both parties to an alliance can agree in advance to swap skills and technologies that the other covets, thereby ensuring a chance for equitable gain. Fourth, the risk of opportunism by an alliance partner can be reduced if the firm extracts a significant credible commitment from its partner in advance.

Managing the Alliance

D) Once a partner has been selected and an appropriate alliance structure has been agreed on, the task facing the firm is to maximize its benefits from the alliance.

Building Trust

E) Part of the trick of managing an alliance successfully seems to be to build interpersonal relationships between the firms' managers.

Learning From Partners

F) After a five-year study of 15 strategic alliances between major multinationals, Gary Hamel, Yves Doz, and C.K. Prahalad concluded that a major determinant of how much a company gains from an alliance is its ability to learn from its alliance partners.

Critical Thinking and Discussion Questions

1. "In a world of zero transportation costs, no trade barriers, and non-trivial differences between nations with regard to factor endowments, firms must expand internationally if they are to survive." Discuss.

Answer: Given differences in countries with respect to factor endowments, the theory of comparative advantage suggests that different activities should take place in the countries that can perform them most efficiently. If there are also no barriers or costs to trade, then it is likely that a lot of industries will be based out of the countries that provide the best set of factor endowments. For a firm that is located in a sub-optimal location, it will either have to expand internationally or switch to a different industry where the factor endowments are in its favor. For firms already located in the countries with the most favorable factor endowments for their industry, however, there may not be a need to expand internationally. Firstly, the firm may be content to simply focus on the domestic market. But if the firm does want to expand internationally, it may be able to do so via licensing or exporting, and need not necessarily undertake FDI. Thus not only in theory, but also in practice many firms are able to survive quite well without having to expand internationally.

2. Plot the position of the following firms on Figure 10.3 - Procter & Gamble, IBM, Coca-Cola, Dow Chemical, US Steel, and McDonald's. In each case justify your answer.

Answer: Procter & Gamble would be located in the middle right-hand portion of the graph. This is a position of high pressures for local responsiveness and moderate pressures for cost reductions. P&G sells personal and home care products, which do face pressures for local responsiveness. Although these products are not commodities, there are many competitors in P&G industries, which implies a moderate degree of cost pressures. IBM would be in the upper middle portion of the graph. This is a position of moderate pressure for local responsiveness and high pressure for cost reductions. There is a moderate amount of pressure for local responsiveness for IBM products, due to language differences and differing voltage requirements for electronic products across countries. IBM is in a very competitive industry, and cost pressures are high. Coca-Cola is a commodity type product, and it would be located in the upper left-hand portion of the graph. This is a position of low pressures for local responsiveness and high pressures for cost reductions. Dow Chemical and U.S. Steel would both be located in the upper left-hand portion of the graph. Both Dow and U.S. Steel sell products that are commodity-like by nature. As a result, cost pressures would be high and local responsiveness pressures would be low for these products. Finally, McDonalds would be located in the middle left-hand portion of the graph. Pressures for local responsiveness would be low, and cost reduction pressures would be moderate. McDonalds sells a semi commodity-like product, but not to the same degree as Dow Chemical of U.S. Steel.

3. Are the following global industries or multidomestic industries: bulk chemicals, pharmaceuticals, branded food products, moviemaking, television manufacture, personal computers, and airline travel?

Answer: Bulk chemicals are a global industry. Pharmaceuticals are a global industry. Branded food products are a multidomestic industry. Moviemaking is a multidomestic industry that is becoming more global. Many American films, for instance, are released overseas after they finish their run in U.S. theatres. These movies typically have to be modified, however, with foreign language subtitles. The commercial appeal for foreign films in America has yet to develop. Television manufacture is a global industry, as is personal computers. These products do have to be slightly modified to meet the language and voltage requirements of their local markets. Airline travel is a global industry.

4. Discuss how the need for control over foreign operations varies with the strategy and core competencies of a firm. What are the implications of this for choice of entry mode?

Answer: The need for control over foreign operations is lower when the cost pressures are lower - when firms are using a multidomestic or international strategy. There is also less need for control when the core competencies of a firm can be exploited without transferring to foreign operations. Thus a firm that is able to maintain its core competencies in its home country and does not require strong control over operations in a country may more likely export initially export than undertake foreign direct investment. This was clearly the case with Toyota in North America initially. Of course in the opposite situations high control and wholly owned subsidiary foreign direct investment are most appropriate

5. What do you see as the main organizational problems that are likely to be associated with the implementation of a transnational strategy?

Answer: Simultaneously trying to achieve cost efficiencies, global learning, and local responsiveness places difficult and contradictory demands on an organization. Managing these conflicting demands requires the setting of control and motivational policies for people and organizations that force balancing of these demands at multiple levels within firms. The organizational challenges involve managing these inherent conflicts to resolutions that serve the best interests of the firm overall.

6. What kinds of companies stand to gain the most from entering into strategic alliances with potential competitors? Why?

Answer: The companies that stand to gain the most from entering into strategic alliances with potential competitors are those that (1) need a partner to gain access to a foreign market, (2) need a partner to share the capital requirements necessary to launch a new product or service, and (3) have only a modest amount of proprietary technology that will be placed at risk by entering into a strategic alliance. These attributes benefit a firm without giving too much away, and may provide a firm a tremendous advantage in terms of gaining access to a foreign markets and/or investment capital.

Internet Exercises

TEXT EXERCISE 1

Overview

This exercise explores strategic issues involved in foreign expansion. In particular, the exercise examines how Yahoo has approached the Japanese market. As noted in the exercise, the company took a rather unorthodox approach to the market.

Suggested Use in the Classroom

Students are asked to examine Yahoo's American site and Japanese site and discuss, using the framework presented in the text, the strategy that Yahoo is following in Japan. Students will probably suggest that that the Internet is changing the way firms approach foreign markets because many of the costs associated with foreign expansion do not exist when that expansion takes place in cyberspace. However, they will probably also agree that companies must be aware of differences between markets and respond accordingly.

TEXT EXERCISE 2

Overview

The Sony Corporation is not usually associated with banking, however, as this exercise points out, the Japanese company feels that expanding into online financial services will prove to be a worthy means of diversification. In addition, Sony feels that its banking effort will allow it to capture synergies as it puts to use its experience in online music distribution.

Suggested Use in the Classroom

Students are asked to consider the effect of Sony's expansion effort on its internal operations. Many students may feel that Sony is too bureaucratic to succeed in the dot com world, however, others may suggest that because aspects of its new line of business are related to its traditional line, the company has to be able to move at a faster, though not necessarily Internet, speed anyway.

WEB EXERCISE 1

Overview

This exercise explores the global cosmetics industry. While many of the key players in global in nature, they frequently sell products only on a regional basis under local names. Other companies have pursued international markets either through joint ventures with local companies, or by selling the same product everywhere.

Suggested Use in the Classroom

Students are asked to analyze the strategies of cosmetics companies, and explain the differences between the strategies that are utilized. In addition, students are asked to comment on how the Internet could change the nature of the business. Most students will probably argue that the Internet will create more potential for global brands—suggesting that its reach will naturally create more homogeneity among consumer preferences. Other students however, will probably take a counter position noting that just because everyone has access to the same products does not necessarily mean everyone likes the same things.

WEB EXERCISE 2

Overview

This exercise extends the previous one by continuing to explore the global cosmetics industry. In particular, the exercise examines how Avon is changing its international strategy in the age of the Internet. Avon's ability to expand its online position must be carefully balanced with its need to maintain its traditional sales force.

Suggested Use in the Classroom

Avon has indicated that its primary target, at least for now, in its online venture will be the younger customer. Students are asked to comment on this strategy, and discuss the challenges Avon will face in cyberspace. This exercise provides a good forum for debate. Some students will feel that Avon is making the right decision in going after the younger consumer, noting that the Internet is more heavily used by the younger generation than older consumers. Others however, may believe that by targeting only younger consumers, Avon runs the risk of alienating its traditional, revenue generating market

CLOSING CASE: Sweden's IKEA

Summary

The closing case describes the expansion and philosophy of IKEA. IKEA's cost focused global strategy served it very well as it expanded across Europe, and provided a growing middle class with furniture at much cheaper prices than the traditional craft-based furniture industry. The strategy was not as successful in the North American market, however, and changes were required. Discussion of the case can be assisted by the following questions:

QUESTION 1: What strategy was IKEA pursuing as it expanded throughout Europe during the 1970s and early 1980s - a multidomestic strategy, a global strategy, or an international strategy?

ANSWER 1: IKEA was pursuing a global strategy focused on providing standardized low cost products worldwide with the assumption that consumer tastes were similar enough that local adaptation was not required.

QUESTION 2: Why do you think this strategy did not work as well in North America as it did in Europe?

ANSWER 2: In Europe IKEA's products represented a significant cost reduction from other products, and consumers were willing to give up some of their preferences for lower costs. Given the greater competition and economies of scale for other furniture manufacturers and retailers in North America, IKEA's cost advantage was not a significant factor for consumers. North American's general preference for bigger everything - from beds to furniture to houses to cars - also limited the appeal of IKEA's products.

QUESTION 3: As of 1998, what strategy is IKEA pursuing? Does this strategy make sense? Can you see any drawbacks to this strategy?

ANSWER 3: IKEA is clearly moving from a purely global strategy to a more transnational strategy. It is allowing stores in different countries to adapt products (and develop new products) in line with local demands. It is also trying to transfer innovations from one country to others, and facilitate global learning. The main drawback of this strategy is that it increases coordination costs and limits IKEA's ability to realize as significant experience curve effects.

Management Focus: Strategy at Clear Vision

Summary

This feature follows the case of Clear Vision through its efforts to profit by becoming an international firm. Clear Vision is a manufacturer and distributor of eyewear. Clear Vision began its move toward becoming a multinational in the 1970s, after a strong dollar made U.S. based manufacturing very expensive. To compete with low cost imports, Clear Vision took its own manufacturing operations overseas, first in Hong

Kong and then in Mainland China. The case describes Clear Vision's experiences in those endeavors, and also discusses Clear Vision's later moves to purchase minority interests in several international eyewear companies.

<u>Suggested Discussion Questions</u>

1. Did Clear Vision have to go global to survive? Explain your answer.

2. Explain why Clear Vision decided to invest in a foreign eyewear firms?

3. Discuss Clear Vision's foreign market strategy. Was the strategy appropriate? Why or why not?

Management Focus: McDonald's Everywhere

<u>Summary</u>

This feature examines Mc Donald's international strategy. McDonald's facing saturation in the US market, sees foreign expansion as a major component in its future growth strategy.

<u>Suggested Discussion Questions</u>

1.What are McDonald's core competencies? How does the company successfully transfer its strategic advantages to new markets?

2. McDonald's rate of foreign expansion is growing rapidly, and its foreign revenues make up an increasingly large share of the chain's overall revenue. Discuss how McDonald's experiences in one market help the company in other markets.

3. McDonald's Homepage: {http://www.mcdonalds.com/}

Management Focus: Procter & Gamble's International Strategy

<u>Summary</u>

This feature focuses on P&G efforts to introduce products into European and Asian markets. Together with Unilever, P&G is a dominant global force in laundry detergents, cleaning products, and personal care products. P&G expanded abroad after World War II by pursuing an international strategy – transferring brands and marketing policies developed in the United States to Western Europe, initially with considerable success. In the 1970s, however, this strategy started to exhibit some flaws. It became clear that the root cause of P&G problems was its propensity to transfer its U.S. marketing and product strategies to overseas markets essentially "intact (without taking into consideration the need for local responsiveness). The case goes on to illustrate P&G miscues in this area in several different instances.

<u>Suggested Discussion Questions</u>

1. Based on what you know about P&G (apart from this case), plot P&G's position on Figure 10.3 in the text. According to the information provided in the case, was P&G's strategy in Europe in the early part of the case consistent with where you just placed P&G on the graph? If not, do you believe that P&G's strategy in Europe was flawed? Explain your answer.

2. What do you think that P&G should do to improve its positions in Europe and Asia? Make your answer as substantive as possible.

3. Of the four basic international strategies described in the textbook (global, international, multidomestic, and transnational), which strategy is the most appropriate for the majority of P&G's products? Why?

4. Procter & Gamble Homepage: {http://www.pg.com/}

Management Focus: Anatomy of a Failed Alliance

Summary

This feature relates the story of a failed joint venture. In June 1984 General Motors and the Daewoo Group of South Korea signed an agreement that called for each to invest $100 million in a Korean-based 50/50 joint venture that would manufacture the Pontiac LeMans (a subcompact car). The venture started out with good intentions. GM felt that it could benefits from the joint venture by gaining access to South Korea's inexpensive labor, and Daewood felt that it could benefit from the joint venture by gaining access to GM's engineering skills. Unfortunately, as the first LeMans was coming off of the assembly line in 1987, the joint venture was turning sour. In the period between 1984 and 1987, South Korea had lurched toward democracy, and workers throughout the country were demanding better wages. Suddenly, it was cheaper to build LeMans vehicles in German than South Korea. From Daewoo's perspective, GM was treating its Korean partners badly. Daewoo Group Chairman Kim Whooshing complained publicly that GM executives were arrogant and treated him shabbily. The joint venture was dissolved in 1992.

Suggested Discussion Questions

1. Describe the attributes of "making an alliance work" that are discussed in the textbook. Did both GM and Daewoo Group show good faith in each of these areas? Explain your answer.

2. From the information provided in the feature, do you get the impression that GM and Daewoo trusted each other? Did the level of trust in the relationship change over time? What steps could have been taken by GM and Daewoo to enhance the level of trust in the relationship?

3. Make a list of the things that went wrong in this joint venture. Could the joint venture have been saved if the parties involved would have worked harder to preserve the relationship? If not, was the dissolution of the relationship the appropriate thing to do?

4. Homepages: General Motors Homepage: {http://www.gm.com/}; Daewoo Group Homepage: {http://www.dwc.co.kr/emain.htm}

Additional Readings and Sources of Information

Carmakers in Japan: Buy or Be Bought: {http://www.businessweek.com/2000/00_02/b36663130.htm}

Getting the Most out of a Partnership: {http://businessweek.com/smallbiz/news/date/9904/f990416g.htm}

Pharmacia-Monsanto: "A Rousing Wave of Skepticism"?:
{http://www.businessweek.com/bwdaily/dnflash/dec1999/nf91220j.htm}

BNP's Boss: The Man Who May Be King: {http://www.businessweek.com/1999/99_27/b3636149.htm}

Cuba: Yahoo!, Stay Home: {http://www.businessweek.com/1999/99_47/b3656172.htm}

CHAPTER 11
ENTERING FOREIGN MARKETS

CHAPTER SUMMARY

INTERNET EXCERCISES

CRITICAL THINKING AND DISCUSSION QUESTIONS

CLOSING CASE: Downey's Soup

Learning Objectives

1. Identify the different modes that firms use to enter a foreign market.

2. Understand the advantages and disadvantages of each entry mode.

3. Appreciate the relationship between strategy and a firm's choice of entry mode.

4. Appreciate some pitfalls of exporting.

5. Be familiar with the steps a firm can take to improve its export performance.

6. Have a good grasp of the mechanics of export and import financing.

Chapter Summary

This chapter focuses on the process of entering foreign markets. The six most common foreign entry strategies are discussed. These are: exporting, turnkey projects, licensing, franchising, establishing a joint venture with a host country firm, and setting up a wholly owned subsidiary in the host country. The advantages and disadvantages of each of these strategies are discussed. A nice table is provided on page 369 of the text that sums up this information. A large portion of the chapter is dedicated strictly to exporting. The promise and pitfalls of exporting are discussed, along with a discussion of the role of export management companies in the internationalization process. The chapter also provides a nice discussion of export financing. In this section, the author discusses the financial devices that have evolved to facilitate exporting including: the letter of credit, the draft (or bill of exchange), and the bill of lading. The chapter ends by providing an example of a typical international trade transaction. This example illustrates the complex nature of international trade transactions.

OPENING CASE: Merrill Lynch in Japan

Summary

The opening case describes the history Merrill Lynch in Japan. The first time Merrill Lynch entered the Japanese market in the 1980s it met with limited success. While it maintained a presence in Japan, Merrill Lynch did not seriously attempt to develop its position in Japan until 1997, when it was able to pick up some of the personnel and assets of the bankrupt Yamaichi Securities. This mode of entry has given Merrill Lynch a broad market presence and a head start on other Western firms considering entry into Japan. The following questions can be helpful in directing the discussion.

QUESTION 1: Why did Merrill Lynch's initial entry into Japan meet with such limited success?

ANSWER 1: Merrill Lynch was entering a market where there was significant customer loyalty, and where investors were cautious about entrusting their savings to a foreign firm. As a foreign firm, they also had difficulty in attracting top employees. The unique advantage Merrill Lynch had, knowledge of foreign investment products, was of little use given regulations restricting foreign investments.

QUESTION 2: What role did changing regulations play in Merrill Lynch's 1997 investment?

ANSWER 2: Changing regulations played an important role in Merrill Lynch's 1997 investment. Japan relaxed foreign exchange controls and removed many other restrictions in line with the WTO agreement on liberalization of financial services. The crash of the stock market led to additional liberalization of regulations on brokerage activities.

QUESTION 3: What remained the major impediments to Merrill Lynch in Japan? What had not changed since its initial entry? Did the new entry strategy address these impediments?

ANSWER 3: One of the factors that limited the initial success, and still was an impediment to business, was Merrill Lynch's lack of a distribution system in Japan. While it could now sell a wide range of its products, without a distribution system, entry would be difficult. By buying assets from Yamaichi, Merrill Lynch was able to quickly take over an established distribution system. Building such a distribution system from scratch would be both very difficult and expensive.

Chapter Outline With Lecture Notes and Teaching Tips

INTRODUCTION

A) This chapter is concerned with three closely related topics: the decision of which foreign markets to enter, when to enter them, and on what scale; the choice of entry mode; and the mechanics of exporting.

B) There are several different options open to a firm that wishes to enter a foreign market, including exporting, licensing or franchising to host country firms, setting up a joint venture with a host country firm, or setting up a wholly owned subsidiary in the host country to serve that market. Each of these options has its advantages and each has its disadvantages.

C) The magnitude of the advantages and disadvantages associated with each entry mode are determined by a number of different factors, including transport costs and trade barriers, political and economic risks, and firm strategy. The optimal choice of entry mode varies from situation to situation depending upon these various factors. Thus while it may make sense for some firms to serve a given market by exporting, other firms might serve the same market by setting up a wholly owned subsidiary in that market, or by utilizing some other entry mode.

BASIC ENTRY DECISIONS

Which Foreign Markets?

A) The choice between different foreign markets must be made on an assessment of their long run profit potential. This is a function of a large number of factors, many of which we have already considered in depth in earlier chapters. Once a set of attractive markets have been identified, it is important to consider the timing of entry. With regard to the **timing of entry**, we say that entry is early when an international business enters a foreign market before other foreign firms, and late when it enters after other international businesses have already established themselves in the market.

B) Other things being equal, the benefit, cost, risk, tradeoff is likely to be most favorable in the case of politically stable developed and developing nations that have free market systems, and where there is not a dramatic upsurge in either inflation rates, or private sector debt. It is likely to be least favorable in the case of politically unstable developing nations that operate with a mixed or command economy, or developing nations where speculative financial bubbles have led to excess borrowing.

Timing of Entry

C) Once a set of attractive markets has been identified, it is important to consider the timing of entry. With regard to the timing of entry, we say that entry is early when an international business enters a foreign market before other foreign firms, and late when it enters after other international businesses have already established themselves in the market.

D) There are several advantages frequently associated with entering a market early. These are commonly known as **first mover advantages**. One first mover advantage is the ability to pre-empt rivals and capture demand by establishing a strong brand name. A second advantage is the ability to build up sales volume in that country and ride down the experience curve ahead of rivals. To the extent that this is possible, it gives the early entrant a cost advantage over later entrants. This cost advantage may enable the early entrant to respond to later entry by cutting prices below the (higher) cost structure of later entrants, thereby driving them out of the market. A third advantage is the ability of early entrants to create switching costs that tie customers into their products or services. Such switching costs make it difficult for later entrants to win business.

E) It is important to realize that there can also be disadvantages associated with entering a foreign market before other international businesses (these are often referred to as **first mover disadvantages**)

F) **Pioneering costs** are costs that an early entrant has to bear that a later entrant can avoid. Pioneering Costs arise when a business system in a foreign country is so different from that in a firm's home market that the enterprise has to devote considerable time, effort and expense to learning the rules of the game. Pioneering costs include the costs of business failure if the firm, due to its ignorance of the foreign environment, makes some major mistakes. Pioneering costs also include the costs of promoting and establishing a product offering, including then cost of educating the customers.

Scale of Entry and Strategic Commitments

G) The final issue that an international business needs to consider when contemplating market entry is the scale of entry. Entering a market on a large scale involves the commitment of resources to that venture. The consequences of entering on a significant scale are associated with the value of the resulting strategic commitments. A **strategic commitment** is a decision that has a long term impact and is difficult to reverse. Deciding to enter a foreign market on a significant scale is a major strategic commitment.
Significant strategic commitments are neither unambiguously good nor bad. Rather, they tend to change the competitive playing field and unleash a number of changes, some of which may be desirable and some of which will not be.

H) Small-scale entry has the advantage of allowing a firm to learn about a foreign market while simultaneously limiting the firm's exposure to that market.

I) It is important to realize that there are no "right" decisions here, just decisions that are associated with different levels of risk and reward.

ENTRY MODES

A) These are basically six different ways to enter a foreign market. Each of these entry strategies is discussed below:

Exporting

B) Most manufacturing firms begin their global expansion as exporters and only later switch to another mode for servicing a foreign market.

Teaching Tip: Dun and Bradstreet provide two excellent publications on the Internet pertaining to the basics of exporting successfully. The publications are entitled How to Plan for Global Growth and Tips to Help You Export Successfully. The publications are available at {hppt://www.dbisna.com/global/hmenue.htm}.

Teaching Tip: Your students may wonder how firms U.S. firms find buyers in foreign countries. To find foreign customers, exporters often use "'trade leads" that are provided by organizations dedicated towards the activity of matching "buyers" and "sellers" in an international context. An example of a site that provides trade leads is the National Trade Data Bank at {http://www.stat-usa.gov/BEN/subject/trade.html}. This service is available on a subscription basis.

Advantages of Exporting

C) Exporting avoids the often substantial cost of establishing manufacturing operations in the host country. Exporting may help a firm achieve experience curve location economies.

Teaching Tip: A site entitled "A Guide to the Best Internet Resources for Small and Medium Sized Exporters" is available at {http://web.ukonline.co.uk/members/jim.hamill/contents.htm}.

Disadvantages of Exporting

D) Exporting from the firm's home base may not be appropriate if there are lower-cost locations for manufacturing the product abroad. High transport costs can make exporting uneconomical. Tariff barriers can make exporting uneconomical. Agents in a foreign country may not act in exporter's best interest.

Turnkey Projects

E) In a **turnkey project,** the contractor agrees to handle every detail of the project for a foreign client, including the training of operating personnel. At completion of the contract, the foreign client is handed the "key" to a plant that is ready for full operation - hence the term turnkey. This is actually a means of exporting process technology to another country.

Lecture Note: Students might enjoy learning more about companies that identify themselves as firms that engage in "turnkey projects." Examples of these companies include: AJS Design and Contracting, Inc.

{http://www.inter-access.com/ajs/index.html} and Construction Specialty Services Inc. {http://www.cssiweb.com/}.

Advantages of Turnkey Projects

F) The main advantage of turnkey projects is that they are a way of earning great economic returns from the know-how required to assemble and run a technologically complex process. Turnkey projects may also make sense in a country where the political and economic environment is such that a longer-term investment might expose the firm to unacceptable political and/or economic risk.

Disadvantages of Turnkey Projects

G) First, by definition, the firm that enters into a turnkey deal will have no long-term interest in the foreign country. Second, the firm that enters into a turnkey project may create a competitor. If the firm's process technology is a source of competitive advantage, then selling this technology through a turnkey project is also selling competitive advantage to potential and/or actual competitors.

Licensing

H) A **licensing agreement** is an arrangement whereby a licensor grants the rights to intangible property to another entity (the licensee) for a specified time period, and in return, the licensor receives a royalty fee from the licensee. Intangible property includes patents, inventions, formulas, processes, designs, copyrights, and trademarks.

Advantages of Licensing Agreements

I) In the typical international licensing deal, the licensee puts up most of the capital necessary to get the overseas operations going. Thus, a primary advantage of licensing is that the firm does not have to bear the development costs and risks associated with opening a foreign market. Licensing is often used when a firm wishes to participate in a foreign market, but is prohibited from doing so by barriers to investment. Licensing is frequently used when a firm possesses some intangible property that might have business applications, but is does not want to develop those applications itself.

Disadvantages of Licensing Agreements

J) First, licensing does not give a firm the tight control over manufacturing, marketing, and strategy that is required for realizing experience curve and location economies. Second, competing in a global market may require a firm to coordinate strategic moves across countries by using profits earned in one country to support competitive attacks in another. Licensing severely limits a firm's ability to do this. A third problem involves the potential loss of proprietary (or intangible) technology or property. One way of reducing the risk of losing proprietary trade secrets is through the use of **cross-licensing agreements**. Under a cross-licensing agreement, a firm might license some valuable intangible property to a foreign partner, but in addition to a royalty payment, the firm might also request that the foreign partner license some of its valuable know-how to the firm.

Franchising

K) **Franchising** is basically a specialized form of licensing in which the franchisor not only sells intangible property to the franchisee, but also insists that the franchisee agree to abide by strict rules as to how it does business.

Advantages of Franchising

L) The advantages of franchising as an entry mode are very similar to those of licensing. Specifically the firm is relieved of many costs and risks of opening up a foreign market.

Disadvantages of Franchising

M) Franchising may inhibit the firm's ability to take profits out of one country to support competitive attacks in another. A more significant disadvantage of franchising is quality control. The geographic distance of the firm from its foreign franchisees can make poor quality difficult for the franchisor to detect.

Joint Ventures

N) A **joint venture** entails establishment of a firm that is jointly owned by two or more otherwise independent firms. Fuji-Xerox, for example, was set up as a joint venture between Xerox and Fuji Photo.

Teaching Tip: There are also a number of publications available that can help managers make good joint venture decisions. A brief description of a book entitled "International Joint Ventures: A Practical Guide" can be accessed at {http://www.westgroup.com/practice/intllaw/intljoin.htm}.

Advantages of Joint Ventures

O) A firm can benefit from a local partner's knowledge of the host country's competitive conditions, culture, language, political systems, and business systems. Second, when the development costs and/or risks of opening a foreign market are high, a firm might gain by sharing these costs and/or risks with a local partner. In many countries, political considerations make joint ventures the only feasible entry mode.

Teaching Tip: There are a number of organizations that try to help companies find joint venture partners. An example is a British organization called "TradeMatch." Information about TradeMatch is available at their web site at {http://www.expo.co.uk/}.

Disadvantages of Joint Ventures

P) First, just as with licensing, a firm that enters into a joint venture risks giving control of its technology to its partner. Second, a joint venture does not give a firm the tight control over subsidiaries that it might need to realize experience curve or location economies. Third, shared ownership arrangements can lead to conflicts and battles for control between the investing firms if their goals and objectives change over time, or if they take different views as to what the venture's strategy should be.

Wholly Owned Subsidiaries

Q) In a **wholly owned subsidiary**, the firm owns 100 percent of the stock. Establishing a wholly owned subsidiary in a foreign market can be done two ways. The firm can either set up a new operation in that country or it can acquire an established firm and use that firm to promote its products in the country's market.

Advantages of a Wholly Owned Subsidiary

R) First, when a firm's competitive advantage is based on technological competence, a wholly owned subsidiary will often be the preferred entry mode, since it reduces the risk of losing control over that competence. Second, a wholly owned subsidiary gives a firm the tight control over operations in different countries that is necessary for engaging in global strategic coordination (i.e., using profits from one country to support competitive attacks in another). Third, a wholly owned subsidiary maybe required if a firm is trying to realize location and experience curve economies.

Disadvantages of a Wholly Owned Subsidiary

S) Establishing a wholly owned subsidiary is generally the most costly method of serving a foreign market. Firms doing this must bear full costs and risks of setting up overseas operations.

SELECTING AN ENTRY MODE

A) Although there are trade-offs involved, it is possible to generalize about the optimal choice of entry mode.

Core Competencies and Entry Mode

B) The optimal entry mode for these firms depends to some degree on the nature of their core competencies. In Particular, a distinction can be drawn between firms whose core competency is in technological know-how and whose core competency is in management know-how.

Technological Know-How

C) If a firm's competitive advantage (its core competence) is based upon control over proprietary technological know-how, licensing and joint venture arrangements should be avoided if possible in order to minimize the risk of losing control over that technology, unless the arrangement can be structured in a way where these risks can be reduced significantly.

D) When a firm perceives its technological advantage as being only transitory, or the firm may be able to establish its technology as the dominant design in the industry, then licensing may be appropriate even if it does involve the loss of know-how. By licensing its technology to competitors, a firm may also deter them from developing their own, possibly superior, technology

Management Know-How

E) The competitive advantage of many service firms is based upon management know-how. For such firms, the risk of loosing control over their management skills to franchisees or joint venture partners is not that great, and the benefits from getting greater use of their brand names can be significant.

Pressures for Cost Reductions and Entry Mode

F) The greater the pressures for cost reductions, the more likely it is that a firm will want to pursue so me combination of exporting and wholly owned subsidiaries. This will allow it to achieve location and scale economies as well as retain some degree of control over its worldwide product manufacturing and distribution

THE PROMISE AND PITFALLS OF EXPORTING

A) The potential benefits from exporting can be great. Regardless what country a firm is based in, the rest of the world is a much larger market than the domestic market. While larger firms may be proactive in seeking out new export opportunities, many smaller firms are reactive and only pursue international opportunities when the customer calls or knocks on the door.

B) Many neophyte exporters have run into significant problems when first trying to do business abroad, souring them on following up on subsequent opportunities.

C) Common pitfalls include poor market analysis, poor understanding of competitive conditions, lack of customization for local markets, poor distribution arrangements, bad promotional campaigns, and a general underestimation of the differences and expertise required for foreign market penetration.

D) If basic business issues weren't enough, the tremendous paperwork and formalities that must be dealt with can be overwhelming to small firms.

IMPROVING EXPORT PERFORMANCE

A) There are a number of ways in which inexperienced exporters can gain information about foreign market opportunities and avoid some of the common pitfalls that tend to discourage and frustrate neophyte exporters.

Government Information Sources

B) Most national governments maintain departments that can help firms establish export opportunities. In the U.S., the most comprehensive source of information is probably the U.S. Department of Commerce.

Utilizing Export Management Companies (EMC)

C) **Export management companies** are export specialists that act as the export marketing department or international department for client firms.

D) One way for first time exporters to identify the opportunities associated with exporting, and to avoid many of the associated pitfalls is to hire an **Export Management Company** (EMC).

E) EMCs normally accept two types of export assignments. EMCs start-up exporting operations for a firm with the understanding that the EMC will have continuing responsibility for selling the firm's products.

F) In theory, the advantage of EMCs is that they are experienced specialists who can help the neophyte exporter identify opportunities and avoid common pitfalls. However, studies have revealed a large variation in the quality of EMCs. Therefore, an exporter should carefully review a number of EMCs, and check references from an EMC's past client, before deciding on a particular EMC.

Exporting Strategy

G) In addition to utilizing EMCs, a firm can reduce the risks associated with exporting if it is careful about its choice of exporting strategy. First, particularly for the neophyte exporter, it does to help to hire an EMC, or at least an experienced export consultant, to help with the identification of opportunities and navigate through the tangled web of paperwork and regulations so often involved in exporting. Second, it often makes sense to initially focus on one, or a handful, of markets. Third, it may make sense to enter a foreign market on a fairly small scale in order to reduce the costs of any subsequent failure. Fourth, the exporter needs to recognize the time and managerial commitment involved in building export sales, and should hire additional personnel to oversee this activity least the existing management of the firm be stretched too thin. Fifth, in many countries it is important to devote a lot of attention to building strong and enduring relationships with local distributors and / or customers. Sixth, it is important to hire local personnel to help the firm establish itself in a foreign market. Finally, it is important for the exporter to keep the option of local production in mind.

EXPORT AND IMPORT FINANCING

A) Mechanisms for financing exports and imports have evolved over the centuries in response to a problem that can be particularly acute in international trade: the lack of trust that exists when one must put faith in a stranger.

Lack of Trust

B) Firms engaged in international trade face a problem - they have to trust someone who may be very difficult to track down if they default on an obligation.

C) Due to the lack of trust, each party to an international transaction has a different set of preference regarding the configuration of the transaction. Figures 15.1 and 15.2 show the preferences for two firms - a US exporter and a French importer.

D) The problems arising from a lack of trust between exporters and importers can be solved by using a third party who is trusted by both - normally a reputable bank. Figure 15.3 illustrates this

Teaching Tip: A menu of resources available on the Internet that deal with financing exports and other international finance issues is available at {http://dylee.keel.econ.ship.edu/intntl/intfin/fin-hom.htm}.

Letter of Credit

E) A **letter of credit**, abbreviated as L/C, stands at the center of international commercial transactions. Issued by a bank at the request of an importer, the letter of credit states the bank will pay a specified sum of money to a beneficiary, normally the exporter, on presentation of particular, specified documents.

Draft

F) A **draft**, sometimes referred to as a bill of exchange, is the instrument normally used in international commerce for payment. A draft is simply an order written by an exporter instructing an importer, or an importer's agent, to pay a specified amount of money at a specified time. A **sight draft** is payable on presentation to the drawee while a **time draft** allows for a delay in payment - normally 30, 60, 90, or 120 days.

Bill of Lading

G) The **bill of lading** is issued to the exporter by the common carrier transporting the merchandise. It serves three purposes: it is a receipt, a contract, and a document of title.

A Typical International Transaction

H) The entire process for conducting an export transaction is summarized in Figure 11.4.

Critical Thinking and Discussion Questions

1. Review Merrill Lynch's 1997 reentry into the Japanese private client market (see the opening case for details). Pay close attention to the timing and scale of entry and the nature of the strategic commitments Merrill Lynch is making in Japan. What are the potential benefits associated with this strategy? What are the costs and risks? Do you think the trade-offs between benefits and risks and costs makes sense? Why?

Answer: It would appear that Merrill Lynch is positioning itself well to sell financial services products to a nation full of savers (big market). The timing of the reentry is driven by macroeconomic changes, regulatory changes, and a specific opportunity to access a distribution channel. It would seem that the strategy is positioning Merrill Lynch to be able to capture a share in a very attractive market, and give Merrill Lynch some important first mover advantages over other foreign entrants. Nevertheless it is not clear that Merrill Lynch (or any foreigner) will be able to succeed in this market, and it could find that it will be unable to attract sufficient customers to justify the investment. Whether students believe the cost benefit tradeoff makes sense is clearly a matter of opinion and proclivity for taking risks.

2. "Licensing propriety technology to foreign competitors is the best way to give up a firm's competitive advantage." Discuss.

Answer: The statement is basically correct - licensing proprietary technology to foreign competitors does significantly risk loss of the technology. Therefore licensing should generally be avoided in these situations. Yet licensing still may be a good choice in some instances. When a licensing arrangement can be structured in such a way as to reduce the risks of a firm's technological know-how being expropriated by licensees, then licensing may be appropriate. A further example is when a firm perceives its technological advantage as being only transitory, and it considers rapid imitation of its core technology by competitors to be likely. In such a case, the firm might want to license its technology as rapidly as possible to foreign firms in order to gain global acceptance for its technology before imitation occurs. Such a strategy has some advantages. By licensing its technology to competitors, the firm may deter them from developing their own, possibly superior, technology. And by licensing its technology the firm may be able to establish its technology as the dominant design in the industry. In turn, this may ensure a steady stream of royalty payments. Such situations apart, however, the attractions of licensing are probably outweighed by the risks of losing control over technology, and licensing should be avoided

3. What kind of companies stand to gain the most from entering into strategic alliances with potential competitors? Why?

Answer: Firms that stand to learn much more from their competitors (or learn more important information) than they expect their competitors to learn from them stand to gain a great deal from a strategic alliance. If a firm is able to team up with a competitor that is in a good position to make significant advances in the near future (either by its own efforts or in conjunction with its partner), then an alliance can also provide significant benefits. More generally, if a strategic alliance greatly eases a firm's entry into a new market, allows it to undertake projects that would have been too risky or costly otherwise, brings together complementary skills to bear on a problem that neither firm would have been able to address individually, or provides an opportunity to set a technological standard, then a firm stands to gain a great deal from an alliance.

4. You are the assistant to the CEO of a small textile firm that manufactures high-quality, premium-priced, stylish clothing. The CEO has decided to see what the opportunities are for exporting and has asked you for advice as to the steps the company should take. What advice would you give the CEO?

Answer: This question is designed to stimulate classroom discussion and/or to encourage your students to "think" about the export process in completing a written answer for this question.
There are a number of approaches that can be pursued in answering this question. The first step might be to tap into some of the government information sources that are available, free of charge, to see if international markets are available for the company's product. There are also a number of resources on the Internet, mentioned throughout the text that can assist companies in learning about the foreign market potential of their products. Another approach would be to contact an export management company for assistance. While this approach may involve some cost, it may be the fastest way to get "up and running" in regard to initiating an export program.

5. A small Canadian firm that has developed a set of valuable new medical products using its own unique biotechnology know-how is trying to decide how best to serve the European Community market. Its choices are as follows. (i) Manufacture the product at home and let foreign sales agents handle marketing. (ii) Manufacture the products at home but set up a wholly owned subsidiary in Europe to handle marketing. (iii) Enter into a strategic alliance with a large European pharmaceutical firm. The product would be manufactured in Europe by a 50/50 joint venture, and then marketed by the European firm. The cost of investment in manufacturing facilities is a major one for the Canadian firm - but it is not outside of the firm's reach. If these were the firm's only options, what option would you advise it to choose? Why?

Answer: If there were no significant barriers to exporting, then option (iii) would seem unnecessarily risky and expensive. After all, the transportation costs required to ship drugs are small relative to the value of the product. Both options (i) and (ii) would expose the firm to less risk of technological loss, and would allow the firm to maintain much tighter control over the quality and costs of the drug. The only other reason to consider option (iii) would be if an existing pharmaceutical firm could also give it much better access to the market and potentially access to its products and technology, and that this same firm would insist on the 50/50 manufacturing joint venture rather than agreeing to be a foreign sales agent. The choice between (i) and (ii) boils down to a question of which way will be the most effective in attacking the market. If a foreign sales agent can be found that is already quite familiar with the market and who will agree to aggressively market the product, the agent may be able to increase market share more quickly than a wholly owned marketing subsidiary that will take some time to get going. On the other hand, in the long run the firm will learn a great deal more about the market and will likely earn greater profits if sets up its own sales operations. And if it is unable to find a sales agent who will aggressively sell the product, than this may be best alternative.

Internet Exercises

TEXT EXERCISE 1

Overview

Managed Care health programs are becoming very common in numerous markets. While the programs have gotten a bad rap in the U.S., other countries are welcoming the. Most countries however, are using alternate terms to describe the programs in an effort to avoid negative press. Today, many of America's healthcare giants are linking up with foreign firms to offer managed care programs in new markets.

Suggested Use in the Classroom

Students are asked to comment on the challenges, faced by service providers as they expand into foreign markets as compared to consumer products companies. Many students will probably suggest that alliances with local companies can help service providers avoid many of the cultural and legal blunders that are commonly associated with international expansion. Students may also recognize the highly personal nature of healthcare and the need to be sensitive to not only the healthcare recipient, but also the healthcare provider.

TEXT EXERCISE 2

Overview

General Motors is actively trying to increase its market position in Asia. To that end, the company has recently formed a number of alliances with local firms, and is considering additional ventures. However, experts stress that the company will still need to develop products targeted toward specific markets, and expand its global distribution network.

Suggested Use in the Classroom

Students are asked to consider GM's Asian strategy. In particular, students should compare and contrast the benefits of using joint ventures versus wholly owned subsidiaries. Many students will probably argue that GM is approaching the Asian market well—that its alliances with local companies will allow it to make quick inroads to the market. Others however, may take the stand that GM is spreading itself to thinly—and that it will end up losing control of this critical market. Students taking this position may suggest that the company cannot possibly treat each alliance as a priority, and what's more, GM may end up cannibalizing sales in some markets.

WEB EXERCISE 1

Overview

This exercise explores Densitron International's joint ventures. The British-based producer of personal computers has established a web-based joint ventures linking a Taiwanese manufacturing firm and its own design team. The company hopes the alliance will help it avoid many of the slow-downs associated with the more traditional process of getting new products to market.

Suggested Use in the Classroom

Students are asked to consider the disadvantages of web-based joint ventures as compared to more traditional relationships. Many students may suggest that because electronic alliances do not allow for the face-to-face contact that form the basis of more traditional alliances, the trust that is so critical to the success of alliances may not exist. However, they will probably also recognize that alliances such as the one described in this exercise offer great competitive potential to firms, and that such alliances may allow firms to pursue strategies that may have otherwise been impossible.

WEB EXERCISE 2

Overview

Thanks to the Internet, today's small companies may have the ability to act like their larger counterparts. This exercise examines the activities of one such company, the Alan Group, a small producer of plastic connectors. The company has made technology a major component in its overall strategy.

Suggested Use in the Classroom

Students are asked to compare the Alan Group's strategy to the more traditional process of international expansion that is described in the text. Many students will suggest that the Alan Group will eventually have to develop some sort of physical presence in key markets—some students may suggest that the company will turn to alliances as a means of continued growth. Students may argue that the company cannot continue to operate like a small company and still achieve the goals of a larger firm.

CLOSING CASE: Downey's soup

Summary

The closing case describes difficulties encountered by Downey's soup when it tried to export soup to Japan. Discussion of the case can be assisted by the following questions:

QUESTION 1: Did Downey Foods' export opportunity occur as a result of proactive action by Downey or was its strategy reactive?

ANSWER 1: Downey's opportunity to export to Japan was entirely reactive - they did not search for the export opportunity. When asked to export to however, they were diligent in trying to react to this opportunity.

QUESTION 2: Why did Downey experience frustrations when trying to export to Japan? What actions might Downey take to improve its prospects of succeeding in the Japanese market?

ANSWER 2: Downey's frustrations mainly came from its lack of understanding of how the process worked, and what it would take to appease Japanese trade officials. Working with a food company experienced in importing food products into Japan would have helped Downey initially, and would have decreased the likelihood of the continued difficulties.

QUESTION 3: You have been hired by Downey Foods to develop an exporting strategy for the firm. What steps do you think Downey should take to increase the volume of its exports?

ANSWER 3: Not being an expert in either the food industry nor in exporting, an appropriate strategy would include utilizing an EMC or export consultants, focusing on only one or a few markets at first and getting them working effectively, starting out on a small scale, and having realistic expectations about the time and commitment required. As the exporting develops, Downey should foster good relations with local distributors and hire local personnel.

Management Focus: Amway goes Astray in China

Summary

This feature explores Amway's experiences in China. Amway, a US direct Sales company selling household and personal products entered the Chinese market in 1995. By early 1998, the company had a presence in 37 cities in Mainland China and had surpassed Avon and Mary Kay as the biggest direct marketer in the country. It's success story came to a grinding halt in April 01 1998 when the Chinese government placed a ban on direct selling. Amway called on the help of US Trade Representative Charlene Barshefsky who negotiated a partial reversal of the ban, however Amway's ability to practice its traditional business model will be severely curtailed.

Suggested Discussion Questions

1. Initially Amway's success in China appeared to be virtually guaranteed. However the company suddenly found its first mover advantages turned to first mover disadvantages when the government introduced new legislation. Discuss Amway's experience in China and how it might affect future international efforts.

2. Amway managed to get a partial reversal on the ban on direct selling by asking for US government assistance. Would a smaller company have been able to achieve similar results? How might your response affect the Foreign Market entry decisions of a smaller company?

3. Amway's homepage: {http://www.amway.com}

Management Focus: Fuji-Xerox

Summary

This feature focuses on the evolution of the joint venture between Xerox (a U.S. manufacturer of photocopiers) and Fuji (a Japanese manufacturer of film products). Initially, Xerox joint ventured with Fuji as a way of gaining access to the Japanese photocopier market. The feature portrays the evolution of the joint venture from the time it was established in 1962 until today. Over the course of time, Fuji's influence over Xerox increased substantially. Fuji recognized the market potential for a small, inexpensive copier in Japan and, over Xerox's objection, designed and introduced a small copier to the Japanese market. The product was a hit. Fuji also championed the use of total quality management and other methods to reduce defect rates and improve quality. As a result of Fuji's successes in these areas, Xerox emulated Fuji and greatly improved its own operations. The feature goes on to discuss the evolution of the copier market in the United States, and the tremendous benefit of the Xerox-Fuji partnership for the Xerox Corporation.

Suggested Discussion Questions

1. Discuss the advantages and disadvantages of a joint venture as a foreign market entry strategy. Which of these advantages and disadvantages manifested themselves in the Fuji-Xerox joint venture?

2. Why did Fuji do a better job at recognizing the market potential for a small, inexpensive copier in the Japanese market than Xerox? What does this tell us about the advantages of having foreign nationals working for a company regardless of its entry strategy?

3. In your opinion, what has made the Fuji-Xerox joint venture one of the most enduring and reportedly successful joint ventures in history between two companies from different countries?

4. Fuji-Xerox Homepage: {http://fujixerox.com/}

Management Focus: Red Spot Paint Varnish

Summary

This feature focuses on Red Spot paint Varnish, a company that produces paints for plastic components used in automobiles. The company relies on foreign markets for some 15-25% of its annual revenue. Generating its foreign sales has not been an easy task according to one employee. The company has found it difficult to hire managers with appropriate international experience and has also struggled with pressures to achieve quick results.

1. How has the Internet made it easier for companies to not only get extra assistance but also find the experienced talent necessary to build an international staff?

2. In an era of "time is money," how can the trusting relationships that are so often critical to the success of a foreign venture be achieved?

3. Red Spot Homepage: {http://www.redspot.com/}

Additional Readings and Sources of Information

The Internet Guide to Small-Business Exporting:
{http://www.businessweek.com/smallbiz/news/columns/97-23/e3530046.htm}

Morgan Stanley's Global Gamble: {http://www.businessweek.com/1996/07/b34621.htm}

How Merrill Lynch is Winning the East: {http://www.businessweek.com/1997/35/b355422138.htm}

CHAPTER 12
GLOBAL MARKETING AND PRODUCT DEVELOPMENT

NEW PRODUCT DEVELOPMENT

The Location of R&D
Integrating R&D, Marketing, and Production
Cross-Functional Teams
Implications for International Business

CHAPTER SUMMARY

INTERNET EXERCISES

CRITICAL THINKING AND DISCUSSION QUESTIONS

CLOSING CASE: Nike - The Ugly American?

Learning Objectives

1. Understand why and how it may make sense to vary the attributes of a product across countries.

2. Appreciate why and how a firm's distribution system might vary across countries.

3. Understand why and how advertising and promotional strategies might vary across countries.

4. Understand why and how a firm's pricing strategy might vary across countries.

5. Understand how the globalization of the world economy is affecting new-product development within international business.

Chapter Summary

This chapter focuses on the marketing and R&D activities of global firms. The chapter begins with a review of the four elements that constitute a firm's marketing mix: product attributes, distribution strategy, communication strategy, and pricing strategy. A firm's marketing mix is the set of choice that if offers its customers. Many firms vary their marketing mix from country to country depending on differences cultures, levels of economic development, product and technical standards, the availability of distribution channels, and so forth. The chapter discusses the strategic implications of each element of the marketing mix for an international firm. The link between marketing and R&D is also discussed. The author stresses the point that selling a product on a global scale may require that a firm vary its products from country to country to satisfy local preferences. This may require a firm to establish R&D centers in different parts of the world, and closely link R&D and marketing in each region to ensure that the company is producing products that its overseas customers will buy.

OPENING CASE: Proctor and Gamble in Japan

Summary

The opening case describes the approach Procter and Gamble (P&G) has taken in Japan. Initially, P&G would typically experience some success in a product category, but then find that domestic competitors would beat it out. P&G realized that it needed to customize its marketing approach and products for the needs of Japanese consumers and the country-specific competition it faced. The following questions can be helpful in directing the discussion.

QUESTION 1: What was P&G's early approach to the Japanese market? Why?

ANSWER 1: P&G original approach was to take basic products developed in the US, and then essentially introducing them unchanged in Japan. Some localization of advertising was done, but the general view was that its products fulfilled universal needs. The basic utility of a diaper is not particularly culturally determined, and the need to clean clothes and dishes is fairly similar across developed countries.

QUESTION 2: Why wasn't this approach successful?

ANSWER 2: One reason is that needs are not entirely universal. Differences exist in washing temperature, types of foods (cleaning needs), and preferred attributes (e.g., trim fit). The existence of local competitors also meant that positioning needed to be localized to respond to local conditions.

QUESTION 3: How is P&G's current approach different? What are the benefits of this approach?

ANSWER 3: P&G is much more locally responsive in its product development and marketing approach. It is willing to develop new products specifically for individual markets. This has led not only to a higher market share in individual markets, but P&G is also learning that products developed for one market may prove valuable in other markets.

Chapter Outline With Lecture Notes and Teaching Tips

INTRODUCTION

A) In this chapter the focus is on how an international business can perform marketing and R&D activities so they will reduce the costs of value creation and add value by better serving customer needs.

B) The tension that exists in most international businesses between, on the one hand, the need to reduce costs, and on the other hand, the need to be responsive to local conditions is particularly predominant in this chapter as we look at the development and marketing of products

Teaching Tip: A broad array of international marketing resources is available on the Internet. A very comprehensive menu of these resources, courtesy of Shippensburg University, is available at {http://dylee.keel.econ.ship.edu/intntl/intbus/intmarke.htm}.

THE GLOBALIZATION OF MARKETS

A) Theodore Levitt waxed lyrically about the globalization of world markets. Levitt's arguments are worth quoting at some length since they have become something of a lightening rod for the debate about the extent of globalization.

B) The current consensus among academics is that although the world is moving towards global markets, the continuing persistence of cultural and economic differences among nations acts as a major brake on any trend toward global consumer tastes and preferences. In addition, trade barriers and differences in product and technical standards also constrain a firm's ability to sell a standardized product to a global market.

Teaching Tip: There are a number of consulting companies that help firms "go global." You students might be interested in knowing a little bit about these companies. One company is the Chicago based Quadral Group. The Quadral Group's web site can be accessed at {http://quadralgroup.com/}.

MARKET SEGMENTATION

A) **Market segmentation** refers to identifying distinct groups of consumers whose purchasing behavior differs from others in important ways. Firms must adjust their marketing mix from segment to segment.

B) In international business, segmentation needs to consider the existence of segments that transcend national borders and understand differences across countries in the structure of segments.

C) For a segment to transcend national borders, consumers in that segment must have some compelling similarities that lead to similarities in purchasing behavior.

D) Where such similarities do not exist, there must be some customization if the firm is to maximize performance in the market. This customization may be in the product, the packaging, or simply the way in which the product is marketed.

E) Global market segments are much likely to exist in industrial products (e.g., memory chips, chemical products, and corporate bonds) than in consumer products.

PRODUCT ATTRIBUTES

A) Products sell well when their attributes match consumer needs. If consumer needs were the same the world over, a firm could simply sell the same product worldwide. But consumer needs vary from country to country depending on culture and the level of economic development.

<u>Cultural Differences</u>

B) Countries differ along a whole range of (cultural) dimensions, including tradition, social structure, language, religion, and education. At the same time, there is some evidence of the trends Levitt talked about. Tastes and preferences are becoming more cosmopolitan

<u>Economic Differences</u>

C) Just as important as differences in culture are differences in the level of economic development. Firms based in highly developed countries tend to build a lot of extra performance attributes into their products. Consumers in less developed nations do not usually demand these extra attributes, where the preference is for more basic products.

<u>Product and Technical Standards</u>

D) Notwithstanding the forces that are creating some convergence of consumer tastes and preferences, Levitt's vision of global markets may still be a long way off due to national differences in product and technological standards.

DISTRIBUTION STRATEGY

A) A critical element of a firm's marketing mix is its distribution strategy, the means it chooses for delivering the product to the consumer.

<u>A typical distribution system</u>

B) Figure 12.2 in the text illustrates a typical distribution system consisting of a channel that includes a wholesale distributor and a retailer. If the firm manufacturers it product in the particular country, it can sell directly to the consumer, to the retailer, or to the wholesaler. The same options are available to a firm that manufacturers outside the country.

<u>Differences Among Countries</u>

C) **Retail Concentration** - In some countries the retail system is very concentrated, whereas in other countries it is fragmented. In a concentrated system, a few retailers supply most of the market.

D) **Channel Length** - Refers to the number of intermediaries between the producer and the consumer. If the producer sells directly to the consumer, the channel is very short. If the producer sells through an import agent, a wholesaler, and a retailer, a long channel exists.

E) **Channel Exclusivity** - An exclusive distribution channel is one that is difficult for outsiders to access. Japan's system is often help up as an example of a very exclusive system.

<u>Choosing a Distribution Strategy</u>

F) A choice of distribution strategy determines which channel the firm will use to reach potential consumers. Since each intermediary in a channel adds its own markup to the products, there is generally a critical link between channel length and the firm's profit margin. However, a long channel also has benefits. One benefit of using a longer channel is that it economizes on selling costs when the retail sector is very fragmented.

COMMUNICATION STRATEGY

A) Another critical element in the marketing mix is communicating the attributes of the product to prospective customers. A number of communication channels are available to a firm; they include direct selling, sales promotion, direct marketing, and advertising.

B) A firm's communications strategy is partly defined by its choice of channel.

<u>Barriers to International Communication</u>

C) International communication occurs whenever a firm uses a marketing message to sell its products in another country. The effectiveness of a firm's international communication can be jeopardized by three potentially critical variables:

Cultural Barriers

D) Cultural barriers can make it difficult to communicate messages across cultures. The best way for a firm to overcome cultural barriers is to develop cross-cultural literacy.

Source Effects

E) Source effects occur when the receiver of the message (the potential consumer) evaluates the message based upon the status or image of the sender. Source effects can be either positive or negative. The class can be stimulated to think of some positive and negative source effects (German autos vs. German wine, Italian cuisine vs. British cuisine)

Noise Levels

F) Noise tends to reduce the chance of effective communication. In this context, noise refers to the amount of other messages that are competing for a potential consumer's attention.

Push versus Pull Strategies

G) The main choice with regard to communication strategy is between a push strategy and a pull strategy. A push strategy emphasizes personnel selling whereas a pull strategy emphasizes mass media advertising. The choice between push and pull strategies depends upon product type and consumer sophistication, channel length, and media availability.

Product Type and Consumer Sophistication

H) A pull strategy is generally favored by firms in consumer goods industries that are trying to sell to a large segment of the market. In contrast, firms that sell industrial products or other complex products favor a push strategy.

Channel Length

I) Using direct selling to push a product through many layers of a distribution channel can be very expensive. In such circumstances, a firm may try to pull its product through the channels by using mass advertising to create consumer demand.

Media Availability

J) A pull strategy relies on access to advertising media. A push strategy is more attractive when access to mass media is limited.

The Push-Pull Mix

K) Push strategies tend to be emphasized more in the following circumstances; 1) for industrial products and/or complex new products, 2) when distribution channels are short and 3) when few print or electronic media are available. Pull strategies tend to be emphasized more in the following circumstances: 1) for consumer goods products, 2) when distribution channels are long and when 3) sufficient print and electronic media are available to carry the marketing message.

Global Advertising

L) In recent years there has been much discussion about the pros and cons of standardized advertising worldwide.

For Standardized Advertising

M) The support for global advertising is threefold. 1) It has significant economic advantages. 2) There is the concern that creative talent is scarce and that one large effort to develop a campaign will produce better results than 40 or 50 smaller efforts. 3) Brand names are global.

Against Standardized Advertising

N) The are two main arguments against globally standardized advertising. 1) Cultural differences among nations are such tat a message that works in one nation can fail miserably in another. 2) Country differences in advertising regulations may block implementation of standardized advertising.

Dealing with Country Differences

O) Some firms have been experimenting with tactics that allow them to capture some of the benefits of global standardization while recognizing differences in countries' cultural and legal environments.

PRICING STRATEGY

A) International pricing strategy is an important component of the overall international marketing mix.

Price Discrimination

B) Price discrimination exists whenever consumers in different countries are charged different prices for the same product. Price discrimination can assist a firm in the process of maximizing its profits.

C) For price discrimination to work the firm must be able to keep national markets separate and different price elasticities of demand must exist in different countries.

The Determinants of Demand Elasticity

D) The elasticity of demand is determined by a number of factors, of which income level and competitive conditions are probably the most important. In general price elasticities tend to be greater in countries with lower income levels and greater numbers of competitors.

Strategic Pricing

E) The concept of **strategic pricing** has three aspects, which we will refer to as predatory pricing, multi-point pricing, and experience curve pricing.

Predatory Pricing

F) **Predatory pricing** involves using the profit gained in one market to support aggressive pricing in another market. The objective is to drive competitors out of the market.

Multi-point Pricing Strategy

G) Multi-point pricing strategy becomes an issue in those situations where two or more international businesses compete against each in two or more distinct (national) markets.

H) The concept of **multi-point pricing** refers to the fact a firm's pricing strategy in one market may have an impact on their rival's pricing strategy in another market. In particular aggressive pricing in one market may elicit a competitive response form a rival in another market that is important to the firm.

I) The managerial message in all of this is that pricing decisions around the world need to be centrally monitored.

Experience Curve Pricing

J) Many firms pursuing an **experience curve pricing** strategy on an international scale price low worldwide in attempting to build global sales volume as rapidly as possible, even if this means taking large losses initially. A firm using experience curve pricing believes that several years in the future, when it has moved down the experience curve, it will be making substantial profits and, moreover, have a cost advantage over its less aggressive competitors.

Regulatory Influences on Prices

K) Firms' abilities to engage in either price discrimination or strategic pricing may be limited by national or international regulations.

Antidumping Regulations

L) **Dumping** occurs whenever a firm sells a product for a price that is less than the cost of producing it.

M) From the perspective of an international business, the important point is that antidumping rules set a floor under export prices and limit firms' ability to pursue strategic pricing.

Competition Policy

N) Most industrialized nations have regulations designed to promote competition and to restrict monopoly practices. These regulations can be used to limit the prices that a firm can charge in a given country.

CONFIGURING THE MARKETING MIX

A) Standardization versus customization is not an all or nothing concept. In reality most firms standardize some things and customize others. When looking at the overall marketing mix and message, one often finds some aspects of standardization and some aspects of customization in all products depending on local requirements and overall cost structures.

Teaching Tip: In the coming years, the Internet will become an increasingly important part of an international businesses' marketing mix. A site entitled "The Internet and International Marketing" {http://web.ukonline.co.uk/members/jim.hamill/wwwlect.htm} is a ten module on-line course covering effective use of the Internet in international marketing.

NEW PRODUCT DEVELOPMENT

A) Firms that successfully develop and market new products can earn enormous returns. Some examples are provided in the textbook.

The Location of R&D

B) Ideas for new products are simulated by the interactions of scientific research, demand conditions, and competitive conditions. Other things being equal, the rate of new-product development seems to be greater in countries where:
    i)   More money is spent on basic and applied research and development.
    ii) Demand is strong.
    iii) Consumers are affluent.
    iv) Competition is intense.

Integrating R&D, Marketing, and Production

C) The need to adequately commercialize new technologies poses special problems in the international business, since commercialization may require different versions of a new product to be produced for different countries.

D) A firm's new product development efforts need to be closely coordinated with the marketing, production, and materials management functions. This integration is critical to making certain that customer needs are met and that the company performs all its value creation activities efficiently

Teaching Tip: For anyone interested in doing a better job keeping up with international news, Interactive Global News is an international electronic news source sponsored by Pangaea Communications. The site provides a substantive and thought provoking series of news briefs and commentaries on global business issues. The site is available to the public at {http://www.pangaea.net/ign/news.htm}.

Cross-Functional Teams

E) One means of achieving cross-functional integration is to have cross-functional product development teams. Effective cross functional teams should be led by a heavyweight project manager with status in the organization, have members from all the critical functional areas, have members located together, have clear goals, and have an effective conflict resolution process.

F) This all becomes more difficult when developing products for multiple worldwide markets. Many large firms have research centers in limited locations, with product development activities more dispersed.

Implications for the International Business

G) The need to integrated R&D and marketing to adequately commercialize new technologies poses special problems in the international business, since commercialization may require different versions of a new product to be produced for different countries.

H) Integrating R&D, marketing, and production in an international business may require R&D centers in North America, Asia, and Europe that are closely linked by formal and informal integrating mechanisms with marketing operations in each country in their regions, and with the various manufacturing facilities.

Critical Thinking and Discussion Questions

1. Imagine you are the marketing manager for a US manufacturer of disposable diapers. Your firm is considering entering the Brazilian. Your CEO believes the advertising message that has been effective in the United States will suffice in Brazil. Outline the possible objections to this strategy. Your CEO also believes that the pricing decisions in Brazil can be left to local managers. Why might she be wrong?

Answer: While babies' behinds serve the same function in all cultures, and the product's technical standards may be similar, sensitivity to bodily functions does vary across cultures. Thus the advertising message may need to be changed for different attitudes towards what is appropriate advertising. Likewise, where it might be progressive to show an ad with a male changing a diaper in some countries, in other countries this message could be lost or misinterpreted. Another consideration would be the noise level created by the advertising message of competitor's products, which may well be different in Brazil. While local demand and price elasticity decisions should play an important role in Brazil, pricing should not be left solely to the discretion of the local managers. Since this is a global business, your firm will likely be competing in Brazil with some of the same competitors as elsewhere. Thus pricing decisions in one country can have an impact on pricing and competition in other markets. Similarly, your firm may want to position and price the brand similarly across different South American countries.

2. Within 20 years we will have seen the emergence of enormous global markets for standardized consumer products. Do you agree with this statement? Justify your answer.

Answer: One could either choose to agree or disagree, while the best answer would likely hedge it somewhere in the middle. There clearly already are enormous global markets already for products like Coke and Levis, while it is questionable whether there will ever be a global consumer market for Norwegian lutefisk. More global consumer markets will likely emerge, but there will continue to be national distinctions for many products.

3. You are the marketing manager of a food products company that is considering entering the South Korean market. The retail system in South Korea tends to be very fragmented. Moreover, retailers and

wholesalers tend to have long-term ties with South Korean food companies, which makes access to distribution channels difficult. What distribution strategy would you advise the company to pursue? Why?

Answer: The firm should sell to either wholesalers or import agents. Because the retail system in South Korea is very fragmented, it would be very expensive for the firm to make contact with each individual retailer. As a result, it would be more economical for the firm to sell to wholesalers or import agents. Import agents may have long-term relationships with wholesalers, retailers, and/or other import agents. Similarly, wholesalers may have long-standing relationships with retailers and, therefore, be better able to persuade them to carry the firm's product than the firm itself would.

4. "Price discrimination in indistinguishable from dumping." Discuss the accuracy of this statement?

Answer: In some specific instances this statement is correct, but as a general rule it is not. When a firm is pricing lower in a foreign country than it is in its domestic market, it can be difficult to distinguish dumping from price discrimination unless it is clear that the firm is selling at below cost in the foreign market. Yet when costs are reasonably well known and all prices are above these, or if the firm is pricing lower in its domestic market than in foreign markets, it can reasonably concluded that price discrimination rather than dumping is occurring.

5. You work for a company that designs and manufactures personal computers. Your company's R&D center is in North Dakota. The computers are manufactured under contract in Taiwan. Marketing strategy is delegated to the heads of three regional groups: a North American group (based in Chicago), a European group (based in Paris), and an Asian group (based in Singapore). Each regional group develops the marketing approach within its region. In order of importance, the largest markets for your products are North America, Germany, Britain, China, and Australia. Your company is experiencing problems in its product development and commercialization process. Products are late to market, the manufacturing quality is poor, and costs are higher than projected, and market acceptance of new products is less than hoped for. What might be the source of these problems? How would you fix them?

Answer: The dispersion of activities makes sense - products are produced in the lowest cost location and marketed by people familiar with local conditions. (The R&D in North Dakota must be a historical fluke.) Yet this makes the coordination task extremely complex, and information required for successful commercialization is likely not being effectively communicated among all the appropriate people. Greater cross-functional integration in the new product development process should help to improve product development and commercialization.

Internet Exercises

TEXT EXERCISE 1

Overview

This exercise explores how L'Oreal, the French cosmetics company, has developed it global marketing strategy. While L'Oreal products can be found across the globe, the company frequently chooses to develop markets by adapting not only the product, but also the brand name to meet local demands.

Suggested Use in the Classroom

Students are asked to discuss the advantages and disadvantages of a standardized marketing strategy versus a customized strategy. In addition, students are asked to comment on how an Internet cosmetics company might compete in global markets. Many students will probably opt for a more standardized strategy by an Internet company citing the global nature of the Internet as the basis for their position. A few students will probably maintain that women's preferences across the globe vary greatly when it comes to cosmetics, and that a successful company will respond to those needs.

TEXT EXERCISE 2

Overview

This exercise extends the previous one by continuing to explore international marketing strategy within the cosmetics industry. This company featured in the exercise, German based Beiersdorf, in contrast to L'Oreal, follows a relatively standardized approach to markets with its Nivea brand of skin cream.

Suggested Use in the Classroom

Students are asked to compare and contrast the strategies of Beiersdorf and L'Oreal, and comment on the success of each firm. Students are also asked to discuss which firm is better positioned to compete in the electronic world of cosmetics. As with the previous exercise, most students will probably suggest that a global brand name will be easier to market via the Internet than a series of customized products.

WEB EXERCISE 1

Overview

American pop culture can be found in all parts of the globe. However, there are indications that not everyone appreciates it to the same degree. Many Hollywood studios are currently considering the wisdom of developing products specifically geared towards certain markets—a departure from their traditional approach of selling American films everywhere.

Suggested Use in the Classroom

In this exercise, students are asked to consider the demand for customized products and the ability of the studios to provide them. Many students will focus on alliances with local companies as a means of bringing a local flavor to products. Other students however, may question the cost involved in developing market-specific products.

WEB EXERCISE 2

Overview

Marks and Spencer, the British retailer, has recently lost market share to foreign companies. The retailer admits that it is out of touch with its customers, and is currently in the process of introducing new products in its foreign locations in an effort to better meet local preferences. In addition, the company sees great potential in its newly established Internet site.

Marks and Spencer, unlike many of its competitors, is proposing to maintain a wide variety of products on its Internet sites—products that are adapted to each location. Students are asked to consider the company's approach to its e-business, and comment on its potential relative to its rivals' more standardized sites. Many students may comment on the ability of rival companies such as the Gap to develop a global brand position by employing a standardized marketing strategy. These students may suggest that Marks and Spencer, with its more localized effort, runs the risk of being a relative unknown by comparison.

Management Focus: MTV Rocks the World

Summary

This feature focuses on the phenomenal success of MTV, a music-orientated television station that is broadcast in over 80 countries. MTV's audience is primarily teens and young adults in their early 20s. These are people who are just formulating their tastes and brand preferences, and constitute a perfect market for companies that are trying to sell a global, standardized product. As a result, some of MTV's largest advertisers are Levi Strauss, Procter & Gamble, Johnson & Johnson, Pepsi-Cola, and Apple Computer. These companies use MTV as a medium to reach a global audience and create a "global" appeal for their standardized products. The case expounds upon how MTV is helping "pave the wave" for increased globalization and standardization of products worldwide.

Suggested Discussion Questions

1. The opening case discusses the misfortunes that P&G experienced by transforming its marketing message for consumer products directly from the United States to parts of Europe and Asia. The message the emerged from this case was that just because a marketing campaign works for P&G in America, that doesn't mean that it will work in other parts of the world. In contrast, the companies that advertise on MTV hope to sell a fairly standardized product to all corners of the world. What is different about P&G's approach in Europe and Asia (as described in the case at the end of the chapter) and what MTV's advertisers are trying to accomplish? Explain your answer.

2. MTV has been successful, in part, because music is a global medium. Can you think of any other global mediums? Where else could companies like Levi Strauss, Johnson & Johnson, and Pepsi-Cola advertise to reach a global audience?

3. MTV's Homepage: {http://www.mtv.com/}

Management Focus: Global Advertising at Polaroid

Summary

This features focuses on the experiences of Polaroid in developing advertising campaigns for its European markets. In the mid-1970s, Polaroid introduced its SX-70 camera to Europe using an advertising campaign designed in the United States. Despite the objections of the company's European personnel, the commercials were not modified for a European audience. The commercials were not a success, and

Polaroid struggled in gaining a foothold in the European market. When Polaroid changed its strategy and decided to reposition its camera to accommodate a more serious platform, the company changed its attitude towards developing commercials for its European markets. This time, Polaroid let its European personnel help design and implement the commercials, and they have been a phenomenal success.

Suggested Discussion Questions

1. What was wrong with Polaroid's first attempt at developing an advertising campaign for its European markets? Explain your answer.

2. Discuss the importance of decentralized decision making in developing advertising campaigns for international markets.

3. Polaroid Homepage: {http://www.polaroid.com/}

Management Focus: Castrol Ltd.

Summary

This feature focuses on the strategies and experience of Castrol Oil in marketing its GTX brand of motor oil around the world. Castrol Oil is the lubricants division of the British chemical, oil, and gas concern Burmah Castrol. Castrol Oil's GTX brand of motor oil is marketed as a premium brand. The feature focuses on the company's entries into the lubricants markets in Thailand and Viet Nam. Castrol has a unique strategy of appealing to consumers who drive motorcycles, in hopes of developing brand loyalty and retaining these customers as their countries develop to the point where cars are more common. This strategy worked well in Thailand, and is currently under way in Viet Nam.

Suggested Discussion Questions

1. In underdeveloped countries like Thailand and Viet Nam, the conventional forms of media that we are accustomed to, like radio and television, are often absent. This problem is particularly pronounced in Viet Nam. Describe how Castrol Oil overcame this challenge. Does their approach seem prudent to you? Explain your answer.

2. Would you describe Castrol Oil's communications strategy in Viet Nam as a push or a pull strategy? Explain your answer.

3. Castrol Oil emphasizes a premium pricing strategy. What elements of the company's communications and distributions strategies support this premium pricing strategy?

Additional Readings and Sources of Information

I'd Like to Buy the World a Coke: {http://www.businessweek.com/1998/15/b3573108.htm}

Nike Opens its Books on Sweatshop Audits:
{http://www.businessweek.com/bwdaily/dnflash/apr2000/nf00472b.htm}

India's Youth: {http://www.businessweek.com/1999/99_41/b3650015.htm}
P&G's Hottest New Product: P&G: {http://www.businessweek.com/1998/40/b3598119.htm}

Danone Hits Its Stride: {http://www.businessweek.com/1999/99_05/b3614009.htm}

CHAPTER 13
GLOBAL OPERATIONS MANAGEMENT

<u>Chapter Outline</u>

OPENING CASE: Li & Fung

INTRODUCTION

STRATEGY, MANUFACTURING, AND MATERIALS MANAGEMENT

WHERE TO MANUFACTURE

Country Factors
Technological Factors
Product Factors
Locating Manufacturing Facilities

THE STRATEGIC ROLE OF FOREIGN FACTORIES

Management Focus: Hewlett Packard in Singapore

MAKE OR BUY DECISIONS

The Advantages of Make
The Advantages of Buy
Management Focus: Make or Buy Decisions at Boeing Company
Trade-offs
Strategic Alliances with Suppliers

COORDINATING A GLOBAL MANUFACTURING SYSTEM

Management Focus: Materials Management at Bose
The Power of Just in Time
The Role of Organization
The Role of Information Technology

CHAPTER SUMMARY

CRITICAL THINKING AND DISCUSSION QUESTIONS

INTERNET EXCERCISES

CLOSING CASE: Timberland

<u>Learning Objectives</u>

1. Be familiar with the important influence that operations management can have on the competitive position of an international business.

2. Understand how country differences, manufacturing technology, and product features all affect the choice of where to locate production operations.

3. Appreciate the factors that influence a firm's decision of whether to source component parts from within the company or purchase them from a foreign supplier.

4. Understand what is required to efficiently coordinate a globally dispersed manufacturing system.

OPENING CASE: Li & Fung

Summary

The opening case describes the role of Li & Fung in managing the supply chain and providing goods for other firms - including The Limited and Gymboree. Li & Fung manages a whole network of suppliers across Southeast Asia, and is able to use these suppliers to provide consumer. The following questions can be helpful in directing the discussion.

QUESTION 1: What is the basic business of Li & Fung?

ANSWER 1: Li & Fung takes orders from customers and sifts through its network of 7000 independent suppliers across 26 countries to put together the right suppliers and manufacturers to fulfill the orders of its customers. It is focused on being able to provide the right products in the right quantities quickly, but relies on customers like The Limited to identify customer trends and market the final products. Li & Fung manages the logistics and arranges for final shipment to customers.

QUESTION 2: Why don't firms like The Limited handle these activities themselves?

ANSWER 2: By working with a number of different retailers like The Limited, Li & Fung is able to have a much larger and diverse supplier base than any one retailer could support. Thus it is able to provide better products more quickly and at a lower cost than a retailer would who did not rely on its services.

Chapter Summary

This chapter explores the issues associated with global operations management. At the outset, the author defines the terms operations, production, and material management, and then goes on to discuss the importance of total quality management (TQM) and ISO 9000. Particular emphasis is placed on the topics of "where" international firms should locate their manufacturing operation and how international firms decided whether to "make-or-buy" component parts. In regard to the former, the author argues that country factors, technological factors, and product factors influence a manufacturers location decision. In regard to make-or-decisions, the author provides a balanced discussion of the advantages and disadvantages of buying components parts (in the world marketplace) opposed to making them in-house.
The chapter concludes with separate discussion of the importance of strategic alliances, just-in-time manufacturing, and information technology to international firms.

Chapter Outline With Lecture Notes and Teaching Tips

INTRODUCTION

A) In this chapter we will be looking at three questions: Where in the world should productive activities be located? Decide how much production should be performed in-house, and how much outsourced? How best to coordinate a globally dispersed supply chain?

STRATEGY, MANUFACTURING, AND MATERIALS MANAGEMENT

A) This chapter focuses on two activities - production and materials management - and attempts to clarify how these activities might be performed internationally to (1) lower the costs of value creation and (2) add value by better serving customer needs.

B) **Production** refers to activities involved in creating a product. **Materials management** refers to activities that control the transmission of physical materials through the value chain, from procurement through production and into distribution. **Logistics** refers to the procurement and physical transmission of material through the supply chain, from suppliers to customers.

C) The objectives of manufacturing and materials management are to lower the costs of value creation and add value by better serving customer needs. This can be accomplished by lowering costs and increase product quality. These two aspects are related.

D) There are three ways in which improved quality control reduces costs. First, productivity increases because time is not wasted manufacturing poor quality products that cannot be sold. This saving leads to a direct reduction in unit costs. Second, increased product quality means lower re-work and scrap costs. Third, greater product quality means lower warranty and re-work costs. The net effect is to lower the costs of value creation by reducing both manufacturing and service costs.

E) The main management technique that companies are utilizing to boost their product quality is Total Quality Management (TQM). TQM is a management philosophy that takes as its central focus the need to improve the quality of a company's products and services.

F) Apart from the rise of TQM, the growth of international standards in some cases focused greater attention on the importance of product quality. In Europe, for example, the European Union requires that the quality of a firm's manufacturing processes and products be certified under a quality standard known as ISO 9000 before the firm is allowed access to the European marketplace.

G) Added to the objectives of lowering costs and improving quality are two further objectives of manufacturing and materials management that take on particular importance for international businesses. First, manufacturing and materials management must be able to accommodate demands for local responsiveness. Second, manufacturing and materials management must be able to respond quickly to shifts in customer demand.

Lecture Note: Each year CIO magazine publishes a list of the "Top 100" companies in terms of Supply Chain/Logistics Management. This list may be helpful in locating companies that are heavily involved in this issue. The current list, which includes global corporations such as Caterpillar, Chrysler, Texas Instruments, Toyota, UPS, and Xerox, can be accessed at {http://www.cio.com/CIO/100winners.html#Supply Chain/Logistics Management}.

WHERE TO MANUFACTURE

A) For the firm that considers international production to a feasible option, three broadly defined factors need to be considered when making a location decision: country factors, technological factors, and product factors

Country Factors

B) As discussed earlier in the book, country factors suggest that a firm should locate it various manufacturing activities in those locations where economic, political, and cultural conditions, including relative factor costs, are most conducive to the performance of that activity. However, regulations affecting FDI and trade can significantly affect the appropriateness of specific countries, as can expectations about future exchange rate changes

Teaching Tip: The United States Central Intelligence Agency has compiled a "country profile" on each country in the world. The country profiles are very informative, and may provide useful information to a company that is contemplating doing business in a particular country. The country profiles are available to the public and can be downloaded at {http://fedstats.gov/index20.html}.

Teaching Tip: For additional information about a particular country, Yahoo provides an easy-to-search bank of linked sources that provide information about almost every country in the world. The site is available at {http://www.yahoo.com/Government/Countries/}.

Technological Factors

C) The type of technology a firm uses in its manufacturing can be pivotal in location decisions. Three characteristics of a manufacturing technology are of interest here: the level of its fixed costs; its minimum efficient scale; and its flexibility.

Fixed Costs

D) In some cases the fixed costs of setting up a manufacturing plant are so high that a firm must serve the world market from a single location or from a very few locations.

Minimum Efficient Scale

E) The larger the minimum efficient scale of a plant, the greater the argument for centralizing production in a single location or a limited number of locations.

Flexible Manufacturing (Lean Production)

F) The term flexible manufacturing technology or **lean production** as it is often called – covers a range of manufacturing technologies that are designed to (i) reduce set up times for complex equipment (ii) increase the utilization of individual machines through better scheduling, and (iii) improve quality control at all stages of the manufacturing process.

G) Flexible manufacturing technologies allow a company to produce a wider variety of end products at a unit cost that at one time could only be achieved through the mass production of a standardized output. The term **mass customization** has been coined to describe this ability. Mass customization implies that a firm may be able to customize its product range to suit the needs of different customer groups without bearing a cost penalty.

H) **Flexible machine cells** are another common flexible manufacturing technology. A flexible machine cell is a grouping of various types of machinery, a common materials handler, and a centralized cell controller (computer).

I) The adoption of flexible manufacturing technologies can help improve the competitive position of firms. Most importantly, from the perspective of an international business, flexible manufacturing technologies can assist in the process of customizing products to different national markets in accordance with demands for local responsiveness.

Summary

J) When fixed costs are substantial, the minimum efficient scale of production is high, and/or flexible manufacturing technologies are available, the arguments for concentrating production at a few choice locations are strong. Alternatively, when both fixed costs and the minimum efficient scale of production are relatively low, and when appropriate flexible manufacturing technologies are not available, the arguments for concentrating production at a few choice locations are not as compelling.

Product Factors

K) Two product factors impact location decisions. The first is the product's value-to-weight ratio because of its influence on transportation costs. If the value-to-weight ratio is high, it is practical to produce the product in a single location and export it to other parts of the world. If the value-to-weight ratio is low, there is greater pressure to manufacture the product in multiple locations across the world.

L) The other product feature that can influence location decisions is whether the product serves **universal needs**, needs that are the same all over the world. Since there are few national differences in consumer taste and preference for such products, the need for local responsiveness is reduced. This increases the attractiveness of concentrating manufacturing in a central location.

Locating Manufacturing Facilities

M) There are two basic strategies for locating manufacturing facilities: concentrating them in the optimal location and serving the world market from there, and decentralizing them in various regional or national locations that are close to major markets. The appropriate strategic choice is determined by the various country, technological, and product factors discussed in this section. A summary of this material is provided in Table 13.3 in the text.

THE STRATEGIC ROLE OF FOREIGN FACTORIES

A) The strategic role of foreign factories can change over time. A factory originally set up to make a standard product to serve a local market, or to take advantage of low cost inputs, can evolve into a facility with advanced design capabilities.

B) Similarly, the strategic advantage of a particular location can change as well, as governmental regulations change and/or countries upgrade their factors of production.

C) As the strategic role of a factory is upgraded and a firm develops centers of excellence in different locations worldwide, it supports the development of a transnational strategy.

MAKE-OR-BUY DECISIONS

A) International businesses face sourcing decisions, decisions about whether they should make or buy the component parts to go into their final product. Make-or-buy decisions are important factors in many firms' manufacturing strategies.

Teaching Tip: An article entitled "Is the Make-Buy Decision Process a Core Competence"? by Charles H. Fine and Daniel E. Whitney of MIT Center for Technology, Policy, and Industrial Development is available at {http://web.mit.edu/ctpid/www/Whitney/morepapers/make_ab.html}.

The Advantages of Make

B) The arguments that support making component parts in-house - vertical integration - are fourfold. Specifically, vertical integration may be associated with lower costs, facilitate investments in highly specialized assets, protect proprietary technology, and facilitate the scheduling of adjacent processes.

Lower Costs

C) It may pay a firm to continue manufacturing a product or component part in-house, as opposed to outsourcing it to an independent manufacturer, if the firm is more efficient at that production activity than any other enterprise.

Facilitating Specialized Investments

D) When substantial investments in specialized assets are required to manufacture a component, the firm will prefer to make the component internally rather than contract it out to a supplier.

Proprietary Product Technology Protection

E) In order to maintain control over its technology, a firm might prefer to make component parts that contain proprietary technology in-house, rather than have them made by independent suppliers.

Improved Scheduling

F) The weakest argument for vertical integration is that production cost savings result from it because it makes planning, coordination, and scheduling of adjacent processes easier.

The Advantage of Buy

G) The advantages of buying component parts from independent suppliers are that it gives the firm greater flexibility, it can help drive down the firm's cost structure, and it may help the firm to capture orders from international customers. .

Strategic Flexibility

H) The greatest advantage of buying component parts from independent suppliers is that the firm can maintain its flexibility, switching orders between suppliers as circumstances dictate. This is particularly important in the international context where changes in exchange rates and trade barriers might alter the attractiveness of various supply sources over time.

Lower Costs

I) Vertical integration into the manufacture of component parts involves an increase in the scope of the organization. The resulting increase in organizational complexity can be costly. There are three reasons for this. First, the greater the number of sub-units within an organization, the greater the problems of coordinating and controlling those units. Second, the firm that vertically integrates into component part manufacture may find that because its internal suppliers have a captive customer in the firm, internal suppliers lack an incentive to reduce costs. Third, leading directly on from the previous point, vertically integrated firms have to determine the appropriate price for goods transferred between sub-units within the firm. Setting appropriate transfer prices is a problem in any firm. The firm that buys its components from independent suppliers can avoid all of these problems.

Offsets

J) Another reason for outsourcing some manufacturing to independent suppliers based in other countries is that it may help the firm capture more orders from that country.

Trade-Offs

K) It is clear that trade offs are involved in make-or-buy decisions. The benefits of manufacturing components in-house seem to be greatest when highly specialized assets are involved, when vertical integration is necessary for protecting proprietary technology, or when the firm is simply more efficient than external suppliers at performing a particular activity.

L) Several firms have tried to capture some of the benefits of vertical integration, without encountering the associated organizational problems, by entering into long-term strategic alliances with key suppliers. Although alliances with suppliers can help the firm to capture the benefits associated with vertical integration without dispensing entirely with the benefits of a market relationship, alliances do have their drawbacks. The firm that enters into a strategic alliance may find its strategic flexibility limited by commitments to alliance partners

Strategic Alliances with Suppliers

M) Several international businesses have tried to reap some of the benefits of vertical integration without the associated organizational problems by entering into strategic alliances with key suppliers.

COORDINATING A GLOBAL MANUFACTURING SYSTEM

A) **Materials management** encompasses the activities necessary to get materials to a manufacturing facility, through the manufacturing process, and out through a distribution system to the end user. The materials management function is complicated in an international business by distance, time, exchange rates, customs barriers, and the like. Efficient materials management can have a major impact upon a firm's bottom line.

Teaching Tip: Stanford University maintains a web site that is a forum for the dissemination of research and practical advice in the area of global supply chain management. The site supplies current information that can help embellish a lecture on global materials management. The site is available at {http://www-leland.standford.edu/group/scformu/}.

The Power of Just-in-Time (JIT)

B) The basic philosophy behind JIT systems is to economize on inventory holding costs by having materials arrive at a manufacturing plant just in time to enter the production process, and not before.

C) Just-in-time systems generate major cost savings from reduced warehousing and inventory holding costs. In addition, JIT systems help the firm to spot defective parts and take them out of the manufacturing process - thereby boosting product quality

The Role of Information Technology

D) Information technology and particularly electronic data interchange, play a major role in materials management. EDI facilitates the tracking of inputs, allows the firm to optimize its production schedule, allows the firm and its suppliers to communicate in real time, and eliminates the flow of paperwork between a firm and its suppliers.

Critical Thinking and Discussion Questions

1. An electronics firm is considering how best to supply the world market for microprocessors used in consumer and industrial electronic products. A manufacturing plant cost approximately $500 million to construct and requires a highly skilled work force. The total value of the world market for this product over the next 10 years is estimated to be between $10 and $15 billion. The tariffs prevailing in this industry are currently low. What kind of manufacturing strategy do you think the firm should adopt - concentrated or decentralized? What kind of location(s) should the firm favor for its plant(s)?

Answer: The firm should pursue a concentrated manufacturing because (1) the tariffs prevailing in the industry are low, (2) the cost of building a plant to produce the microprocessors is high, and (3) the product's value-to-weight ratio is high. All of these factors favor a concentrated vs. a decentralized manufacturing strategy. In terms of location, the company should consider three factors: country factors, technology factors, and product factors. First, in terms of country factors, the firm should locate its plant in a country that has a highly skilled pool of workers available. That criteria probably limits the firm to developed nations. Second, in terms of technology factors, the firm is compelled to limit the number of its manufacturing facilities because of the high cost of constructing a plant. Third, in terms of product factors, the firm can manufacturer its product in a central location due to the relatively high value-weight ratio and the universal appeal of the product.

2. A chemical firm is considering how best to supply the world market for sulfuric acid. A manufacturing plant costs approximately $20 million to construct and requires a moderately skilled work force. The total value of the world market for this product over the new 10 years is estimated to be between $20 and $30 billion. The tariffs prevailing in this industry are moderate. Should the firm favor concentrated manufacturing or decentralized manufacturing? What kind of location(s) should the firm seek for its plant(s)?

Answer: This question is a tougher call than the scenario depicted in Question #1. The firm should probably pursue a limited decentralized manufacturing strategy (meaning that the firm should not set up a plant in every country that it sells to, but should set up plants in several "regions" of the world). This strategy makes sense because (1) The tariffs prevailing in the industry are moderate (rather than low), (2) the cost of constructing a facility is relatively modest ($20 million), and (3) only a moderately skilled work force is needed (which is probably available in many low-cost regions of the world). The firm should select its location based on country factors, technology factors and product factors. In terms of country factors, the firm should find locations where semi-skilled labor is inexpensive. In terms of technology factors, the firm is not constrained by a high fixed costs associated with its product, so technology is not a pervasive issue. Finally, product factors favor the firm locating in several locations throughout the world. The company's product has a low value-weight ratio, making it unattractive to produce the product in a central location and export it across the world.

3. A firm must decide whether to make a component part in-house or to contract it out to an independent supplier. Manufacturing the part requires a nonrecoverable investment in specialized assets. The most efficient suppliers are located in countries with currencies that many foreign exchange analysts expect to appreciate substantially over the next decade. What are the pros and cons of (a) manufacturing the component in-house and (b) outsourcing manufacture to an independent supplier? Which option would you recommend? Why?

Answer: Manufacturing in-house:
      reduce risk of currency appreciation - rising costs from independent suppliers
      specialized asset investment would make firm dependent on specific suppliers
      protect technological know-how
      improved scheduling
    Out-sourcing:
      if the product using the component fails in the market, the supplier will bear the cost of the non-recoverable investment
      preserve flexibility in case a better component can be designed or bought
      lower organizational and coordination costs
Based on what we know, manufacturing in house may be slightly preferred, but other information could tip the decision the other way.

4. Explain how an efficient materials management function can help an international business compete more effectively in the global marketplace.

Answer: Given the complexity involved in coordination of material and product flows in a multinational enterprise (purchases, currency exchange, inbound and outbound transportation, production, inventory, communication, expediting, tariffs and duties), a materials management function can help to assure that these flows take place in the most efficient manner possible. A related advantage is that by having a materials management function, a firm may obtain improved information about the costs of different transport alternatives, and choose to reconfigure some of its flows to better take advantage of these costs. By being better able to utilize just in time techniques, the cost of production can be lowered while the quality is increased. The materials management function can also help an international business to develop information technology systems that allow it to better track the flow of goods throughout the firm.

Internet Exercises

TEXT EXERCISE 1

Overview

The business-to-business segment is Asia's fastest growing area of e-commerce. One player in the market, Aaeon Technology, is spending half a million dollars to update its software system so that it can compete effectively on the Internet.

<u>Suggested Use in the Classroom</u>

Aaeon Technology is hoping its new software system will allow it to manage components of the supply chain electronically. Students are asked to consider the notion of moving supply chain management to the Internet and its effect on the physical, cultural, economic and/or political distance that may complicate international materials management. Most students will probably argue that while there may be disadvantages to such a move, especially in terms of the loss of personal relationships, that firms that do not make such adjustments will soon find themselves in an uncompetitive situation.

TEXT EXERCISE 2

<u>Overview</u>

Network computing, according to the experts, will be a necessary strategic component in the new millennium. By leveraging the Internet and developing intranets and extranets, even small companies can now compete on a global scale.

<u>Suggested Use in the Classroom</u>

Students are asked to discuss the advantages of incorporating the Internet into a business. Many students will focus on the marketing applications associated with the Internet, but it is important to recognize the operational issues as well.

WEB EXERCISE 1

<u>Overview</u>

This exercise explores the new customs declaration process that was recently adopted by the European Union. Companies exporting to the market will allow for virtual warehousing greatly facilitating the clearing process. However, to take full advantage of the new systems, companies will need to establish corporate intranets and extranets (see previous exercise).

<u>Suggested Use in the Classroom</u>

Students are asked to use the framework presented in the text and consider the implications of Europe's new customs declaration process. Many students may suggest that the new system could result in companies reducing the number of manufacturing sites. In addition, the new system has the potential to bring huge cost savings to firms of all sizes.

WEB EXERCISE 2

<u>Overview</u>

This exercise examines Heineken's Spanish operations. The company recently acquired a Spanish brewery, but in order to gain approval for the takeover, Heineken is being asked to make cuts in some of storage facilities and sell several brands. _

Suggested Use in the Classroom

Students are asked to consider the process of determining the location of production facilities, and in particular, what challenges consumer products firms face as compared to companies producing industrial products. Most students will probably suggest that especially for culturally bound products, the challenge is much greater for consumer products companies because they may need to be in certain locations in order to meet customer expectations, whereas an industrial products firm has much more flexibility in its location decisions.

CLOSING CASE: Timberland

Summary

This case focuses on Timberland, a New Hampshire based manufacturer of rugged, high-quality shoes. Because of the quality and uniqueness of its shoes, Timberland has experienced rapid growth in both America and international markets. Along with Timberland's growth in sales has come a growth in its system of logistics. Unfortunately, during a large part of its growth era, Timberland did not grow its logistics system very effectively. As a result, by the early 1990s Timberland found itself confronted with an extremely complex global manufacturing and logistics network. The case describes how Timberland overcame this challenge and how its new logistics and manufacturing system is facilitating, rather than hindering, its global growth initiatives.

QUESTION 1: What caused Timberland's logistical problems in the 1990s? What do you think were the competitive and financial consequences of these problems?

ANSWER 1: Timberland's materials management system grew on an as needed basis, with new facilities developed in response to increasing demands. There was no overall strategic plan for materials management, and the resulting system was overly complex and inefficient. The company lacked information systems to coordinate and control the dispersed production and distribution network, and small shipment sizes resulted in a large number of orders that were not shipped via the most cost effective method. Financially this was very expensive, and customer service suffered. Thus Timberland not only spent more than needed, its growth was also constrained by the system.

QUESTION 2: What was the key to solving Timberland's logistical problems? Why? What are the consequences of this solution likely to be for Timberland's competitive position and financial performance?

ANSWER 2: The key to solving the problem was in developing an information system that would allow Timberland to track shipments from the factory to the stores. Once tracking was possible, then the information was available to simplify the system and reduce costs. This should lead to lower costs and better on time delivery of goods.

QUESTION 3: Timberland makes almost no products in the United States. Instead, it manufactures some products in the Dominican Republic, and Puerto Rico, while outsourcing the remaining products from third party manufacturers. Explain the probable linking behind this strategy. Why does the company not outsource all production? Why does the company make shoes in the Dominican Republic and Puerto Rico, but not on the mainland of the United States?

ANSWER 3: Part of the reason for the company owned and operated plants is historic, as Timberland started plants there (and maintains them) due to the low costs relative to the mainland of the United States. Company owned facilities also give Timberland a location where they can test out new models and new production techniques. If a quick production run of a particular product is required to serve a very important customer, having company operated facilities also makes it easier for Timberland to fill these needs than if they would have to rearrange the production schedule at one of the third party suppliers.

Management Focus: Hewlett Packard in Singapore

Summary

This feature explores the strategic decision making involved in establishing Hewlett Packard's Singapore plant. The company initially used the plans as a low cost location to manufacture electronic components. Later, entire products were produced in Singapore, Later still, the Singapore plant was involved not only in production but also product design. Today, the plant is an important part of Hewlett Packard's global network responsible for manufacturing and also product development and design.

Suggested Discussion Questions

1) What factors were important in Hewlett Packard's initial decision to open a plant in Singapore? How did these factors contribute to the decision to increase responsibilities at the Singapore plant?

2) Today, the Singapore plant is considered to be a "lead plant" for Hewlett Packard. How can the company help the plant continue to be a key component in Hewlett Packard's global network?

3) Hewlett Packard's homepage: {http://hewlettpackard.com}

Management Focus: Make-or-Buy Decisions at Boeing

Summary

This feature focuses on the process of generating "make-or-buy" decisions at Boeing. The Boeing Company is the world's largest manufacturer of commercial jet aircraft with a 60 percent share of the global market. Due to decreasing demand for its aircraft and cost constraints on the part of its buyers, Boeing has been forced to find ways to become more price competitive. One strategy that Boeing has utilized is outsourcing. The feature describes Boeing's outsourcing criteria, which involves making a determination whether it is better for Boeing to "make" or "buy" a particular component part. For Boeing this is serious business. On the one hand, Boeing does not want to take unnecessary strategic risks and become too dependent on outside suppliers for critical component parts. On the other hand, Boeing can outsource certain component parts and realize a substantial cost saving. The case illustrates the nature of this dilemma at Boeing.

Suggested Discussion Questions

1. Describe Boeing's criteria for determining whether a component part should be "outsourced" or whether it should be manufactured in-house. Are Boeing's criteria appropriate? Why or why not?

2. What could go wrong with Boeing's strategy of outsourcing? Has Boeing taken the necessary precautions? Are there any hazards in the company's strategy?

3. In the future do you believe that Boeing will be doing more or less outsourcing? Justify your answer.

4. Boeing Homepage: {http://www.boeing.com}

Management Focus: Materials Management at Bose

Summary

This feature focuses on the manner in which Bose Corporation has made its materials management function an important part of its overall competitiveness. Bose's core competence is in its electronic engineering skills, but the company attributes much of its business success to tightly coordinated materials management. Bose purchases most of its electronic and nonelectronic components from independent suppliers scattered around North America, the Far East, and Europe. The case describes the manner in which Bose has capitalized on this strategy by making its materials management function extremely efficient and effective.

Suggested Discussion Questions

1. Why is materials management so important to Bose? Explain your answer.

2. How important is the role of information technology to Bose's materials management and logistics operations?

3. Bose Homepage: {http://www.bose.com/}

Additional Readings and Sources of Information

Why the Productivity Revolution Will Spread: {http://www.businessweek.com/2000/00_07/b3668015.htm}

How a Korean Electronics Giant Came Out of the Crisis Stronger Than Ever:
{http://www.businessweek.com/1999/99_51/b3660005.htm}

Time For a Reality Check in Asia: {http://www.businessweek.com1996/49/b35041.htm}

CHAPTER 14
GLOBAL HUMAN RESOURCE MANAGEMENT

Chapter Outline

OPENING CASE: Global Human Resource Management at Coca-Cola

INTRODUCTION

STAFFING POLICY

Types of Staffing Policy
The Expatriate Problem
Management Focus: Managing Expatriates at Shell International Petroleum

TRAINING AND MANAGEMENT DEVELOPMENT

Training for Expatriate Managers
Repatriation of Expatriates
Management Focus: Monsanto's Repatriation Program
Management Development and Strategy

PERFORMANCE APPRAISAL

Performance Appraisal Problems
Guidelines for Performance Appraisal

COMPENSATION

National Differences in Compensation
Management Focus: Executive Pay Policies for Global Managers
Expatriate Pay

INTERNATIONAL LABOR RELATIONS

The Concerns of Organized Labor
The Strategy of Organized Labor
Approaches to Labor Relations

CHAPTER SUMMARY

CRITCAL THINKING AND DISCUSSION QUESTIONS

INTERNET EXERCISES

CLOSING CASE: Global HRM at Colgate Palmolive, Inc.

Learning Objectives

1. Be familiar with the pros and cons of different approaches to staffing policy in international businesses.

2. Understand why management may fail to thrive in foreign postings.

3. Understand what can be done to increase an executive's change of succeeding in a foreign posting.

4. Appreciate the role that training, management development, and compensation practices can play in effectively managing human resources within an international business.

Chapter Summary

This closing chapter focuses on the challenging topic of global human resource management (HRM). The term expatriate manager is introduced, which refers to a citizen of one country who is working abroad in one of his or her firm's subsidiaries. The task of staffing foreign subsidiaries is discussed. In this area, firms typically pursue either an ethnocentric, polycentric, or geocentric approach. This section is followed with an explanation of the challenges involved in selecting expatriate managers. Expatriate often fail in their overseas assignments for a variety of reasons, ranging from the inability of their spouses to adjust to living overseas to a manager's personal or emotional maturity. Techniques that can be used to reduce expatriate failure are presented and discussed. The chapter also discusses a number of other HRM topics in the context of global management. The topics of training and management development are discussed, along with performance appraisal and compensation.

OPENING CASE: Global Human Resource Management at Coca-Cola

Summary

This feature describes how Coca Cola manages the human resource function across its global operations. In essence, the firm uses HRM as the glue that binds its widely diverse group of divisions into a cohesive family. This is accomplished first, by propagating a common human resources philosophy within the company, and second, by developing a group of internationally minded midlevel executives for future senior management responsibilities. The feature goes on to describe the firm's international compensation policy and how Coca Cola continually trains its international managers.

Suggested Discussion Questions

QUESTION 1: What was is the general staffing philosophy of Coca-Cola when selecting personnel for management positions in foreign markets?

ANSWER 1: Coca-Cola primarily staffs management positions in its foreign operations with individuals local to the culture. It tries to pay wages competitive with the best companies in the local market in order to attract the best local talent.

QUESTION 2: What role do expatriates play in the overall staffing approach of Coca-Cola?

ANSWER 2: In spite of the preference for hiring local personnel, expatriates are used in two circumstances. One is when a particular individual has a specific set of skills that are required for a particular position. The second circumstance is when it will assist in the personal development of a particular individual. Coca-Cola believes that because it is a global company, senior managers should have some experience working in countries outside their home base. By moving some individuals around to different locations not only do these individuals benefit, but they also bring a different perspective that can be shared with local employees.

QUESTION 3: Given that Coca-Cola operates in so many different countries with very different labor laws and cultural norms affecting the relationship between a firm and its employees, how can a corporate HRM group provide any relevant service to local operations?

ANSWER 3: The HRM group can help local operations by providing training on the overall philosophy of Coca-Cola. It is then left to the local HRM staff to translate this philosophy into local policies. Since Coca-Cola works with many of the same suppliers (e.g., for cans) and customers (e.g., McDonald's) across the world, it is important that employees in different countries have similar approaches and understanding of Coca-Cola values. The HRM group can also help share information across groups on best practices and approaches to solving common problems. When it is necessary to find individuals for, and place individuals in, expatriate assignments, the HRM group can serve as a valuable liaison in matching individuals and positions.

Chapter Outline With Lecture Notes and Teaching Tips

INTRODUCTION

A) **Human resource management** refers to the activities an organization carries out to utilize its human resources effectively. These activities include determining the firm's human resource strategy, staffing, performance evaluation, management development, compensation, and labor relations.

Challenges Involved

B) The role of HRM is complex enough in a purely domestic firm, but it is more complex in an international business, where staffing, management development, performance evaluation, and compensation activities are complicated by profound differences between countries in labor markets, culture, legal systems, economic systems, and the like.

C) If it is to build a cadre of international managers, the HRM function must deal with a host of issues related to **expatriate managers** (citizens of one country working abroad).

Teaching Tip: There are a number of private HRM firms that provide selection, training and repatriation services for expatriate managers. An example of one of these companies can be found at {http://www.global-dynamics.com/expatria.htm}.

Lecture Note: According to a new survey by William M. Mercer, Inc. {http://www.relojournal.com/june97/mercer.htm}, the number of expatriate managers living outside their home countries is growing. The majority (90%) of the large multinationals surveyed predicted that the number of expatriate managers that they employ would increase over the next two years.

STAFFING POLICY

A) Staffing policy is concerned with the selection of employees who have the skills required to perform a particular job. Staffing policy can be viewed as a major tool for developing and promoting a corporate culture.

B) Research has identified three main approaches to staffing policy within international businesses. These have been characterized as an ethnocentric approach, a polycentric approach and a geocentric approach.

The Ethnocentric Approach

C) An **ethnocentric approach** to staffing policy is one in which key management positions in an international business are filled by parent-country nationals. The policy makes most sense for firms pursuing an international strategy.

D) Firms pursue an ethnocentric staffing policy for three reasons: First, the firm may believe there is a lack of qualified individuals in the host country to fill senior management positions. Second, the firm may see an ethnocentric staffing policy as the best way to maintain a unified corporate culture. Third, if the firm is trying to create value by transferring core competencies to a foreign operation, as firms pursuing an international strategy are, it may believe that the best way to do this is to transfer parent country nationals who have knowledge of that competency to the foreign operation. Despite the rationale for pursing an ethnocentric staffing policy, the policy is now on the wane in most international businesses. There are two reasons for this. First, an ethnocentric staffing policy limits advancement opportunities for host country nationals. Second, an ethnocentric policy can lead to "cultural myopia."

The Polycentric Approach

E) A **polycentric** staffing policy is one in which host country nationals are recruited to manage subsidiaries in their own country, while parent country nationals occupy the key positions at corporate head quarters. While this approach may minimize the dangers of cultural myopia, it may also help create a gap between home and host country operations. The policy is best suited to firms pursuing a multidomestic strategy

F) Advantages of polycentric approach: First, the firm is less likely to suffer from cultural myopia, and second, this staffing approach may be less expensive to implement than an ethnocentric policy. There are two important disadvantages to polycentric staffing approach however. First, host country nationals have limited opportunities to gain experience outside their own country and thus cannot progress beyond senior positions in their own subsidiaries. Second, a gap can form between host country managers and parent country managers.

The Geocentric Approach

G) A **geocentric** staffing policy is one in which the best people are sought for key jobs throughout the organization, regardless of nationality. This approach is consistent with building a strong unifying culture and informal management network. It is well suited to firms pursuing either a global or transnational strategy. The immigration policies of national governments may limit the ability of a firm to pursue this policy.

H) The advantages of a geocentric approach to staffing include enabling the firm to make the best use of its human resources and build a cadre of international executives who feel at home working in a number of different cultures. The disadvantages of geocentric approach include difficulties with immigration laws and costs associated with implementing the strategy.

Summary

I) The advantages and disadvantages of each of the three main approaches to staffing policy are summarized in Table 14.1

The Expatriate Problem

J) A prominent issue in the international staffing literature is **expatriate failure** - the premature return of an expatriate manager to his or her home country.

Teaching Tip: the Integrated Resources Group at {http://www.expat-repat.com/text/home.html} provides a broad array of information about expatriate performance. This site is well worth a visit and can provide good lecture material

Expatriate Failure Rates

K) The costs of expatriate failure can be substantial. The main reasons for expatriate failure among Western firms seems to be 1) an inability of an expatriate's spouse to adapt to a foreign culture, 2) inability of the employee to adjust, 3) other family-related reasons, 4) manager's personal or emotional maturity, and 5) inability to cope with larger overseas responsibilities.

L) Managers of European firms gave only one reason consistently to explain expatriate failure: the inability of the manager's spouse to adjust to a new environment. For the Japanese firms, the reasons for failure, in descending order of importance, were inability to cope with larger overseas responsibility, difficulties with new environment, personal or emotional problems, lack of technical competence, and the inability of spouse to adjust.

Lecture Note: A recent survey by William M. Mercer, Inc., illustrates some of the problems that contribute to expatriate failure. For instance, only 50% of the companies that participated in the survey have structured procedures for selecting candidates for international assignments, fewer than 10% use any form of testing to screen clients, only slightly more than 50% provide expatriates with any form of cultural briefing, and only 45% have a formal repatriation process at the end of the assignment. More examples of issues that contribute to expatriate failure can be found at the Mercer website at {http://www.relojournal.com/june97/mercer.htm}.

Expatriate Selection

M) One way of reducing expatriate failure rates is through improved selection procedures. Mendenhall and Oddou identified four dimensions that seem to predict success in a foreign posting: self-orientation, others-orientation, perceptual ability, and cultural toughness.

N) **Self-orientation** attributes strengthen the expatriate's self-esteem, self-confidence, and mental well-being. **Perceptual ability** refers to the ability to understand why people of other countries behave the way they do. **Cultural toughness** refers to the fact that how well an expatriate adjusts to a particular posting tends to be related to the country of assignment.

TRAINING AND MANAGEMENT DEVELOPMENT

A) Selection is just the first step in matching a manager with a job. The next step involves training the manager to do the job. Training begins where selection ends and it focuses upon preparing the manager for a specific job.

B) Management development is a rather broader concept. Management development is concerned with developing the skills of the manager over his or her career with the firm.

Training for Expatriate Managers

C) Cultural training, language training, and practical training all seem to reduce expatriate failure. However, according to one study only about 30 percent of managers sent on one- to five-year expatriate assignments received training before their departure.

Teaching Tip: A forum for international trade training is available online at {http://www.fitt.ca/}. Established in 1992, the Forum for International Trade Training (FITT) is a not-for-profit organization mandated by the Canadian government in partnership with private industry to remedy the shortage of people with the skills necessary to succeed in overseas markets.

Cultural Training

D) Cultural training seeks to foster an appreciation for the host country's culture.

Language Training

E) Despite the prevalence of English, an exclusive reliance on English diminishes an expatriate manager's ability to interact with host country nationals.

Practical Training

F) Practical Training is aimed at helping the expatriate manager and her family ease themselves into day-to-day life in the host country.

Repatriation of Expatriates

G) A largely overlooked but critically important issue in the training and development of expatriate managers is to prepare them for reentry into their home country organization.

H) The HRM function needs to develop good program for re-integrating expatriates back into work life within their home country organization once their foreign assignment is over, and for utilizing the knowledge they acquired while abroad.

Management Development and Strategy

I) Management development programs are designed to increase the overall skill levels of managers through a mix of ongoing management education and rotations of managers through a number of jobs within the firm to give them varied experiences.

J) Management development is often used as a strategic tool to build a strong unifying culture and informal management network, both of which are supportive of a transnational and global strategy

PERFORMANCE APPRAISAL

Performance Appraisal Problems

A) Unintentional bias makes it difficult to evaluate the performance of expatriate managers objectively. In most cases, two groups evaluate the performance of expatriate managers - host nation managers and home office managers - and both are subject to bias.

B) Frequently home country managers must rely more on hard data when evaluating expatriates, and host country managers can be biased towards their own frame of reference.

Guidelines for Performance Appraisal

C) Several things can reduce bias in the performance appraisal. First, most expatriates appear to believe more weight should be given to an on-site manager's appraisal than to an off-site manager's appraisal. Second, a former expatriate who served in the same location should be involved in the appraisal process to help reduce bias. Finally, when the policy is for foreign on-site mangers to write performance evaluations, home office managers should probably be consulted before an on-site manager completes a formal termination evaluation.

COMPENSATION

National Differences in Compensation

A) Substantial differences exist in the compensation of executives at the same level in various countries. These differences in compensation practices raise a perplexing question for an international business: should the firm pay executives in different countries according to the prevailing standards in each country, or should it equalize pay on a global basis?

Expatriate Pay

B) The most common approach to expatriate pay is the balance sheet approach. This approach equalizes purchasing power across countries so employees can enjoy the same standard in their foreign positing that they enjoyed at home.

C) A further component of the balance sheet approach is to provide financial incentives and allowances to offset qualitative differences between assignment locations.

D) The components of the typical expatriate compensation package are: 1) Base salary, 2) A foreign service premium, 3) Allowances of various types, 4) Tax differentials, 5) Benefits.

Base Salary

E) An expatriate's base salary is normally in the same range as the base salary for a similar position in the home country.

Foreign Service Premium

F) A foreign service premium is extra pay the expatriate receives for working outside his or her country of origin. It is offered as an inducement to accept foreign postings.

Allowances

G) Four types of allowances are often included in an expatriate's compensation package: hardship allowances, housing allowances, cost-of-living allowances, and education allowances.

Taxation

H) Unless a host country has a reciprocal tax treaty with the expatriate's home country, the expatriate may have to pay income tax to both the home country and the host-country governments. When a reciprocal tax treaty is not in force, the firm typically pays the expatriate's income tax in the host country.

Benefits

I) Many firms also ensure that their expatriates receive the same level of medical and pension benefits abroad that they received at home.

INTERNATIONAL LABOR RELATIONS

A) A key issue in international labor relations is the degree to which organized labor is able to limit the choices available to an international business. A firm's ability to pursue a transnational or global strategy can be significantly constrained by the actions of labor unions.

The Concerns of Organized Labor

B) A principal concern of organized labor is that the multinational can counter union bargaining power by threatening to move production to another country. Another concern is that multinationals will try to import and impose unfamiliar labor practices from other countries.

The Strategy of Organized Labor

C) Organized labor has responded to the increased bargaining power of multinational corporations by taking three actions; (1) trying to set-up their own international organizations, (2) lobbying for national legislation to restrict multinationals, and (3) trying to achieve regulations of multinationals through international organization such as the United Nations. However, none of these efforts have been that successful.

Approaches to Labor Relations

D) Traditional labor relations have been decentralized to individual subsidiaries within multinationals. Now there is a trend towards greater centralization. This enhances the bargaining power of the multinational via-a-vis organized labor.

E) There is a growing realization that the way in which work is organized within a plant can be a major source of competitive advantage.

Critical Thinking and Discussion Questions

1. What are the main advantages and disadvantages of the ethnocentric, polycentric, and geocentric

approaches to staffing policy? When is each approach appropriate?

Answer: The answer to this question is contained in Table 14.1 in the text. An ethnocentric staffing policy is one in which all key management positions are filled by parent country nationals. The advantages of the ethnocentric approach are: (1) Overcomes lack of qualified managers in host country, (2) Unified culture, and (3) Helps transfer core competencies. The disadvantages of the ethnocentric approach are: (1) Produces resentment in host country, and (2) Can lead to cultural myopia. An ethnocentric approach is typically appropriate for firms utilizing an international strategy. A polycentric staffing policy requires host country nationals to be recruited to manage subsidiaries, while parent country nations occupy key positions at corporate headquarters. The advantages of the polycentric approach are: (1) Alleviates cultural myopia, and (2) It is inexpensive to implement. The disadvantages of the polycentric approach are: (1) Limits career mobility, and (2) Isolates headquarters from foreign subsidiaries. A polycentric approach is typically appropriate for firms utilizing a multidomestic strategy. A geocentric staffing policy seeks the best people for key jobs throughout the organization, regardless of nationality. The advantages of a geocentric approach are: (1) Uses human resources efficiently, (2) Helps build strong culture and informal management network. The disadvantages of the geocentric staffing policy are: (1) National immigration policies may limit implementation, and (3) It is expensive to implement. A geocentric approach is typically appropriate for firms unitizing a global or transnational strategy.

2. Research suggests that many expatriate employees encounter problems that limit both their effectiveness in a foreign posting and their contribution to the company when they return home. What are the main causes and consequences of these problems, and how might a firm reduce the occurrence of such problems?

Answer: The primary causes of expatriate problems are the inability of the spouse to adjust, inability of the employee to adjust, other family problems, personal/emotional maturity, and an inability to cope with the larger overseas responsibilities. The consequences of such problems are that an employee can be ineffective or detrimental overseas, and/or may return prematurely before the assigned job tasks are completed. A firm can reduce the occurrence of expatiate problems by developing an effective selection process, training, and repatriation program. The most successful expatriates seem to be those who have high self-esteem and self-confidence, get along well with others, are willing to attempt to communicate in a foreign language, and can empathize with people of other cultures. An expatriate training program should include cultural, language, and practical training. Cultural training seeks to foster an appreciation of the host country's culture so that the expatriate behaves accordingly. Language training involves training in local language both from a business and personal perspective. Practical training is aimed at assisting the expatriate manager and her family to ease themselves into day-to-day life in the host country. The sooner a day-to-day routine is established, the better the prospects are that the expatriate and family will adapt successfully. Before leaving, however, specific plans and procedures should be in place for the repatriation of the employee.

3. What is the link between an international business's strategy and its human resource management policies, particularly with regard to the use of expatriate employees and their pay scale?

Answer: In firms pursuing a multidomestic strategy, a polycentric staffing approach is most common and there are relatively few expatriates or the associated pay issues. Expatriates are more common in firms with international strategies, and an ethnocentric staffing approach is utilized. In this situation the pay is often based on home country levels, with adjustments as required for differing living costs and taxes as outlined by the balance sheet approach. Firms pursuing global or transnational strategies most often use a geocentric approach to staffing, where the best individuals (regardless of nationality) are chosen fill positions in any country. Here the pay issues for expatiates can become particularly complex, as allowance must be made for home country norms, host country costs and expectations, and global norms across the company.

4. In what ways can organized labor constrain the strategic choices of an international business? How can an international business limit these constraints?

Answer: Organized labor can significantly constrain the choices firms make with respect to location. International firms (or domestic ones for that matter) often choose to locate new facilities in places where there is relative labor peace and harmonious working relations. Labor can also raise objections and threaten disruptive behavior if a firm decides to move some activities to other locations - which in some cases only reinforces the need for relocating the activities. Organized labor has also attempted to (i) set-up their own international organizations, (ii) lobby for national legislation to restrict multinationals, and (iii) achieve regulation of multinationals through international organization such as the United Nations. However, none of these broader efforts have been that successful. International businesses have the advantage of being able to provide or take away jobs, and in today's labor market that gives them considerable power. As a condition of opening or expanding a facility, firms can negotiate favorable conditions with local unions and force unions to compete against each other for the gains in membership

Internet Exercises

TEXT EXERCISE 1

Overview

As the Internet begins to take off in Europe, demand is rising for managers with skills in e-commerce. The shortage of people with dot com experience is so great that headhunters are taking a global approach to seeking new management, often turning to the U.S. as a source of talent.

Suggested Use in the Classroom

Students are asked to consider how the Internet is changing the job search process. Most students will recognize that finding information on job opportunities both domestically and abroad is significantly easier now than in pre-Internet days. They will probably also note that the global, free nature of the Internet also has the potential to increase the competition for new jobs.

TEXT EXERCISE 2

Overview

This exercise extends the previous one by considering the challenges expatriates face as they begin jobs in new countries. Today's expatriates have the advantage of using the Internet both as a source of information about new locations, and also a means of communicating with other expatriates about their experiences.

Suggested Use in the Classroom

Students are asked to discuss how to best prepare for a foreign assignment. Students will probably recognize that the more knowledge they have about a new location, the easier the adjustment process is likely to be. Most will also recognize the value of support groups in managing culture shock, and will probably suggest the support groups that can be found on the Internet have the potential to be very valuable.

WEB EXERCISE 1

Overview

This exercise explores the labor side of human resource development, and in particular the use of sweatshop factories, and other types of inappropriate labor practices. Students on some campuses across the U.S. are beginning to take issue with companies such as Nike and the Gap that have been accused of such wrongdoings.

Suggested Use in the Classroom

Students are asked to consider their role in the fight against inferior working conditions in offshore factories. Many students may believe that while student groups have the potential to publicize a company's inappropriate practices on a small scale, such groups lack the power to make a significant difference. Other students however, may argue that student organizations have the potential to force at least certain types of companies (those catering to typical college students such as the Gap) to improve their labor practices.

WEB EXERCISE 2

Overview

This exercise extends the previous exercise by continuing to explore international labor issues. In particular, this exercise questions whether companies that have been publicly censured for their labor practices are indeed taking advantage of foreign workers.

Suggested Use in the Classroom

As with the previous exercise, students are likely to take different positions on this issue. Some students may argue that while labor practices in certain countries may be inferior by U.S. standards, as long as companies obey local laws, they should not be criticized. Others however, may take the perspective that companies should treat labor as well as possible regardless of local practices. Some students may note that in some instances, even those cases where labor practices are comparatively poor, workers may prefer to have some sort of job to no job.

CLOSING CASE: Global HRM at Colgate Palmolive

Summary

The closing case describes the approach of Colgate-Palmolive in developing a cadre of mangers with international experience and an understanding of the challenges inherent in a global firm. Discussion of the case can be assisted by the following questions:

QUESTION 1: What is the relationship between HRM and strategy at Colgate-Palmolive?

ANSWER: Colgate is trying to develop an HRM strategy that facilitates its international strategy. According to the case, Colgate is pursuing a transnational strategy. A transnational strategy calls for a geocentric approach to staffing global operations, which is what Colgate is presently doing. Colgate is also trying to develop a compensation program that facilitates its transnational strategy. So far, the compensation program has experienced mixed success. The managers that are selected for the company's international training program are all compensated similarly, which avoids the possibility of resentments over pay developing among this group of managers. However, the locally hired managers (in the host countries) do not receive the same level of compensation as the expatriate managers that come out of the international training program. Colgate needs to find a way to narrow this disparity.

QUESTION 2: How do you think Colgate-Palmolive's international training program might improve its economic performance?

ANSWER: The international training program provides Colgate with a cadre of managers who have specialized training in international business and who have been fully socialized into the Colgate culture. As these managers move into their overseas assignments, it is less likely that they will make costly mistakes and it is more likely that they will maximize the potential of their overseas assignments than managers who have not had a similar level of training.

QUESTION 3: What potential problem and pitfalls do you see with Colgate-Palmolive's international training program?

ANSWER: The advantage of the program is that is provides Colgate a group of international managers who have extensive international training and are fully socialized into the Colgate culture. By doing this, Colgate is in effect establishing an "elite" group of managers that have been identified as having high potential to succeed in overseas assignments. The disadvantage of the program is that it can create resentments among locally hired mangers of subsidiaries in overseas markets and other Colgate employees as a result of the generous compensation provided to the "elite" group of managers. Also, the Colgate employees that are "passed over" for admittance to the training program may see their future potential at Colgate as limited, and may leave Colgate to work for another company.

Management Focus: Managing Expatriates at Shell International Petroleum

Summary

This feature examines how Shell International, a global petroleum company employing over 100,000 people manages its expatriates. The international mobility of its workforce is an important part of Shell's overall philosophy. However, in the early 1990's, the company found that it was having an increasingly difficult time recruiting personnel for foreign postings.

Suggested Discussion Questions

1. Shell's commitment to the success of its foreign assignments is demonstrated by its efforts to uncover expatriate concerns. Discuss the results of Shell's survey to its present and past expatriates and families. How do these results compare to the results of other studies exploring expatriate failure?

2. Shell has implemented several changes to its expatriate program including providing education assistance to families with children, and establishing a Spouse Employment Center to help locate employment opportunities. In your opinion, will these programs "solve" Shell's problems, or is there still more to be done?

c) Shell's homepage {http://www.shell.com}

Management Focus: Monsanto's Repatriation Program

Summary

This feature describes Monsanto's repatriation program for its expatriate managers. The program is very sophisticated, and is designed to provide a supportive environment for the company's managers who are returning from overseas assignments. The feature describes the details of the repatriation program, which is a model program for the repatriation of expatriate managers.

Suggested Discussion Questions

1. How does Monsanto's repatriation program provide an incentive for high-potential managers to accept overseas assignments?

2. According to the feature, after they return home, Monsanto's expatriate managers are given the opportunity to showcase their experience to their peers, subordinates, and superiors, in special information exchange. Why is this important? What function does this serve in the repatriation process?

3. How does Monsanto's repatriation program help an expatriate manager adjust his personal life to returning home? Is this an important component of a firm's repatriation program?

Management Focus: Executive Pay Policies for Global Managers

Summary

This feature discusses how several international firms compensate their expatriate managers. The discussion illustrates the fact that there is no one single approach to compensating expatriate managers. This is a complicated issue that companies resolve according to the specifics of their programs.

Suggested Discussion Questions

1. Discuss Hewlett-Packard's expatriate compensation program? Does it make sense to establish a different program for short-term expatriates and long-term expatriate managers? Explain your answer.

2. Compare and contrast Hewlett-Packard's expatriate compensation program with 3M's program. If you were an expatriate manager, which program would you prefer? Why?

Additional Readings and Sources of Information

Coke and Cadbury? Some Foreign Regulators May Not Swallow It: {http://www.businessweek.com/bwdaily/dnflash/apr1999/nf90407d.htm}

Riding the Mobile Net to Riches?: {http://www.businessweek.com/2000/00_10/b3671020.htm}

They're Sending You Where?: {http://www.businessweek.com/1998/40/b3598037.htm}

HP's Carly Fiorina: The Boss: {http://www.businessweek.com/1999/99_31/b3640001.htm}

TEST BANK

Chapter 1 Globalization

True/False Questions

1. The global economy is moving progressively towards a world in which national economies are relatively isolated from each other.

   Answer: False   Difficulty: Easy   Page: 4

2. Commonly referred to as globalization, the trend toward a more integrated global economic system is a recent development.

   Answer: False   Difficulty: Easy   Page: 4

3. An advantage of globalization is that it narrows the range of issues that a manager has to deal with.

   Answer: False   Difficulty: Medium   Page: 5

4. Because of the global presence of widely accepted products like Citicorp credit cards, Coca-Cola, and Levi's jeans, national markets are all but disappearing.

   Answer: False   Difficulty: Medium   Page: 6

5. Realistically, a company has to be a multinational firm to benefit from the globalization of markets.

   Answer: False   Difficulty: Easy   Page: 6

6. Currently the most global of markets are for industrial goods and materials that serve a universal need the world over.

   Answer: True   Difficulty: Hard   Page: 7

7. Although many companies have lowered their overall cost structure and have improved the quality of their products by dispersing their production activities to locations around the world, this activity is confined primarily to large firms.

   Answer: False   Difficulty: Medium   Page: 7

8. The acronym GATT stands for General Agreement on Tariffs and Trade.

   Answer: True   Difficulty: Medium   Page: 8

Chapter 1 Globalization

9. In addition to reducing trade barriers, many countries have also been progressively removing restrictions on barriers to foreign direct investment.

   Answer: True   Difficulty: Hard   Page: 8

10. There is very little evidence that suggests that the lowering of trade barriers has facilitated the globalization of production.

    Answer: False   Difficulty: Easy   Page: 9

11. According to data from the World Trade Organization, the volume of world output has grown faster than the volume of world trade since the 1950s.

    Answer: False   Difficulty: Medium   Page: 9

12. Surprisingly, despite the importance of technology in our everyday lives, technological change has played only a minor role in the globalization of markets.

    Answer: False   Difficulty: Medium   Page: 11

13. If we look 20 years into the future, most forecasts now predict a rapid rise in world output accounted for by developing nations such as China, India, and South Korea, and a rapid decline in the share enjoyed by rich industrialized countries such as Britain and the United States.

    Answer: True   Difficulty: Medium   Page: 17

14. South Korea is an example of a developing nation.

    Answer: True   Difficulty: Easy   Page: 17

15. The stock of foreign direct investment refers to the total cumulative value of foreign investments in a country.

    Answer: True   Difficulty: Medium   Page: 18

16. In the 1960s global business activity was dominated by large Japanese multinational corporations.

    Answer: False   Difficulty: Medium   Page: 20

Chapter 1 Globalization

17. Although most international trade and investment is still conducted by large firms, small to medium sized firms are increasingly involved in international trade and investment.

   Answer: True   Difficulty: Medium   Page: 21

18. Although there are many benefits to globalization, economists argue that increased international trade and cross-border investments will result in higher prices for goods and services.

   Answer: False   Difficulty: Hard   Page: 24

19. It is commonly believed that globalization stimulates economic growth, creates jobs, and raises income levels.

   Answer: True   Difficulty: Medium   Page: 24

20. An international business is any firm that engages in international trade or investment.

   Answer: True   Difficulty: Easy   Page: 28

Multiple Choice Questions

21. Commonly referred to as _____, the trend toward a more integrated global economic system has been in place for many years.
   A) market standardization
   B) cross-border integration
   C) globalization
   D) nationalization

   Answer: C   Difficulty: Easy   Page: 4

22. The trend towards more integrated global markets has _____.
   A) accelerating in recent years
   B) decelerating in recent years
   C) remained the same in recent years
   D) accelerating for services in recent years, but decelerating for manufactured goods

   Answer: A   Difficulty: Medium   Page: 4

Chapter 1 Globalization

23. The two main components of globalization are:
    A) the globalization of markets and the globalization of production
    B) the globalization of production and the globalization of finance
    C) the standardization of technology and the globalization of markets
    D) the globalization of finance and the globalization of accounting

    Answer: A Difficulty: Medium Page: 6

24. The two main components of globalization are the globalization of markets and the globalization of:
    A) finance
    B) accounting standards
    C) information systems
    D) production

    Answer: D Difficulty: Medium Page: 6

25. The globalization of markets refers to the fact that in many industries historically distinct and separate markets are merging into:
    A) several distinct regional markets
    B) markets defined by a common culture
    C) one huge marketplace
    D) markets defined by a common language

    Answer: C Difficulty: Medium Page: 6

26. The merging of historically distinct and separate national markets into one huge global marketplace is referred to as the _____.
    A) melding of markets
    B) integration of markets
    C) transformation of commerce
    D) globalization of markets

    Answer: D Difficulty: Easy Page: 6

27. Nearly _____ of US companies that export are small firms.
    A) 25 percent
    B) 47 percent
    C) 71 percent
    D) 97 percent

    Answer: D Difficulty: Hard Page: 6

Chapter 1 Globalization

28. The most global of markets is in the area of:
    A) services
    B) consumer goods
    C) industrial goods
    D) intellectual capital

    Answer: C Difficulty: Hard Page: 6

29. The most global of markets are not markets for _____, where national differences in tastes and preferences are still often important enough to act as a break on globalization.
    A) services
    B) consumer goods
    C) insurance and banking
    D) industrial goods

    Answer: B Difficulty: Medium Page: 6

30. Globalization results in a greater degree of _____ across markets than would be present otherwise.
    A) diversification
    B) diversity
    C) homogeneity
    D) heterogeneity

    Answer: C Difficulty: Easy Page: 7

31. The globalization of _____ refers to the tendency among many firms to source goods and services from different locations around the globe in an attempt to take advantage of national differences in the cost and quality of factors of production (such as labor, energy, land, and capital).
    A) information technology
    B) process design
    C) markets
    D) production

    Answer: D Difficulty: Easy Page: 7

Chapter 1 Globalization

32. The sourcing of goods and services from different locations around the globe to take advantage of national differences in the cost and quality of factors of production is referred to as:
    A) the globalization of distribution
    B) the globalization of production
    C) the globalization of sourcing
    D) the globalization of purchasing

    Answer: B Difficulty: Easy Page: 7

33. In producing its electronics products, Sony Corporation sources goods and services from different locations around the globe in an attempt to take advantage of national differences in the cost and quality of factors of production. This practice is made possible by the globalization of:
    A) finance
    B) production
    C) markets
    D) process design

    Answer: B Difficulty: Medium Page: 7

34. According to former Secretary of Labor Robert Reich, the propensity of firms to outsource many of their productive activities to different suppliers around the world has resulted in the creation of _____ products.
    A) multi-domestic
    B) cross-national
    C) global
    D) cross-cultural

    Answer: C Difficulty: Easy Page: 7

35. Which of the following is not an impediment to the optimal dispersion of productive activities to different locations around the world?
    A) transportation costs
    B) issues associated with political risk
    C) informal barriers to trade between countries
    D) reductions in the barriers to foreign direct investment

    Answer: D Difficulty: Hard Page: 8

Chapter 1 Globalization

36. The two macro factors that seem to underlie the trend toward greater globalization are:
    A) the increase in global economic stability, and the slowdown in technological change
    B) the increase in barriers to the free flow of goods, services, and capital that has occurred since the end of World War II, and global economic stability
    C) the decline in barriers to the free flow of goods, services, and capital that has occurred in the past 10 years, and the slowdown in technological change
    D) the decline in barriers to the free flow of goods, services, and capital that has occurred since the end of World War II, and technological change

    Answer: D   Difficulty: Hard   Page: 8

37. The two macro factors that seem to underlie the trend towards greater globalization are the decline in barriers to the free flow of goods, services, and capital that has occurred since the end of World War II and:
    A) technological change
    B) global economic stability
    C) societal change
    D) global political stability

    Answer: A   Difficulty: Medium   Page: 8

38. Cisco Systems exports a number of products to consumers in other countries. This practice is referred to as _____.
    A) world exchange
    B) international trade
    C) cross-national barter
    D) situational commerce

    Answer: B   Difficulty: Medium   Page: 8

39. The exporting of goods or services to consumers in another country is referred to as _____.
    A) situational commerce
    B) world exchange
    C) international trade
    D) cross-national barter

    Answer: C   Difficulty: Easy   Page: 8

40. Although Gillette is an American company, it has invested substantial business resources in activities outside the United States. This practice is referred to as:
    A) transnational commerce
    B) foreign direct investment
    C) international trade
    D) organizational diversification

    Answer: B   Difficulty: Medium   Page: 8

41. The investing of resources in business activities outside a firm's home country is referred to as:
    A) international trade
    B) domestic direct investment
    C) transnational barter
    D) foreign direct investment

    Answer: D   Difficulty: Easy   Page: 8

42. The _____ is a treaty designed to remove barriers to the free flow of goods, services, and capital between nations.
    A) Global Agreement on Tariffs and Commerce
    B) United Nations Treaty on Trade
    C) General Agreement on Tariffs and Trade
    D) Multi-National Agreement on Tariffs and Commerce

    Answer: C   Difficulty: Medium   Page: 8

43. Under the umbrella of GATT there have been eight rounds of negotiations among member states. The most recent round of negotiations was referred to as the

    _____.
    A) Uruguay Round
    B) Malaysian Symposium
    C) German Round
    D) New Zealand Symposium

    Answer: A   Difficulty: Medium   Page: 8

Chapter 1 Globalization

44. Which of the following was not an outcome of the Uruguay Round of the GATT?
    A) increased trade barriers
    B) extended GATT to cover services as well as manufactured goods
    C) established the World Trade Organization
    D) provided extended protection for patents, trademarks, and copyrights

    Answer: A   Difficulty: Medium   Page: 8

45. All of the following were accomplishments of the 1993 Uruguay Round, with the exception of:
    A) eliminating tariffs on all consumer goods
    B) extended GATT to cover services as well as manufactured goods
    C) further reducing trade barriers
    D) established a World Trade Organization

    Answer: A   Difficulty: Hard   Page: 8

46. The acronym GATT stands for:
    A) Global Agreement on Taxation and Tariffs
    B) Global Association of Technology and Trade
    C) General Agreement on Taxation and Trademarks
    D) General Agreement of Tariffs and Trade

    Answer: D   Difficulty: Easy   Page: 8

47. The agency established at the 1993 Uruguay Round to police the international trading system is the _____.
    A) Global Trade Enforcement Administration
    B) World Tariff and Trade Bureau
    C) International Trade Enforcement Agency
    D) World Trade Organization

    Answer: D   Difficulty: Medium   Page: 8

Chapter 1 Globalization

48. Suppose Royal Dutch/Shell, an international oil company, had a complaint about a trade issue. The _____, a governing body established at the Uruguay Round in 1993 to police the international trading system, is an organization that Royal Dutch Shell could take its complaint to.
    A) World Trade Organization
    B) International Trade Monitoring Bureau
    C) World Tariff and Trade Agency
    D) International Trade Monitoring Agency

    Answer: A Difficulty: Medium Page: 8

49. The acronym WTO stands for:
    A) Western Trade Organization
    B) World Tax Organization
    C) World Trade Organization
    D) World Tariff Organization

    Answer: C Difficulty: Easy Page: 8

50. Under the conditions of the 1993 Uruguay agreement, average tariff rates worldwide will approach _____.
    A) percent
    B) 22.0 percent
    C) 6.75 percent
    D) 3.9 percent

    Answer: D Difficulty: Hard Page: 8

51. Approximately 95 percent of the changes that countries have made pertaining to foreign direct investment regulations have:
    A) made it harder for foreign companies to enter their markets
    B) made it easier for foreign companies to enter their markets
    C) had no effect on the ease upon which foreign companies can enter their markets
    D) made it easier to foreign producers of raw materials to enter their markets but more difficult for foreign producers of finished products to enter their markets

    Answer: B Difficulty: Medium Page: 9

Chapter 1 Globalization

52. Which of the following statement is consistent with data from the World Trade Organization?
    A) the volume of world trade has grown faster than the volume of world output since the 1950s.
    B) the volume of world trade has grown slower than the volume of world output since the 1950s.
    C) the volume of world trade and the volume of world output have grown at approximately the same rate since the 1950s.
    D) the volume of world trade and the volume of world output have remained constant since the 1950s.

    Answer: A   Difficulty: Hard   Page: 9

53. According to data from the World Trade Organization, the volume of world trade has grown faster than the volume of world output since the 1950s. This relationship suggests all of the following except:
    A) more firms are dispersing different parts of their overall production process to different locations around-the globe to drive down production costs.
    B) nations are becoming increasingly self-sufficient for important goods and services
    C) FDI is playing an increasing role in the global economy
    D) more firms are dispersing different parts of their overall production process to different locations around-the globe to increase quality.

    Answer: B   Difficulty: Medium   Page: 9

54. Exports now account for _____ of world production, up from 8 percent in 1950.
    A) 16.5 percent
    B) 26.4 percent
    C) 40.0 percent
    D) 52.6 percent

    Answer: B   Difficulty: Hard   Page: 9

55. Evidence suggests that FDI is playing a(n):
    A) decreasing role in the world economy
    B) increasing role in the world economy for services but a decreasing role in the world economy for manufactured goods
    C) increasing role in the world economy for manufactured goods but a decreasing role in the world economy for services
    D) increasing role in the world economy

    Answer: D   Difficulty: Medium   Page: 9

Chapter 1 Globalization

56. The primary purpose of the December 1999 meeting of the World Trade Organization in Seattle was to:
    A) consider the admission of 27 new nations into the organization
    B) pass regulations governing international e-commerce
    C) launch a new round of talks aimed at further reductions in cross-border barriers to trade and investment
    D) discuss the role of "technological change" in the globalization of the world economy

    Answer: C Difficulty: Hard Page: 10

57. According to our textbook, the growing integration of the world economy is:
    A) increasing the intensity of competition in a wide range of manufacturing and service industries
    B) decreasing the intensity of competition in manufacturing industries, and increasing the intensity of competition in services
    C) increasing the intensity of competition in manufacturing industries, and decreasing the intensity of competition in services
    D) narrowing the scope of competition in a wide range of service, commodity, and manufacturing industries

    Answer: A Difficulty: Medium Page: 10

58. According to our textbook, the single most important innovation has been the development of the _____.
    A) telegraph
    B) microprocessor
    C) airplane
    D) telephone

    Answer: B Difficulty: Easy Page: 11

59. The theory that predicts that the power of microprocessor technology doubles and the cost of production falls every 18 months is referred to as:
    A) Brennan's Theorem
    B) Bailey's Law
    C) Moore's Law
    D) Ivan's Law

    Answer: C Difficulty: Medium Page: 11

Chapter 1 Globalization

60. According to our textbook, by the year 2003 there may be _____ Internet users worldwide.
    A) 100 million
    B) 150 million
    C) 250 million
    D) 350 million

    Answer: D Difficulty: Hard Page: 11

61. Web based electronic commerce is called:
    A) e-commerce
    B) I-commerce
    C) c-commerce
    D) cyper-commerce

    Answer: A Difficulty: Easy Page: 12

62. Which of the following was not mentioned in our textbook as major innovation in transportation technology?
    A) commercial jet aircraft
    B) superfreighters
    C) e-commerce
    D) the introduction of containerization

    Answer: C Difficulty: Medium Page: 12

63. Due to containerization, the transportation costs associated with the globalization of production have:
    A) remained the same
    B) increased dramatically
    C) declined
    D) increased slightly

    Answer: C Difficulty: Easy Page: 13

64. As a result of a variety of innovations, the real costs of information processing and communication have _____ over the past two decades.
    A) fallen slightly
    B) increased slightly
    C) remained constant
    D) fallen dramatically

    Answer: D Difficulty: Easy Page: 13

Chapter 1 Globalization

65. Although the characteristics of the global economy have changed dramatically over the past 30 years, as late as the 1960s all of the following demographic characteristics were true except:
   A) the U.S. dominated the world economy
   B) small, U.S. entrepreneurial firms dominated the international business scene
   C) the U.S. dominated the world foreign direct investment picture
   D) roughly half the world was governed by centrally planned economies of the Communist world

   Answer: B   Difficulty: Medium   Page: 16

66. In the early 1960s, the world's most dominant industry power was:
   A) Japan
   B) the United Kingdom
   C) Germany
   D) the United States

   Answer: D   Difficulty: Easy   Page: 16

67. In 1963, the U.S. accounted for _____ of world manufacturing output.
   A) 80.0
   B) 12.8
   C) 65.6
   D) 40.3

   Answer: D   Difficulty: Hard   Page: 16

68. In recent years, all of the following countries have seen their share of world output fall except:
   A) United States
   B) France
   C) Germany
   D) China

   Answer: D   Difficulty: Hard   Page: 16

Chapter 1 Globalization

69. In recent years, all of the following countries have seen their share of world output increase except:
    A) Malaysia
    B) Germany
    C) China
    D) South Korea

    Answer: B Difficulty: Hard Page: 16

70. As of 1998, the world's largest exporter was:
    A) United States
    B) China
    C) Japan
    D) Germany

    Answer: A Difficulty: Medium Page: 17

71. If we look 20 years into the future, most forecasts now predict a _____ in world output accounted for by developing nations such as China, India, Indonesia, and South Korea, and a _____ in the share enjoyed by rich industrialized countries such as Britain, Japan, and the United States.
    A) rapid rise, rapid decline
    B) slight rise, slight decline
    C) rapid decline, rapid rise
    D) rapid rise, slight decline

    Answer: A Difficulty: Medium Page: 17

72. The following is an example of a developing nation.
    A) Thailand
    B) Britain
    C) Japan
    D) United States

    Answer: A Difficulty: Easy Page: 16

73. All of the following are examples of developing nations with the exception of:
    A) China
    B) India
    C) South Korea
    D) Japan

    Answer: D Difficulty: Medium Page: 16

Chapter 1 Globalization

74. Which of the following is not considered to be a "developing" nation?
    A) Brazil
    B) India
    C) China
    D) France

    Answer: D Difficulty: Medium Page: 17

75. The World Bank has estimated that if current trends continue, by 2020 the
    _____ economy could be 40 percent larger than that of the United States.
    A) Russian
    B) Chinese
    C) Japanese
    D) British

    Answer: B Difficulty: Hard Page: 17

76. In the 1960s, the two most dominant countries in the world economy were:
    A) United States and Japan
    B) Britain and the United States
    C) United States and Germany
    D) Britain and Japan

    Answer: B Difficulty: Hard Page: 18

77. During the 1970s and 1980s, the foreign direct investment by non-U.S. firms was
    motivated primarily by the following two factors:
    A) the desire to disperse production activities to optimal locations; and the desire to
       build a direct presence in major foreign markets
    B) the desire to disperse production activities to optimal locations; and the desire to
       influence foreign exchange rates
    C) the desire to influence foreign exchange rates; and the desire to influence political
       developments in foreign countries
    D) the desire to build a direct presence in major foreign markets; and the desire to
       influence political developments in foreign countries

    Answer: A Difficulty: Medium Page: 18

Chapter 1 Globalization

78. During the 1970s and the 1980s, the foreign direct investment by non-U.S. firms was motivated primarily by the desire to disperse production activities to optimal locations and the desire to:
    A) build a direct presence in foreign markets
    B) influence foreign exchange rates
    C) influence political developments in foreign countries
    D) influence sociocultural developments in foreign countries

    Answer: A Difficulty: Medium Page: 18

79. The total cumulative value of foreign investments is referred to as the _____.
    A) accumulation of foreign direct investments
    B) portfolio of foreign direct investments
    C) stock of foreign direct investments
    D) set of foreign direct investments

    Answer: C Difficulty: Easy Page: 18

80. The amount of investments made across national boarders each years is called the

    _____.
    A) international foreign direct investment totality
    B) inclusive foreign direct investments
    C) totality of foreign direct investments
    D) flow of foreign direct investments

    Answer: D Difficulty: Easy Page: 19

81. During the 1990s, the percentage of foreign direct investment inflows accounted for by developing countries has:
    A) decreased
    B) never been determined
    C) remained constant
    D) increased

    Answer: D Difficulty: Easy Page: 19

Chapter 1 Globalization

82. During the 1990s, the percentage of foreign direct investment inflows accounted for by developed countries has:
   A) remained constant
   B) fluctuated wildly
   C) increased
   D) decreased

   Answer: D   Difficulty: Easy   Page: 19

83. The country that has received the greatest volume of inward FDI in recent years has been _____.
   A) Britain
   B) South Korea
   C) China
   D) United States

   Answer: C   Difficulty: Medium   Page: 19

84. A _____ enterprise is any business that has productive activities in two or more countries.
   A) cross-cultural
   B) multinational
   C) varied-national
   D) diverse-national

   Answer: B   Difficulty: Easy   Page: 19

85. A multinational enterprise is any business that has productive activities in:
   A) two or more countries
   B) five or more countries
   C) at lease one industrialized countries
   D) Europe, Asia, and North America

   Answer: A   Difficulty: Medium   Page: 19

Chapter 1 Globalization

86. General Electric Corporation has productive activities in a number of countries. As a result, it would be appropriate to refer to General Electric as a _____ corporation.
    A) transnational
    B) diverse-national
    C) crossnational
    D) multinational

    Answer: D Difficulty: Easy Page: 19

87. Since the 1960s, there have been two notable trends in the demographics of the multinational enterprise. These two trends have been:
    A) the rise of non-U.S. multinationals and the disappearance of mini-multinationals
    B) the decline of non-U.S. multinationals and the decline of mini-multinationals
    C) the decline of non-U.S. multinationals and the growth of mini-multinationals
    D) the rise of non-U.S. multinationals and the growth of mini-multinationals

    Answer: D Difficulty: Medium Page: 19

88. Since the 1960s, there have been two notable trends in the demographics of the multinational enterprise. These two trends have been the rise of non-U.S. multinationals and the:
    A) declining importance of multinationals
    B) declining profitability of multinationals
    C) growth of mini-multinationals
    D) disappearance of mini-multinationals

    Answer: C Difficulty: Medium Page: 19

89. The decline of the U.S. in its dominance of the global economy can be explained by two factors. These are:
    A) the globalization of the world economy and China's rise to the top rank of economic powers
    B) the fall of communism in Eastern Europe and the republics of the former Soviet Union and Japan's rise to the top rank of economic powers
    C) the globalization of the world economy and Japan's rise to the top rank of economic powers
    D) a decrease in trade barriers worldwide and China's rise in economic power

    Answer: C Difficulty: Medium Page: 20

Chapter 1 Globalization

90. Mini-multinationals are:
    A) multinational firms from relatively small countries
    B) multinational firms that have been involved in international business for less than five years
    C) multinational firms that operate in three or less foreign countries
    D) Medium-sized and small multinationals

    Answer: D   Difficulty: Easy   Page: 21

91. Apex Engineering is a small firm that operates in several different foreign countries. It would be appropriate to refer to Apex as a:
    A) aspiring-multinational
    B) mini-multinational
    C) insignificant-multinational
    D) emerging-multinational

    Answer: B   Difficulty: Easy   Page: 21

92. Which of the following statements is not true regarding potential business opportunities in the former Communist nations of Europe and Asia?
    A) the economies of most of the former Communist states are very strong
    B) many of the former Communist nations of Europe and Asia share a commitment to free market economies
    C) as a result of disturbing signs of growing unrest and totalitarian tendencies, the risks involved in doing business in these countries is very high
    D) for about half a century these countries were essentially closed to Western international business

    Answer: A   Difficulty: Medium   Page: 21

93. Which of the following statements is not true regarding the majority of Latin American countries?
    A) governments are selling state-owned enterprises to private investors
    B) foreign investment is welcome
    C) debt and inflation are down
    D) neither democracy nor free market reforms have seemed to take hold

    Answer: D   Difficulty: Medium   Page: 21

Chapter 1 Globalization

94. The last quarter of the 20th century experienced _____ in the global economy.
    A) increased stability
    B) slow-moving
    C) virtually no changes
    D) rapid changes

    Answer: D   Difficulty: Medium   Page: 23

95. Economists argue that increased international trade and cross-border investments will result in _____ prices for goods and services.
    A) higher
    B) stable
    C) lower
    D) unstable

    Answer: C   Difficulty: Easy   Page: 24

96. Which of the following is not a benefit of globalization?
    A) lower prices for goods
    B) raises the incomes of consumers
    C) slows economic growth
    D) helps to create jobs in all countries that choose to participate

    Answer: C   Difficulty: Medium   Page: 24

97. One frequently voiced concern about the effects of globalization is that it may:
    A) slow economic growth
    B) increase prices for goods
    C) lower the income of consumers
    D) destroy manufacturing jobs in wealthy advanced economies such as the U.S.

    Answer: D   Difficulty: Medium   Page: 25

Chapter 1 Globalization

98. One frequently voiced concern about globalization is that it destroys manufacturing jobs in wealthy advanced economies such as the U.S. The basic thrust of the critics' argument is:
    A) developing nations will recruit employees from the more advanced economies, thereby depleting their labor pools
    B) globalization increases the pace of the shift from a world economy based on manufactured goods to a world economy based on services
    C) falling trade barriers allows firms to move their manufacturing activities offshore to countries where wage rates are much lower
    D) the governments of developing countries will heavily subsidize their primary industries, making competing products produced in advanced economies less attractive

    Answer: C Difficulty: Hard Page: 25

99. Critics use the following argument to suggest that globalization is a contributing factor to an increase in pollution.
    A) globalization results in an increase in the amount of activity that takes place in companies that do not have adequate pollution controls
    B) globalization results in increased commerce between countries, which results in an increase in the amount of transportation activity (e.g. trains, barges, air cargo, trucks, etc.)
    C) firms that operate in countries that have adequate pollution regulations have a tendency to move their manufacturing operations to countries that have less stringent or no pollution controls to avoid the cost of regulation
    D) globalization results in increased production, which has the undesirable side-effect of increased pollution

    Answer: C Difficulty: Hard Page: 26

100. NAFTA stands for:
    A) North American Free Trade Agreement
    B) North Atlantic Free Trade Agency
    C) North American Federation of Trade Advocates
    D) National Alliance for Technology Advancement

    Answer: A Difficulty: Easy Page: 27

Chapter 1 Globalization

101. What is the primary purpose of the World Trade Organization?
    A) arbitrate trade disputes
    B) act as a "watchdog" for countries that lower their pollution standards in an effort to attract more foreign manufacturing activity
    C) set tariffs for countries that signed the GATT agreement
    D) monitor the implementation of trade agreements such as NAFTA

    Answer: A   Difficulty: Medium   Page: 27

102. In what way can the World Trade Organization (WTO) penalize member countries that are found to be engaged in unfair trade practices?
    A) the WTO can impose sanctions on the transgressor
    B) the WTO can bring the employees of offending companies to court
    C) the WTO can restrict the membership of the offending country in other world organizations such as the United Nations
    D) the WTO panel can issue a ruling instructing a member state to change trade policies that violate GATT regulations, and if the policies are not changed, allow other states to impose sanctions

    Answer: D   Difficulty: Medium   Page: 27

103. The minimum that a firm has to do to engage in international business is to:
    A) export or import
    B) invest directly in operations in another country
    C) establish joint ventures or strategic alliances with companies in other countries
    D) license products to companies in other countries

    Answer: A   Difficulty: Easy   Page: 28

104. Managing an international business is different from managing a purely domestic business for all of the following reasons except:
    A) countries are different
    B) international transactions involve converting money into different currencies
    C) the range of problems confronted by a manager in an international business are narrower than those confronted by a manager in a domestic business
    D) an international business must find ways to work within the limits imposed by government intervention in the international trade and investment system

    Answer: C   Difficulty: Medium   Page: 29

Chapter 1 Globalization

105. The _____ of production makes it increasingly irrelevant to talk about "American" products, "Japanese" products, or "German" products, since these products are made through components parts produced throughout the world.
    A) standardization
    B) alignment
    C) simplification
    D) globalization

    Answer: D Difficulty: Easy Page: 30

Essay Questions

106. Describe the concept of globalization. What are the major opportunities and challenges that globalization has created for business organization?

    Difficulty: Easy Page: 4

    Answer:
    Globalization refers to a fundamental shift that is occurring in the world economy. The world is progressively moving away from a structure in which national economies are relatively isolated from each other, towards a structure in which national economies are merging into one huge interdependent global economic system. This trend is commonly referred to as globalization.

    The trend towards globalization is creating many opportunities for businesses to expand their revenues, drive down their costs, and boost their profits. For example, many American firms are now exporting to previously closed foreign markets. By doing so, these firms are simultaneously expanding their sales and driving down their costs through additional economies of scale. Globalization has also created challenges for business organizations. For example, managers now have to grapple with a wide range of globalization related issues. Examples of these issues include: should we export, should we build a plant in a foreign country, should we modify our products to suite the tastes of each of our foreign customers, and how do we respond to foreign competition? These questions often do not have easy answers, but are very important to the future competitiveness of business organizations.

Chapter 1 Globalization

107. Describe the two main components of globalization. Explain how each of these components of globalization has helped create the shift towards a more integrated world economy.

Difficulty: Medium   Page: 6

Answer:
The two main components of globalization are the globalization of markets and the globalization of production. The globalization of markets refers to the fact that in many industries historically distinct and separate national markets are merging into one huge global marketplace. The globalization of production refers to the tendency among many firms to source goods and services from different locations around the world in an attempt to take advantage of national differences in the cost and quality of factors of production (such as labor, energy, and capital).

Both of these components of globalization have helped create the shift towards a more integrated world economy. The globalization of markets has created a "global" interest in many products, such as Coca-Cola, the Sony Walkman, and Levi jeans. This "sharing of interest" in products across national boarders has facilitated the trend towards a more integrated world economy. The globalization of production has resulted in a substantial increase in the number of business relationships between companies from different countries. This increase in the number and intensity of interrelationships between companies from different countries has also facilitated the trend towards a more integrated world economy.

108. Describe the meaning of the term "trade barriers"? What measures have been taken by the world community to reduce the impact of trade barriers on international trade?

Difficulty: Hard   Page: 8

Answer:
Trade barriers are the regulations, tariffs, and other activities that are put in place by governments for the purpose of protecting their domestic industries from "foreign competition." For example, a country may impose a stiff tariff on the import of foreign produced automobiles. That makes it very difficult (i.e., creates a substantial barrier) for foreign produced cars to be sold in their country.

Chapter 1 Globalization

The world community has taken a number of measures to not only lessen the impact of trade barriers on international trade, but to remove trade barriers altogether. The General Agreement on Tariffs and Trade (GATT) has been an ongoing effort to remove and reduce trade barriers worldwide. Under the umbrella of GATT, there have been eight rounds of negotiations among member states, which now number 120, designed to lower and/or reduce all forms of trade barriers. To provide the GATT treaty some teeth, the recently completed Uruguary Round of GATT established the World Trade Organization (WTO) which polices the international trading system. Although the WTO cannot compel a nation to comply with the GATT treaty, it can recommend that other member nations impose sanctions on the offending party.

Other business organizations, governments, trade groups, and not-for-profit organizations are working hard to reduce and remove trade barriers. As mentioned in the textbook, between 1991 and 1996 alone, more than 100 countries, rich and poor, made 599 changes to their laws governing investment by foreign businesses in their countries. Some 95 percent of these changes involved liberalizing a country's foreign investment regulations to make it easier for foreign companies to enter their markets.

109. Describe the impact of the development of the World Wide Web on global commerce?

Difficulty: Easy   Page: 12

Answer:
Viewed globally, the Web is emerging as the great equalizer. It is a powerful dislocating force that rolls back some constraints of location, scale, and time zones. The Web allows businesses, both small and large, to expand their global presence at a lower cost than ever before.

110. Define the term "foreign direct investment (FDI)." How does the term "foreign direct investment" differ from the term "international trade?"

Difficulty: Medium   Page: 18

Answer:
Foreign direct investment occurs when a firm invests resources in business activities outside its home country. For example, an American firm may invest in a production facility in Italy. International trade occurs when a firm exports goods or services to consumers in another country. The difference between the terms is that the term "international trade" does not necessarily mean that a firm is investing resources in business activities outside its home country. the firm could be simply exporting domestically produced products to a foreign country.

Chapter 1 Globalization

111. What is a multinational enterprise? What have been the two most notable trends in multinational enterprises since the 1960s? What is a mini-multinational? Do you expect the role of mini-multinationals to gain momentum or wane in the future? Why?

Difficulty: Easy   Page: 19

Answer:
A multinational enterprise is any business that has productive activities in two or more countries. There are many multinational enterprises, including General Motors, Sony, General Electric, Exxon, and Toyota. The two most notable trends in multinational enterprises since the 1960s have been (1) the rise of non-U.S. multinationals, particularly Japanese multinationals; and (2) the growth of mini-multinationals.

Mini-multinationals are small and medium-sized international firms. The role of these firms is likely to gain momentum in the future. Many small and medium-sized companies are becoming increasingly involved in international trade, in a variety of different contexts. As these companies expand their international activities, they will increasingly take their place as mini-multinationals on the world stage.

112. Discuss the primary advantages and disadvantages of globalization. Do you believe the advantages outweigh the disadvantages? How can the effects of the disadvantages of globalization be reduced?

Difficulty: Medium   Page: 24

Answer:
There are many advantages of globalization. From a broad perspective, globalization creates economic activity (which stimulates economic growth), creates jobs, raises income levels, and provides consumers with more choices in regard to the products and services that are available to them. From the perspective of an individual firm, globalization has the potential to increase revenues (through expanded market potential), drive down costs (through additional economies of scale), and boost profits.

Chapter 1 Globalization

Conversely, critics argue that globalization destroys manufacturing jobs in wealthy countries and contributes to pollution. In regard to destroying manufacturing jobs, the basic thrust of the critics argument is that falling trade barriers allow firms in industrialized countries to move their manufacturing activities offshore to countries where wage rates are much lower. This activity, if it occurs, has the undesirable side-effect of eliminating manufacturing jobs in the industrialized country. In regard to pollution, the critics of globalization argue that globalization encourages firms from advanced nations to move manufacturing facilities offshore to less developed countries to avoid the more stringent pollution controls in place in their home countries. This activity increases worldwide pollution.

The final section of the question is designed to encourage classroom discussion and/or to encourage students to "think" about how these undesirable side-effects of globalization can be reduced.

Chapter 2 Country Differences in Politics

True/False Questions

1. The term collectivism refers to a system that stresses the primacy of collective goals over individual goals.

   Answer: True   Difficulty: Easy   Page: 41

2. Political systems that emphasize collectivism tend to be totalitarian, while political systems that place a high value on individualism tend to be democratic.

   Answer: True   Difficulty: Hard   Page: 41

3. There is essentially no relationship between collectivism and socialism.

   Answer: False   Difficulty: Easy   Page: 41

4. Individualism is similar to collectivism. In a political sense, individualism refers to a philosophy that an individual should have freedom in his or her economic and political pursuits.

   Answer: False   Difficulty: Medium   Page: 43

5. Totalitarianism is a form of government in which one person or political party exercises absolute control over all spheres of human life, and opposing political parties are prohibited.

   Answer: True   Difficulty: Medium   Page: 44

6. The four major forms of totalitarianism are: communist totalitarianism, theocratic totalitarianism, tribal totalitarianism, and right-wing totalitarianism.

   Answer: True   Difficulty: Medium   Page: 45

7. Tribal totalitarianism is found in states where political power is monopolized by a party, group, or individual that governs according to religious principles.

   Answer: False   Difficulty: Hard   Page: 45

Chapter 2 Country Differences in Politics

8. In a market economy the goods and services that a country produces, and the quantity in which they are produced, is not planned by anyone. Rather, it is determined by the interaction of supply and demand and signaled to producers through the price system.

    Answer: True   Difficulty: Easy   Page: 45

9. For a market economy to work, there must be no restrictions on supply.

    Answer: True   Difficulty: Medium   Page: 46

10. In a pure command economy, the goods and services that a country produces, the quantity in which they are produced, and the prices at which they are sold are all planned by the government.

    Answer: True   Difficulty: Medium   Page: 46

11. Command economies are relatively common among the states of Western Europe, although they are becoming less so. France, Italy, and Sweden can all be classified as command economies.

    Answer: False   Difficulty: Medium   Page: 46

12. A copyright grants the inventor of a new product or process exclusive right to the manufacture, use, or sales of that invention.

    Answer: False   Difficulty: Easy   Page: 50

13. A patent grants the investor of a new product or process exclusive rights to the manufacture, use, or sale of that invention.

    Answer: True   Difficulty: Easy   Page: 50

14. Patents are designs and names, often officially registered, by which merchants or manufacturers designate and differentiate their products (e.g., Christian Dior clothes).

    Answer: False   Difficulty: Medium   Page: 50

15. Historically, the enforcement of intellectual property rights has been fairly consistent across countries.

    Answer: False   Difficulty: Medium   Page: 50

Chapter 2 Country Differences in Politics

16. The Paris Convention for the Protection of Industrial Property is an international agreement signed by 96 countries to protect intellectual property rights.

    Answer: True   Difficulty: Medium   Page: 50

17. Civil law is based on a very detailed set of laws that are organized into codes.

    Answer: True   Difficulty: Easy   Page: 54

18. The Human Development Index is based on three measures: per capita income, life expectancy, and poverty rate.

    Answer: False   Difficulty: Hard   Page: 57

19. Privatization refers to the selling of state-owned enterprises to private investors.

    Answer: True   Difficulty: Medium   Page: 60

20. The Foreign Corrupt Practices Act is a U.S. law enacted in 1977 that prohibits U.S. companies from making "corrupt" payments to foreign officials for the purpose of obtaining or retaining business.

    Answer: True   Difficulty: Medium   Page: 78

Multiple Choice Questions

21. Every country has a political, economic, and legal system. Collectively we refer to these systems as constituting the _____ economy of a country.
    A) domestic
    B) civic
    C) administrative
    D) political

    Answer: D   Difficulty: Easy   Page: 41

Chapter 2 Country Differences in Politics

22. England, France, and Germany all have unique political, economic, and legal systems. A country's political, economic, and legal system is collectively referred to as its _____ economy.
    A) political
    B) formal
    C) administrative
    D) official

    Answer: A Difficulty: Easy Page: 41

23. A nation's system of government is referred to as its _____ system.
    A) political
    B) administrative
    C) economic
    D) bureaucratic

    Answer: A Difficulty: Easy Page: 41

24. Political systems can be assessed according to two related dimensions. These are:
    A) the degree to which they emphasize individualism opposed to totalitarian and the degree to which they are individualistic verses democratic
    B) the degree to which they are market orientated opposed to production orientated and the degree to which they are democratic verses individualistic
    C) the degree to which they emphasize social democracy opposed to communism and the degree to which they emphasize collectivism opposed to individualism
    D) the degree to which they emphasize collectivism opposed to individualism and the degree to which they are democratic or totalitarian

    Answer: D Difficulty: Hard Page: 41

25. Political systems can be assessed according to two related dimensions. These are the degree to which they emphasize collectivism opposed to individualism and:
    A) the degree to which they are democratic or totalitarian
    B) the degree they are market oriented opposed to production oriented
    C) the degree to which they are Muslin or Christian
    D) the degree to which they are proactive or reactive

    Answer: A Difficulty: Medium Page: 41

Chapter 2 Country Differences in Politics

26. The term _____ refers to a system that stresses the primacy of collective goals over individual goals.
    A) collectivism
    B) capitalism
    C) individualism
    D) totalitarian

    Answer: A   Difficulty: Easy   Page: 41

27. When _____ is practiced, the needs of society as a whole are generally viewed as being more important than individual freedoms.
    A) totalitarianism
    B) collectivism
    C) individualism
    D) capitalism

    Answer: B   Difficulty: Easy   Page: 41

28. Which of the following political systems is consistent with the notion that an individual's right to do something may be restricted because it runs counter to "the good of society" or "the common good."
    A) totalitarian
    B) collectivism
    C) autocratic
    D) capitalism

    Answer: B   Difficulty: Medium   Page: 41

29. _____ trace their intellectual roots to Karl Marx.
    A) Separatists
    B) Capitalists
    C) Individualists
    D) Socialists

    Answer: D   Difficulty: Medium   Page: 41

Chapter 2 Country Differences in Politics

30. The group that believed that socialism could be achieved only through violent revolution and totalitarian dictatorship were referred to as:
    A) communists
    B) fascists
    C) political democrats
    D) collectivists

    Answer: A   Difficulty: Medium   Page: 41

31. Followers of socialists ideology who commit themselves to achieving socialism through democratic reforms are called:
    A) communists
    B) social democrats
    C) individualists
    D) political democrats

    Answer: B   Difficulty: Medium   Page: 42

32. The group that was committed to achieving socialism by democratic means were referred to as:
    A) collectivists
    B) communists
    C) social democrats
    D) fascists

    Answer: C   Difficulty: Medium   Page: 42

33. The last major Communist power left is _____.
    A) Finland
    B) China
    C) Brazil
    D) South Korea

    Answer: B   Difficulty: Easy   Page: 42

34. Social democracy has had its greatest influence in the following group of countries:
    A) Canada, United States, Mexico, and Spain
    B) India, Pakistan, Burma, Nepal, Sri Lanka, and Bhutan
    C) Brazil, Chile, Uruguay, Ecuador, Columbia, and French Guiana
    D) Australia, Britain, France, Germany, Norway, Spain, and Sweden

    Answer: D   Difficulty: Hard   Page: 42

Chapter 2 Country Differences in Politics

35. Experience has demonstrated that state ownership of the means of production:
    A) often runs in parallel with the public interest
    B) is the most profitable way to organize production
    C) is the most efficient way to organize production
    D) often runs counter to the public interest

    Answer: D   Difficulty: Medium   Page: 42

36. Which of the following definitions best describes the concept of individualism?
    A) Political philosophy that an individual should have freedom over his or her economic and political pursuits.
    B) Political system in which government is by the people, exercised either directly or through elected representatives.
    C) Political system that stresses the primacy of collective goals over individual goals.
    D) Form of government in which one person or political party exercises absolute control over all spheres of human life and in which opposing political parties are prohibited.

    Answer: A   Difficulty: Medium   Page: 42

37. The philosophy that is based on the idea that an individual should have freedom in his or her economic pursuits is called:
    A) individualism
    B) socialism
    C) totalitarianism
    D) collectivism

    Answer: A   Difficulty: Easy   Page: 42

38. In contrast to collectivism, _____ stresses that the interests of the individual should take precedence over the interests of the state.
    A) totalitarianism
    B) socialism
    C) individualism
    D) collectivism

    Answer: C   Difficulty: Easy   Page: 42

Chapter 2 Country Differences in Politics

39. Individualism is built on two central tenets:
    A) socialism is the preferred political philosophy and an emphasis on the importance of collective interests over individual interests
    B) an emphasis on the importance of collective interests over individual interests and the belief that the welfare of society is best served by letting a collective body determine what is in society's best interest rather than individuals
    C) the needs of society as a whole are more important than individual freedoms and the welfare of society is best served by letting a collective body determine what is in society's best interest rather than individuals
    D) an emphasis on the importance of guaranteeing individual freedom and self expression and the belief that the welfare of society is best served by letting people pursue their own economic self-interest.

    Answer: D Difficulty: Medium Page: 43

40. The Cold War was essentially a war between _____, championed by the now-defunct Soviet Union, and _____, championed by the United States.
    A) collectivism, individualism
    B) democracy, socialism
    C) socialism, totalitarianism
    D) individualism, collectivism

    Answer: A Difficulty: Medium Page: 44

41. The political system in which government is by the people, exercised either directly or through elected representatives is referred to as:
    A) despotism
    B) democracy
    C) totalitarianism
    D) collectivism

    Answer: B Difficulty: Easy Page: 44

42. _____ is a form of government in which one person or political party exercises absolute control over all spheres of human life, and opposing political parties are prohibited.
    A) Capitalism
    B) Totalitarianism
    C) Democracy
    D) Collectivism

    Answer: B Difficulty: Easy Page: 44

43. Which of the following political philosophies go "hand-in-hand?"
    A) democracy and individualism
    B) collectivism and individualism
    C) totalitarianism and democracy
    D) democracy and collectivism

    Answer: A Difficulty: Medium Page: 44

44. A political system in which citizens periodically elect individuals to represent them is referred to as a _____.
    A) participatory collective
    B) totalitarianism democracy
    C) representative democracy
    D) socialistic democracy

    Answer: C Difficulty: Easy Page: 44

45. To guarantee that elected representatives can be held accountable for their actions by the electorate, an ideal representative democracy has a number of safeguards. Which of the following is not an example of a safeguard in a ideal respresentative democracy?
    A) a fair court system that is independent from the political system
    B) universal adult suffrage
    C) an individual's right to freedom of expression, opinion, and organization
    D) a political police force and armed services

    Answer: D Difficulty: Medium Page: 44

46. A form of totalitarianism that advocates achieving socialism through totalitarian dictatorship is called _____.
    A) tribal totalitarianism
    B) democratic totalitarianism
    C) communist totalitarianism
    D) collective totalitarianism

    Answer: C Difficulty: Medium Page: 45

Chapter 2 Country Differences in Politics

47. There are four major forms of totalitarianism in the world today. These are:
    A) collective, Marxist, right-wing, and ancestral
    B) theocratic, democratic, tribal, and communist
    C) communist, theocratic, tribal, and right-wing
    D) ancestral, Marxist, left-wing, and compiled

    Answer: C Difficulty: Hard Page: 45

48. All of the following are forms of totalitarianism except:
    A) right-wind
    B) ancestral
    C) theocratic
    D) tribal

    Answer: B Difficulty: Medium Page: 45

49. A form of totalitarianism in which political power is monopolized by a party, group, or individual that governs according to religious principles is called _____.
    A) right-wing totalitarianism
    B) theocratic totalitarianism
    C) ancestral totalitarianism
    D) tribal totalitarianism

    Answer: B Difficulty: Medium Page: 45

50. In which region of the world is tribal totalitarianism found?
    A) Africa
    B) Australia
    C) South America
    D) Asia

    Answer: A Difficulty: Hard Page: 45

51. Right-wing _____ generally permits individual economic freedom, but restricts individual political freedom on the grounds that it would lead to a rise of communism.
    A) socialism
    B) collectivism
    C) capitalism
    D) totalitarianism

    Answer: D Difficulty: Medium Page: 45

Chapter 2 Country Differences in Politics

52. The four broad types of economic systems are:
    A) market economy, combined economy, production economy, and service economy
    B) market economy, command economy, mixed economy, and state-directed economy
    C) combined economy, separate economy, mixed economy, and production economy
    D) ordinance economy, production economy, political economy, and separate economy

    Answer: B Difficulty: Medium Page: 45

53. Which of the following is not one of the four broad types of economic system?
    A) state-directed economy
    B) command economy
    C) mixed economy
    D) progressive economy

    Answer: D Difficulty: Medium Page: 45

54. In a pure _____ economy the good and services that a country products, and the quantity in which they are produced, is not planned by anyone. Rather it is determined by the interaction of supply and demand and signaled to producers through the price system.
    A) ordinance
    B) market
    C) command
    D) combined

    Answer: B Difficulty: Easy Page: 45

55. In a pure command economy the goods and services that a country produces, the quantity in which they are produced, and the prices at which they are sold are all planned by:
    A) private industry
    B) local trade associations
    C) individual entrepreneurs
    D) the government

    Answer: D Difficulty: Medium Page: 46

Chapter 2 Country Differences in Politics

56. An economic system in which the goods and services produced, the quantity in which they are produced, and the prices at which they are sold are all planned by the government is referred to as a:
    A) civic economy
    B) administrative economy
    C) command economy
    D) market economy

    Answer: C Difficulty: Easy Page: 46

57. In a pure _____ economy all businesses are state owned so the government can direct them to make investments that are in the best interests of the nation as a whole, rather than in the interest of private individuals.
    A) command
    B) mixed
    C) market
    D) state-directed

    Answer: A Difficulty: Medium Page: 46

58. In a _____ economy, certain sectors of the economy are left to private ownership and free market mechanisms, while in other sectors there is significant state ownership and government planning.
    A) command
    B) combined
    C) mixed
    D) political

    Answer: C Difficulty: Easy Page: 47

59. _____ economies are relatively common in Western Europe, although they are becoming less so.
    A) Mixed
    B) State-directed
    C) Command
    D) Market

    Answer: A Difficulty: Medium Page: 47

Chapter 2 Country Differences in Politics

60. A _____ economy is one in which the state plays a significant in directing investment activities of private enterprise through "industrial policy" and in otherwise regulating business activity in accordance with national goals.
    A) market
    B) state-directed
    C) mixed
    D) command

    Answer: B   Difficulty: Medium   Page: 47

61. Which of the following countries are frequently cited as examples of state-directed economies?
    A) Germany and France
    B) Canada and the United States
    C) Brazil and Mexico
    D) South Korea and Japan

    Answer: D   Difficulty: Hard   Page: 47

62. The _____ of a country refers to the rules that regulate behavior, along with the processes by which the laws of a country are enforced and through which redress for grievances is obtained.
    A) political system
    B) administrative system
    C) economic structure
    D) legal system

    Answer: D   Difficulty: Easy   Page: 48

63. _____ rights refer to the bundle of legal rights over the use to which a resource is put and over the use made of any income that may be derived form that resource.
    A) Statutory
    B) Asset
    C) Taxable
    D) Property

    Answer: D   Difficulty: Easy   Page: 49

64. Which of the following describes the concept of intellectual property?
    A) Exclusive legal rights of authors, composers, playwrights, artists, and publishers to publish and dispose of their work as they see fit.
    B) Property, such as computer software, screenplays, musical scores, or chemical formulas for new drugs, that is the product of intellectual activity.
    C) Designs and names, often officially registered, by which merchants or manufacturers designate and differentiate their products.
    D) Document giving the inventor of a new product or process exclusive rights to the manufacturer, use, or sales of that invention.

    Answer: B Difficulty: Medium Page: 50

65. Suppose you invent a new product and want to obtain the exclusive rights to manufacture the product. To protect yourself, you should apply for a _____ on the product.
    A) trust
    B) patent
    C) copyright
    D) trademark

    Answer: B Difficulty: Easy Page: 5

66. Suppose 3-M corporation develops a new type of adhesive tape. 3-M can protect its invention through _____ protection.
    A) warrant
    B) patent
    C) copyright
    D) trademark

    Answer: B Difficulty: Medium Page: 50

67. A _____ grants the inventor of a new product or process exclusive rights to the manufacture, use, or sale of that invention.
    A) trademark
    B) warrant
    C) patent
    D) copyright

    Answer: C Difficulty: Easy Page: 50

68. _____ are the exclusive legal rights of authors, composers, playwrights, artists, and publishers to publish and dispose of their work as they see fit.
   A) Patents
   B) Copyrights
   C) Trusts
   D) Licenses

   Answer: B   Difficulty: Easy   Page: 50

69. A composer is able to protect an original musical score from being copied and sold by someone else through _____ protection.
   A) patent
   B) warrant
   C) trademark
   D) copyright

   Answer: D   Difficulty: Medium   Page: 50

70. _____ are designs and names, often officially registered, by which merchants or manufacturers designate and differentiate their products.
   A) Copyrights
   B) Patents
   C) Warrants
   D) Trademarks

   Answer: D   Difficulty: Easy   Page: 50

71. The Nike "swoosh" logo is protected from being used by any other shoe manufacturer as a result of _____ protection.
   A) trademark
   B) copyright
   C) patent
   D) warrant

   Answer: A   Difficulty: Medium   Page: 50

72. Patents, copyrights, and trademarks are examples of _____ property laws.
   A) intellectual
   B) administrative
   C) official
   D) central

   Answer: A   Difficulty: Medium   Page: 50

Chapter 2 Country Differences in Politics

73. "Windows" is a computer operating system that is an exclusive _____ of the Microsoft corporation.
    A) sticker
    B) hallmark
    C) registry
    D) trademark

    Answer: D Difficulty: Easy Page: 50

74. According to our textbook, the _____ industry suffers the most from lax enforcement of intellectual property rights.
    A) book
    B) consumer electronics
    C) computer software
    D) prescription drug

    Answer: C Difficulty: Hard Page: 51

75. _____ liability involves holding a firm and its officers responsible when a product causes injury, death, or damage.
    A) Turnout
    B) Contract
    C) Product
    D) Outcome

    Answer: C Difficulty: Easy Page: 52

76. A _____ is a document that specifies the conditions under which an exchange is to occur, and details the rights and obligations of the parties involved.
    A) patent
    B) compact
    C) treaty
    D) contract

    Answer: D Difficulty: Easy Page: 53

77. There are two main legal traditions found in the world today. These are:
    A) administrative law system and civil law system
    B) common law system and mutual law system
    C) interdependent law system and independent law system
    D) common law system and civil law system

    Answer: D Difficulty: Medium Page: 52

78. The legal system that is based on a detailed set of laws, organized into codes, that is used in more than 80 countries is referred to as:
    A) civil law system
    B) criminal law system
    C) multi-level system
    D) administrative law system

    Answer: A Difficulty: Medium Page: 53

79. The legal system based on tradition, precedent, and custom that evolved in England over hundreds of years and is now found in Britain's former colonies, including the United States, is called:
    A) multi-level legal system
    B) civil law system
    C) common law system
    D) administrative law system

    Answer: C Difficulty: Medium Page: 54

80. Which of the following statement is true?
    A) Civil law tends to be relatively ill-specified
    B) Criminal law is the body of law that governs contract enforcement
    C) Civil law is based on a very detailed set of laws that are organized into codes
    D) The civil law system evolved in England over one hundred years ago. It is now found in most of Britain's former colonies, including the United States.

    Answer: C Difficulty: Hard Page: 54

81. GDP is an acronym that stands for:
    A) gross domestic profile
    B) gross domestic product
    C) gradual demographic profile
    D) general domestic productivity

    Answer: B Difficulty: Easy Page: 54

82. PPP is an acronym that stands for:
    A) power purchasing procedures
    B) procurement priority procedures
    C) priority patent procedures
    D) purchasing power parity

    Answer: D Difficulty: Medium Page: 54

83. The United Nations _____ index is based on life expectancy, literacy rates, and whether average incomes are sufficient to meet the basic needs of life in a country.
    A) Human Development
    B) Standard of Living
    C) Quality of Life
    D) Economic Development

    Answer: A Difficulty: Medium Page: 57

84. The United Nations Human Development index is based on the following three measures.
    A) standard of living, quality of transportation, and life expectancy
    B) access to medical care, access to education, and life expectancy
    C) access to education, literacy rates, and whether average incomes, based on PPP estimates, are sufficient to meet the basic needs of life in a country.
    D) life expectancy, literacy rates, and whether average incomes, based on PPP estimates, are sufficient to meet the basic needs of life in a country

    Answer: D Difficulty: Hard Page: 57

85. The Human Development Index is scaled from 0 to 100. Countries scoring less than _____ are classified as low human development (the quality of life is poor).
    A) 25
    B) 50
    C) 75
    D) 33.3

    Answer: B Difficulty: Hard Page: 57

86. There is general agreement that _____ is the engine of long-run economic growth.
    A) small business
    B) government
    C) innovation
    D) agriculture

    Answer: C Difficulty: Medium Page: 57

Chapter 2 Country Differences in Politics

87. The process through which people create new products, new processes, new organization, new management practices, and new strategies is called:
    A) bureaucracy
    B) administration
    C) development
    D) innovation

    Answer: D   Difficulty: Easy   Page: 57

88. It has been argued that the economic freedom associated with a _____ economy creates greater incentives for innovation than either a planned or mixed economy.
    A) production
    B) market
    C) commercial
    D) manufacturing

    Answer: B   Difficulty: Medium   Page: 60

89. The process of selling state-owned enterprises to private investors is called:
    A) political-economic divestiture
    B) privatization
    C) downsizing
    D) ownership-transfer

    Answer: B   Difficulty: Easy   Page: 60

90. _____ is the process of selling state-owned enterprises to private investors.
    A) Downsizing
    B) Capitalization
    C) Ownership-transfer
    D) Privatization

    Answer: D   Difficulty: Easy   Page: 60

91. Privatization refers to:
    A) the selling of state-owned enterprises to private investors
    B) the selling of public corporations to private investors
    C) guarding company secrets from the general public
    D) transferring political power from the government to private citizens

    Answer: A   Difficulty: Medium   Page: 60

Chapter 2 Country Differences in Politics

92. Since the late 1980s two major trends have emerged in the political economies of many of the world's national states. These are:
    A) a wave of communist revolutions have swept the world and there has been a strong move away from free market economies toward more centrally planned economies.
    B) a wave of socialistic revolutions have swept the world and there has been a strong move away from free market economies toward more centrally planned and mixed economies.
    C) a wave of democratic revolutions have swept the world and there has been a strong move away from centrally planned and mixed economies toward more free market economies.
    D) a wave of totalitarian revolutions have swept the world and there has been a strong move away from centrally planned and mixed economies toward more free market economies.

    Answer: C Difficulty: Hard Page: 63

93. Which of the following is not one of the three main reasons for the spread of democracy worldwide?
    A) the spread of democracy has been unchallenged worldwide
    B) in many countries the economic advances of the past 25 years have led to the emergence of increasingly prosperous middle and working classes, which have pushed for democratic reforms
    C) the spread of new information and communications technology
    D) many totalitarian regimes failed to deliver economic progress to most of their populations

    Answer: A Difficulty: Hard Page: 65

94. _____ involves removing legal restrictions to the free play of markets, the establishment of private enterprises, and the manner in which private enterprises operate.
    A) Privatization
    B) Simplification
    C) Deregulation
    D) Socialism

    Answer: C Difficulty: Medium Page: 69

Chapter 2 Country Differences in Politics

95. The _____ movement started in Britain in the early 1980s when then-Prime Minister Margaret Thatcher started to sell state-owned assets.
    A) modification
    B) simplification
    C) privatization
    D) deregulation

    Answer: C Difficulty: Medium Page: 71

96. Advantages that accrue to early entrants into a business market are referred to as:
    A) standard-class advantages
    B) first-mover advantages
    C) prime-mover advantages
    D) first-stage advantages

    Answer: B Difficulty: Easy Page: 74

97. _____ accrue to early entrants into a business market.
    A) Prime-mover advantages
    B) Standard-class advantages
    C) First-class advantages
    D) First-mover advantages

    Answer: D Difficulty: Easy Page: 74

98. Handicaps suffered by late entrants into a business market are referred to as:
    A) late-mover disadvantages
    B) last-class disadvantages
    C) late-mover stumbling blocks
    D) late-mover difficulties

    Answer: A Difficulty: Easy Page: 74

99. In the language of business strategy, early entrants into potential future economic stars may be able to reap substantial _____ advantages, while late entrants may fall victim to _____ disadvantages.
    A) first-mover, late-mover
    B) initial-mover, last-mover
    C) first-class, final-class
    D) economic, financial

    Answer: A Difficulty: Medium Page: 74

100. The likelihood that political forces will cause drastic changes in a country's business environment that adversely affect the profit and other goals of a particular business enterprise is referred to as:
    A) political risk
    B) democratic risk
    C) administrative risk
    D) governmental risk

    Answer: A   Difficulty: Easy   Page: 75

101. The likelihood that economic mismanagement will cause drastic changes in a country's business environment that adversely affect the profit and other goals of a business enterprise is called:
    A) industrial risk
    B) commercial risk
    C) legal risk
    D) economic risk

    Answer: D   Difficulty: Medium   Page: 75

102. _____ is defined as the likelihood that economic mismanagement will cause drastic changes in a country's business environment that adversely affect the profit and other goals of a business enterprise.
    A) Financial risk
    B) Commercial risk
    C) Industrial risk
    D) Economic risk

    Answer: D   Difficulty: Medium   Page: 75

103. The likelihood that a trading partner will opportunistically break a contract or expropriate property rights is called:
    A) legitimate risk
    B) permissible risk
    C) constitutional risk
    D) legal risk

    Answer: D   Difficulty: Easy   Page: 76

Chapter 2 Country Differences in Politics

104. The _____ is a U.S. law enacted in 1977 that prohibits U.S. companies from making "corrupt" payments to foreign officials for the purpose of obtaining or retaining business.
    A) Foreign Corrupt Practices Act
    B) Federal Mercenary Practices Act
    C) Federal Corrupt Behavior Act
    D) Foreign Mercenary Practices Act

    Answer: A Difficulty: Easy Page: 78

105. The Foreign Corrupt Practices Act is a U.S. law enacted in 1977 that prohibits U.S. companies from:
    A) making products in overseas markets that do not comply with the same safety and environmental regulations as domestically produced products.
    B) exporting to countries that do not comply with United Nations human rights regulations.
    C) making "corrupt" payments to foreign officials for the purpose of obtaining or retaining business.
    D) exporting to countries that are not members of the World Trade Organization
    E) selling products for corrupt, unethical, or illegal purposes

    Answer: C Difficulty: Hard Page: 78

Essay Questions

106. What is meant by the term "political system?" What are the two related dimensions by which a political system can be assessed?

    Difficulty: Easy Page: 41

    Answer:
    A country's "political system" is its system of government. Political systems can be assessed according to two related dimensions. The first is the degree to which they emphasize collectivism as opposed to individualism. The second dimension is the degree to which they are democratic or totalitarian.

Chapter 2 Country Differences in Politics

107. Describe the difference between collectivism and individualism. Are these two ideologies compatible or in direct conflict? Which ideology seems to be gaining ground and which ideology is waning? Is this good news or bad news for international commerce? Explain your answer.

Difficulty: Medium   Page: 41

Answer:
The term collectivism refers to a political system that stresses the primacy of collective goals over individual goals. The general ideal is that the needs of society as a whole are more important than individual freedoms. As a result, in a collectivist society, an individual's right to do something may be restricted because it runs counter to "the good of the society" or the "common good."

108. Individualism refers to a philosophy that an individual should have freedom in his or her economic and political pursuits. Moreover, individualism stresses that the interests of the individual should take precedence over the interests of the state.

The ideals exposed by individualism and collectivism are in direct conflict with one another. Over the past two decades, collectivism has been waning and individualism has been gaining steam. A wave of democratic ideals and free market economics is currently sweeping away socialism and communism worldwide. Evidence of this can be seen in Eastern Europe and the republics of the former Soviet Union. According to the author of the textbook, this represent good news for international business, since the pro-business and pro-free trade values of individualism create a favorable environment within which international business can thrive.
Draw a distinction between democracy and totalitarianism. Which political system facilitates the development of a free market economic system? Why?

Difficulty: Medium   Page: 44

Answer:
Democracy and totalitarianism are at different ends of the political spectrum. Democracy refers to a political system in which government is by the people, exercised either directly or through elected representatives. Totalitarianism is a form of government in which one person or political parties exercise absolute control over all spheres of human life, and opposing political parties are prohibited. Most modern democratic states practice what is commonly referred to as representative democracy. In a representative democracy, citizens periodically elect individuals to represent them. There are four major forms of totalitarianism, including communist totalitarianism, theocratic totalitarianism, tribal totalitarianism, and right-wing totalitarianism.

Chapter 2 Country Differences in Politics

109. A democratic political system facilitates the development of a free market economy. A democratic system favors the primacy of individual goals over collective goals, which facilitates the development of free markets.
Draw a distinction between democracy and totalitarianism. Which political system facilitates the development of a free market economic system? Why?

Difficulty: Medium   Page: 44

Answer:
Democracy and totalitarianism are at different ends of the political spectrum. Democracy refers to a political system in which government is by the people, exercised either directly or through elected representatives. Totalitarianism is a form of government in which one person or political parties exercise absolute control over all spheres of human life, and opposing political parties are prohibited. Most modern democratic states practice what is commonly referred to as representative democracy. In a representative democracy, citizens periodically elect individuals to represent them. There are four major forms of totalitarianism, including communist totalitarianism, theocratic totalitarianism, tribal totalitarianism, and right-wing totalitarianism.

110. A democratic political system facilitates the development of a free market economy. A democratic system favors the primacy of individual goals over collective goals, which facilitates the development of free markets.
What is intellectual property? What is the philosophy behind intellectual property law? Why is it so important to protect intellectual property rights? Are the laws that protect intellectual property rights fairly consistent across nations, or do they vary widely? Is this a problem?

Difficulty: Medium   Page: 50

Answer:
Intellectual property refers to property, such as computer software, a screenplay, a music score, or the chemical formula for a new drug, that is the product of intellectual activity. The philosophy behind intellectual property law is to reward the originator of a new invention, book, musical record, clothes design, and the like for his or her new idea. Without strict intellectual property laws, there would be very little incentive for an individual to work hard to create these types of items. For instance, a person could work very hard and spend huge amounts of money to create a new animated film, and have someone else duplicate the film for the cost of a film duplicating machine and a blank tape.

Chapter 2 Country Differences in Politics

111. Unfortunately, the protection of intellectual property rights varies greatly from country to country. This is a problem. Weak laws or the weak enforcement of intellectual property laws in foreign countries encourages the piracy of intellectual property. The world community is addressing this problem, but a satisfactory solution to this problem has yet to be found.

    How important is innovation?. Does innovation have a better chance of catching hold in a market economy or a planned economy? Explain your answer.

    Difficulty: Easy   Page: 57

    Answer:
    There is general agreement that innovation is the engine of long-run economic growth in virtually any country. Innovation has a much better chance of catching hold in a market economy opposed to a planned economy. The individual freedom (and opportunity for personal gain) associated with a market economy (like the economy in the U.S.) creates greater incentives for innovation than either a planned or mixed economy. In a market economy, anyone who has an innovative idea is free to try to develop the idea, and has the potential to reap substantial personal gain. This feature of a market economy provides a powerful incentive for people to work on innovative ideas. In contrast, in a planned economy the state owns all means of production. Consequently there is no incentive or opportunity for entrepreneurial individuals to try to develop valuable new innovations, since it is the state, rather than the individual, that captures all of the gains.

112. What is the difference between political risk, economic risk, and legal risk?

    Difficulty: Hard   Page: 75

    Answer:
    Political risk is the likelihood that political forces will cause drastic changes in a country's business environment that adversely affect the profit and other goals of a business enterprise. In contrast, economic risk is the likelihood that economic mismanagement will cause drastic changes in a country's business environment that adversely affect the profit and other goals of a business enterprise. Finally, legal risk is the likelihood that a trading partner will opportunistically break a contract or expropriate property rights.

Chapter 2 Country Differences in Politics

113. One major ethical dilemma facing firms from Western democracies is whether they should do business in totalitarian countries that routinely violate the human rights of their citizens. What is the principle argument on both sides of this issue? What is your opinion?

Difficulty: Medium   Page: 76

Answer:
This question is designed to stimulate classroom discussion and/or encourage your students to think about a difficult ethical issue. The two sides to the debate alluded to above are as follows:

Arguments against Western democracies doing business in totalitarian countries:
Some people argue that investing in totalitarian countries provides comfort to dictators and can help prop up repressive regimes that abuse basic human rights. Moreover, these critics argue that without the participation of Western investors in their economies, many repressive regimes would collapse and be replaced by more democratically inclined governments.

Arguments in favor of Western democracies doing business in totalitarian countries:
In contrast, there are those who argue that investment by a Western firm, by raising the level of economic development of a totalitarian country, can help change it from within. They note that economic well being and political well being often go hand-in-hand.

Chapter 3 Differences in Culture

True/False Questions

1. Culture is a system of values and norms that are shared among a group of people and that when taken together constitute a design for living.

   Answer: True   Difficulty: Easy   Page: 88

2. Norms are abstract ideas about what a group believes to be good, right, and desirable.

   Answer: False   Difficulty: Medium   Page: 88

3. Folkways are the routine conventions of everyday life.

   Answer: True   Difficulty: Easy   Page: 88

4. Mores are norms that are central to the functioning of a society and to its social life.

   Answer: True   Difficulty: Easy   Page: 89

5. In terms of social structure, Western societies tend to emphasize the primacy of the group, while individuals tend to figure much larger in many other societies.

   Answer: False   Difficulty: Medium   Page: 90

6. A group is an association of two or more individuals who have a shared sense of identity and who interact with each other in structured ways on the basis of a common set of expectations about each other's behavior.

   Answer: True   Difficulty: Easy   Page: 91

7. Class consciousness refers to a condition where people tend to perceive themselves in terms of their class background, and this shapes their relationships with members of other classes.

   Answer: True   Difficulty: Medium   Page: 95

8. The relationship among religion, ethics, and society is straightforward and relatively easy to discern.

   Answer: False   Difficulty: Hard   Page: 95

9. Religion is a system of shared beliefs and rituals that are concerned with the realm of the sacred.

    Answer: True   Difficulty: Easy   Page: 95

10. Some sociologists have argued that of the two main branches of Christianity - Catholicism and Protestantism - the former has the most important economic implications.

    Answer: False   Difficulty: Hard   Page: 97

11. The past two decades have witnessed a surge in what is often referred to as "Islamic fundamentalism."

    Answer: True   Difficulty: Medium   Page: 98

12. Many of the economic principles of Islam are anti-free enterprise.

    Answer: False   Difficulty: Medium   Page: 99

13. One economic principle of Islam that has received particular attention is the prohibition of the payment or receipt of interest.

    Answer: True   Difficulty: Medium   Page: 101

14. According to Max Weber, the ascetic principles embedded in Hinduism do not encourage the kind of entrepreneurial activity found in Protestantism.

    Answer: True   Difficulty: Hard   Page: 101

15. Because Buddhists, like Hindus, stress spiritual achievement rather than involvement in the world, the emphasis on wealth creation that is embedded in Protestantism is not found in Buddhism. Thus, in Buddhist societies we do not see the same kind of cultural stress on entrepreneurial behavior that we see in the Protestant West.

    Answer: True   Difficulty: Hard   Page: 102

16. Countries that have more than one language typically have only one culture.

    Answer: False   Difficulty: Medium   Page: 104

Chapter 3 Differences in Culture

17. Unspoken language refers to nonverbal communication.

    Answer: True   Difficulty: Easy   Page: 104

18. The most famous study of how culture relates to values in the workplace was undertaken by Geert Hofstede.

    Answer: True   Difficulty: Easy   Page: 108

19. Hofstede's study isolated four dimensions that he claimed summarized different cultures. These dimensions included aggressive versus passive, power distance, individualism versus collectivism, and masculinity versus femininity.

    Answer: False   Difficulty: Medium   Page: 108

20. According to Hofstede, high power distance cultures are found in countries that let inequalities grow over time into inequalities of power and wealth. Ans: T

    Answer: True   Difficulty: Medium   Page: 108

Multiple Choice Questions

21. An understanding of how cultural differences across and within nations can affect the way in which business is practiced is referred to as:
    A) cross-cultural literacy
    B) cultural business sensitivity
    C) cross-national awareness
    D) cross-border sensitivity

    Answer: A   Difficulty: Medium   Page: 86

22. _____, an expert on cross-cultural differences and management, defined culture as "the collective programming of the mind which distinguishes the members of one human group from another."
    A) David Ricardo
    B) Michael Porter
    C) Geert Hofstede
    D) Raymond Vernon

    Answer: C   Difficulty: Medium   Page: 88

Chapter 3 Differences in Culture

23. A _____ is a system of values and norms that are shared among a group of people and that when taken together constitute a design for living.
    A) society
    B) clique
    C) fraternity
    D) culture

    Answer: D Difficulty: Easy Page: 88

24. _____ is that complex whole that includes knowledge, beliefs, art, morals, laws, customs, and other capabilities acquired by people as members of society.
    A) Clique
    B) Society
    C) Organization
    D) Culture

    Answer: D Difficulty: Easy Page: 88

25. Which of the following statements defines the concept of culture?
    A) System of values and norms that are shared among a group of people and that when taken together constitute a design for living.
    B) Abstract ideas about what a group believes to be good, right, and desirable.
    C) Social rules and guidelines that prescribe appropriate behavior in particular situations.
    D) Routine conventions of everyday life

    Answer: A Difficulty: Medium Page: 88

26. The two central components of culture are:
    A) ethics and laws
    B) values and norms
    C) religious beliefs and family tradition
    D) class consciousness and social mobility

    Answer: B Difficulty: Medium Page: 88

Chapter 3 Differences in Culture

27. A _____ is an abstract idea about what a group believes to be good, right, and desirable.
    A) criterion
    B) value
    C) culture
    D) norm

    Answer: B Difficulty: Easy Page: 88

28. Abstract ideas about what a group believes to be good, right, and desirable are referred to as _____.
    A) values
    B) norms
    C) cultures
    D) principles

    Answer: A Difficulty: Easy Page: 88

29. A _____ is a social rule or guideline that prescribes appropriate behavior in a particular situation.
    A) value
    B) norm
    C) pattern
    D) culture

    Answer: B Difficulty: Easy Page: 88

30. Social rules and guidelines that prescribe appropriate behavior in particular situations are referred to as _____.
    A) ethics
    B) norms
    C) principles
    D) models

    Answer: B Difficulty: Easy Page: 88

Chapter 3 Differences in Culture

31. Norms are:
    A) social rules and guidelines that prescribe appropriate behavior in particular situations
    B) abstract ideas about what a group believes to be good, right, and desirable
    C) groups of people who share common sets of values and ideas
    D) unusual forms of conduct

    Answer: A   Difficulty: Medium   Page: 88

32. A _____ is a group of people who share a common set of values and norms.
    A) cohort
    B) society
    C) fellowship
    D) fraternity

    Answer: B   Difficulty: Easy   Page: 88

33. Folkways and mores are forms of _____.
    A) conduct
    B) culture
    C) norms
    D) values

    Answer: C   Difficulty: Hard   Page: 88

34. The two major categories of norms are:
    A) routines and values
    B) conduct and culture
    C) rites and rituals
    D) folkways and mores

    Answer: D   Difficulty: Medium   Page: 88

35. _____ are social conventions concerning things such as the appropriate dress code in a particular situation, good social manners, eating with the correct utensils, neighborly behavior, and the like.
    A) Rites
    B) Rituals
    C) Mores
    D) Folkways

    Answer: D   Difficulty: Medium   Page: 88

36. _____ are norms that are central to the functioning of a society and to its social life.
    A) Mores
    B) Codes
    C) Procedures
    D) Policies

    Answer: A   Difficulty: Medium   Page: 89

37. Although there are many different aspects of social structure, two main dimensions stand out when explaining differences between cultures. These are:
    A) the degree to which the basic unit of social organization is the group; and the degree to which the basic unit of society is a clique
    B) the degree to which the basic unit of social organization is the individual; and the degree to which a society is heterogeneous
    C) the degree to which the basic unit of social organization is the extended family; and the degree to which the basic unit of society is heterogeneous
    D) the degree to which the basic unit of social organization is the individual; and the degree to which a society is stratified into classes or castes

    Answer: D   Difficulty: Hard   Page: 90

38. Although there are many different aspects of social structure, two main dimensions stand out when explaining differences between cultures. These are the degree to which the basic unit of social organization is the individual and:
    A) the degree to which a society is stratified into classes or castes
    B) the degree to which the basic unit of society is a clique
    C) the degree to which a society is heterogeneous
    D) the degree to which the basic unit of social organization is the extended family

    Answer: A   Difficulty: Medium   Page: 90

39. A society's _____ refers to its basic social organization.
    A) "social bureaucracy"
    B) "social regime"
    C) "social structure"
    D) "social hierarchy"

    Answer: C   Difficulty: Easy   Page: 90

Chapter 3 Differences in Culture

40. A _____ is an association of two or more individuals who have a shared sense of identity and who interact with each other in structured ways on the basis of a common set of expectations about each other's behavior.
    A) assemblage
    B) group
    C) norm
    D) society

    Answer: B   Difficulty: Easy   Page: 91

41. According to our textbook, while groups are found in all societies, societies differ according to the degree to which the group is viewed as:
    A) the primary means of social mobility
    B) the primary means of determining social psychology
    C) the primary means of determining social norms
    D) the primary means of social organization

    Answer: D   Difficulty: Hard   Page: 91

42. The high level of entrepreneurial activity in the United States can be attributed in part to the high level of emphasis place on the _____ in the American society.
    A) group
    B) cadre
    C) community
    D) individual

    Answer: D   Difficulty: Hard   Page: 91

43. A focus on the "individual" rather than the "group" is evident in many _____ cultures.
    A) Asian
    B) Western
    C) South American
    D) African

    Answer: B   Difficulty: Medium   Page: 91

Chapter 3 Differences in Culture

44. In contrast to the Western emphasis on the _____, in many other societies the _____ is the primary unit of social organization.
    A) individual, group
    B) group, clan
    C) coterie, individual
    D) clan, group

    Answer: A   Difficulty: Medium   Page: 92

45. A central value of the Japanese culture is the importance attached to:
    A) individualism
    B) group membership
    C) personal distinctiveness
    D) personal individuality

    Answer: B   Difficulty: Medium   Page: 92

46. All societies are stratified on a hierarchical basis into social categories, or:
    A) social strata
    B) norm based strata
    C) social segments
    D) norm based associations

    Answer: A   Difficulty: Easy   Page: 93

47. The term _____ refers to the extent to which individuals can move out of the strata into which they are born.
    A) vertical mobility
    B) social potential
    C) social mobility
    D) vertical potential

    Answer: C   Difficulty: Easy   Page: 93

48. The most rigid system of stratification is a _____ system.
    A) degree
    B) caste
    C) cross-cultural
    D) class

    Answer: B   Difficulty: Medium   Page: 93

Chapter 3 Differences in Culture

49. A _____ system is a closed system of stratification in which social position is determined by the family into which a person is born, and change in that position is usually not possible during an individual's lifetime.
    A) rank
    B) caste
    C) criterion
    D) position

    Answer: B   Difficulty: Medium   Page: 93

50. Although the number of societies with caste systems has diminished rapidly during the 20th century, one major example still remains. This example is:
    A) China
    B) Japan
    C) Britain
    D) India

    Answer: D   Difficulty: Medium   Page: 94

51. A class system is a form of _____ in which the position a person has by birth can be changed through his or her own achievements or luck.
    A) horizontal stratification
    B) closed stratification
    C) open stratification
    D) vertical stratification

    Answer: C   Difficulty: Easy   Page: 94

52. A _____ system is a form of open stratification in which the position a person has by birth can be changed through his or her own achievements and/or luck.
    A) class
    B) caste
    C) more
    D) norm

    Answer: A   Difficulty: Medium   Page: 94

53. Historically, British society has been divided into three main classes:
    A) the upper class, the middle class, and the working class
    B) the topmost class, the central class, and the bottom class
    C) the preferred class, the medium class, and the lower class
    D) the higher class, the central class, and the lower class

    Answer: A   Difficulty: Hard   Page: 94

54. _____ consciousness refers to a condition where people perceive themselves in terms of their class background, and this shapes their relationships with members of other classes.
    A) Social
    B) Rank
    C) Class
    D) Norm

    Answer: C   Difficulty: Easy   Page: 95

55. Many people perceive themselves in terms of their class background, and this shapes their relationships with members of other classes. This form of perception is called:
    A) social awareness
    B) category mindfulness
    C) denominational awareness
    D) class consciousness

    Answer: D   Difficulty: Medium   Page: 95

56. The system of shared beliefs and rituals that are concerned with the realm of the sacred is referred to as _____.
    A) religion
    B) persuasion
    C) norming
    D) divinity

    Answer: A   Difficulty: Easy   Page: 95

Chapter 3 Differences in Culture

57. _____ systems refer to a set of moral principles, or values, that are used to guide and shape behavior.
    A) Class
    B) Ethical
    C) Social
    D) Norming

    Answer: B   Difficulty: Easy   Page: 95

58. Most of the world's ethical systems are the product of:
    A) economic heritage
    B) political heritage
    C) historical norms
    D) religions

    Answer: D   Difficulty: Medium   Page: 95

59. While there are thousands of different religions in the world, four dominate. These are:
    A) Christianity, Islam, Confucianism, and Shinto
    B) Judaism, Islam, Shinto, and Confucianism
    C) Christianity, Islam, Hinduism, and Buddhism
    D) Confucianism, Shinto, Taoism, and Islam

    Answer: C   Difficulty: Hard   Page: 95

60. According to the textbook, the most widely practiced religion in the world is probably _____.
    A) Christianity
    B) Buddhism
    C) Islam
    D) Confucianism

    Answer: A   Difficulty: Medium   Page: 97

61. The vast majority of Christians live in:
    A) Europe and the Americas
    B) Asia and Australia
    C) North and South America
    D) Eastern Europe and Asia

    Answer: A   Difficulty: Easy   Page: 97

Chapter 3 Differences in Culture

62. In 1904, a German sociologist, _____, made a connection between Protestant ethics and "the spirit of capitalism."
    A) Abram Maslow
    B) Max Weber
    C) George Williams
    D) John Wesley

    Answer: B   Difficulty: Hard   Page: 97

63. In 1904, Max Weber, a German sociologist, made a connection between Protestant ethics and "the spirit of _____."
    A) specialization
    B) capitalism
    C) communism
    D) socialism

    Answer: B   Difficulty: Medium   Page: 97

64. Which of the following pairs of religious beliefs are most likely to lead to economic development and growth?
    A) Hinduism and Buddhism
    B) Islam and Christianity
    C) Christianity and Shinto
    D) Confucianism and Islam

    Answer: B   Difficulty: Hard   Page: 97

65. Which of the following lists correctly identifies the world's major religions by size of following (from highest to lowest)?
    A) Hinduism, Islam, Christianity, Confucianism, Buddhism
    B) Christianity, Islam, Hinduism, Buddhism, Confucianism
    C) Christianity, Hinduism, Islam, Confucianism, Buddhism
    D) Buddhism, Islam, Christianity, Hinduism, Confucianism

    Answer: B   Difficulty: Hard   Page: 98

Chapter 3 Differences in Culture

66. With close to 1 billion adherents, _____ is the second largest of the world's major religions.
    A) Christianity
    B) Confucianism
    C) Islam
    D) Buddhism

    Answer: C   Difficulty: Hard   Page: 98

67. Which of the following is not one of the major principles of Islam?
    A) being pretentious
    B) being generous but not a squanderer
    C) avoiding killing except for justifiable causes
    D) dealing justly and equitably with other

    Answer: A   Difficulty: Medium   Page: 98

68. The _____ lives in a social structure that is shaped by Islamic values and norms of moral conduct.
    A) Buddhist
    B) Christian
    C) Confucian
    D) Muslim

    Answer: D   Difficulty: Medium   Page: 98

69. The country in which the Islamic fundamentalists have been the most successful is _____.
    A) China
    B) India
    C) Iran
    D) South Korea

    Answer: C   Difficulty: Medium   Page: 98

70. Which of the following principles is not consistent with the teachings of the Koran?
    A) the protection of the rights of private property
    B) earning a legitimate profit through trade economics
    C) free enterprise
    D) earning profit through the exploitation of others

    Answer: D   Difficulty: Medium   Page: 98

Chapter 3 Differences in Culture

71. The Koran _____ of free enterprise and of earning legitimate profit through trade and commerce.
    A) speaks approvingly
    B) does not address the issue
    C) speaks critically
    D) forbids the practice

    Answer: A   Difficulty: Hard   Page: 99

72. Islamic countries are likely to be receptive to international business as long as those businesses _____.
    A) employ Islamic people
    B) have property in an Islamic nation
    C) behave in a manner that is consistent with Islamic ethics
    D) adhere to Islamic beliefs

    Answer: C   Difficulty: Medium   Page: 99

73. One economic principle of _____ that has received particular attention is the prohibition of the payment or receipt of interest, which is considered usury.
    A) Islam
    B) Christianity
    C) Hinduism
    D) Confucianism

    Answer: A   Difficulty: Medium   Page: 99

74. Which of the following religions prohibits the payment or receipt of interest?
    A) Christianity
    B) Islam
    C) Confucianism
    D) Hinduism

    Answer: B   Difficulty: Medium   Page: 101

75. The world's oldest major religion is:
    A) Buddhism
    B) Islam
    C) Confucianism
    D) Hinduism

    Answer: D   Difficulty: Hard   Page: 101

Chapter 3 Differences in Culture

76. _____ has approximately 500 million adherents, most of them in the Indian subcontinent.
    A) Confucianism
    B) Buddhism
    C) Islam
    D) Hinduism

    Answer: D   Difficulty: Medium   Page: 101

77. _____ believe there is a moral force in society that requires the acceptance of certain responsibilities, called *dharma*.
    A) Muslims
    B) Hindus
    C) Christians
    D) Confucians

    Answer: B   Difficulty: Medium   Page: 101

78. The terms dharma, karma, and nirvana are associated with the _____ religion.
    A) Hindu
    B) Christian
    C) Buddhist
    D) Islamic

    Answer: A   Difficulty: Medium   Page: 101

79. Under the teachings of _____, the most able individuals in a business organization may find their route to the higher levels of the organization blocked simply because they come from lower casts.
    A) Hinduism
    B) Christianity
    C) Islam
    D) Buddhism

    Answer: A   Difficulty: Medium   Page: 101

Chapter 3 Differences in Culture

80. _____ was founded in India in the sixth century BC by Shiddhartha Gautama, an Indian prince who renounced his wealth to pursue an ascetic lifestyle and spiritual perfection.
    A) Confucianism
    B) Islam
    C) Christianity
    D) Buddhism

    Answer: D Difficulty: Medium Page: 102

81. Buddhists are found primarily in the following areas:
    A) The Middle East and Eastern Africa
    B) Central and Southwest Asia, China, Korea, and Japan.
    C) Western Europe and North America
    D) South America

    Answer: B Difficulty: Medium Page: 102

82. For more than 2,000 years until the 1949 Communist revolution, _____ was the official ethical system of China.
    A) Buddhism
    B) Hinduism
    C) Confucianism
    D) Christianity

    Answer: C Difficulty: Medium Page: 102

83. Individuals that following the teaching of Confucius are found primarily in:
    A) North America and Western Europe
    B) Eastern Europe and the republics of the former Soviet Union
    C) The Middle East and Eastern Africa
    D) China, Korea, and Japan

    Answer: D Difficulty: Medium Page: 102

84. The religion that is built around a comprehensive ethical code that establishes guidelines for relationships with others is called _____.
    A) Buddhism
    B) Hinduism
    C) Confucianism
    D) Christianity

    Answer: C Difficulty: Medium Page: 102

Chapter 3 Differences in Culture

85. The values of loyalty, reciprocal obligations, and honesty are central to the _____ system of ethics.
    A) Buddhist
    B) Islamic
    C) Hindu
    D) Confucian

    Answer: D Difficulty: Medium Page: 102

86. The most widely spoken language in the world is:
    A) German
    B) English
    C) French
    D) Spanish

    Answer: B Difficulty: Medium Page: 104

87. The most famous study of how culture relates to values in the workplace was undertaken by _____.
    A) George Williams
    B) Thomas Peters
    C) Geert Hofstede
    D) Michael Porter

    Answer: C Difficulty: Easy Page: 103

88. The language of international business is increasingly becoming:
    A) Spanish
    B) English
    C) French
    D) Japanese

    Answer: B Difficulty: Medium Page: 104

89. Based on recent trends in international business, when Japanese and German businesspeople get together to do business, it is almost certain that they will communicate in:
    A) French
    B) German
    C) Japanese
    D) English

    Answer: D Difficulty: Medium Page: 104

Chapter 3 Differences in Culture

90. Unspoken language is referred to as:
    A) discrete communication
    B) nonverbal communication
    C) silent communication
    D) passive communication

    Answer: B   Difficulty: Medium   Page: 105

91. Geert Hofstede isolated four dimensions that he claimed summarized different cultures. Which of the following is not one of Hofstede's dimensions?
    A) capitalistic versus socialistic
    B) masculinity versus femininity
    C) power distance
    D) uncertainty avoidance

    Answer: A   Difficulty: Medium   Page: 106

92. The most famous study of how culture relates to values in the workplace was undertaken by:
    A) Geert Hofstede
    B) Thomas Peters
    C) Michael Porter
    D) George Baker

    Answer: A   Difficulty: Easy   Page: 108

93. Geert Hofstede isolated four dimensions that be claimed summarized different:
    A) religions
    B) ethical systems
    C) cultures
    D) languages

    Answer: C   Difficulty: Medium   Page: 108

Chapter 3 Differences in Culture

94. In his studies, Hofstede isolated four dimensions that he claimed summarized different cultures. These were:
    A) individualism versus collectivism, power distance, tolerant versus intolerant, and aggressive verses passive
    B) uncertainty avoidance, masculinity versus femininity, individual versus group oriented, forward versus reserved
    C) aggressive verses passive, tolerant versus intolerant, power distance, and individual versus group oriented
    D) power distance, individualism versus collectivism, uncertainty avoidance, and masculinity versus femininity

    Answer: D   Difficulty: Medium   Page: 108

95. Which of the following is not one of the four dimensions that Hofstede claimed summarized different cultures?
    A) uncertainty avoidance
    B) aggressive versus passive
    C) masculinity versus femininity
    D) individualism versus collectivism

    Answer: B   Difficulty: Easy   Page: 108

96. Hofstede's _____ dimension focused on how a society deals with the fact that people are unequal in physical and intellectual capabilities.
    A) individualism versus collectivism
    B) uncertainty avoidance
    C) power distance
    D) masculinity versus femininity

    Answer: C   Difficulty: Medium   Page: 108

97. Hofstede's _____ dimension focused on the relationship between the individual and his or her followers.
    A) individualism versus collectivism
    B) aggressive versus passive
    C) masculinity versus femininity
    D) power distance

    Answer: A   Difficulty: Medium   Page: 108

98. Hofstede's _____ dimension measured the extent to which different cultures socialized their members into accepting ambiguous situations and tolerating uncertainty.
    A) masculinity versus femininity
    B) power distance
    C) individualism versus collectivism
    D) uncertainty avoidance

    Answer: D Difficulty: Medium   Page: 109

99. Hofstede's _____ dimension looked at the relationship between gender and work roles.
    A) power distance
    B) masculinity versus femininity
    C) individualism versus collectivism
    D) uncertainty avoidance

    Answer: B Difficulty: Medium   Page: 109

100. According to Hofstede's Model, which group of nations score high on the individualism scale and low on the power distance scale?
    A) advanced western nations such as the United States, Canada, and Britain
    B) South American nations such as Brazil, Peru, and Ecuador
    C) Asian nations such as Japan, South Korea, and Singapore
    D) African nations such as Zaire, Sudan, and Chad

    Answer: A Difficulty: Hard   Page: 109

101. According to Hofstede's Model, what country stands out as having a culture with strong uncertainty avoidance and high masculinity?
    A) United States
    B) Japan
    C) Australia
    D) Germany

    Answer: B Difficulty: Hard   Page: 109

Chapter 3 Differences in Culture

102. Ethnocentrism is a belief in the:
    A) superiority of one's own ethnic group or culture
    B) superiority of one's own legal system compared to others
    C) superiority of one's own religious beliefs over others
    D) superiority of individualism versus collectivism

    Answer: A Difficulty: Easy Page: 113

103. Acting on the belief in the superiority of one's own ethnic group or culture is referred to as _____ behavior.
    A) collectivist
    B) intolerant
    C) individualistic
    D) ethnocentric

    Answer: D Difficulty: Medium Page: 113

104. Suppose an international executive from Italy consistently acted in a manner that indicated that he believed that his ethnic group and culture is superior to any others. If this was the case, the executive would be exhibiting _____ behavior.
    A) synergistic
    B) plyocentric
    C) ethnocentric
    D) individualistic

    Answer: C Difficulty: Medium Page: 113

105. Many businesses falter in their attempts to establish markets overseas because they act like their culture is superior to the cultures of other countries. This belief and attitude is referred to as:
    A) culturalism
    B) parochialism
    C) nationalism
    D) ethnocentrism

    Answer: D Difficulty: Medium Page: 113

Chapter 3 Differences in Culture

Essay Questions

106. Describe what is meant by the term "culture?" Differentiate between the terms culture, values, and norms.

    Difficulty: Easy   Page: 88

    Answer:
    Culture can be defined as a system of values and norms that are shared among a group of people and that when taken together constitute a design for living. Values and norms are the underpinnings of culture. Values are abstract ideas about what a group believes to be good, right, and desirable. Put differently, values are shared assumptions about how things ought to be. Norms are the social rules and guidelines that prescribe appropriate behavior in a particular situation.

107. What are the two dimensions of a society's social structure that stand out as being of particular importance when explaining differences between cultures?

    Difficulty: Medium   Page: 90

    Answer:
    The first is the degree to which the basic unit of social organization is the individual, as opposed to the group. Western societies tend to emphasize the primacy of the individual, while groups tend to figure much larger in many other societies. The second dimension is the degree to which a society is stratified into classes or castes. Some societies are characterized by a relatively high degree of social stratification and relatively low mobility between strata (e.g., Indian), while other societies are characterized by a low degree of social stratification and high mobility between strata (e.g. American).

108. Describe the concept of social mobility. Does social mobility vary significantly from society to society? Describe the extremes in terms of a society that has low social mobility and a society that has high social mobility. Would you rather live in a society with a high level or a low level of social mobility? Why?

    Difficulty: Medium   Page: 93

Answer:
Social mobility refers to the extent to which individuals can move out of the strata into which they are born. For instance, in a society with a low level of social mobility, it would be very difficult (if not impossible) for someone that is born into a family of laborers to become a manager. Social mobility varies significantly from society to society. The most rigid system of stratification is a caste system. A caste system is a closed system of stratification in which social position is determined by the family into which a person is born, and change in that position is usually not possible during an individual's lifetime. At the other extreme is the American "class" system (i.e. upper class, middle class, and lower-middle class). In this system, class membership is determined mainly by an individual's own efforts and achievements, rather than his or her family heritage. Thus, an individual in American, through effort and achievement, can move smoothly from the lower-middle class (or the working class) to the upper class.

Your students will undoubtedly say that they would rather live in a society with a high level of social mobility. The clear advantage of such a society is that a person's position is determined by his or her own individual effort.

109. What is meant by the term "class consciousness?" Under what circumstances can class consciousness be bad?

Difficulty: Medium   Page: 95

Answer:
The term class consciousness refers to a condition where people tend to perceive themselves in terms of their class background, and this shapes their relationships with members of other classes. Class consciousness can be bad if it leads to hostility and animosity between classes. For example, if the "upper-class" in a society (in terms of economic stature) tries to dominate the "lower-class," it can lead to hostility and a mutual antagonism between the classes. This typically makes it difficult to achieve cooperation between management and labor, if the "upper-class" is typically in management and the "lower-class" constitutes the majority of the laborers.

110. What is meant by the Protestant work ethic? What impact has the Protestant work ethic had on the emergence of modern day capitalism?

Difficulty: Easy   Page: 97

Answer:
In 1904 a German sociologist, named Max Weber, made a connection between Protestant ethics and "the spirit of capitalism." Weber drew this conclusion by observing that, in Western Europe, the business leaders and owners of capital were overwhelmingly Protestant. This relationship led Weber to conclude that there was a link between Protestantism and the emergence of modern capitalism. Weber argued that Protestant ethics emphasized the importance of hard work and wealth creation, which are the essential components of capitalism. Thus, Weber coined the term "Protestant work ethic" to denote the tendency on the part of Protestants to work hard and accumulate wealth, which are the underpinnings of capitalism.

111. What are some of the similarities between Islam and Christianity as they related to the practice of business?

Difficulty: Medium   Page: 97

Answer:
Having the same roots, Islam and Christianity share many similarities regarding the conduct of business. Many of the economic principles of Islam are pro free enterprise and hostile to socialist ideals. In both Islamic and Christian societies, it is appropriate to earn a profit through trade and commerce, as long as the profit is justly earned and not based on the exploitation of others. In addition, the principles of honesty, respect for the rights of others, and dealings justly and equitable with others are found in both religions.

112. Hofstede isolated four dimensions that he claimed charaterized the cultures of different countries. Briefly describe each of Hofstede's four dimensions. Should Hofstede's dimensions be used by managers to determine how cultures differ and what that might mean for management practices?

Difficulty: Hard   Page: 108

Answer:
Hostede's four dimension are: power distance, individualism versus collectivism, uncertainty avoidance, and masculinity versus femininity. Each of these dimensions is briefly described below.

Power Distance: This dimension focuses on how a society deals with the fact that people are unequal in physical and intellectual capabilities. According to Hofstede, high power distance cultures are found in countries that let inequalities grow over time into inequalities of power and wealth. Low power distance cultures are found in societies that try to play down such inequalities as much as possible.

Chapter 3 Differences in Culture

Individualism versus Collectivism: This dimension focuses on the relationship between the individual and his or her fellows. In individualistic societies, the ties between individuals are loose and individual achievement and freedom are highly valued. In societies where collectivism is emphasized, the ties between individuals are tight.

Uncertainty Avoidance: This dimension measures the extent to which different cultures socialize their members into accepting ambiguous situations and tolerating uncertainty. Members of high uncertainty avoidance cultures place a premium on job security, career patterns, retirement benefits, and so on. Lower uncertainty avoidance cultures are characterized by a greater readiness to take risks and less emotional resistance to change.

Masculinity versus Femininity: Finally, this dimension looks at the relationship between gender and work roles. In masculine cultures, sex roles are sharply differentiated and traditional "masculine values," such as achievement and the effective exercise of power, determines cultural ideals. If feminine cultures, sex roles are less sharply distinguished, and little differentiation is made between men and women in the same job.

Hofstede used these dimensions to develop charts that provided descriptive information about cultures. These charts were intended to be used by managers to understand the dynamics of different cultures.

As articulated in the textbook, Hofstede's model has some weaknesses, and should not be used as the sole determinant of how one interfaces with individuals from other cultures. On the other hand, Hofstede's model is a tool that can provide a manager insight that he or she might not otherwise have relative to cultural issues.

113. What is ethnocentric behavior? Is ethnocentrism a desirable of an undesirable attribute for the manager of an international firm?

Difficulty: Medium   Page: 113

Answer:
Ethnocentrism is a belief in the superiority of one's own ethnic group or culture. Often, this leads to behavior that reflects a disregard or contempt for the cultures of other countries. Ethnocentric behavior is not a desirable attribute for the manager of an international firm. International managers must have a healthy respect for other and a balanced perspective.

Chapter 4 International Trade Theory

True/False Questions

1. Propagated in the 16th and 17th centuries, mercantilism advocated that countries should discourage both imports and exports.

    Answer: False   Difficulty: Easy   Page: 125

2. Free trade refers to a situation where a government does not attempt to influence through quotas or duties what its citizens can buy from another country or what they can produce and sell to another country.

    Answer: True   Difficulty: Easy   Page: 125

3. The great strength of the theories of Smith, Ricardo, and Heckscher-Ohlin is that they identify the specific benefits of international trade.

    Answer: True   Difficulty: Medium   Page: 125

4. The first theory of international trade emerged in England in the mid-16th century. Referred to as the theory of comparative advantage, its principle assertion was that gold and silver were the mainstays of national wealth and essential to vigorous commerce.

    Answer: False   Difficulty: Medium   Page: 128

5. The flaw with mercantilism was that it viewed trade as a zero-sum gain.

    Answer: True   Difficulty: Hard   Page: 129

6. A positive-sum game in a situation in which a gain by one country results in a loss by another.

    Answer: False   Difficulty: Easy   Page: 126

7. A country has an absolute advantage in the production of a product when it is more efficient than any other country is producing it.

    Answer: True   Difficulty: Easy   Page: 129

8. In his 1776 landmark book The Wealth of Nations, Adam Smith supported the mercantilist assumption that trade is a zero-sum game.

   Answer: True   Difficulty: Medium   Page: 129

9. Smith's basic argument was that a country should never produce goods at home that it can buy at a lower cost from other countries.

   Answer: True   Difficulty: Medium   Page: 129

10. To an even greater degree than the theory of comparative advantage, the theory of absolute advantage suggests that trade is a positive-sum game in which all can gain.

    Answer: False   Difficulty: Hard   Page: 129

11. The basic message of the theory of comparative advantage is that the potential world production is greater with unrestricted free trade than it is with restricted free trade.

    Answer: True   Difficulty: Medium   Page: 134

12. According to evidence compiled by the World Bank, free trade has a positive effect on economic growth.

    Answer: True   Difficulty: Medium   Page: 137

13. Like Ricardo's theory, the Heckscher-Ohlin theory argues that free trade is beneficial. Unlike Ricardo's theory, however, the Heckscher-Ohlin theory argues that the pattern of international trade is determined by differences in factor endowments, rather than differences in productivity.

    Answer: True   Difficulty: Medium   Page: 138

14. The Heckscher-Olin theory would predict that the United States should be a primary importer of capital goods.

    Answer: False   Difficulty: Medium   Page: 138

15. Most economists prefer the Heckscher-Ohlin theory to Ricardo's theory because it makes fewer simplifying assumptions, and it has been subjected to many empirical tests.

    Answer: True   Difficulty: Medium   Page: 138

Chapter 4 International Trade Theory

16. The Heckscher-Ohlin theory has been one of the least influential in international economics.

    Answer: False   Difficulty: Medium   Page: 138

17. Raymond Vernon's theory of the Product Life-Cycle was based on the observation that for most of the 20th century a very large proportion of the world's new products were developed by U.S. firms and sold first in the U.S. market.

    Answer: True   Difficulty: Medium   Page: 139

18. The new trade theorists argue that in those industries where the existence of substantial economies of scale imply that the world market will profitable support only a few firms, countries may export certain products simply because they have a firm that was an early entrant into that industry.

    Answer: True   Difficulty: Medium   Page: 142

19. In sum, Porter's argument is that the degree to which a nation is likely to achieve international success in a certain industry is a function of the combined impact of factor endowments, domestic demand conditions, related and supporting industries, and degree of government support.

    Answer: False   Difficulty: Medium   Page: 143

20. The new trade theory suggests the importance to firms of building and exploiting first-mover advantages.

    Answer: True   Difficulty: Medium   Page: 149

Multiple Choice Questions

21. Propagated in the 16th and 17th centuries, _____ advocated that countries should simultaneously encourage exports and discourage imports.
    A) ethnocentrism
    B) capitalism
    C) collectivism
    D) mercantilism

    Answer: D   Difficulty: Easy   Page: 123

Chapter 4 International Trade Theory

22. Propagated in the 16th and 17th centuries, mercantilism advocated that countries should:
    A) simultaneously encourage exports and discourage imports
    B) simultaneously discourage exports and encourage imports
    C) encourage both imports and exports
    D) discourage both imports and exports

    Answer: A Difficulty: Medium Page: 125

23. Which of the following statements accurately characterizes mercantilism?
    A) it is a new but largely discredited doctrine
    B) it is a new, highly credible doctrine
    C) it is an old yet highly credible doctrine
    D) it is an old and largely discredited doctrine

    Answer: D Difficulty: Medium Page: 125

24. Adam Smith advanced the theory of _____.
    A) absolute advantage
    B) capitalism
    C) similar opportunity
    D) mercantilism

    Answer: A Difficulty: Easy Page: 125

25. Which of the following international trade scholars was the first to explain why unrestricted free trade is beneficial to a country?
    A) Adam Smith
    B) Bertil Ohlin
    C) Eli Heckscher
    D) Paul Krugman

    Answer: A Difficulty: Medium Page: 125

26. _____ refers to a situation where a government does not attempt to influence through quotas or duties what its citizens can buy from another country or what they can produce and sell to another country.
    A) Autonomous trade
    B) Free trade
    C) Clear commerce
    D) Unencumbered commerce

    Answer: B Difficulty: Easy Page: 125

Chapter 4 International Trade Theory

27. Which of the following international management scholars argued that the "invisible hand" of the market mechanism, rather than government policy, should determine what a country imports and what it exports?
    A) David Ricardo
    B) Eli Heckscher
    C) Michael Porter
    D) Adam Smith

    Answer: D   Difficulty: Hard   Page: 125

28. Adam Smith argued that the _____ of the market mechanism, rather than government policy, should determine what a country imports and what it exports.
    A) invisible hand
    B) blunt force
    C) economic realities
    D) ups and downs

    Answer: A   Difficulty: Medium   Page: 125

29. The theory of comparative advantage, advanced by _____, is the intellectual basis of the modern argument for unrestricted free trade.
    A) Michael Porter
    B) David Ricardo
    C) Bertil Ohlin
    D) Adam Smith

    Answer: B   Difficulty: Hard   Page: 125

30. According to the textbook, the _____ contains the intellectual basis of the modern argument for unrestricted free trade.
    A) Product Life-Cycle theory
    B) Heckscher-Ohlin theory
    C) theory of comparative advantage
    D) theory of absolute advantage

    Answer: C   Difficulty: Medium   Page: 125

Chapter 4 International Trade Theory

31. In terms of explaining why some countries export automobiles, consumer electronics, and machine tools, while other countries export chemicals, watches, and jewelry, David Ricardo's theory of comparative advantage offer an explanation in terms of:
    A) international differences in intellectual capital
    B) international differences in labor productivity
    C) the interplay between the proportions in which the factors of production (such as land, labor, and capital) are available in different countries and the proportions in which they are needed for producing particular goods
    D) the cultural histories of the exporting nations

    Answer: B Difficulty: Hard Page: 125

32. In explaining why some countries export oil while others export textiles, the Heckscher-Ohlin theory:
    A) emphasizes the interplay between the proportions in which the factors of production (such as land, labor, and capital) are available in different countries
    B) emphasizes international differences in labor productivity
    C) emphasizes international differences in intellectual capital
    D) emphasizes international differences in cultural histories

    Answer: A Difficulty: Hard Page: 126

33. One early response to the failure of the Heckscher-Ohlin theory to explain the observed pattern of international trade was the _____.
    A) theory of rising costs
    B) product life-cycle theory
    C) theory of comparative advantage
    D) theory of cultural constraints

    Answer: B Difficulty: Medium Page: 126

34. The _____ was an early response to the failure of the Hecksher-Ohlin theory to explain the observed pattern of international trade.
    A) theory of absolute advantage
    B) new trade theory
    C) theory of comparative advantage
    D) product life-cycle theory

    Answer: D Difficulty: Medium Page: 126

Chapter 4 International Trade Theory

35. Which of the following choices correctly matches a scholar with the theory that he or she proposed?
    A) Adam Smith / Comparative Advantage
    B) David Ricardo / New Trade
    C) Raymond Vernon / Product Life Cycle
    D) Eli Heckscher / Absolute Advantage

    Answer: C   Difficulty: Medium   Page: 126

36. The Product Life Cycle Theory is associated with the work of:
    A) Raymond Vernon
    B) Eli Heckscher
    C) Adam Smith
    D) Michael Porter

    Answer: A   Difficulty: Medium   Page: 126

37. The _____ theory stresses that in some cases countries specialize in the production and export of particular products not because of underlying differences in factor endowments but because in certain industries the world market can support only a limited number of firms.
    A) balanced trade
    B) Heckscher-Olin
    C) new trade
    D) product life-cycle

    Answer: C   Difficulty: Medium   Page: 127

38. The New Trade Theory is associated with the work of:
    A) Michael Porter
    B) Raymond Vernon
    C) Paul Krugman
    D) Adam Smith

    Answer: C   Difficulty: Medium   Page: 127

39. The _____ stresses that in some cases countries specialize in the production and export of particular products not because of underlying differences in factor endowments, but because in certain industries the world market can support only a limited number of firms.
    A) product life cycle theory
    B) theory of absolute advantage
    C) Heckscher-Ohlin theory
    D) new trade theory

    Answer: D Difficulty: Medium Page: 127

40. The theory of _____, developed by Michael Porter, focuses on the importance of country factors such as domestic demand and domestic rivalry in explaining a nation's dominance in the production and export of particular products.
    A) new trade
    B) absolute advantage
    C) comparative advantage
    D) national competitive advantage

    Answer: D Difficulty: Medium Page: 128

41. Which of the following scholars (or teams of scholars) is not associated with the theory that follows his name?
    A) Michael Porter / National Competitive Advantage
    B) Adam Smith / Absolute Advantage
    C) David Ricardo / Comparative Advantage
    D) Eli Heckscher and Bertil Ohlin / Product Life Cycle

    Answer: D Difficulty: Hard Page: 128

42. Which of the following two theories justify some limited and selective government intervention to support the development of certain export-oriented industries?
    A) the theory of national competitive advantage and the Heckscher-Ohlin theory
    B) the theory of absolute advantage and the new trade theory
    C) the Heckscher-Ohlin theory and theory of comparative advantage
    D) the new trade theory and theory of national competitive advantage

    Answer: D Difficulty: Hard Page: 128

Chapter 4 International Trade Theory

43. The first theory of international trade emerged in England in the mid-16th century. Referred to as _____, its principal assertion was that gold and silver were the mainstays of national wealth and essential to vigorous commerce.
    A) collectivism
    B) mercantilism
    C) capitalism
    D) economic conservatism

    Answer: B Difficulty: Easy Page: 128

44. The main tenet of mercantilism was that it was in a country's best interest to maintain a trade _____.
    A) balance
    B) embargo
    C) surplus
    D) deficit

    Answer: C Difficulty: Medium Page: 128

45. The flaw with mercantilism was that it viewed trade as a _____.
    A) zero-sum game
    B) economic necessity
    C) non essential economic activity
    D) threat to a government's independence

    Answer: A Difficulty: Medium Page: 128

46. Which of the following is not consistent with the central beliefs of mercantilism?
    A) government should intervene to achieve a surplus in the balance of trade
    B) policies should be put in place to minimize exports and maximize imports
    C) imports should be limited by tariffs and quotas
    D) exports should be subsidized

    Answer: B Difficulty: Hard Page: 128

47. A situation in which a gain by one party results in a loss by another is called a _____.
    A) transfer of wealth
    B) unbalanced scorecard
    C) zero-sum game
    D) positive-sum game

    Answer: C Difficulty: Easy Page: 129

Chapter 4 International Trade Theory

48. A _____ is a situation in which a gain by one country results in a loss by another.
    A) positive-sum game
    B) transfer of wealth
    C) zero-sum game
    D) unbalanced scorecard

    Answer: C Difficulty: Easy Page: 129

49. A situation in which all countries can benefit, even if some benefit more than others, is called a _____.
    A) near equivalent-result game
    B) positive-sum game
    C) balanced scorecard
    D) zero-sum game

    Answer: B Difficulty: Easy Page: 129

50. In his 1776 landmark book The Wealth of Nations, _____ attacked the mercantilist assumption that trade is a zero-sum game.
    A) Geert Hofstede
    B) Max Weber
    C) Michael Porter
    D) Adam Smith

    Answer: D Difficulty: Easy Page: 127

51. In his 1776 landmark book _____, Adam Smith attacked the mercantilist assumption that trade is a zero-sum game.
    A) The Wealth of Nations
    B) The Free Trade Manifesto
    C) A Commentary on Free Trade and Globalization
    D) Free Trade and Mercantilism

    Answer: A Difficulty: Medium Page: 129

Chapter 4 International Trade Theory

52. According to Smith, countries should specialize in the production of goods for which they have an absolute advantage and then:
    A) retain these goods for strictly domestic sales
    B) trade these goods for the goods produced by other countries
    C) sell these goods to the highest domestic or international bidder
    D) prohibit the import of these goods from other countries

    Answer: B   Difficulty: Hard   Page: 129

53. _____ basic argument, articulated through the theory of absolute advantage, is that a country should never produce goods at home that it can buy at a low cost from another country.
    A) David Ricardo's
    B) Michael Porter's
    C) Bertil Ohlin's
    D) Adam Smith's

    Answer: D   Difficulty: Medium   Page: 130

54. A situation in which one country is more efficient at producing a product than any other country is referred to as:
    A) absolute advantage
    B) relative advantage
    C) comparative advantage
    D) pertinent advantage

    Answer: A   Difficulty: Medium   Page: 130

55. In his 1817 book entitled Principles of Political Economy, _____ introduced the theory of comparative advantage.
    A) Adam Smith
    B) David Ricardo
    C) Raymond Vernon
    D) Max Weber

    Answer: B   Difficulty: Medium   Page: 133

Chapter 4 International Trade Theory

56. In his 1817 book entitled the _____, David Ricardo introduced the theory of comparative advantage.
    A) The Free Trade Advocate
    B) The Folly of Mercantilism
    C) The Principles of National Competitiveness
    D) The Principles of Political Economy

    Answer: D Difficulty: Medium Page: 133

57. A situation in which a country specializes in producing the goods it produces most efficiently and buys the products it produces less efficiently from other countries, even if it could produce the good more efficiently itself is referred to as:
    A) comprehensive advantage
    B) pertinent advantage
    C) comparative advantage
    D) absolute advantage

    Answer: C Difficulty: Medium Page: 133

58. According to Ricardo's theory of _____, it makes sense for a country to specialize in the production of those goods that it produces most efficiently and to buy the goods that it produces less efficiently from other countries, even if this means buying goods from other countries that it could produce more efficiently itself.
    A) competitive advantage
    B) comparative advantage
    C) pertinent advantage
    D) absolute advantage

    Answer: B Difficulty: Medium Page: 133

59. The basic message of the theory of comparative advantage is that:
    A) potential world production is greater with unrestricted free trade than it is with restricted trade
    B) potential world production is not significantly affected by trade policy
    C) potential world production is greater with restricted trade.
    D) it makes sense for a country to specialize in the production of those goods that it produces most efficiently and to buy the goods that it products less efficiently from other countries, unless this means buying goods from other countries that it could produce more efficiently itself

    Answer: A Difficulty: Hard Page: 133

Chapter 4 International Trade Theory

60. The basic message of the theory of _____ is that potential world production is greater with unrestricted free trade than it is with restricted free trade.
    A) mercantilism
    B) comparative advantage
    C) the Leontief Paradox
    D) absolute advantage

    Answer: B Difficulty: Medium Page: 133

61. To an even greater degree than the theory of absolute advantage, the theory of _____ suggests that trade is a positive-sum game in which all gain.
    A) total advantage
    B) mercantilism
    C) comparative advantage
    D) paradoxical advantage

    Answer: C Difficulty: Medium Page: 133

62. Ricardo's theory of comparative advantage suggests that consumers in all nations can consume more if there are:
    A) trade restrictions on services only
    B) no trade restrictions
    C) severe trade restrictions
    D) trade restrictions on manufactured goods only

    Answer: B Difficulty: Medium Page: 134

63. The theory of comparative advantage:
    A) provides a strong rationale for encouraging international trade
    B) provides a strong rationale for discouraging international trade
    C) neither encourages nor discourages international trade
    D) provides a weak rationale for discouraging international trade

    Answer: A Difficulty: Medium Page: 134

64. Dynamic gains in both the stock of a country's resources and the efficiency with which resources are utilized will cause a country's PPP to:
    A) shift inward
    B) shift outward
    C) make no appreciable change
    D) no longer be influential

    Answer: B Difficulty: Hard Page: 137

65. Swedish economists _____ and _____ advanced a theory of trade that argued that comparative advantage arises from differences in national factor endowments.
    A) Durbin, Coles
    B) Hecksher, Ohlin
    C) Delhomme, Rivette
    D) Mouton, Penn

    Answer: B   Difficulty: Medium   Page: 138

66. The theory that argues that comparative advantage arises from differences in national factor endowments was advanced by the Swedish economists _____ and

    _____.
    A) Toussaint, Coles
    B) Leblanc, Cormier
    C) Wills, Theler
    D) Hecksher, Ohlin

    Answer: D   Difficulty: Medium   Page: 138

67. The _____ theory predicts that countries will export those goods that make intensive use of those factors that are locally abundant, while importing goods that make intensive use of factors that are locally scarce.
    A) Hecksher-Cormier
    B) Ricardo-Olin
    C) Hecksher-Olin
    D) Carrier-Roller

    Answer: C   Difficulty: Medium   Page: 138

Chapter 4 International Trade Theory

68. Which of the following statements is a fair comparison of the Heckscher-Ohlin theory and the Ricardo theory (i.e. comparative advantage) of free trade?
    A) both theories argues that the pattern of international trade is determined by currency exchange rates
    B) the Heckscher-Olin theory argues that the pattern of international trade is determined by trade endowments, while the Ricardo theory argues that the pattern of international trade is determined by differences in productivity
    C) both theories argue that the pattern of international trade is determined by differences in productivity
    D) the Heckscher-Olin theory argues that the pattern of international trade is determined by differences in productivity, while the Ricardo theory argues that the pattern of international trade is determined by trade endowments

    Answer: B Difficulty: Hard Page: 138

69. According to the textbook, most economists prefer the Heckscher-Ohlin theory to Ricardo's theory (i.e. comparative advantage) because of two factors. These factors are:
    A) it makes fewer simplifying assumptions and it has been subjected to many empirical tests
    B) it has been subjected to many empirical tests and it has stood the test of time
    C) it makes fewer simplifying assumptions and it has been acknowledged by the World Trade Organization as the better of the two theories
    D) it has been acknowledged as the better of the two theories by the World Trade Organization, and it has stood the test of time

    Answer: A Difficulty: Medium Page: 138

70. The Hecksher-Olin theory argues that the pattern of international trade is determined by differences in:
    A) productivity
    B) political interests
    C) factor endowments
    D) national priorities

    Answer: C Difficulty: Medium Page: 138

Chapter 4 International Trade Theory

71. Contrary to what the Heckscher-Ohlin theory would predict, the United States has been a primary importer rather than an exporter of capital goods. This phenomenon is referred to as the _____ paradox.
    A) Theler
    B) Leontief
    C) Cormier
    D) Ricardo

    Answer: B Difficulty: Easy Page: 136

72. _____ initially proposed the product life-cycle theory in the mid-1960s.
    A) Cormier
    B) Heckscher
    C) Vernon
    D) Smith

    Answer: C Difficulty: Easy Page: 137

73. Raymond Vernon initially proposed the _____ in the mid-1960s.
    A) new trade theory
    B) theory of absolute advantage
    C) product life-cycle theory
    D) theory of comparative advantage

    Answer: C Difficulty: Easy Page: 139

74. Raymond Vernon initially proposed the product life-cycle theory in:
    A) the mid-1940s
    B) the mid-1950s
    C) the mid-1960s
    D) the mid-1970s

    Answer: C Difficulty: Hard Page: 139

75. Vernon's product life-cycle theory was based on the observation that for most of the 20th century a very large proportion of the world's new products had been developed by U.S. firms and sold first in the _____ market.
    A) Japanese
    B) Western European
    C) U.S.
    D) Canadian

    Answer: C Difficulty: Medium Page: 139

Chapter 4 International Trade Theory

76. Vernon's product life-cycle theory was based on the observation that for most of the 20th century a very large proportion of the world's new products had been developed by _____ firms and sold first in the U.S. market.
    A) Mexican
    B) Canadian
    C) Western European
    D) U.S.

    Answer: D   Difficulty: Medium   Page: 139

77. Which theory of international trade suggests that the production of products is likely to switch from advanced countries to developing countries over time?
    A) new trade
    B) comparative advantage
    C) Hecksher-Ohlin
    D) product life-cycle

    Answer: D   Difficulty: Medium   Page: 139

78. According to the textbook, historically the product-life-cycle theory is an:
    A) accurate explanation of international trade patterns for manufactured goods but not for services
    B) accurate explanation of international trade patterns
    C) accurate explanation of international trade patterns in some countries but not in others
    D) inaccurate explanation of international trade patterns

    Answer: B   Difficulty: Medium   Page: 139

79. The _____ theory argues that in many industries, because of substantial economies of scale, there are increasing returns to specialization.
    A) Leontief's paradox
    B) product life-cycle
    C) new trade
    D) Heckscher-Ohlin

    Answer: C   Difficulty: Medium   Page: 142

Chapter 4 International Trade Theory

80. The _____ theory argues that due to the presence of substantial scale economies, world demand will support only a few firms in many industries.
    A) Heckscher-Ohlin
    B) Leontief's paradox
    C) product life-cycle
    D) new trade

    Answer: D   Difficulty: Medium   Page: 142

81. The theory that argues that due to the presence of substantial scale economies, world demand will support only a few firms in many industries in referred to as the:
    A) theory of comparative advantage
    B) product life-cycle theory
    C) theory of absolute advantage
    D) new trade theory

    Answer: D   Difficulty: Medium   Page: 142

82. The theory that argues that due to the presence of substantial scale economies, world demand will support only a few firms in the aircraft industry, is referred to as the:
    A) theory of absolute advantage
    B) theory of comparative advantage
    C) new trade theory
    D) product life-cycle theory

    Answer: C   Difficulty: Medium   Page: 142

83. Which theory of international trade directly explains why there are only two to three producers of airlines in the world today?
    A) absolute advantage
    B) new trade
    C) comparative advantage
    D) product life cycle

    Answer: B   Difficulty: Medium   Page: 142

84. The economic and strategic advantages that accrue to early entrants in an industry are called:
   A) first-mover advantages
   B) initial-class advantages
   C) early-entrant advantages
   D) first-stage benefits

   Answer: A   Difficulty: Easy   Page: 142

85. _____ advantages are the economic and strategic advantages that accrue to early entrants into an industry.
   A) Initial-class
   B) First-mover
   C) First-stage
   D) Early-entrant

   Answer: B   Difficulty: Easy   Page: 142

86. The new trade theorists argue that the United States leads in exports of commercial jet aircraft not because it is better endowed with the factors of production required to manufacture aircraft, but because:
   A) U.S. built commercial jet aircraft have the best safety record
   B) the U.S. commercial jet aircraft industry has a lower wage rate than foreign competitors
   C) the World Trade Organization has given preferential treatment to the U.S. commercial jet aircraft industry
   D) two of the first movers in the industry were U.S. firms

   Answer: D   Difficulty: Hard   Page: 142

87. The new trade theorists argue that the United States leads in exports of commercial jet aircraft not because it is better endowed with the factors of production required to manufacture aircraft, but because:
   A) U.S. built commercial jet aircraft have the best safety record
   B) the U.S. commercial jet aircraft industry has a lower wage rate than foreign competitors
   C) the World Trade Organization has given preferential treatment to the U.S. commercial jet aircraft industry
   D) two of the first movers in the industry were U.S. firms

   Answer: D   Difficulty: Hard   Page: 142

Chapter 4 International Trade Theory

88. The economic and strategic advantages that accrue to early entrants into an industry are referred to as:
    A) first-mover advantages
    B) initial-shaker advantages
    C) preemptive advantages
    D) first-in advantages

    Answer: A   Difficulty: Easy   Page: 142

89. According to the new trade theorists, because early entrants are able to gain _____, the early entrants into an industry may get a lock on the world market that discourages subsequent entry.
    A) high brand awareness
    B) highly skilled employees
    C) high legitimacy
    D) economies of scale

    Answer: D   Difficulty: Medium   Page: 142

90. New trade theorists stress the role of the following three variables in giving a firm first-mover advantages?
    A) availability of capital, entrepreneurship, and favorable government policies
    B) entrepreneurship, favorable foreign exchange rates, and innovation
    C) luck, entrepreneurship, and innovation
    D) modernization, luck, and the availability of capital

    Answer: C   Difficulty: Hard   Page: 143

91. New trade theorists stress the role of entrepreneurship, innovation, and _____ is giving a firm first-mover advantages.
    A) luck
    B) creativity
    C) factor endowments
    D) capital

    Answer: A   Difficulty: Medium   Page: 143

92. In 1990 _____ of Harvard Business School published the results of an intensive research effort that attempted to determine why some nations succeed and others fail in international competition.
    A) Eli Heckscher
    B) Michael Porter
    C) Bertil Ohlin
    D) Raymond Vernon

    Answer: B Difficulty: Easy Page: 143

93. According to Michael Porter, a nation's position in factors of production such as skilled labor or the infrastructure necessary to compete in a given industry are referred to as:
    A) demand endowments
    B) factor endowments
    C) factor competencies
    D) demand conditions

    Answer: B Difficulty: Hard Page: 143

94. In 1990, Michael Porter of the Harvard Business School, published the results an intensive research effort that attempted to determine why some nations succeed and others fail in international competition. The name of the book was _____.
    A) The Comparable Advantage of Trade and Globalization
    B) The Wealth of Nations
    C) The Competitive Advantage of Nations
    D) The Absolute Advantages of Globalization

    Answer: C Difficulty: Medium Page: 143

95. In his book The Competitive Advantage of Nations, Porter's thesis was that four broad attributes of a nation shape the environment in which local firms compete, and that these attributes promote or impede the creation of competitive advantage. Which of the following is not one of these attributes?
    A) factor endowments
    B) customs
    C) firm strategy, structure, and rivalry
    D) related and supporting industries

    Answer: B Difficulty: Hard Page: 143

Chapter 4 International Trade Theory

96. In his study dealing with the competitive advantage of nations, Porter argued that in regard to factor endowments, _____ factors are the most significant for competitive advantage.
    A) standard
    B) basic
    C) advanced
    D) complementary

    Answer: C Difficulty: Medium Page: 145

97. In his study dealing with the competitive advantage of nations, Porter argued that in regard to demand conditions, a nation's firms' gain competitive advantage if their domestic consumers are _____ and _____.
    A) unpretentious, passive
    B) modest, passive
    C) exacting, unpretentious
    D) sophisticated, demanding

    Answer: D Difficulty: Medium Page: 145

98. Which of the following theorists argued that successful industries within a country tend to be grouped into "clusters" of related industries?
    A) Porter
    B) Vernon
    C) Ricardo
    D) Heckscher

    Answer: A Difficulty: Medium Page: 145

99. In his study, Porter observed that there are a disproportionate number of people with finance backgrounds on the top management teams of many _____ industries.
    A) Japanese
    B) French
    C) United States
    D) South Korean

    Answer: C Difficulty: Hard Page: 145

Chapter 4 International Trade Theory

100. In sum, Porter concluded that the degree to which a nation is likely to achieve international success in a certain industry is a function of the combined impact of factor endowments, domestic demand conditions, related and supporting industries, and _____.
    A) domestic wage rates
    B) membership in the World Trade Organization
    C) availability of capital
    D) firm strategy, structure, and rivalry

    Answer: D   Difficulty: Medium   Page: 145

101. Porter's "diamond" of the determinants of national competitive advantage includes factor endowments, related and supporting industries, firm strategy, structure, and rivalry, and _____.
    A) demand conditions
    B) membership in the World Trade Organization
    C) domestic wage rates
    D) government support

    Answer: A   Difficulty: Medium   Page: 145

102. Porter's "diamond" of the determinants of national competitive advantage includes demand conditions, related and supporting industries, firm strategy, structure, and rivalry, and _____.
    A) domestic wage rates
    B) government support
    C) factor endowments
    D) membership in the World Trade Organization

    Answer: C   Difficulty: Medium   Page: 145

103. If Porter is correct, we would expect his model to predict:
    A) currency exchange rates
    B) membership in the World Trade Organization
    C) the pattern of international trade
    D) factor endowments

    Answer: C   Difficulty: Medium   Page: 148

Chapter 4 International Trade Theory

104. According to the new trade theory, firms that establish a _____ advantage with regard to the production of a particular new product may subsequently dominate global trade in that product.
    A) initial-class
    B) early entrant
    C) first-mover
    D) initial-entrant

    Answer: C Difficulty: Medium Page: 149

105. According to the textbook, it has been often argued that in recent years that _____ firms, rather than their European or North American competitors, seem to have been prepared to undertake the vast investments and bear the years of losses required to build a first-mover advantage.
    A) Chinese
    B) South Korean
    C) Japanese
    D) Australian

    Answer: C Difficulty: Hard Page: 150

Essay Questions

106. What is meant by the term "free trade?" Was Adam Smith an advocate or critic of free trade? Is free trade compatible with the concept of mercantilism? Explain your answer.

    Difficulty: Easy Page: 125

    Answer:
    Free trade refers to a situation where a government does not attempt to influence through quotas or duties what its citizens can buy from another country or what they can produce and sell to another country. This concept was supported by Adam Smith, who argued that the "invisible hand" of the market mechanism, rather than government policy, should determine what a country imports and what it exports. The concept of mercantilism is not compatible with the concept of free trade. The main tenet of mercantilism is that it is in a country's best interests to maintain a trade surplus by exporting more than it imports. Consistent with this belief, the mercantilist doctrine advocated government intervention to achieve a surplus in the balance of trade.

Chapter 4 International Trade Theory

107. When does free trade occur?

Difficulty: Easy   Page: 125

Answer:
Free trade occurs when a government does not attempt to influence through quotas or duties what its citizens can buy from another country or what they can produce and sell to another country.

108. Describe Adam Smith's concept of absolute advantage.

Difficulty: Medium   Page: 129

Answer:
According to Smith, countries should specialize in the production of goods for which they have an absolute advantage and then trade those goods for the goods produced by other countries. For instance, during Smith's time, England had an absolute advantage in the production of textiles, and France had an absolute advantage in the production of wine. According to the concept of absolute advantage, it then only makes sense for England to produce textiles (and export them to France), and France to produce wine (and export it to England). Smith's basic argument, therefore, was that a country should never produce goods at home that it can buy at a lower cost from other countries. Moreover, Smith argued that by specializing in the production of goods in which each has an absolute advantage, both countries benefit by engaging in trade.

109. Describe the Heckscher-Ohlin theory of international trade. Is the Heckscher-Ohlin theory consistent with the notion of free trade? Why or why not?

Difficulty: Medium   Page: 138

Answer:
The Heckscher-Ohlin theory predicts that countries will export those goods that make intensive use of those factors that are locally abundant, while importing goods that make intensive use of factors that are locally scarce. Thus, the Heckscher-Ohlin theory attempts to explain the pattern of international trade that we see in the world economy. The Heckscher-Ohlin theory is consistent with the notion of free trade. It also has commonsense appeal, and there are many examples of international commerce that are supportive of the theory.

Chapter 4 International Trade Theory

110. Describe the central tenant of the product life-cycle theory.

Difficulty: Medium   Page: 139

Answer:
Proposed by Raymond Vernon, the product life-cycle theory suggests that early in their life cycle, most new products are produced in an exported from the country in which they were developed. As a new product becomes widely accepted internationally, production starts in other countries. As a result, the theory suggests, the product may ultimately be exported back to the country of its innovation.

111. Describe the new trade theory. How does the new trade theory help us to understand why the United States is dominant in the world market for commercial aircraft exports?

Difficulty: Hard   Page: 142

Answer:
The new trade theory stresses that in some cases countries specialize in the production and export of particular products not because of underlying differences in factor endowments, but because in certain industries, the world market can support only a limited number of firms. In such industries, firms that enter the market first build a competitive advantage that is difficult to challenge. Thus, the observed pattern of trade between nations may in part be due to the ability of firms to capture first-mover advantages.
This theory helps us understand why the United States is dominant in the world market for commercial aircraft exports. American firms such as Boeing were first movers in the world market in the commercial aircraft industry. As a result, Boeing and to a lesser extent other American firms built a competitive advantage that has subsequently been difficult for firms from countries with equally favorable factor endowments to challenge.

112. Describe what is meant by first-mover advantages?

Difficulty: Easy   Page: 142

Answer:
First mover advantages are the economic and strategic advantages that accrue to early entrants into an industry. Because they are able to gain economies of scale, early entrants may get a lock on the world market that discourages subsequent entry. In other words, the ability of first-movers to reap economies of scale creates a barrier to entry. In the commercial aircraft industry, for example, the fact that Boeing and Airbus are already in the industry and have achieved substantial economies of scale effectively discourages new entrants.

113. In an extensive study that was published in a book entitled The Competitive Advantage of Nations, Michael Porter concluded that four broad attributes of a nation shape the environment in which local firms compete, and that these attributes promote or impede the creation of competitive advantage. Identify and describe the four attributes advanced by Porter. What did Porter conclude from his analysis?

Difficulty: Medium   Page: 143

Answer:
The four attributes identified by Porter are as follows:

- Factor Endowments: A nation's position in factors of production such as skilled labor or the infrastructure necessary to compete in a given industry.
- Demand Conditions: The nature of home demand for the industry's product or service.
- Related or Supporting Industries: The presence or absence in a nation of supplier industries and related industries that are internationally competitive.
- Firm Strategy, Structure, and Rivalry: The conditions in the nation governing how companies are created, organized, and managed and the nature of domestic rivalry.

Porter speaks of these four attributes as constituting the diamond. He argues that firms are most likely to succeed in industries or industry segments where the diamond is most favorable.

Chapter 5 The Political Economy of International Trade

True/False Questions

1. Free trade refers to a situation where a government does not attempt to restrict what its citizens can buy from another country or what they can sell to another country.

   Answer: True   Difficulty: Easy   Page: 158

2. Tariffs are relatively new instruments of trade policy.

   Answer: False   Difficulty: Medium   Page: 159

3. A tariff is a tax levied on imports.

   Answer: True   Difficulty: Easy   Page: 160

4. Specific tariffs are leveled as a proportion of the value of the imported good (for example, 5% of the value of a new car).

   Answer: True   Difficulty: Medium   Page: 160

5. A tariff raises the cost of imported products relative to domestic products.

   Answer: True   Difficulty: Medium   Page: 160

6. The main gains from subsidies accrue to importers, whose international competitiveness is increased as a result of them.

   Answer: False   Difficulty: Medium   Page: 161

7. An import quota is a direct restriction on the quantity of some good that may be imported into a country.

   Answer: True   Difficulty: Easy   Page: 162

8. Quotas benefit consumers.

   Answer: False   Difficulty: Easy   Page: 162

9. A local content requirement demands that some specific fraction of a good be produced domestically.

   Answer: True   Difficulty: Medium   Page: 162

Chapter 5 The Political Economy of International Trade

10. A quota on trade imposed by the exporting country, typically at the request of the importing country, is referred to as a voluntary export restraint.

    Answer: True   Difficulty: Medium   Page: 165

11. Administrative trade policies are bureaucratic rules that are designed to make it easy for imports to enter a country.

    Answer: False   Difficulty: Medium   Page: 164

12. One common political argument for government intervention is that it is necessary for protecting jobs and industries from "unfair" foreign competition.

    Answer: True   Difficulty: Medium   Page: 165

13. Countries sometimes argue that it is important to protect certain industries for reasons of national security.

    Answer: True   Difficulty: Medium   Page: 165

14. The D'Amato Act is legislation that allows Americans to sue foreign firms that use property in Cuba confiscated from them after the 1959 revolution.

    Answer: False   Difficulty: Hard   Page: 167

15. The infant industry argument is the oldest economic argument for government intervention.

    Answer: True   Difficulty: Medium   Page: 169

16. The intellectual case for free trade goes back to the late 18th century and the work of Adam Smith.

    Answer: True   Difficulty: Medium   Page: 172

17. In its early years GATT was by most measures unsuccessful.

    Answer: False   Difficulty: Medium   Page: 173

Chapter 5 The Political Economy of International Trade

18. Against the background of rising pressures for protectionism, in 1986 the members of the GATT embarked on their eighth round of negotiations to reduce tariffs, the Brussels Round.

    Answer: False   Difficulty: Medium   Page: 174

19. Until the Uruguay Round GATT rules had applied only to industrial goods.

    Answer: True   Difficulty: Medium   Page: 175

20. According to the textbook, the world is better off with a GATT deal than without it.

    Answer: True   Difficulty: Medium   Page: 175

Multiple Choice Questions

21. _____ refers to a situation where a government does not attempt to restrict what its citizens can buy from another country or what they can sell to another country.
    A) Free trade
    B) Unencumbered trade
    C) Sovereign trade
    D) Autonomous trade

    Answer: A   Difficulty: Easy   Page: 158

22. Which of the following is not an example of one of the main instruments in trade policy used by governments around the world.
    A) tariffs
    B) political mandate
    C) subsidies
    D) import quotas

    Answer: B   Difficulty: Medium   Page: 159

23. _____ are the oldest and simplest instrument of trade policy.
    A) Subsidies
    B) Administrative policies
    C) Tariffs
    D) Voluntary export restraints

    Answer: C   Difficulty: Medium   Page: 160

Chapter 5 The Political Economy of International Trade

24. A _____ is a tax levied on imports.
    A) tariff
    B) special assessment
    C) penalty
    D) globalization assessment

    Answer: A Difficulty: Easy Page: 160

25. A tariff is a tax levied on _____.
    A) domestically produced goods
    B) imports
    C) services
    D) exports

    Answer: B Difficulty: Easy Page: 160

26. Tariffs fall into two categories. These are:
    A) specific tariffs and ad valorem tariffs
    B) global tariffs and domestic tariffs
    C) general tariffs and specific tariffs
    D) flexible tariffs and ad valorem tariffs

    Answer: A Difficulty: Medium Page: 160

27. The oldest form of _____ is a tariff.
    A) political policy
    B) administrative policy
    C) trade policy
    D) agricultural policy

    Answer: C Difficulty: Medium Page: 160

28. According to the author of the textbook, tariffs cause the most damage to _____, because this group bears the economic brunt of tariffs.
    A) trade associations
    B) governments
    C) consumers
    D) producers

    Answer: C Difficulty: Medium Page: 160

29. According to the author of the textbook, tariffs benefit the following two groups:
    A) government and producers
    B) consumers and trade associations
    C) government and consumers
    D) producers and consumers

    Answer: A Difficulty: Medium Page: 160

30. _____ are levied as a fixed charge for each for each unit of a good imported.
    A) Specific tariffs
    B) General tariffs
    C) Ad valorem tariffs
    D) Global tariffs

    Answer: A Difficulty: Easy Page: 160

31. Taxes levied as a fixed charge for each unit of good imported are referred to as:
    A) ad valorem tariffs
    B) global tariffs
    C) special tariffs
    D) general tariffs

    Answer: C Difficulty: Easy Page: 160

32. While _____ tariffs are levied as a fixed charge for each unit of a good imported, _____ tariffs are levied as a proportion of the value of the imported good.
    A) general, special
    B) ad valorem, special
    C) global, special
    D) specific, ad valorem

    Answer: D Difficulty: Medium Page: 160

33. An example of a(n) _____ tariff is the 25 percent tariff the U.S. government placed on imported light trucks in the 1980s.
    A) general
    B) ad valorem
    C) special
    D) global

    Answer: B Difficulty: Medium Page: 160

34. According to the author of the textbook, tariffs are unambiguously _____ and _____.
   A) pro-producer and pro consumer
   B) anti-consumer and pro-producer
   C) anti-consumer and anti-producer
   D) pro-producer and anti-consumer

   Answer: D Difficulty: Hard Page: 160

35. A _____ is a government payment to a domestic producer.
   A) duty
   B) subsidy
   C) quota
   D) tariff

   Answer: B Difficulty: Easy Page: 160

36. A government payment to a domestic producer is called a:
   A) subsidy
   B) tariff
   C) duty
   D) quota

   Answer: A Difficulty: Easy Page: 160

37. The main gains from subsidies accrue to _____, whose international competitiveness is increased as a result of them.
   A) domestic producers
   B) consumers
   C) governments
   D) importers

   Answer: A Difficulty: Medium Page: 161

38. According to official national figures, government subsidies to industry in most industrialized countries during the late 1980s amounted to between:
   A) 40% and 50% of the value of industrial output
   B) 15% and 20% of the value of industrial output
   C) 2% and 3.5% of the value of industrial output
   D) 10% and 15% of the value of industrial output

   Answer: C Difficulty: Hard Page: 161

39. An import quota is a direct restriction on the quantity of some good that may be:
    A) subsidized by a country
    B) imported into a country
    C) exported out of a country
    D) produced in a country

    Answer: B Difficulty: Easy Page: 162

40. Both import quotas and VERs benefit _____ by limiting import competition, but they result in higher prices, which hurts _____.
    A) domestic producers, consumers
    B) governments, consumers
    C) consumers, foreign producers
    D) foreign producers, governments

    Answer: A Difficulty: Hard Page: 162

41. An _____ is a direct restriction on the quantity of some goods that may be imported into a country.
    A) specialization quota
    B) production quota
    C) import quota
    D) export quota

    Answer: C Difficulty: Easy Page: 162

42. A _____ is a quota on trade imposed by the exporting country, typically at the request of the importing country's government.
    A) voluntary export restraint
    B) involuntary export restraint
    C) trade reconciliation
    D) refereed export restraint

    Answer: A Difficulty: Medium Page: 162

43. A quota on trade imposed by the exporting country, typically at the request of the importing country, is called a:
    A) involuntary import restraint
    B) trade reconciliation
    C) voluntary export restraint
    D) refereed export restraint

    Answer: C Difficulty: Medium Page: 162

44. One of the most famous examples of a _____ is the limitation on auto exports to the United States enforced by Japanese automobile producers in 1981.
    A) involuntary import restraint
    B) voluntary export restraint
    C) trade reconciliation
    D) referred export restraint

    Answer: B Difficulty: Hard Page: 162

45. Local content requirements benefit the _____ of component parts, but they raise prices of imported components, which hurts _____.
    A) consumers, producers
    B) producers, governments
    C) consumers, governments
    D) producers, consumers

    Answer: D Difficulty: Hard Page: 162

46. A _____ demands that some specific fraction of a good be produced domestically.
    A) international content requirement
    B) local content requirement
    C) specific content requirement
    D) ad valorem content requirement

    Answer: B Difficulty: Easy Page: 162

47. A government order that some specific fraction of a good be produced domestically is called a:
    A) local content requirement
    B) ad valorem content requirement
    C) international content requirement
    D) specific content requirement

    Answer: A Difficulty: Easy Page: 162

Chapter 5 The Political Economy of International Trade

48. If Ford Motor decided to produce cars in Italy, and the Italian government stipulated that 50% of the component parts that went into Ford's vehicles must be produced locally, that requirement would be an example of a:
    A) ad valorem content requirement
    B) international content requirement
    C) specific content requirement
    D) local content requirement

    Answer: D   Difficulty: Medium   Page: 162

49. If Boeing won an order to sell 50 of its new Boeing 777 airplanes to China, but the Chinese government stipulated that 20 percent of the component parts of the 777s that it purchased must be produced in China, that stipulation would be an example of a:
    A) ad valorem content requirement
    B) specific content requirement
    C) ad hoc content requirement
    D) local content requirement

    Answer: D   Difficulty: Medium   Page: 162

50. For a domestic producer of component parts, local content requirements provide protection in the same way an import quota does: _____.
    A) by limiting foreign competition
    B) by increasing tariffs
    C) by eliminating foreign competition
    D) by encouraging foreign competition

    Answer: A   Difficulty: Medium   Page: 163

51. In the context of international trade, _____ is defined as selling goods in a foreign market at a price below their costs of production or as selling goods in a foreign market at below their "fair" market price.
    A) slicing
    B) dumping
    C) slashing
    D) subsidizing

    Answer: B   Difficulty: Easy   Page: 163

52. An alleged example of _____ occurred in 1997, when two Korean manufacturers of semiconductors, LG Semicon and Hyundai Electronics, were accused of selling dynamic random access memory chips in the U.S. market at below their costs of production.
    A) dumping
    B) forcing
    C) slicing
    D) subsidizing

    Answer: A   Difficulty: Medium   Page: 163

53. A charge of "dumping" can be levied against a foreign firm if one of the two following conditions exist:
    A) goods are being sold that do not meet local content requirements or goods are being sold that do not meet local quality standards
    B) goods are being sold at predatory prices or goods are being sold that do not meet local product safety standards
    C) goods are being sold without the consent of the host government or goods are being sold that do not meet local quality standards
    D) goods are being sold at below their cost of production or goods are being sold at below their "fair" market value

    Answer: D   Difficulty: Hard   Page: 163

54. _____ are designed to punish foreign firms that engage in dumping.
    A) Antidumping policies
    B) Couterdumping policies
    C) Statutory dumping policies
    D) Civil dumping policies

    Answer: A   Difficulty: Easy   Page: 163

55. The ultimate objective of antidumping policies is to:
    A) protect consumers from predatory pricing
    B) protect host governments from the loss of legitimate tax revenue
    C) protect domestic producers from "unfair" foreign competition
    D) protect foreign producers from "unfair" local competition

    Answer: C   Difficulty: Medium   Page: 163

56. In the United States, if a domestic producer believes that a foreign firm is dumping production in the U.S. market, it can file a petition with the following two government agencies:
    A) Treasury Department and the Senate Committee on Fair Trade
    B) Department of Agricultural and the Department of Labor
    C) Department of State and the Treasury Department
    D) Commerce Department and International Trade Commission

    Answer: D   Difficulty: Hard   Page: 164

57. Bureaucratic rules that are designed to make it difficult for imports to enter a country are referred to as:
    A) situational trade policies
    B) ad valorem trade policies
    C) supplemental trade policies
    D) administrative trade policies

    Answer: D   Difficulty: Easy   Page: 164

58. An administrative policy is an informal instrument or bureaucratic rule that can be used to restrict imports and boost exports. Such policies benefit _____ but hurt

    _____.
    A) trade associations, producers
    B) consumers, producers
    C) consumers, trade associations
    D) producers, consumers

    Answer: D   Difficulty: Medium   Page: 164

59. Consider the following scenario. The Netherlands exports tulip bulbs to almost every country in the world except Japan. The reason is that Japanese customs inspectors insist on checking every tulip bulb by cutting it down the middle (which destroys the bulb). The insistence on the part of the Japanese to inspect the bulbs in this manner (which makes it impractical for the Netherlands to export to Japan) is an example of an:
    A) administrative trade policy
    B) ad valorem trade policy
    C) contingent trade policy
    D) supplemental trade policy

    Answer: A   Difficulty: Medium   Page: 164

60. At one time, the French government required that all imported videocassette recorders arrive in France through a small customs entry point that was both remote and poorly staffed. This policy, which in effect made it impractical for a foreign company to import videocassette recorders to France, is an example of an:
    A) supplemental trade policy
    B) contingent trade policy
    C) administrative trade policy
    D) ad valorem trade policy

    Answer: C Difficulty: Medium Page: 164

61. If a country restricted the import of a particular good to a remote seaport that made it extremely difficult for any other country to import the good profitably, that would be an example of an _____ that limits imports.
    A) ad valorem trade policy
    B) administrative trade policy
    C) situational trade policy
    D) directional trade policy

    Answer: B Difficulty: Medium Page: 164

62. _____ are bureaucratic rules that are designed to make it difficult for imports to enter a country.
    A) Ad valorem trade policies
    B) Supplemental trade policies
    C) Contingent trade policies
    D) Administrative trade policies

    Answer: D Difficulty: Easy Page: 164

63. In general, there are two types of arguments for government intervention into the free flow of trade. These are:
    A) patriotic and sociocultural
    B) sociocultural and legal
    C) political and economic
    D) legal and patriotic

    Answer: C Difficulty: Medium Page: 164

Chapter 5 The Political Economy of International Trade

64. In general, there are two types of arguments for government intervention into the free flow of trade. These are: (1) political and (2)
    A) technological
    B) sociocultural
    C) legal
    D) economic

    Answer: D   Difficulty: Medium   Page: 164

65. The two main types of arguments for government intervention into the free flow of trade are economic and _____.
    A) sociocultural
    B) legal
    C) political
    D) technological

    Answer: C   Difficulty: Medium   Page: 164

66. _____ arguments for government intervention into international trade are typically concerned with boosting the overall wealth of a nation.
    A) Economic
    B) Political
    C) Legal
    D) Sociocultural

    Answer: A   Difficulty: Easy   Page: 164

67. Perhaps the most common political argument for government intervention into the free flow of trade is that:
    A) it protects national pride
    B) politicians and their constituents tend to think that domestically produced products are superior to products produced in another country
    C) it is necessary for protecting jobs and industries from foreign competition
    D) it is necessary to maintain domestic economic stability

    Answer: C   Difficulty: Medium   Page: 167

68. The _____ is legislation that allows Americans to sue foreign firms that use property in Cuba confiscated from them after the 1959 revolution.
    A) Frederick-Peterson Act
    B) D'Amato-Perkins Act
    C) Perkins-Dole Act
    D) Helms-Burton Act

    Answer: D   Difficulty: Hard   Page: 167

69. The _____ is legislation that is similar to the Helms-Burton Act, but is aimed at Libya and Iran.
    A) Perkin's Act
    B) D'Amato Act
    C) Williams Act
    D) Cato Act

    Answer: B   Difficulty: Hard   Page: 167

70. _____ status allows countries to export goods to the U.S. under favorable terms.
    A) Most favored nation
    B) Preferential partner
    C) Fully qualified
    D) Cleared nation

    Answer: A   Difficulty: Medium   Page: 168

71. The _____ argument is by far the oldest economic argument for government intervention into the free flow of trade.
    A) mature industry
    B) infant industry
    C) declining industry
    D) proprietary industry

    Answer: B   Difficulty: Easy   Page: 168

72. The oldest economic argument for government intervention into the free flow of trade is referred to as the:
    A) infant industry argument
    B) strategic trade policy argument
    C) proprietary industry argument
    D) declining industry argument

    Answer: A   Difficulty: Easy   Page: 169

73. According to the _____ argument, many developing countries have a potential comparative advantage in manufacturing, but new manufacturing industries there cannot initially compete with well-established industries in developed countries. To allow manufacturing to get a toehold, the argument is that governments should temporarily support new industries (with tariffs, import quotas, and subsidies) until they have grown strong enough to meet international competition.
    A) proprietary industry
    B) strategic trade policy
    C) mature industry
    D) infant industry

    Answer: D   Difficulty: Medium   Page: 169

74. Primarily as a result of pressure from the developing world, the GATT recognized the _____ argument as a legitimate reason for protectionism.
    A) declining industry
    B) infant industry
    C) strategic trade policy
    D) mature industry

    Answer: B   Difficulty: Medium   Page: 169

75. According to the _____ argument, a government should use subsidies to support promising firms that are active in newly emerging industries.
    A) strategic trade policy
    B) infant industry
    C) declining industry
    D) mature industry

    Answer: A   Difficulty: Medium   Page: 169

76. The infant industry argument has been recognized as a legitimate reason for protectionism by the:
    A) GATT
    B) North Atlantic Treaty Organization
    C) United Nations
    D) International Monetary Fund

    Answer: A   Difficulty: Medium   Page: 169

Chapter 5 The Political Economy of International Trade

77. The strategic trade policy argument of the new trade theorists advances an _____ justification for government intervention in international trade.
    A) technological
    B) sociocultural
    C) economic
    D) political

    Answer: C Difficulty: Medium Page: 169

78. The _____ arguments of the new trade theorists suggest an economic justification for government intervention in international trade.
    A) mature industry
    B) declining industry
    C) infant industry
    D) strategic trade policy

    Answer: D Difficulty: Hard Page: 169

79. According to the strategy trade policy argument, a government should use subsidies to:
    A) support promising firms in emerging industries
    B) support established firms in key industries
    C) support the import of goods that a country cannot produce domestically
    D) support the export of agricultural products

    Answer: A Difficulty: Medium Page: 169

80. An important component of _____ is that it might pay governments to intervene in an industry if it helps domestic firms overcome the barriers to entry created by foreign firms that have already reaped first-mover advantages.
    A) tactical trade policy
    B) strategic trade policy
    C) administrative trade policy
    D) comparative trade policy

    Answer: B Difficulty: Medium Page: 170

81. According to the textbook, Paul Krugman, a professor at MIT, predicts that a country that attempts to use strategic trade policy to establish a domestic firm (or firms) in a dominant position in a global industry will probably:
    A) succeed fairly smoothly
    B) be viewed favorable in the international community
    C) provoke retaliation
    D) be successful if the policy is in force for at least three years

    Answer: C Difficulty: Medium   Page: 170

82. Free trade as a government policy was first officially embraced by Great Britain in 1846, when the British Parliament repealed the _____.
    A) Corn Laws
    B) Steel Laws
    C) Coal Laws
    D) Apparel Laws

    Answer: A Difficulty: Medium   Page: 172

83. The Corn Laws:
    A) were repealed after record harvests in Britain
    B) placed a high tariff on corn imported into Britain
    C) were repealed after a stinging speech in parliament by David Ricardo where he outlined the theory of comparative advantage
    D) were enacted by the U.S. government after defeating Britain in the War of Independence

    Answer: B Difficulty: Hard   Page: 172

84. Aimed at avoiding rising unemployment by protecting domestic industry and diverting consumer demand away from foreign products, the _____ tariff erected an enormous wall of tariff barriers.
    A) Smott-Hawley Act
    B) Porter-Ricardo Act
    C) Heckscher-Ohlin
    D) Smith-Krugman

    Answer: A Difficulty: Hard   Page: 172

Chapter 5 The Political Economy of International Trade

85. The General Agreement on Tariffs and Trade (GATT) was established in _____.
    A) 1867
    B) 1908
    C) 1947
    D) 1983

    Answer: C Difficulty: Medium Page: 173

86. Founded in 1947, the _____ was a multilateral agreement whose objective was to liberalize trade by eliminating tariffs, subsidies, import quotas, and the like.
    A) General Agreement of Tariffs and Trade
    B) World Trade Supervisory Authority
    C) United Nations
    D) International Trade Organization

    Answer: A Difficulty: Easy Page: 173

87. The latest round of the GATT agreement, referred to as the _____, was launched in 1986 and completed in December 1993.
    A) Uruguay Round
    B) German Round
    C) Japanese Round
    D) Brazilian Round

    Answer: A Difficulty: Medium Page: 173

88. The _____ was a multilateral agreement whose objective was to liberalize trade by eliminating tariffs, subsidies, import quotas, and the like.
    A) Multinational Agreement on Globalization
    B) United Nations Charter on Free Trade
    C) World Agreement on Trade and Free Commerce
    D) General Agreement on Trade and Tariffs

    Answer: D Difficulty: Medium Page: 173

89. In its early years, GATT was by most measures:
    A) very unsuccessful
    B) slightly unsuccessful
    C) slightly successful
    D) very successful

    Answer: D Difficulty: Medium Page: 173

90. Which of the following is not one of the main reasons that protectionist pressures arose around the world during the 1980s?
    A) many countries found ways to get around GATT regulations
    B) the opening of Japanese markets to imports
    C) the economic successes of Japan
    D) the persistent trade deficit in the United States

    Answer: B Difficulty: Hard Page: 174

91. One of the best known examples of _____ is the agreement between the United States and Japan, under which Japanese producers promised to limit their auto imports to the United States as a way of defusing growing trade tensions.
    A) voluntary export restraint
    B) import quotas
    C) local content requirement
    D) ad valorem tariffs

    Answer: A Difficulty: Medium Page: 174

92. One of the best-known examples of voluntary export restraints is the agreement between the United States and Japan, under which Japanese producers promised to limit their _____ to the United States as a way of defusing growing trade tensions.
    A) camera imports
    B) VCR imports
    C) auto imports
    D) steel imports

    Answer: D Difficulty: Medium Page: 174

93. In 1986 GATT members embarked on their eighth round of negotiations to reduce tariffs. The negotiations were referred to as the _____ Round (so named because they took place in this country).
    A) German
    B) Australian
    C) Brazilian
    D) Uruguay

    Answer: D Difficulty: Easy Page: 174

Chapter 5 The Political Economy of International Trade

94. The eighth (and most recent) round of the GATT negotiations was referred to as the:
    A) Finland Round
    B) Uruguay Round
    C) New Zealand Round
    D) French Round

    Answer: B Difficulty: Easy Page: 174

95. Which of the following is not a component of the Uruguay Round agreement?
    A) GATT rules will be much clearer and stronger.
    B) GATT fair trade and market access rules will be extended to cover a wider range of services.
    C) agricultural subsidies will be substantially reduced.
    D) tariffs on industrial goods will be increased by more the one-half

    Answer: D Difficulty: Hard Page: 175

96. Which of the following statement is not a component of the Uruguay Round agreement?
    A) tariffs on industrial goods will be reduced by more than one-third
    B) barriers on trade in textiles will be significantly reduced over 10 years
    C) a World Trade Organization will be created to implement the GATT agreement
    D) agricultural subsidies will be substantially increased

    Answer: D Difficulty: Hard Page: 175

97. The World Trade Organization was created by the _____ of the GATT negotiations.
    A) Cyprus Round
    B) Canadian Round
    C) Norway Round
    D) Uruguay Round

    Answer: D Difficulty: Medium Page: 175

98. As a result of the Uruguay Round agreement, the _____ was created to arbitrate trade disputes and monitor the trade policies of member countries.
    A) United Trade Authority
    B) World Trade Organization
    C) Global Commerce Authority
    D) International Trade Authority

    Answer: B Difficulty: Medium Page: 175

Chapter 5 The Political Economy of International Trade

99. What is the main effect of the Uruguay Round Agreement on Agricultural products?
    A) consumers will face higher prices
    B) farm subsidies will be reduced
    C) inefficient producers will be better off
    D) nothing - the Uruguay Round failed to make progress on this issue

    Answer: B   Difficulty: Medium   Page: 175

100. The acronym WTO stands for:
    A) World Trade Organization
    B) World Technology Outlook
    C) Western Trade Alliance
    D) World Trade Outlook

    Answer: A   Difficulty: Easy   Page: 175

101. According to the textbook, the WTO's policing and enforcement mechanisms are having _____ on world trade.
    A) a positive effect
    B) a negative effect
    C) no effect
    D) a very slight effect

    Answer: A   Difficulty: Medium   Page: 177

102. Trade barriers _____ the cost of exporting products to a country.
    A) have no effect on
    B) raise
    C) lower
    D) eliminate

    Answer: B   Difficulty: Medium   Page: 182

103. _____ may limit a firm's ability to serve a country from locations outside of that country.
    A) Statutory export restraints
    B) Voluntary export restraints
    C) Involuntary export restraints
    D) Legal export restraints

    Answer: B   Difficulty: Medium   Page: 182

104. Which of the following is not a disadvantage of government intervention in trade policy?
    A) intervention can be self-defeating, since it tends to protect the inefficient rather than help firms become efficient global competitors
    B) intervention in the form of tariffs, quotas, and subsidies can help firms and industries establish a competitive advantage in the world economy
    C) intervention is unlikely to be well executed, since it may invite retaliation and trigger a trade war
    D) intervention is dangerous, since it may invite retaliation and trigger a trade war

    Answer: B   Difficulty: Medium   Page: 182

105. According to our textbook, government intervention in trade policy is unlikely to be well-executed for the following reason:
    A) inexperience
    B) the costs associated with intervention
    C) the impact of special interest groups
    D) because of the high turnover of officials in government industries

    Answer: C   Difficulty: Medium   Page: 182

Essay Questions

106. What is a tariff? Describe the difference between specific tariffs and ad valorem tariffs.

    Difficulty: Easy   Page: 160

    Answer:
    A tariff is a tax levied on imports. Specific tariffs are levied as a fixed charge for each unit of a good imported (for example, $500 for each automobile). Ad valorem tariffs are levied as a proportion of the value of the imported good. An example of an ad valorem tariff is the 25 percent tariff that the U.S. government placed on imported light trucks (including pickup trucks, four-wheel-drive vehicles, and minivans) in the late 1980s.

Chapter 5 The Political Economy of International Trade

107. Who gains and who losses from the imposition of a tariff on an imported good? How can it be determined whether the net gain from the tariff exceeds the net loss?

Difficulty: Medium   Page: 160

Answer:
The government gains, because the tariff increases government revenues. Domestic producers gain, because the tariff gives them some protection against foreign competitors by increasing the cost of imported foreign goods. Consumers lose because they must pay more for certain imports. Whether the gains to the government and domestic producers exceeds the loss to consumers depends on various factors such as the amount of the tariff, the importance of the imported good to domestic consumers, the number of jobs saved in the protected industry, and so on.

108. What is a subsidy? Provide some examples of the forms that subsidies take. How do subsidies help domestic producers?

Difficulty: Medium   Page: 160

Answer:
A subsidy is a government payment to a domestic producer. Subsidies take many forms including cash grants, low-interest loans, tax breaks, and government equity participation in domestic firms. By lowering costs, subsidies help domestic producers in two ways: they help them compete against low-cost foreign imports and they help them gain export markets.

109. What is a voluntary export restraint? Can countries use voluntary export restraints to avoid trade retaliation? Explain your answer.

Difficulty: Medium   Page: 162

Answer:
A voluntary export restraint is a "voluntary" quota on trade imposed by the exporting company (on itself) typically at the request of the importing country's government. One of the most famous examples is the limitation on auto exports to the United States enforced by the Japanese automobile producers in 1981. In response to direct pressure from the U.S. government, this voluntary export restraint limited Japanese automobile imports to no more than 1.68 million vehicles per year.

Clearly, voluntary export restraints can be used to "head off" higher tariffs, more restrictive formal quotas, and other forms of trade retaliation.

Chapter 5 The Political Economy of International Trade

110. What is a local content requirement? How are local content requirements typically expressed?

Difficulty: Medium   Page: 162

Answer:
A local content requirement calls for a specific fraction of a good (produced by a multinational firm in a foreign country) to be produced locally. This requirement can be expressed in physical terms (e.g., 75 percent of component parts must be produced locally) or in value terms (e.g., 75 percent of the value of this product must be produced locally).

111. What are administrative trade policies? Are these trade policies deliberately designed to restrict the flow of imports into a country, or do they simply reflect the complexity of the bureaucracies in many foreign countries? Provide at least one example of an "administrative trade policy."

Difficulty: Medium   Page: 164

Answer:
Administrative trade policies are bureaucratic rules that are almost always deliberately designed to restrict the flow of a particular import into a country. For instance, a country may design some administrative rule that makes it totally impractical for a foreign company to import a particular product into its country. An example that is provided in the textbook is tulip bulbs. The Netherlands exports tulip bulbs to almost every country of the world except Japan. The reason is that Japanese customs inspectors insist on checking every tulip bulb by cutting it vertically down the middle, which in effect ruins the bulb. Other examples are equally as compelling. For example, a country might insist that every VCR that is imported into the country be thoroughly tested to make sure that it will not subject the user to an "electric shock." If it took several weeks for these tests to be completed, it would be very difficult to make money importing VCRs into this country.

Obviously, these types of administrative trade policies are informal tariffs and are designed to block specific imports from entering a country.

Chapter 5 The Political Economy of International Trade

112. What are the principle political and economic arguments for government intervention into international trade? Please describe these arguments. In your opinion, which set of arguments are the most compelling?

Difficulty: Hard   Page: 164

Answer:
Political Arguments: The political arguments cover a range of issues, including protecting jobs, protecting industries deemed important for national security, and retaliating against unfair foreign competition. In regard to protecting jobs, this is the most common political argument for government intervention. For example, the Japanese quotas on rice imports are aimed at protecting jobs in that country's agricultural sector. In terms of protecting industries deemed important for national security, countries sometimes argue that it is necessary to protect certain industries (like aerospace, steel, advanced electronics, etc.) because they are important for national security. Finally, in regard to retaliating against foreign competition, some people argue that governments should use the threat to intervene in trade policy as a bargaining tool to help open foreign markets and force trading partners to "play by the rules of the game."

Economic arguments: The economic arguments in favor of government intervention include the infant industry argument and strategic trade policy. The infant industry argument is most often used by developing countries. According to this argument, many developing countries have a potential comparative advantage in manufacturing, but new manufacturing industries there can not initially compete with well-established industries in developed countries. To allow manufacturing to get a toehold, the argument is that governments should temporarily support new industries (with tariffs, import quotas, and subsidies) until they have grown strong enough to meet international standards. The strategy trade policy argument is more complex, but basically argues that governments should use their trade policies to help certain domestic firms dominate their global industries and gain first-mover advantages, and that it might pay government to intervene in an industry if it helps domestic firms overcome the barriers to entry created by foreign firms that have already reaped first-mover advantages.

The author of the textbook clearly believes that the economic arguments for government intervention into international trade are the most compelling. This question presents an interesting and engaging topic for classroom discussion.

113. The World Trade Organization (WTO) was created by the recently completed Uruguay Round of the GATT negotiations. According to the textbook, has the WTO gotten off to a good start or a poor start? Do you believe that the WTO will be effective in the long run? Why or why not?

Difficulty: Medium   Page: 172

Answer:
According to the textbook, the early life of the WTO suggests that its policing and enforcement mechanisms are having a positive effect. Countries are using the WTO to settle trade disputes, which represents an important vote of confidence in the organization's dispute resolution procedures. So far, the users of the system have included both developed and developing countries, which is also a promising development. In addition, some powerful developed countries, including the United States, have been willing to accept WTO ruling that have gone against them, which attests to the organization's legitimacy.

The second part of this question - do you believe that the WTO will be effective in the long run - is designed to provide a forum for classroom discussion and/or ask your students to "think" about the role of an organization like the WTO in settling international commerce disputes.

Chapter 6 Foreign Direct Investment

True/False Questions

1. Foreign direct investment occurs when a firm invests directly in new facilities to produce and/or market a product in a foreign country.

   Answer: True   Difficulty: Easy   Page: 192

2. The stock of foreign direct investment refers the total accumulated value of foreign-owned assets at a given time.

   Answer: True   Difficulty: Medium   Page: 193

3. The flow of foreign investment refers to the number of countries a firm is investing in at any given point in time.

   Answer: False   Difficulty: Easy   Page: 193

4. There has been a rapid decrease in the total volume of FDI over the past 20 years.

   Answer: False   Difficulty: Medium   Page: 193

5. Recently, FDI inflows into the world's developing nations have been on the decline.

   Answer: False   Difficulty: Medium   Page: 194

6. Gross fixed capital formation summarizes the total amount of capital invested in factories, stores, office buildings, and the like.

   Answer: True   Difficulty: Medium   Page: 196

7. Japan is the largest source country for FDI.

   Answer: False   Difficulty: Medium   Page: 198

8. The eclectic paradigm is a theory of FDI that combines two other perspectives into a single holistic explanation of FDI.

   Answer: True   Difficulty: Hard   Page: 200

9. Licensing involves granting a foreign entity the right to produce and sell the firm's product in return for a royalty fee on every unit the foreign entity sells.

    Answer: True Difficulty: Medium Page: 200

10. In general, foreign direct investment is less expensive and less risky than either licensing or exporting.

    Answer: False Difficulty: Medium Page: 200

11. FDI is expensive because a firm must establish production facilities in a foreign country or acquire a foreign enterprise.

    Answer: True Difficulty: Medium Page: 200

12. FDI is risky because of the problems associated with doing business in a different culture where the "rules of the game" may be very different.

    Answer: True Difficulty: Medium Page: 200

13. There is a branch of economic theory known as internationalization theory that seeks to explain why firms often prefer exporting to foreign direct investment.

    Answer: False Difficulty: Medium Page: 201

14. A rationale for wanting control over the operations of a foreign entity is that the firm might wish to take advantage of differences in factor costs across countries, producing only part of its final product in a given country, while importing other parts from where they can be produced at a lower cost.

    Answer: True Difficulty: Hard Page: 201

15. A firm will favor foreign direct investment over exporting as an entry strategy when transportation costs or trade barriers make exporting unattractive.

    Answer: True Difficulty: Medium Page: 202

16. An oligopoly is an industry composed of a large number of large firms.

    Answer: False Difficulty: Medium Page: 203

Chapter 6 Foreign Direct Investment

17. Raymond Vernon's view of foreign direct investment is that firms undertake FDI at particular stages in the life cycle of a product they have pioneered.

    Answer: True   Difficulty: Hard   Page: 213

18. The eclectic paradigm has come under sharp criticism by British economist John Dunning.

    Answer: False   Difficulty: Hard   Page: 205

19. Knowledge spillovers that occur when companies in the same industry locate in the same area are called externalities.

    Answer: True   Difficulty: Medium   Page: 206

20. In practice, many countries have adopted neither a radical policy nor a free market policy toward FDI, but instead a policy that can best be described as pragmatic nationalism.

    Answer: True   Difficulty: Medium   Page: 208

Multiple Choice Questions

21. _____ occurs when a firm invests directly in new facilities to produce and/or market a product in a foreign country.
    A) Reciprocal foreign investment
    B) Cross-boarder international investment
    C) International capital investment
    D) Foreign direct investment

    Answer: D   Difficulty: Easy   Page: 192

22. FDI is an acronym that stands for:
    A) Federation of Direct Investors
    B) Federal Diversification Initiative
    C) Foreign Direct Investment
    D) Formal Direct Internationalization

    Answer: C   Difficulty: Easy   Page: 192

Chapter 6 Foreign Direct Investment

23. According to the U.S. Department of Commerce, _____ occurs whenever a U.S. citizen, organization, or affiliated group takes an interest of 10 percent or more in a foreign business entity.
    A) cross-boarder international investment
    B) foreign direct investment
    C) reciprocal foreign investment
    D) international capital investment

    Answer: B Difficulty: Medium Page: 192

24. If General Electric, a U.S. based corporation, purchased a 50% interest in a company in Italy, that purchase would be an example of:
    A) multinational investment
    B) reciprocal foreign investment
    C) foreign direct investment
    D) cross-boarder international investment

    Answer: C Difficulty: Medium Page: 192

25. If Siemens, a German firms, purchased a 20% interest in a manufacturing firm in the United States, Siemens would be engaging in:
    A) foreign direct investment
    B) global entrepreneurship
    C) cross-boarder international investment
    D) multinational investment

    Answer: A Difficulty: Medium Page: 192

26. A _____ is a company that conducts business in more than one country.
    A) cross-cultural enterprise
    B) synergistic enterprise
    C) multinational enterprise
    D) international conglomerate

    Answer: C Difficulty: Easy Page: 192

27. A company that conducts business in more than one country is referred to as a:
    A) synergistic enterprise
    B) multinational enterprise
    C) international conglomerate
    D) statutory enterprise

    Answer: B Difficulty: Easy Page: 192

Chapter 6 Foreign Direct Investment

28. The _____ of foreign direct investment refers to the amount of FDI undertaken over a given period (normally a year). The _____ of foreign direct investment refers to the total accumulated value of foreign-owned assets at any time.
    A) portfolio, current
    B) flow, stock
    C) stock, flow
    D) stockpile, portfolio

    Answer: B   Difficulty: Medium   Page: 193

29. The _____ of foreign direct investment refers to the amount of FDI undertaken over a given period (normally a year).
    A) register
    B) stock
    C) portfolio
    D) flow

    Answer: D   Difficulty: Easy   Page: 193

30. The _____ of foreign direct investment refers to the total accumulated value of foreign-owned assets at a given time.
    A) stock
    B) flow
    C) register
    D) portfolio

    Answer: A   Difficulty: Easy   Page: 193

31. The flow of foreign direct investment out of a country is referred to as the:
    A) forfeiture of national investment
    B) loss of national investment
    C) expenditure of FDI
    D) outflow of FDI

    Answer: D   Difficulty: Easy   Page: 193

32. The flow of foreign direct investment into a country is referred to as the:
    A) inflow of FDI
    B) FDI capture
    C) FDI gain
    D) accrual of FDI

    Answer: A   Difficulty: Easy   Page: 193

33. During the past 20 years there has been a:
    A) increase in the stock but not in the flow of FDI in the world economy
    B) marked increase in both the flow and stock of FDI in the world economy
    C) marked decrease in both the flow and stock of FDI in the world economy
    D) increase in flow but not the stock of FDI in the world economy

    Answer: C Difficulty: Medium Page: 193

34. Which of the following two statements accurately reflects the trend in foreign direct investments over the past 20 years?
    A) there has been a rapid increase in the total volume of FDI undertaken and there has been a change in the importance of various countries as sources for FDI
    B) there has been a rapid increase in the total volume of FDI undertaken and the countries that have been instrumental as sources of FDI have remained the same
    C) there has been a rapid decrease in the total volume of FDI undertaken and there has been a change in the importance of various countries as sources for FDI.
    D) there has been a rapid decrease in the total volume of FDI undertaken and the countries that have been instrumental as sources of FDI have remained the same

    Answer: A Difficulty: Medium Page: 193

35. The average yearly outflow of FDI increased from about $25 billion in 1975 to a record _____ billion in 1998.
    A) $45
    B) $380
    C) $644
    D) $905

    Answer: C Difficulty: Hard Page: 195

36. Between 1984 and 1998 the total flow of FDI from all countries increased by more than _____, while world trade grew by 91% and world output by 27%
    A) 75%
    B) 300%
    C) 700%
    D) 1000%

    Answer: D Difficulty: Hard Page: 195

Chapter 6 Foreign Direct Investment

37. Which of the following factors has not contributed to the increase in FDI over the past several years?
    A) dramatic shifts towards free market economies
    B) business firms still fear protectionist pressures
    C) the globalization of the world economy
    D) dramatic shift towards socialist and communist political institutions

    Answer: D Difficulty: Medium Page: 193

38. Historically, most FDI has been directed at the _____ nations of the world as firms based in advanced countries invested in _____.
    A) underdeveloped, underdeveloped countries
    B) developed, underdeveloped countries
    C) developed, each other's markets
    D) underdeveloped, each other's markets

    Answer: C Difficulty: Hard Page: 194

39. In 1997, the two largest recipients of FDI in the world were:
    A) Japan and Germany
    B) the United States and China
    C) China and Japan
    D) South Korea and the United States

    Answer: B Difficulty: Hard Page: 195

40. _____ summarizes the total amount of capital invested in factories, stores, office buildings, and the like.
    A) Gross fixed capital formation
    B) Total investment capital
    C) Total tangible investment
    D) Gross depreciable investments

    Answer: A Difficulty: Medium Page: 196

41. In general, FDI accounts for between _____ percent of worldwide gross fixed capital formation.
    A) .5 and 2 percent
    B) 3 and 5 percent
    C) 6 and 8 percent
    D) 10 and 12 percent

    Answer: B Difficulty: Hard Page: 196

Chapter 6 Foreign Direct Investment

42. For most of the period after World War II, (the)_____ was by far the largest source country for foreign direct investment.
    A) Japan
    B) China
    C) United States
    D) England

    Answer: C Difficulty: Medium Page: 198

43. Which of the following is not a reason that helped propel Japanese FDI outflows to record levels from the mid 1980s to the early 1990s?
    A) strong corporate performance
    B) a strong economy
    C) the threat that foreign countries might erect trade barriers against Japanese exports
    D) high domestic interest rates

    Answer: D Difficulty: Hard Page: 199

44. A theory of foreign direct investment that combines two other perspectives into a single holistic explanation of FDI is referred to as the:
    A) versatile model
    B) internationalization model
    C) globalization paradigm
    D) eclectic paradigm

    Answer: D Difficulty: Easy Page: 200

45. A theory of _____ that combines two other perspectives in a single holistic explanation is referred to as the eclectic paradigm.
    A) foreign direct investment
    B) political economy
    C) globalization
    D) regional economic integration

    Answer: A Difficulty: Medium Page: 200

46. _____ involves producing goods at home and then shipping them to the receiving country for sale.
    A) Foreign direct investment
    B) Licensing
    C) Franchising
    D) Exporting

    Answer: D   Difficulty: Easy   Page: 200

47. If 3M, and American firm, produces adhesive tape in St. Paul, Minnesota, and ships the tape to South Korea to be sold, that is an example of:
    A) exporting
    B) licensing
    C) franchising
    D) cross-boarder investing

    Answer: A   Difficulty: Easy   Page: 200

48. The practice of producing goods at home and then shipping them to another country for sales is called:
    A) franchising
    B) exporting
    C) licensing
    D) foreign direct investment

    Answer: B   Difficulty: Easy   Page: 200

49. _____ involves granting a foreign entity the right to produce and sell the firm's product in return for a royalty fee on every unit sold.
    A) Franchising
    B) Exporting
    C) Licensing
    D) Foreign Direct Investment

    Answer: C   Difficulty: Easy   Page: 200

Chapter 6 Foreign Direct Investment

50. The practice of granting foreign entities the right to produce and sell your own product in return for a royalty fee on every unit sold is called:
    A) exporting
    B) licensing
    C) foreign direct investment
    D) importing

    Answer: B   Difficulty: Easy   Page: 200

51. When transportation costs are added to production costs, it becomes unprofitable to ship some products over a large distance. This is particularly true of products that have a:
    A) high value-to-weight ratio
    B) moderate value-to-weight ratio
    C) low value-to-weight ratio
    D) extremely high value-to-weight ratio

    Answer: C   Difficulty: Hard   Page: 200

52. In return for licensing one of its products to a foreign firm, the licensor:
    A) gets preferential trade treatment from the country of the licensee
    B) gets a special subsidy from the country of the licensee
    C) collects a royalty fee on every unit the licensee sells
    D) gets a one time payment from the licensee

    Answer: C   Difficulty: Medium   Page: 200

53. _____ involves producing goods at home and then shipping them to the receiving country for sale. _____ involves granting a foreign entity the right to produce and sell the firm's product in return for a royalty fee on every unit sold.
    A) Exporting, Licensing
    B) Importing, Foreign direct investment
    C) Licensing, Exporting
    D) Foreign direct investment, Licensing

    Answer: A   Difficulty: Medium   Page: 200

Chapter 6 Foreign Direct Investment

54. According to the textbook, FDI is expensive because:
    A) a firm must pay a high franchising fee to participate in foreign direct investment in most countries
    B) a firm must pay the transportation costs to ship domestically produced products overseas
    C) a firm must establish production facilities in a foreign country or acquire a foreign enterprise
    D) a firm must pay a high licensing fee to participate in foreign direct investment in most countries

    Answer: C Difficulty: Medium Page: 200

55. Compared to exporting and licensing, FDI is expensive because:
    A) of the high cost of labor in most countries
    B) a firm must bear the costs of establishing production facilities in a foreign country or of acquiring a foreign enterprise
    C) of high tariffs
    D) of high tax rates worldwide

    Answer: B Difficulty: Medium Page: 200

56. Much foreign direct investment is undertaken as a response to actual or threatened:
    A) trade barriers
    B) economic sanctions
    C) legal action
    D) international appeals

    Answer: A Difficulty: Medium Page: 201

57. A branch of economics knows as _____ seeks to explain why firms often prefer foreign direct investment to licensing as a strategy for entering foreign markets.
    A) comparative advantage theory
    B) globalization theory
    C) cosmopolitan theory
    D) internationalization theory

    Answer: D Difficulty: Medium Page: 201

58. _____ explains why firms prefer foreign direct investment over licensing when entering foreign markets.
    A) Internationalization theory
    B) Home market theory
    C) Host market theory
    D) Domestic preference theory

    Answer: A   Difficulty: Easy   Page: 201

59. Internationalization theory explains why firms prefer _____ over _____ when entering foreign markets.
    A) foreign direct investment, exporting
    B) foreign direct investment, licensing
    C) exporting, foreign direct investment
    D) exporting, licensing

    Answer: B   Difficulty: Medium   Page: 201

60. Internationalization theory explains why firms prefer foreign direct investment over _____ when entering foreign markets.
    A) exporting
    B) strategic alliances
    C) licensing
    D) importing

    Answer: C   Difficulty: Medium   Page: 201

61. Internationalization theory explains why firms prefer _____ over licensing when entering foreign markets.
    A) joint ventures
    B) foreign direct investment
    C) exporting
    D) importing

    Answer: B   Difficulty: Medium   Page: 201

62. According to internationalization theory, licensing has three major drawbacks as a strategy for exploiting foreign market opportunities. Each of the following is a drawback of licensing except:
A) licensing may result in a firm's giving away valuable technological know-how to a potential foreign competitor.
B) licensing does not give a firm the tight control over manufacturing, marketing, and strategy in a foreign country that may be required to maximize its profitability.
C) licensing helps a firm avoid making a direct foreign investment in a foreign country.
D) when a firm's competitive advantage is based not so much on its products as on the management, marketing, and manufacturing capabilities that produce those produces, licensing fails to capture those advantages

Answer: C Difficulty: Hard Page: 201

63. A specific disadvantage of _____ is that it may result in a firm giving away valuable technological know-how to a potential foreign competitor.
A) importing
B) foreign direct investment
C) licensing
D) exporting

Answer: C Difficulty: Medium Page: 201

64. A specific disadvantage of _____ is that it does not give a firm the tight control over manufacturing, marketing, and strategy in a foreign country that may be required to maximize its profitability.
A) foreign direct investment
B) licensing
C) importing
D) exporting

Answer: B Difficulty: Medium Page: 201

65. High transportation costs and/or tariffs imposed on imports help explain why many firms prefer _____ over _____.
A) foreign direct investment or licensing, exporting
B) foreign direct investment or licensing, joint ventures
C) exporting, foreign direct investment or licensing
D) strategic alliances, foreign direct investment or licensing

Answer: A Difficulty: Hard Page: 201

Chapter 6 Foreign Direct Investment

66. According to the textbook, a firm will favor FDI over exporting as an entry strategy when:
    A) interest rates or government policy make exporting unattractive
    B) transportation costs or trade barriers make exporting unattractive
    C) cultural barriers or trade barriers make exporting unattractive
    D) cultural barriers or government policy make exporting unattractive

    Answer: B Difficulty: Hard Page: 202

67. According to the textbook, a firm will favor _____ over _____ when transportation costs or trade barriers make exporting unattractive.
    A) foreign direct investment, exporting
    B) foreign direct investment, importing
    C) exporting, foreign direct investment
    D) licensing, foreign direct investment

    Answer: A Difficulty: Hard Page: 202

68. According to out textbook, a firm will favor _____ over _____ when it wishes to maintain control over its technological know-how, or over its operations and business strategy.
    A) foreign direct investment, exporting
    B) licensing, foreign direct investment
    C) foreign direct investment, licensing
    D) exporting, foreign direct investment

    Answer: C Difficulty: Hard Page: 202

69. One theory used to explain foreign direct investment patterns is based on the idea that firms follow their domestic competitors overseas. First expounded by _____, this theory has been developed with regard to oligopolistic industries.
    A) F.T. Knickerbocker
    B) William P. Smith
    C) Michael Porter
    D) Eli Heckscher

    Answer: A Difficulty: Medium Page: 203

70. One theory used to explain foreign direct investment patterns is based on the idea that firms follow their domestic competitors overseas. First expounded by F.T. Knickerbocker, this theory has been developed with regard to _____ .
    A) oligopolistic industries
    B) cartels
    C) monopolistic industries
    D) syndicated industries

    Answer: A   Difficulty: Medium   Page: 203

71. A(n) _____ is an industry composed of a limited number of large firms (i.e. an industry in which four firms control 80 percent of a domestic market)
    A) syndicate
    B) cartel
    C) oligopoly
    D) monopoly

    Answer: C   Difficulty: Easy   Page: 203

72. An industry composed of a limited number of large firms (i.e. in which four firms control 80 percent of the domestic market), is referred to as a(n):
    A) syndicate
    B) monopoly
    C) cartel
    D) oligopoly

    Answer: D   Difficulty: Easy   Page: 203

73. Several studies of U.S. enterprises suggest that firms based in _____ industries tend to imitate each other's foreign direct investment patterns.
    A) oliogopolistic
    B) monopolistic
    C) syndicated
    D) munificent

    Answer: A   Difficulty: Medium   Page: 203

74. Raymond Vernon's view of foreign direct investment is that firms undertake FDI at:
    A) unpredictable stages in the life cycle of a product they have pioneered
    B) late stages in their corporate histories
    C) early stages in their corporate histories
    D) particular stages in the life cycle of a product they have pioneered

    Answer: D Difficulty: Medium Page: 204

75. The eclectic paradigm has been championed by the British economist _____.
    A) John Dunning
    B) Edward Luty
    C) William Spencer
    D) Andrew Ferguson

    Answer: A Difficulty: Medium Page: 205

76. Advantages that arise from using resource endowments or assets that are tied to a particular location and that a firm finds valuable to combine with its own unique assets are referred to as:
    A) geographic specific preferences
    B) unique geographic advantages
    C) locale-specific preferences
    D) location-specific advantages

    Answer: D Difficulty: Medium Page: 205

77. By _____, Dunning means the advantages that arise from utilizing resource endowments or assets that are tied to a particular foreign location and that a firm finds valuable to combine with its own unique assets.
    A) location-specific advantages
    B) locale-specific preferences
    C) unique geographic advantages
    D) geographic specific preferences

    Answer: A Difficulty: Medium Page: 205

Chapter 6 Foreign Direct Investment

78. Knowledge spillovers that occur when companies in the same industry locate in the same area are referred to as:
    A) inward overflows
    B) cognitive overflows
    C) concentric overflows
    D) externalities

    Answer: D   Difficulty: Medium   Page: 206

79. The _____ view traces its roots to Marxist political and economic theory.
    A) radical
    B) free market
    C) pragmatic nationalism
    D) conservative

    Answer: A   Difficulty: Medium   Page: 206

80. The _____ view argues that international production should be distributed among countries according to the theory of comparative advantage.
    A) conservative
    B) pragmatic nationalism
    C) free market
    D) radical

    Answer: C   Difficulty: Medium   Page: 207

81. The _____ view is that FDI has both benefits and costs.
    A) radical
    B) conservative
    C) free market
    D) pragmatic nationalism

    Answer: D   Difficulty: Medium   Page: 208

Chapter 6 Foreign Direct Investment

82. Three main benefits of inward FDI for a host country are:
   A) the resource-transfer effect, the employment effect, and the balance-of-payments effect
   B) the capital-transfer effect, the technology effect, and the currency exchange effect
   C) the cultural awareness effect, the technology effect, and the balance-of-payments effect
   D) the resource-transfer effect, the technology effect, and the currency exchange effect

   Answer: A   Difficulty: Medium   Page: 209

83. The three main benefits of inward FDI for a host country are the resource-transfer effect, the employment effect, and the:
   A) currency exchange effect
   B) economic impact effect
   C) balance-of-payments effect
   D) technology-transfer effect

   Answer: C   Difficulty: Medium   Page: 209

84. The three main benefits of inward FDI for a host country are the employment effect, the balance-of-payments effect, and the:
   A) currency exchange effect
   B) economic impact effect
   C) technology-transfer effect
   D) resource-transfer effect

   Answer: D   Difficulty: Medium   Page: 209

85. A country's _____ tracks both its payments to and its receipts from other countries.
   A) pulses and minuses account
   B) debits and credits account
   C) checks and balances account
   D) balance-of-payments account

   Answer: D   Difficulty: Easy   Page: 211

86. The record of a country's export and import of goods and services is referred to as its:
    A) current account
    B) foreign account
    C) internal account
    D) tariff account

    Answer: A Difficulty: Medium Page: 211

87. Three main costs of inward FDI concern host countries. These are:
    A) the employment effect, the perceived loss of national sovereignty and autonomy, and the resource transfer effect
    B) the possible adverse effects of FDI on competition with the host country, the resource transfer effect, and the perceived loss of national sovereignty and autonomy
    C) the resource transfer effect, the employment effect, and the possible adverse effects of FDI on competition within the host country
    D) the possible adverse effects of FDI on competition within the host country, adverse effects on the balance of payments, and the perceived loss of national sovereignty and autonomy

    Answer: D Difficulty: Hard Page: 212

88. Three main costs of inward FDI concern host countries: the possible adverse effects of FDI on competition within the host nation, adverse effects on the balance of payments, and _____.
    A) the resource transfer effect.
    B) the technology transfer effect
    C) the perceived loss of national sovereignty and autonomy
    D) the employment effect

    Answer: C Difficulty: Medium Page: 212

89. Three main costs of inward FDI concern host countries: the possible adverse effects of FDI on competition within a host nation, the perceived loss of national sovereignty and autonomy, and _____.
    A) the resource transfer effect
    B) the technology transfer effect
    C) the adverse effects on the balance of payments
    D) the employment effect

    Answer: C Difficulty: Medium Page: 212

Chapter 6 Foreign Direct Investment

90. The most important concerns regarding the costs of FDI for the home country center around:
    A) the balance-of-payments and employment effects of outward FDI
    B) the technology capture effect and the perceived loss of national sovereignty
    C) the resource transfer effect and the inflationary pressures caused by FDI
    D) the perceived loss of national sovereignty and inflationary pressures caused by FDI

    Answer: A Difficulty: Medium Page: 214

91. The most important concerns regarding the costs of FDI for the home country center around the balance-of-payments effects and the:
    A) inflationary pressures caused by FDI
    B) perceived loss of national sovereignty
    C) employment effects
    D) technology capture effects

    Answer: C Difficulty: Medium Page: 214

92. The most important concerns regarding the costs of FDI for the home country center around the employment effect and the:
    A) balance of payments effects
    B) perceived loss of national sovereignty
    C) inflationary pressures caused by FDI
    D) technology capture effects

    Answer: A Difficulty: Medium Page: 214

93. The most serious concerns about _____ arise when FDI is seen as a substitute for domestic production.
    A) inflation
    B) economic stability
    C) the loss of national sovereignty
    D) employment

    Answer: D Difficulty: Medium Page: 214

Chapter 6 Foreign Direct Investment

94. International trade theory tells us that home country concerns about the negative economic effects of offshore production:
    A) are typically right on
    B) may be misplaced
    C) are typically irrelevant
    D) are typically negligible

    Answer: B Difficulty: Hard Page: 214

95. Many Investor nations now have government backed insurance programs to cover major types of foreign investment risk. The types of risks insurable through these programs include all of the following except:
    A) the risk of expropriation
    B) war losses
    C) the inability to transfer profits back home
    D) strategic business blunders

    Answer: D Difficulty: Medium Page: 215

96. As a further incentive to encourage domestic firms to undertake FDI, many countries have eliminated double taxation of foreign income. Double taxation of foreign income refers to:
    A) taxation of income in both the host country and the home country
    B) double taxation of income in the host country
    C) double taxation of income in the home country
    D) taxation that must be paid to both the host country and the IMF

    Answer: A Difficulty: Hard Page: 215

97. It is increasingly common for governments to:
    A) offer incentives to firms that invest in their countries
    B) penalize firms that invest in their countries
    C) offer incentives to firms from developed countries to invest in their countries, but not to firm from developing countries
    D) offer incentives to firms from developing countries to invest in their countries, but not to firms from developed countries

    Answer: A Difficulty: Medium Page: 216

98. Which of the following was not mentioned in the textbook as a common incentive that governments offer foreign firms to invest in their countries?
    A) grants or subsidies
    B) free media advertising
    C) low-interest loans
    D) tax concessions

    Answer: B Difficulty: Hard Page: 216

99. Host government use a range of controls to restrict FDI. The two most common are:
    A) monetary restraints and performance requirements
    B) technology transfer restraints and employment restraints
    C) ownership restraints and performance requirements
    D) employment restraints and repatriation limitations

    Answer: C Difficulty: Hard Page: 216

100. Host governments use a range of controls to restrict FDI. The two most common are ownership restraints and:
    A) performance restraints
    B) monetary restraints
    C) technology transfer restraints
    D) media restraints

    Answer: A Difficulty: Medium Page: 216

101. The _____ is a Paris-based intergovernmental organization of "wealthy" nations whose purpose is to provide its 29 member states with a forum in which governments can compare their experiences, discuss the problems they share, and seek solutions that can be applied within their own national contexts.
    A) Council for Economic Strength
    B) Federation of Emerging Nations
    C) Organization for Economic Cooperation and Development
    D) Organization for Economic Strength and Global Leadership

    Answer: C Difficulty: Medium Page: 217

Chapter 6 Foreign Direct Investment

102. The members of the Organization for Economic Cooperation and Development include:
    A) most South American countries, Japan, France, and Germany
    B) most North American countries, Great Britain, France, and Germany
    C) most Asian countries, the United States, Canada, and Mexico
    D) most European countries, the United States, Canada, Japan, and South Korea

    Answer: D Difficulty: Hard Page: 217

103. McDonalds has expanded into foreign markets primarily through:
    A) franchising
    B) licensing
    C) FDI
    D) exporting

    Answer: A Difficulty: Medium Page: 218

104. Franchising is essentially the service industry version of _____ - although it normally involves much longer-term commitments.
    A) exporting
    B) licensing
    C) FDI
    D) turnkey projects

    Answer: B Difficulty: Medium Page: 219

105. The product life-cycle theory and Knickerbocker's theory of FDI tend to be less useful from a business perspective because they:
    A) are descriptive rather than analytical
    B) have not stood the test of time
    C) because they are not widely known
    D) because they have not been empirically validated

    Answer: A Difficulty: Hard Page: 220

Chapter 6 Foreign Direct Investment

Essay Questions

106. What is meant by the term Foreign Direct Investment? Describe the difference between the flow of foreign direct investment and the stock of foreign direct investment.

Difficulty: Easy   Page: 192

Answer:
Foreign direct investment (FDI) occurs when a firm invests directly in new facilities to produce and/or market a product in a foreign country. To be more precise, the U.S. Department of Commerce describes FDI as follows: FDI occurs whenever a U.S. citizen, organization, or affiliated group takes an interest of 10 percent or more in a foreign business entity.

The flow of foreign direct investment refers to the amount of FDI undertaken over a given period (normally a year). The stock of foreign direct investment refers to the total accumulated value of foreign-owned assets at a given time.

107. Describe what is meant by the eclectic paradigm? Who is its principle champion? Does this paradigm make sense as a rationale for FDI?

Difficulty: Hard   Page: 200

Answer:
The principle champion of the eclectic paradigm is British economist John Dunning. Dunning argues that in addition to other factors, location-specific advantages are also of considerable importance in explaining both the rationale for and the direction of foreign direct investment. By location-specific advantages, Dunning means the advantages that arise from utilizing resource endowments or assets that are tied to a particular foreign location and that a firm finds valuable to combine with its own unique assets. Dunning accepts the arguments of internationalization theory, that it is difficult for a firm to license its own unique capabilities and know-how. Therefore, he argues that combining location-specific assets or resource endowments and the firm's own unique capabilities often requires FDI in production facilities.

Chapter 6 Foreign Direct Investment

This paradigm does make sense as a rationale for FDI. For example, as described in the text, an obvious example of Dunning's arguments is natural resources, such as oil and other minerals, which are specific to certain locations. Dunning suggests that to exploit such foreign resources a firm must undertake FDI. Many U.S. oil companies have done this. They have had to invest in refineries in the areas of the world where the oil is located in order to combine their technological and managerial capabilities with this valuable location-specific resources. Another example is California's Silicon Valley, where a substantial portion of the world's R&D in terms of computer technology is taking place. It might make sense for a foreign producer of computer chips to locate their R&D facility in the Silicon Valley to be near this community of computer chip researchers and manufacturers.

108. Despite its advantages, FDI has been described as an "expensive" and "risky" international growth strategy. Other things being equal, why is FDI expensive and risky? Compare the risks involved with FDI to the risks involved with exporting and licensing.

Difficulty: Medium   Page: 200

Answer:
FDI is expensive because a firm must bear the costs of establishing production facilities in a foreign country or of acquiring a foreign enterprise. FDI is risky because of the problems associated with doing business in another culture where the "rules of the game" may be very different. As a result, relative to firms native to a culture, there is a greater probability that a firm undertaking FDI in a foreign culture will make costly mistakes due to ignorance. When a firm exports, it need not bear the costs of FDI, and the risks associated with selling abroad can be reduced by using a native sales agent. Similarly, when a firm licenses its know-how, it need not bear the costs or risks of FDI, since there are born by the native firm that licenses the know-how.

109. How do transportation costs affect the attractiveness of exporting?

Difficulty: Medium   Page: 200

Answer:
When transportation costs are added to production costs, it becomes unprofitable to shift some products over a long distance. This is particularly true of products that have a low value-to-weight ratio and can be produced at almost any location (e.g., cement, soft drinks, beer, etc.). For such products, relative to either FDI or licensing, the attractiveness of exporting decreases. For products with a high value-to-weight ratio, however, transport costs are normally a very minor component of total landed costs (e.g. jewelry, medical equipment, computer chips). In such cases, transportation costs have little impact on the attractiveness of exporting.

Chapter 6 Foreign Direct Investment

110. Name three reasons that licensing may not be an attractive option.

Difficulty: Medium   Page: 201

Answer:
First, licensing may result in a firm's giving away its know-how to a potential foreign competitor. There are many documented cases of where licensees learned how to produce a product from its licensor, and quickly exited the licensing agreement and started producing a similar product on its own. Second, licensing does not give a firm the tight control over manufacturing, marketing, and strategy in a foreign country that may be required to profitably exploit its advantage in know-how. With licensing, control over production, marketing, and strategy is granted to a licensee in return for a royalty fee. However, for both strategic and operational reasons, a firm may want to retain control over these functions. Third, a firm's know-how may not be amenable to licensing. This is particularly true of management and marketing know-how.

111. What are the benefits of inward FDI (i.e. FDI coming into a country from foreign sources) for the host country? Are these benefits compelling?

Difficulty: Medium   Page: 209

Answer:
The three main benefits of FDI for the host country are the resources-transfer effect, the employment effect, and the balance-of-payments effect. These potential benefits are explained in more detail below.

The Resource-Transfer Effect: FDI can make a positive contribution to a host country by supplying capital, technology, and management resources that would otherwise not be available. The provision of these skills by a multinational company (through FDI) may boost s country's intellectual capital and economic growth rate.

The Employment Effects: The beneficial employment effects claimed for FDI is that foreign direct investment brings jobs to a host country that would otherwise not be created there. For instance, the Japanese auto factories in the United States have provided thousands of jobs for U.S. workers.

Chapter 6 Foreign Direct Investment

The Balance-of-Payment Effects: The effect of FDI on a country's balance-of-payments account in an important policy issue for most host governments. Governments typically like to see a balance-of-payments surplus rather than a deficit. There are two ways that FDI can help a host country experience a balance-of-payments surplus. First, if the FDI is a substitute for imports of goods or services, it can improve a country's balance of payments. For example, the Japanese auto plants in the U.S. produce cars that act as "substitutes" for Japanese imports. Second, FDI may result in an increase in exports. A portion of the goods and services that are produced as a result of FDI may be exported to other countries.

These arguments are compelling, but must be weighed against the costs of FDI. The arguments against FDI include: the possible adverse effects of FDI on competition within the host nation, adverse effects on the balance-of-payments, and the perceived loss of national sovereignty and autonomy.

112. How does a potential host government's attitude toward FDI affect a company's willingness to engage in FDI in that country? Should a host government's attitude toward FDI be a major consideration when making a FDI decision? Why?

Difficulty: Medium   Page: 215

Answer:
A host government's attitude toward FDI should be an important variable in making decisions about where to locate foreign production facilities and where to make a FDI. According to the author of the textbook, other things being equal, investing in countries that have permissive policies toward FDI is clearly preferable to investing in countries that resist FDI.

However, this issue is not straightforward. Many countries have a rather businesslike stance toward FDI. In such cases, a firm considering FDI usually must negotiate the specific terms of the investment with the host government. Such negotiations typically center on two issues. First, if the host country is trying to attract FDI, the negotiations will typically focus on the kind of incentives the host government is prepared to offer the foreign firm and what the firm will commit in exchange. On the other hand, if the host government is leery of FDI, the central issue is likely to be the concessions the firm will make to be allowed to go forward with its project.

Chapter 7 Regional Economic Integration

True/False Questions

1. One notable trend in the global economy in recent years has been the accelerated movement toward global economic integration.

   Answer: False   Difficulty: Easy   Page: 226

2. The last decade has witnessed an unprecedented proliferation of regional trade agreements.

   Answer: True   Difficulty: Easy   Page: 226

3. As predicted by the theory of comparative advantage, there should be a substantial net gain from regional free trade agreements.

   Answer: True   Difficulty: Medium   Page: 226

4. Several levels of economic integration are possible in theory. From most integrated to the least integrated they are area free trade area, a customs union, a common market, an economic union, and finally, a full political union.

   Answer: False   Difficulty: Medium   Page: 228

5. In a free trade area all barriers to the trade of goods and services among member countries are removed.

   Answer: True   Difficulty: Easy   Page: 228

6. In a free trade area, the member nations collectively determine their trade policies with regard to nonmembers.

   Answer: False   Difficulty: Medium   Page: 232

7. The most enduring free trade area in the world is the European Free Trade Association.

   Answer: True   Difficulty: Hard   Page: 228

8. A customs union eliminates trade barriers between member countries and adopts a common external trade policy.

   Answer: True   Difficulty: Medium   Page: 229

Chapter 7 Regional Economic Integration

9. A full common market requires a common currency, harmonization of the member countries' tax rates, and a common monetary and fiscal policy.

   Answer: False   Difficulty: Medium   Page: 229

10. In a theoretically ideal common market, labor and capital are free to move, as there are no restrictions on immigration, emigration, or cross-border flows of capital between markets.

    Answer: True   Difficulty: Medium   Page: 229

11. Although the European Union is the best known, a number of successful common markets exist throughout the world.

    Answer: False   Difficulty: Medium   Page: 229

12. An economic union involves the free flow of products and factors of production between members and the adoption of a common external trade policy.

    Answer: True   Difficulty: Medium   Page: 229

13. The EU is on the road towards political union.

    Answer: True   Difficulty: Hard   Page: 229

14. Most attempts to achieve regional economic integration have been very amicable.

    Answer: False   Difficulty: Easy   Page: 230

15. Trade creation occurs when lower-cost external suppliers are replaced by higher-cost suppliers within the free trade area.

    Answer: False   Difficulty: Medium   Page: 231

16. Europe now has two trade blocs: the European Union and the European Free Trade Association.

    Answer: True   Difficulty: Medium   Page: 233

17. The Single European Act was born out of frustration among EC member countries that the community was not living up to its promise.

    Answer: True   Difficulty: Medium   Page: 235

Chapter 7 Regional Economic Integration

18. To signify the importance of the Single European Act, the European Union decided to change its name to the European Community once the act took effect.

    Answer: False   Difficulty: Hard   Page: 236

19. The first year after NAFTA turned out to be a largely negative experience for all three countries.

    Answer: False   Difficulty: Medium   Page: 244

20. The Andean Pact was formed in 1969 when Bolivia, Chile, Ecuador, Colombia, and Peru signed the Cartagena Agreement.

    Answer: True   Difficulty: Hard   Page: 245

Multiple Choice Questions

21. An agreement between countries in a geographic region to reduce tariff and nontariff barriers to the free flow of goods, services, and factors of production between each other is referred to as:
    A) regional economic integration
    B) cross-cultural economic integration
    C) geographic economic-political integration
    D) cross-cultural economic-political integration

    Answer: A   Difficulty: Easy   Page: 226

22. By _____ we mean agreements between groups of countries in a geographic region to reduce, and ultimately remove, tariff and nontariff barriers to the free flow of goods, services, and factors of production between each other.
    A) geographic economic-political integration
    B) regional economic integration
    C) cross-cultural economic integration
    D) cross-cultural economic-political integration

    Answer: B   Difficulty: Easy   Page: 226

Chapter 7 Regional Economic Integration

23. Over three-quarters of the operational regional agreements in existence today were established between:
    A) 1945 and 1955
    B) 1960 and 1968
    C) 1985 and 1990
    D) 1992 and 1999

    Answer: D   Difficulty: Hard   Page: 226

24. According to the textbook, by entering into _____, groups of countries aim to reduce trade barriers more rapidly than can be achieved under the WTO.
    A) regional agreements
    B) synergistic agreements
    C) global agreements
    D) transnational agreements

    Answer: A   Difficulty: Medium   Page: 227

25. Nowhere has the movement toward regional economic integration been more successful than in _____.
    A) Africa
    B) South America
    C) Asia
    D) Europe

    Answer: D   Difficulty: Medium   Page: 227

26. On January 1, 1993, the _____ effectively became a single market with 340 million consumers.
    A) European Union
    B) South American Union
    C) North American Union
    D) Southeast Asia Union

    Answer: A   Difficulty: Medium   Page: 227

27. The following three countries recently implemented the North American Free Trade Agreement (NAFTA):
    A) Panama, Mexico, and the United States
    B) Canada, Brazil, and the United States
    C) United States, Argentina, and Mexico
    D) Canada, Mexico, and the United States

    Answer: D   Difficulty: Medium   Page: 227

28. NAFTA stands for:
    A) North Asian Free Trade Agreement
    B) North African Free Trade Association
    C) North Atlantic Free Trade Agreement
    D) North American Free Trade Association

    Answer: D   Difficulty: Medium   Page: 227

29. The free trade area known as MERCOSUR consists of the following four countries:
    A) Chile, Mexico, Columbia, and Paraguay
    B) Argentina, Brazil, Paraguay, and Uruguay
    C) Chile, Brazil, Uruguay, and Columbia
    D) Mexico, Columbia, Paraguay, and Uruguay

    Answer: B   Difficulty: Hard   Page: 227

30. Which of the following statement is not accurate in regard to the European Union?
    A) members of the European Union have plans to establish a single currency
    B) members of the European Union are moving toward a closer political union
    C) members of the European Union are discussing enlargement of the EU from the current 15 countries to include another 15 Eastern European states
    D) members of the European Union are discussing a common language

    Answer: D   Difficulty: Medium   Page: 227

31. As predicted by the theory of comparative advantage, there should be a _____ from regional trade agreements.
    A) substantial net gain
    B) minor net gain
    C) no economic impact
    D) substantial net loss

    Answer: A   Difficulty: Medium   Page: 227

32. Which of the following selections accurately depicts the levels of economic integration from least integrated to most integrated?
    A) common market, economic union, full political union, free trade area, and customs union
    B) common market, economic union, full political union, free trade area, and customs union
    C) free trade area, customs union, common market, economic union, and full political union
    D) full political union, free trade area, common market, customs union, and economic union

    Answer: C Difficulty: Hard Page: 228

33. Which of the following selections accurately depicts the levels of economic integration from most integrated to least integration?
    A) full political union, economic union, common market, customs union, and free trade area
    B) free trade area, common market, customs union, full political union, and economic union
    C) common market, economic union, full political union, customs union, and free trade area
    D) economic union, common market, full political union, free trade area, and customs union

    Answer: A Difficulty: Medium Page: 228

34. In a free trade area:
    A) barriers to the trade of goods and services among member nations are removed
    B) a common currency is adopted
    C) a single Parliament determines political and foreign policy
    D) a common external trade policy is adopted

    Answer: A Difficulty: Medium Page: 228

35. The most enduring free trade area in the world is the:
    A) Asian Free Trade Association
    B) MERCOSUR
    C) European Free Trade Association
    D) North American Trade Association

    Answer: C Difficulty: Medium Page: 228

36. The European Free Trade Association (EFTA) is the:
    A) largest free trade in the world
    B) most affluent free trade area in the world
    C) most enduring free trade area in the world
    D) newest free trade area in the world

    Answer: C Difficulty: Hard Page: 228

37. The European Free Trade Association currently includes the following four countries:
    A) Ireland, Iceland, Denmark, and Belgium
    B) Norway, Iceland, Switzerland, and Liechtenstein
    C) Finland, Great Britain, Belgium, and Denmark
    D) Sweden, Norway, Austria, and Finland

    Answer: B Difficulty: Hard Page: 228

38. The European Free Trade Association's emphasis has been on free trade in:
    A) services
    B) agricultural products
    C) industrial goods
    D) consumer goods

    Answer: C Difficulty: Hard Page: 228

39. In a theoretically ideal _____, no discriminatory tariffs, quotas, subsidies, or administrative impediments are allowed to distort trade between member nations. Each country, however, is allowed to determine its own trade policies with regard to nonmembers.
    A) common market
    B) economic union
    C) political union
    D) free trade area

    Answer: D Difficulty: Medium Page: 228

40. A _____ eliminates trade barriers between member countries and adopts a common external trade policy.
    A) free trade area
    B) global union
    C) tariff union
    D) customs union

    Answer: D Difficulty: Medium Page: 229

Chapter 7 Regional Economic Integration

41. The Andean Pact is a _____ .
    A) political union
    B) free trade area
    C) customs union
    D) economic union

    Answer: C Difficulty: Hard Page: 229

42. Like a customs union, the theoretically ideal _____ has no barriers to trade between member countries and a common external trade policy.
    A) free trade area
    B) common market
    C) tariff union
    D) external market

    Answer: B Difficulty: Medium Page: 229

43. A common market includes all of the following characteristics except:
    A) factors of production are allowed to move freely between members
    B) there are no restrictions on immigration between members
    C) full economic integration
    D) there are no restrictions on the cross-border flow of capital between members

    Answer: C Difficulty: Medium Page: 229

44. Which of the following is not an attribute of a common market?
    A) harmonization of the member countries' tax rates
    B) there are no restrictions on the cross-border flow of capital between member nations
    C) there are no restrictions on immigration between member nations
    D) factors of production are allowed to move freely between member nations

    Answer: A Difficulty: Medium Page: 229

45. The European Union is currently a _____ .
    A) common market
    B) customs union
    C) economic union
    D) political union

    Answer: A Difficulty: Medium Page: 229

Chapter 7 Regional Economic Integration

46. Which of the following statements in true in regard to common markets?
    A) the EU is the only successful common market ever established
    B) common markets are prevalent in Africa and South America
    C) the popularity of common markets has waned over the years, and there are less than five successful common markets in existence today
    D) the popularity of common markets is on the increase worldwide, and there are now over 20 successful common markets in existence

    Answer: A   Difficulty: Medium   Page: 229

47. Like the common market, a _____ involves the free flow of products and factors of production between members and the adoption of a common external trade policy.
    A) free trade area
    B) economic union
    C) global union
    D) customs union

    Answer: B   Difficulty: Medium   Page: 229

48. Which of the following is not an attribute of an economic union?
    A) political union
    B) common currency
    C) harmonization of members' tax rates
    D) free flow of products and factors of production between member countries

    Answer: A   Difficulty: Medium   Page: 229

49. Which of the following statements is true in regard to economic unions?
    A) the NAFTA is the only successful economic union in the world today
    B) the popularity of economic unions has increased over the years, and there are now more than 10 successful economic unions in existence
    C) the EU is the only successful economic union in the world today
    D) there are no true economic unions in the world today

    Answer: D   Difficulty: Medium   Page: 229

Chapter 7 Regional Economic Integration

50. The _____, which is playing an every more important role in the EU, has been directly elected by citizens of the EU countries since the late 1970s.
    A) North Atlantic Parliament
    B) North Atlantic Trade Commission
    C) European Parliament
    D) European Trade Commission

    Answer: C Difficulty: Hard Page: 229

51. According to the textbook, most attempts to achieve regional economic integration have been:
    A) extremely successful
    B) amicable and friendly
    C) contentious and halting
    D) uneventful

    Answer: C Difficulty: Medium Page: 230

52. Economic theories suggest that free trade and investment is a positive-sum game, in which:
    A) all participating countries stand to gain
    B) more participating countries gain than lose
    C) at least one participating country gains
    D) most participating countries lose

    Answer: A Difficulty: Medium Page: 230

53. According to the textbook, in regard to international trade, the theoretical ideal is:
    A) barriers to trade for developing nations, but not for industrial nations
    B) an absence of barriers to the free flow of goods, services, and factors of production among nations
    C) barriers to trade for industrial nations, but not for developing nations
    D) heavy barriers to the free flow of goods, services, and factors of production among nations

    Answer: B Difficulty: Medium Page: 230

Chapter 7 Regional Economic Integration

54. Because many governments have accepted part or all of the case for intervention, unrestricted free trade and FDI have proved to be:
    A) only an ideal
    B) a reality
    C) a goal which should be realized soon
    D) a goal that there is no rationale for

    Answer: A   Difficulty: Medium   Page: 230

55. The European Community was established in:
    A) 1945
    B) 1957
    C) 1966
    D) 1979

    Answer: B   Difficulty: Hard   Page: 230

56. The two main reasons that have made _____ difficult to achieve are cost and concerns over national sovereignty.
    A) economic integration
    B) sociological integration
    C) religious integration
    D) cultural integration

    Answer: A   Difficulty: Medium   Page: 231

57. The two main reasons that have made economic integration difficult to achieve are concerns over economic integration and:
    A) concerns over costs
    B) concerns over economic stability
    C) concerns over immigration and emigration
    D) concerns over the safety of travel from one nation to another

    Answer: A   Difficulty: Medium   Page: 231

58. The two main reasons that have made economic integration difficult to achieve are:
    A) concerns over the safety of travel from one nation to another and concerns over dissimilar political ideologies
    B) concerns over costs and concerns over national sovereignty
    C) concerns over immigration and emigration and concerns over economic and political ideologies
    D) concerns over the safety of travel from one nation to another and concerns over national sovereignty

    Answer: B Difficulty: Medium Page: 231

59. In the context of regional trade integration, concern about _____ arise because close economic integration demands that countries give up some degree of their control over such key policy issues as monetary policy, fiscal policy, and trade policy.
    A) cost
    B) national sovereignty
    C) financial stability
    D) cultural uniformity

    Answer: B Difficulty: Hard Page: 231

60. _____ occurs when high-cost domestic producers are replaced by low-cost producers within the free trade area.
    A) Trade alteration
    B) Trade qualification
    C) Trade diversion
    D) Trade creation

    Answer: D Difficulty: Medium Page: 231

61. The phenomenon that occurs when high-cost domestic producers are replaced by low-cost producers within the free trade are is called:
    A) trade alteration
    B) trade qualification
    C) trade creation
    D) trade diversion

    Answer: C Difficulty: Medium Page: 231

62. _____ occurs when lower-cost external suppliers are replaced by higher-cost suppliers within the free trade area.
    A) Trade diversion
    B) Trade qualification
    C) Trade synergy
    D) Trade creation

    Answer: A   Difficulty: Medium   Page: 231

63. The phenomenon that occurs when lower-cost external suppliers are replaced by higher-cost suppliers within the free trade area is called:
    A) trade diversion
    B) trade creation
    C) trade synergy
    D) trade qualification

    Answer: A   Difficulty: Medium   Page: 231

64. _____ occurs when high-cost domestic producers are replaced by low-cost producers. _____ occurs when lower-cost external suppliers are replaced by higher-cost suppliers within the free trade area.
    A) Trade synergy, Trade qualification
    B) Trade qualification, Trade synergy
    C) Trade creation, Trade diversion
    D) Trade diversion, Trade creation

    Answer: C   Difficulty: Hard   Page: 231

65. In theory, _____ rules should ensure that a free trade agreement does not result in trade diversion.
    A) International Monetary Fund
    B) World Bank
    C) United Nations
    D) World Trade Organization

    Answer: D   Difficulty: Hard   Page: 233

66. There are now two trade blocs in Europe. These are the:
    A) European Union and the European Free Trade Association
    B) European Federation and the North Atlantic Trade Block
    C) North Atlantic Trade Block and the European Union
    D) European Federation and the European Trade Association

    Answer: A   Difficulty: Hard   Page: 233

67. There are now two trade blocs in Europe. The European Union and the _____.
    A) North Atlantic Federation
    B) European Free Trade Association
    C) North Atlantic Trade Block
    D) European Federation

    Answer: B   Difficulty: Medium   Page: 233

68. There are now two trade blocs in Europe. The European Free Trade Association and the _____.
    A) North Atlantic Federation
    B) European Federation
    C) North Atlantic Trade Block
    D) European Union

    Answer: D   Difficulty: Medium   Page: 233

69. Of the two trade blocks in Europe, the _____ is by far the more significant, not just in terms of membership, but also in terms of economic and political influence in the world economy.
    A) European Free Trade Association
    B) North Atlantic Trade Block
    C) European Union
    D) European Federation

    Answer: C   Difficulty: Medium   Page: 233

70. The original forerunner of the EU, the _____ was formed in 1951 by Belgium, France, West Germany, Italy, Luxembourg, and the Netherlands.
    A) European Union
    B) European Coal and Steel Community
    C) European Agricultural and Energy Union
    D) European Textiles and Agricultural Community

    Answer: B   Difficulty: Hard   Page: 233

Chapter 7 Regional Economic Integration

71. The European Coal and Steel Community was the original forerunner of the
    _____.
    A) European Federation
    B) North Atlantic Treaty Organization
    C) European Union
    D) North Atlantic Trade Area

    Answer: C   Difficulty: Hard   Page: 233

72. With the signing of the Treaty of Rome in 1957, the _____ was established.
    A) European Community (or Union)
    B) European Free Trade Association
    C) European Coal and Steel Community
    D) European Textiles and Coal Community

    Answer: A   Difficulty: Medium   Page: 233

73. With the signing of the _____ in 1957, the European Community was
    established.
    A) Treaty of Paris
    B) Treaty of Brussels
    C) Treaty of Switzerland
    D) Treaty of Rome

    Answer: D   Difficulty: Hard   Page: 233

74. How many countries are members of the European Union?
    A) 4
    B) 9
    C) 15
    D) 36

    Answer: C   Difficulty: Hard   Page: 234

75. The acronym EC stands for:
    A) Eastward Community
    B) Eastern Europe Community
    C) Eastern Conference
    D) European Community

    Answer: D   Difficulty: Easy   Page: 234

Chapter 7 Regional Economic Integration

76. The acronym EU stands for:
    A) Eastern Europe Union
    B) European Union
    C) Eastward Union
    D) Eastern Union

    Answer: B Difficulty: Easy   Page: 234

77. The purpose of the _____ was to have a single market in place by December 31, 1992.
    A) North Atlantic Sovereignty Act
    B) Single European Act
    C) European Primacy Act
    D) European Sovereignty Act

    Answer: B Difficulty: Medium   Page: 235

78. The purpose of the Single European Act was to:
    A) have a single market in place by December 31, 1992
    B) establish a common currency among European Union Nations
    C) establish common tax laws among European Union Nations
    D) have a single government in place by December 31, 1992

    Answer: A Difficulty: Medium   Page: 235

79. To signify the importance of the _____, the European Community decided to change its name to the European Union once the act took effect.
    A) European Unification Act
    B) European Common Commerce Act
    C) Single European Act
    D) European Free Trade Act

    Answer: C Difficulty: Medium   Page: 235

80. To signify the importance of the Single European Act, the _____ decided to change its name to the European Union once the act took effect.
    A) North Atlantic Community
    B) North Atlantic Trade Federation
    C) European Federation
    D) European Community

    Answer: D Difficulty: Medium   Page: 235

Chapter 7 Regional Economic Integration

81. Which of the following was not one of the purposes of the Single European Act?
    A) remove all frontier controls between EU countries
    B) remove the principle of "mutual recognition" as it pertains to product standards
    C) open public procurement to nonnational suppliers
    D) lift barriers to competition in the EC's retail banking and insurance businesses

    Answer: B   Difficulty: Hard   Page: 235

82. The implications of the Single European Act are:
    A) unknown
    B) enormous
    C) negligible
    D) moderately important

    Answer: B   Difficulty: Hard   Page: 236

83. According to our textbook, the move to a single currency in Europe should:
    A) have no effect on the cost of doing business in Europe
    B) significantly increase the cost of doing business in Europe
    C) significantly decrease the cost of doing business in Europe
    D) moderately increase the cost of doing business in Europe for North American nations, and significantly increase the cost of doing business in the EU for the rest of the world

    Answer: C   Difficulty: Medium   Page: 237

84. For participating countries, a drawback of a single currency in Europe is that:
    A) costs for doing business will increase
    B) it will be more difficult to attract imports
    C) national authorities will lose control over monetary policy
    D) it will be more difficult to compare prices across Europe

    Answer: C   Difficulty: Hard   Page: 238

85. No other attempt at regional integration comes close to (the) _____ in its boldness or its potential implications for the world economy.
    A) EU
    B) NAFTA
    C) Andean Pact
    D) MERCOSUR

    Answer: A   Difficulty: Medium   Page: 241

Chapter 7 Regional Economic Integration

86. In 1988 the governments of the United States and Canada agreed to enter in a _____, which went into effect on January 1, 1989.
    A) economic union
    B) common market
    C) political union
    D) free trade agreement

    Answer: D   Difficulty: Medium   Page: 241

87. The agreement that is designed to abolish within 10 years tariffs on 99 percent of the goods traded between Mexico, Canada, and the United states is called the:
    A) North American Free Trade Agreement
    B) American Federation
    C) American Community
    D) North Atlantic Trade Federation

    Answer: A   Difficulty: Easy   Page: 241

88. According to the textbook, one likely short-term effect of NAFTA will be that many U.S. and Canadian firms will move some production to Mexico to take advantage of:
    A) cheaper transportation costs
    B) lower interest rates
    C) lower labor costs
    D) a higher skilled labor force

    Answer: C   Difficulty: Medium   Page: 241

89. According to our textbook, the first year that NAFTA became a reality turned out to be:
    A) a largely positive experience for all three countries
    B) a largely negative experience for all three countries
    C) a largely positive experience for Mexico, and largely negative experience for the U.S. and Canada
    D) a largely positive experience for the U.S. and Canada, and a largely negative experience for Mexico

    Answer: A   Difficulty: Medium   Page: 242

Chapter 7 Regional Economic Integration

90. The principle argument of those that opposed NAFTA centered around the fear that ratification would result in:
    A) higher interest rates in the U.S.
    B) many U.S. jobs transferred to Mexico
    C) the move towards a common currency for NAFTA member nations
    D) retaliation from the European Union

    Answer: B Difficulty: Medium Page: 243

91. The early euphoria over NAFTA was snuffed out in December 1994 when the _____ was shaken by a financial crisis.
    A) U.S. economy
    B) Mexican economy
    C) Brazilian economy
    D) Canadian economy

    Answer: B Difficulty: Medium Page: 244

92. The _____ was formed in 1969 when Bolivia, Chile, Ecuador, Columbia, and Peru signed the Cartagena Agreement.
    A) Andean Pact
    B) Bolivian Pact
    C) NW South America Group
    D) South American Federation of Independent States

    Answer: A Difficulty: Medium Page: 245

93. The Andean Pact was formed in 1969 when _____ signed the Cartagena Agreement.
    A) Bolivia, Chile, Argentina, French Guiana, and Venezuela
    B) Brazil, Venezuela, Argentina, and Peru
    C) Bolivia, Chile, Ecuador, Colombia, and Peru
    D) Argentina, Chile, Ecuador, Columbia, and Guyana

    Answer: C Difficulty: Hard Page: 245

94. The initial principles of The Andean Group included all of the following except:
    A) internal tariff reduction program
    B) common external tariff
    C) transportation policy
    D) common currency among member nations

    Answer: D Difficulty: Hard Page: 245

Chapter 7 Regional Economic Integration

95. MERCOSUR originated in 1988 as a free trade pact between _____.
    A) Mexico and Brazil
    B) Peru and Brazil
    C) Brazil and Argentina
    D) Venezuela and Peru

    Answer: C Difficulty: Medium Page: 246

96. MERCOSUR originated in 1988 as a free trade pact between Brazil and _____.
    A) Mexico
    B) Peru
    C) Columbia
    D) Argentina

    Answer: D Difficulty: Medium Page: 246

97. MERCOSUR originated in 1988 as a free trade pact between Argentina and
    _____.
    A) Brazil
    B) Mexico
    C) Peru
    D) Columbia

    Answer: A Difficulty: Medium Page: 246

98. Currently, the four member states of MERCOSUR include:
    A) Peru, Chile, Brazil, and Mexico
    B) Columbia, Chile, Brazil, and Paraguay
    C) Argentina, Mexico, Chile, and Brazil
    D) Brazil, Argentina, Paraguay, and Uruguay

    Answer: D Difficulty: Hard Page: 246

99. Formed in 1967, ASEAN currently includes:
    A) Indonesia, Hong Kong, Singapore, Taiwan, Thailand, Malaysia, and Japan
    B) Brunei, Indonesia, Malaysia, Philippines, Singapore, Thailand, and Vietnam
    C) Japan, Taiwan, Hong Kong, Singapore, China, Thailand, and Malaysia
    D) Brunei, Indonesia, Hong Kong, Thailand, Cambodia, Malaysia, and Japan

    Answer: B Difficulty: Hard Page: 248

Chapter 7 Regional Economic Integration

100. The most recent countries to become a members of ASEAN are:
    A) China, Vietnam, and Cambodia
    B) Vietnam, Laos, and Malaysia
    C) Brunei, China, and Thailand
    D) Japan, South Korea, and Thailand

    Answer: B   Difficulty: Hard   Page: 248

101. The United States, Japan, and China are among 18 members of an trade organization referred to as:
    A) AAFTC (American Asian Free Trade Congress)
    B) APEC (Asia Pacific Economic Cooperation)
    C) USAEU (United States Asian Economic Union)
    D) ANAEPC (Asian-North American Economic and Political Coop)

    Answer: B   Difficulty: Medium   Page: 248

102. APEC currently has _____ members including such economic powerhouses as the United States, Japan, and China.
    A) 6
    B) 18
    C) 25
    D) 44

    Answer: B   Difficulty: Hard   Page: 248

103. According to the textbook, currently the most significant developments in regional economic integration are taking place in _____.
    A) Europe and South America
    B) Asia and North America
    C) Europe and North America
    D) Asia and South America

    Answer: C   Difficulty: Medium   Page: 249

104. According to the textbook, currently the most significant developments in regional economic integration are taking place in Europe and:
    A) North America
    B) South America
    C) Asia
    D) The Middle East

    Answer: A   Difficulty: Medium   Page: 249

Chapter 7 Regional Economic Integration

105. The term "Fortress Europe" refers to:
   A) the military prowess of European nations
   B) the perception that the European Union is designed to protect the European continent from the import of foreign produced goods
   C) the unwillingness of European nations to consider forming trade relationships
   D) the economic stability of the European continent

   Answer: B Difficulty: Medium Page: 250

Essay Questions

106. Describe the concept of regional economic integration. Do you believe that regional economic integration is a good thing? Explain your answer.

   Difficulty: Easy Page: 226

   Answer:
   Regional economic integration refers to agreements made by groups of countries in geographic regions to reduce, and ultimately remove, tariff and nontariff barriers to the free flow of goods, services, and factors of production between each other. The North American Free Trade Agreement, which is an agreement between the United States, Mexico, and Canada to reduce and eliminate tariffs between the three countries, is an example of regional economic integration.

   Ask your students to comment on whether regional economic integration is a good thing. In general, the observers of international trade believe that regional economic integration is a positive development. Countries that have participated in regional trade agreements have typically experienced nontrivial gains in trade from other member countries. In addition, as predicted by the theory of comparative advantage (explained in Chapter 4), there should be a substantial net gain from regional trade agreements.

Chapter 7 Regional Economic Integration

107. Please briefly explain the following forms of economic integration: free trade area, customs union, common market, economic union, and full political union. Provide an example of each form of economic integration.

Difficulty: Hard   Page: 228

Answer:
Free Trade Area: In a free trade area, all barriers to the trade of goods and services among member countries are removed. In a theoretically ideal free trade area, no discriminatory tariffs, quotas, subsidies, or administrative impediments are allowed to distort trade between member nations. Each country, however, is allowed to determine its own trade policies with regard to nonmembers. The European Free Trade Association, involving Norway, Iceland, and Switzerland, is an example of a free trade area.

Customs Union: A customs union eliminates trade barriers between member countries and adopts a common external policy. The Andean Pack, which involves Bolivia, Columbia, Ecuador, and Peru, is an example of a customs union.

Common Market: A common market eliminates trade barriers between member countries and adopts a common external policy. In addition, factors of production are also allowed to move freely between member countries. Thus, labor and capital are free to move, as there are no restrictions on immigration, emigration, or cross-border flows of capital between members. Hence, a much closer union is envisaged in a common market than a customs union. The European Union is currently a common market, although its goal is full economic union.

Economic Union: An economic union eliminates trade barriers between members nations, adopts a common external policy, and permits factors of production to move freely between member countries. In addition, a full economic union requires a common currency, harmonization of the member countries' tax rates, and a common monetary and fiscal policy. There are no true economic unions in the world today.

Political Union: A political union is the bringing together of two or more previously separate countries into essentially one country. As a result, all of the components of an economic union would apply, in addition to the political coupling of the countries involved. The United States is an example of a political union, in which previously separate "states" combined into one country. If Puerto Rico ever becomes the 51st state, the political coupling of the present United States with Puerto Rico would be an example of a political union

Chapter 7 Regional Economic Integration

108. Describe the difference between a free trade area and a common market?

Difficulty: Medium   Page: 228

Answer:
In a free trade area all barriers to the trade of goods and services among member countries are removed. In a common market, the factors of production are also allowed to move freely between member countries and a common external trade policy is adopted. In addition, in a common market, labor and capital are free to move because there are no restrictions on immigration, emigration, or cross-border flows of capital between member nations.

109. What are the primary impediments to integration? Are these impediments difficult to overcome? Explain your answer.

Difficulty: Medium   Page: 231

Answer:
Even though there may be a clear rationale for economic integration, there are two impediments that make integration difficult in many cases. First, although economic integration typically benefits the majority of the people in a country, certain groups may lose. For example, according to the author of the textbook, as a result of the 1994 establishment of NAFTA some Canadian and U.S. workers in such industries as textiles, which employ low-cost, low-skilled labor, will lose their jobs as Canadian and U.S. firms move their production to Mexico. As a result, even though the population as a whole may gain as a result of an agreement like NAFTA, these individuals may lose. If these individuals have enough political clout, they may be able to stop a NAFTA type agreement.

The second impediment to integration arises from concerns over national sovereignty. For example, for a full economic union to become a reality, the countries involved have to establish a common currency. The citizens of many countries view their currencies as symbols of national sovereignty and pride. As a result, the desire to maintain a sovereign currency may prohibit a country from joining an economic union. Similar examples prevent countries from entering into all of the forms of regional integration.

In many cases, these impediments to integration are very difficult to overcome. For instance, it is very easy to sympathize with someone who might lose their job as the result of a trade agreement. Similarly, many people become very intransigent on issues involving national sovereignty, which make some forms of regional integration almost impossible to achieve.

Chapter 7 Regional Economic Integration

110. Define trade creation and trade diversion with respect to regional economic integration. Given that integration can both create and divert trade, under what circumstances will regional integration be in the best interest of the world economy?

Difficulty: Medium   Page: 231

Answer:
Trade creation occurs when high-cost domestic producers are replaced by low-cost producers within the free trade area. It may also occur when higher-cost external producers are replaced by lower-cost external producers with the free trade area. Trade diversion occurs when lower-cost external suppliers are replaced by higher-cost suppliers within the free trade area. A regional free trade agreement will benefit the world only if the amount of trade it creates exceeds the amount it diverts.

111. From the standpoint of business and international trade, what are the advantages of a single currency within a trade block (like the EU)?

Difficulty: Medium   Page: 236

Answer:
The gains to business from a single currency arise from decreased exchange costs and reduced risk of disruption from unexpected variations in the value of different currencies. A single currency would also help firms reduce administrative costs, as fewer resources would be required for accounting, treasury management, and the like. Finally, a single currency would make it difficult for companies to charge different prices in different countries in the trade block.

112. What is meant by the term "Fortress Europe?" Is this term fair, or is it an exaggeration?

Difficulty: Medium   Page: 240

Answer:
There are presently two trade blocks in Europe: the European Union (EU) and the European Free Trade Association (EFTA). The EFTA has three members, including Norway, Iceland, and Switzerland. The European Union has 15 members, with more countries trying to get in. The fear on the part of non-European nations is that as regional integration in Europe continues to spread and deepen, the European countries will become more dependent upon one another and more protectionist in terms of their trade practices with other parts of the world. Thus, the term "Fortress Europe."

It is too early to tell whether this characterization is fair or not. What is particularly worrisome to Asia and the West, is that the EU, in particular, might increase external protection as weaker members attempt to offset their loss of protection against other EU countries by arguing for limitations on outside competition.

113. Describe the arguments for and against the North American Free Trade Agreement (NAFTA). In your opinion, is the recent ratification of NAFTA a positive development or a negative development for the citizens of the countries involved?

Difficulty: Medium   Page: 243

Answer:
This question is designed to provide a forum for classroom discussion and/or to ask students' to think about the pluses and minuses of the NAFTA. In general, the proponents of NAFTA have argued that NAFTA should be seen as an opportunity to create an enlarged and more efficient productive based for the entire North American region. The proponents concede that some lower-income jobs will move from the United States and Canada to Mexico. However, they argue that in the end, this will benefit all three countries involved because the movement of jobs to Mexico will create employment and economic growth, and as Mexico's economy grows the demand for U.S. and Canadian products in Mexico will increase. In addition, the international competitiveness of U.S. and Canadian firms that move production to Mexico to take advantage of lower labor costs will be enhanced, enabling them to better compete against Asian and European rivals.

Those that oppose NAFTA claim that U.S. and Canadian citizens will lose their jobs in alarming numbers as low-income positions are moved to Mexico to take advantage of lower wage rates. To date, the movement of jobs from the U.S. and Canada has not reached the numbers that NAFTA's critics envisioned. Environmentalists have also voiced concerns about NAFTA. Because Mexico has more lenient environmental protection laws than either the U.S. or Canada, there is a concern that U.S. and Canadian firms will relocate to Mexico to avoid the cost of protecting the environment. Finally, there is continued opposition in Mexico to NAFTA from those who fear a loss of national sovereignty. Mexican critics fear that NAFTA will allow their country to be dominated by U.S. and Canadian multinationals, and use Mexico as a low-cost assembly site, while keeping their higher-paying jobs in their own countries.

Chapter 8 Foreign Exchange Markets

True/False Questions

1. The international reserve market is a market for converting the currency of one country into that of another country.

   Answer: False   Difficulty: Easy   Page: 258

2. Without the foreign market exchange, international trade and international investment on the scale that we see today would be impossible.

   Answer: True   Difficulty: Easy   Page: 258

3. An exchange rate is simply the rate at which one currency is converted into another.

   Answer: True   Difficulty: Easy   Page: 258

4. In international trade, the risk of not getting paid for a product that is exported from one country to another is referred to foreign exchange risk.

   Answer: False   Difficulty: Medium   Page: 259

5. The market through which an individual or institution exchanges one currency into another is called the foreign exchange market.

   Answer: True   Difficulty: Medium   Page: 260

6. Currency speculation typically involves the short-term movement of funds from one currency to another in the hopes of profiting from shifts in exchange rates.

   Answer: True   Difficulty: Medium   Page: 260

7. When a U.S. tourist in Edinburgh goes to a bank to convert her dollars in pounds, the exchange rate is the forward exchange rate.

   Answer: False   Difficulty: Medium   Page: 261

8. Spot exchange rates change daily as determined by the relative demand and supply for difference currencies.

   Answer: True   Difficulty: Medium   Page: 261

9. A forward exchange occurs when two parties agree to exchange currency and execute the deal at some specific date in the future.

    Answer: True   Difficulty: Easy   Page: 264

10. Arbitrage is the process of buying a currency high and selling it low.

    Answer: False   Difficulty: Medium   Page: 266

11. At the basic level, exchange rates are determined by the demand and supply of one currency relative to the demand and supply for another.

    Answer: True   Difficulty: Easy   Page: 266

12. The law of fixed price states that identical products sold in different countries must sell for the same price when their price is expressed in the same currency in competitive markets free of transportation costs and barriers to trade.

    Answer: True   Difficulty: Medium   Page: 267

13. An efficient market has significant impediments to the free flow of goods and services.

    Answer: False   Difficulty: Easy   Page: 267

14. According to the International Fisher Effect, for any two countries, the spot exchange rate should change in an equal amount but in the opposite direction to the difference in the nominal interest rates between the two countries.

    Answer: True   Difficulty: Hard   Page: 271

15. Fundamental analysis uses price and volume data to determine past trends, which are expected to continue into the future.

    Answer: True   Difficulty: Medium   Page: 275

16. Technical analysis draws on economic theory to construct sophisticated econometric models for predicting exchange rate movements.

    Answer: False   Difficulty: Medium   Page: 276

17. A currency is said to be externally convertible when only nonresidents may convert it into foreign currency without limitations.

    Answer: True   Difficulty: Medium   Page: 286

18. A country's currency is said to be freely convertible when neither residents nor nonresidents are allowed to convert it into a foreign currency.

    Answer: False   Difficulty: Medium   Page: 276

19. The majority of the countries in the world have currency that is freely convertible.

    Answer: False   Difficulty: Medium   Page: 276

20. Countertrade refers to a range of barterlike agreements by which goods and services can be traded for other goods and services.

    Answer: True   Difficulty: Easy   Page: 277

Multiple Choice Questions

21. The _____ is a market for converting the currency of one country into that of another.
    A) foreign exchange market
    B) cross-cultural interchange
    C) financial barter market
    D) monetary replacement market

    Answer: A   Difficulty: Easy   Page: 258

22. The rate at which one currency is converted into another is called the _____.
    A) replacement percentage
    B) resale rate
    C) exchange rate
    D) interchange ratio

    Answer: C   Difficulty: Easy   Page: 258

Chapter 8 Foreign Exchange Markets

23. Without the _____ market, international trade and international investment on the scale that we see today would be impossible.
    A) foreign exchange
    B) financial barter
    C) foreign resale
    D) monetary replacement

    Answer: A Difficulty: Easy Page: 258

24. An _____ is simply the rate at which one currency is converted into another.
    A) replacement percentage
    B) resale rate
    C) interchange ratio
    D) exchange rate

    Answer: D Difficulty: Easy Page: 258

25. The _____ is the lubricant that enables companies based in countries that use different currencies to trade with each other.
    A) World Bank
    B) foreign currency exchange
    C) foreign exchange market
    D) foreign monetary mart

    Answer: B Difficulty: Easy Page: 258

26. One function of the foreign exchange market is to provide some insurance against the risks that arise from changes in exchange rates, commonly referred to as:
    A) foreign market hazard
    B) global jeopardy
    C) foreign exchange risk
    D) commerce uncertainty

    Answer: C Difficulty: Medium Page: 258

27. Which of the following statements is true?
    A) the existence of the foreign exchange market has removed all forms of foreign exchange risk for business organizations
    B) despite the existence of the foreign exchange market, firms do suffer losses because of unpredicted changes in exchange rates, although these occasions are rare
    C) the foreign exchange market eliminates very little foreign exchange risk
    D) despite the existence of the foreign exchange market, it is not unusual for international businesses to suffer losses because of unpredicted changes in exchange rates

    Answer: D Difficulty: Hard Page: 258

28. The foreign exchange market serves two main functions. These are:
    A) collect duties on imported products and convert the currency of one country into the currency of another
    B) insure companies against foreign exchange risk and set interest rates charged to foreign investors
    C) collect duties on imported products and set interest rates charged to foreign investors
    D) convert the currency of one country into the currency of another and provide some insurance against foreign exchange risk

    Answer: D Difficulty: Medium Page: 259

29. The foreign exchange market converts the currency of one country into the currency of another and:
    A) provides some insurance against foreign exchange risk
    B) collects duties on imported products
    C) sets interest rates charged to foreign investors
    D) arbitrates disputes between trade partners

    Answer: A Difficulty: Medium Page: 259

30. The foreign exchange market provides some insurance of foreign exchange risk and:
    A) arbitrates disputes between trade partners
    B) converts the currency of one country into the currency of another
    C) collects duties on imported products
    D) set interest rates charged to foreign investors

    Answer: B Difficulty: Medium Page: 259

Chapter 8 Foreign Exchange Markets

31. Which of the following correctly matches a country with its currency?
    A) South Korea, the pound
    B) France, the deutsche mark
    C) Japan, the yen
    D) Great Britain, the franc

    Answer: C Difficulty: Hard Page: 266

32. Which of the following correctly matches a country with its currency?
    A) Japan, franc
    B) South Korea, the deutsche mark
    C) Canada, the yen
    D) Great Britain, the pound

    Answer: D Difficulty: Hard Page: 259

33. Which of the following is the currency of Japan?
    A) yen
    B) deutsche mark
    C) dollar
    D) pound

    Answer: A Difficulty: Medium Page: 259

34. Which of the following is the currency of France?
    A) pound
    B) deutsche mark
    C) dollar
    D) franc

    Answer: D Difficulty: Medium Page: 259

35. When a tourist exchanges one currency into another, she is participating in the:
    A) foreign barter market
    B) foreign exchange market
    C) foreign replacement market
    D) foreign swap market

    Answer: B Difficulty: Easy Page: 260

36. The _____ is the rate at which the market converts one currency into another.
    A) international conversion factor
    B) world barter factor
    C) foreign exchange rate
    D) global replacement percentage

    Answer: C Difficulty: Medium Page: 260

37. Which of the following is not one of the four main uses that international businesses have for the foreign exchange market?
    A) international businesses use foreign exchange markets to convert money they earn in foreign currencies to their home currencies
    B) international businesses use foreign exchange markets in determining domestic wage rates
    C) international businesses use foreign exchange markets when they have spare cash that they wish to invest for short terms in money markets
    D) currency speculation

    Answer: B Difficulty: Hard Page: 260

38. _____ typically involves the short-term movement of funds from one currency to another in the hopes of profiting from shifts in exchange rates.
    A) Capital venturing
    B) Currency speculation
    C) Monetary risk taking
    D) Investment contemplation

    Answer: B Difficulty: Easy Page: 260

39. Currency speculation typically involves the _____ movements of funds from one currency to another in the hopes of profiting from shifts in exchange rates.
    A) medium-term
    B) long-term
    C) historical
    D) short-term

    Answer: D Difficulty: Medium Page: 260

40. Currency speculation typically involves:
    A) the short-term movement of funds from one currency to another in the hopes of profiting from shifts in exchange rates
    B) the permanent movement of funds from one currency to another in the hopes of profiting from long-term investment in a particular country
    C) the simultaneous purchase of currencies from several countries in hopes of profiting from increasing economic prosperity
    D) the liquidation of currency in favor of precious metals as a hedge against inflation

    Answer: A Difficulty: Medium Page: 260

41. When two parties agree to exchange currency and execute the deal immediately, the transaction is referred to as a _____.
    A) point-in-time exchange
    B) temporal exchange
    C) spot exchange
    D) forward exchange

    Answer: C Difficulty: Easy Page: 261

42. The _____ is the rate at which a foreign exchange dealer converts one currency into another currency on a particular day.
    A) spot exchange rate
    B) reference point exchange rate
    C) point-in-time exchange rate
    D) forward exchange rate

    Answer: A Difficulty: Medium Page: 261

43. When two parties agree to exchange currency and execute the deal _____, the transaction is referred to as a spot exchange.
    A) in 90 days
    B) in 60 days
    C) in 30 days
    D) immediately

    Answer: D Difficulty: Medium Page: 261

44. When a U.S. tourist in Japan goes to a bank to convert her dollars into Japanese yen, the exchange rate is the:
   A) forward exchange rate
   B) regulated exchange rate
   C) sanctioned exchange rate
   D) spot exchange rate

   Answer: D Difficulty: Medium Page: 261

45. It is necessary to use a _____ exchange rate to execute a transaction immediately.
   A) real time
   B) spot
   C) statutory
   D) sanctioned

   Answer: B Difficulty: Medium Page: 261

46. The value of a currency is determined by:
   A) the interaction between the demand and supply of that currency relative to the demand and supply of other currencies
   B) a consortium of international currency traders
   C) the World Trade Organization
   D) negotiations between the central banks of the leading five industrial powers of the world

   Answer: A Difficulty: Medium Page: 261

47. A _____ exchange occurs when two parties agree to exchange currency and execute the deal at some specific date in the future.
   A) reverse
   B) spot
   C) hedge
   D) forward

   Answer: D Difficulty: Medium Page: 262

Chapter 8 Foreign Exchange Markets

48. _____ exchange rates represent market participants' collective predictions of likely spot exchange rates at specified future dates.
    A) Reciprocal
    B) Hedge
    C) Reverse
    D) Forward

    Answer: D   Difficulty: Medium   Page: 262

49. An exchange in which two parties agree to exchange currency and execute the deal at some specific date in the future is called a:
    A) forward exchange
    B) hedge exchange
    C) reverse exchange
    D) spot exchange

    Answer: A   Difficulty: Medium   Page: 262

50. Rates for currency exchange quoted for 30, 90, or 180 days into the future are referred to as _____.
    A) forward exchange rates
    B) foreign exchange quotes
    C) united trade rates
    D) generic exchange quotes

    Answer: A   Difficulty: Easy   Page: 264

51. The foreign exchange market:
    A) is not located in any one place
    B) is located in New York City
    C) has offices in the Capitols of the five most powerful industrialized nations in the world
    D) is located in London

    Answer: A   Difficulty: Medium   Page: 264

Chapter 8 Foreign Exchange Markets

52. When the dollar buys more francs on the spot market than the 30-day forward market, we say the dollars is selling at a _____. Conversely, when the dollars buys less francs on the spot market than the 30-day forward market, we say the dollar is selling at a _____.
    A) premium, discount
    B) handicap, bonus
    C) discount, premium
    D) subsidy, handicap

    Answer: C   Difficulty: Hard   Page: 264

53. The most important trading centers for the foreign exchange market are in:
    A) London, New York, and Tokyo
    B) San Paulo, New York, and Paris
    C) San Francisco, Tokyo, and Singapore
    D) New York, Hong Kong, and Paris

    Answer: A   Difficulty: Hard   Page: 264

54. The largest trading center in the foreign exchange market is _____.
    A) Hong Kong
    B) London
    C) San Paulo
    D) Paris

    Answer: B   Difficulty: Hard   Page: 264

55. The process of buying a currency low and selling it high is called:
    A) forward exchange
    B) skimming
    C) profiteering
    D) arbitrage

    Answer: D   Difficulty: Easy   Page: 266

56. _____ is the process of buying a currency low and selling it high.
    A) Situational exchange
    B) Inward exchange
    C) Arbitrage
    D) Skimming

    Answer: C   Difficulty: Easy   Page: 266

57. Although a foreign exchange transaction can involve any two currencies, some 87% of transactions involve:
    A) Japanese yen
    B) British pounds
    C) U.S. dollars
    D) French francs

    Answer: C   Difficulty: Medium   Page: 266

58. At the most basic level, exchange rates are determined by the demand and supply of one currency relative to the:
    A) permanent value of another
    B) 30-day average of another
    C) 90-day average of another
    D) demand and supply of another

    Answer: D   Difficulty: Medium   Page: 266

59. Most economic theories suggest that three import factors have an important impact on future exchange rate movements in a country's currency. These factors are:
    A) the country's price inflation, its interest rate, and its market philosophy
    B) the country's rate of GNP, its unemployment rate, and its economic policy
    C) the country's participation in the World Trade Organization, its monetary policy, and its market philosophy
    D) the country's rate of economic growth, its participation in the World Trade Organization, and its economy policy

    Answer: A   Difficulty: Hard   Page: 267

60. The three factors that have the most important impact on future exchange rate movement include the country's price inflation, its market philosophy, and its
    _____.
    A) rate of economic growth
    B) unemployment rate
    C) interest rate
    D) participation in the World Trade Organization

    Answer: C   Difficulty: Medium   Page: 267

Chapter 8 Foreign Exchange Markets

61. The three factors that have the most important impact on future exchange rate movement include the country's interest rate, its market philosophy, and its

    _____.
    A) price inflation
    B) participation in the World Trade Organization
    C) unemployment rate
    D) rate of economic growth

    Answer: A   Difficulty: Medium   Page: 267

62. The _____ states that in competitive markets free of transportation costs and barriers to trade, identical products sold in different countries must sell for the same price when their price is expressed in terms of the same currency.
    A) law of one price
    B) principle of consistent pricing
    C) model of fair pricing
    D) principle of equitable pricing

    Answer: A   Difficulty: Medium   Page: 267

63. According to the _____, identical products sold in different countries must sell for the same price when their price is expressed in the same currency in competitive markets free of transportation costs and barriers to trade.
    A) model of fair pricing
    B) law of one price
    C) principle of equitable pricing
    D) principle of consistent pricing

    Answer: B   Difficulty: Medium   Page: 267

64. PPP theory stands for:
    A) Productivity Power Premium theory
    B) Process Productivity Predictor theory
    C) Purchasing Power Parity theory
    D) Personal Power Predictor theory

    Answer: C   Difficulty: Medium   Page: 267

65. A(n) _____ has no impediments to the free flow of goods and services.
    A) classical market
    B) efficient market
    C) traditional market
    D) inefficient market

    Answer: B   Difficulty: Easy   Page: 267

66. A market that has no impediments to the free flow of goods and services is called a(n) _____ market.
    A) inefficient
    B) classical
    C) tolerant
    D) efficient

    Answer: D   Difficulty: Easy   Page: 267

67. If the law of one price were true for all goods and services, the _____ exchange rate could be found from any individual set of prices.
    A) stability power similarity (SPS)
    B) purchasing ability adeptness (PAA)
    C) buying prowess equality (BPE)
    D) purchasing power parity (PPP)

    Answer: D   Difficulty: Hard   Page: 267

68. A _____ is a market in which few impediments to international trade and investment exist.
    A) relatively efficient market
    B) consistently inefficient market
    C) absolutely free market
    D) absolutely closed

    Answer: A   Difficulty: Medium   Page: 268

69. The _____ theory tells us that a country with a high inflation rate will see deprecation in its currency exchange rate.
    A) law of one price
    B) monetary system
    C) PPP
    D) price inflation

    Answer: C   Difficulty: Hard   Page: 268

70. In essence, PPP theory predicts that:
    A) there is no relationship between changes in relative prices and changes in exchange rates
    B) changes in relative prices will result in stability in exchange rates
    C) stability in relative prices will result in a change in exchange rates
    D) changes in relative prices will result in a change in exchange rates

    Answer: D   Difficulty: Hard   Page: 268

71. A less extreme version of the PPP theory states that given _____, that is, markets in which few impediments to international trade and investment exist-the price of a "basket of goods" should be roughly equivalent in each country.
    A) relatively efficient markets
    B) statutory markets
    C) stable markets
    D) absolutely free markets

    Answer: A   Difficulty: Hard   Page: 268

72. In essence, the _____ theory predicts that changes in relative prices will result in a change in exchange rates.
    A) buying power equality (BPE)
    B) purchasing power parity (PPP)
    C) stability power similarity (SPS)
    D) buying prowess equality (BPE)

    Answer: B   Difficulty: Hard   Page: 268

73. In essence, purchasing power parity predicts that changes in relative prices will result in a change in _____ rates.
    A) unemployement
    B) exchange
    C) interest
    D) gross domestic product

    Answer: B   Difficulty: Medium   Page: 268

74. PPP theory predicts that changes in _____ will result in a change in exchange rates.
    A) relative prices
    B) interest rates
    C) unemployment rates
    D) statutory prices

    Answer: A Difficulty: Medium Page: 268

75. Inflation is a _____ phenomenon.
    A) legal
    B) political
    C) monetary
    D) social

    Answer: C Difficulty: Medium Page: 268

76. According to our textbook, when the growth in a country's money supply is faster than the growth in its output, _____ is fueled.
    A) economic growth
    B) unemployment
    C) inflation
    D) per capita savings

    Answer: C Difficulty: Hard Page: 268

77. The PPP theory tells us that a country with a high inflation rate will see:
    A) a depreciation in its currency exchange rate
    B) an appreciation in its currency exchange rate
    C) no change in its currency exchange rate as a result of the inflation rate
    D) economic stability as a result of high inflation

    Answer: A Difficulty: Medium Page: 268

78. According to our textbook, _____ determines whether the rate of growth in a country's money supply is greater than the rate of growth in output.
    A) the international monetary authority
    B) market mechanisms
    C) the private sector
    D) government policy

    Answer: D Difficulty: Hard Page: 270

79. PPP theory predicts that changes in _____ will result in a change in exchange rates.
    A) relative prices
    B) interest rates
    C) unemployment rates
    D) statutory prices

    Answer: A Difficulty: Medium Page: 270

80. According to the textbook, PPP theory does not seem to be a particularly good predictor of exchange rate movements for time spans of:
    A) one year or less
    B) five years or less
    C) ten years or less
    D) twenty years or less

    Answer: B Difficulty: Hard Page: 270

81. For time periods of _____, PPP theory does not seem to be a particularly good predictor of exchange rate movements.
    A) twenty years or less
    B) ten years or less
    C) five years or less
    D) one year or less

    Answer: C Difficulty: Hard Page: 270

82. The PPP theory seems to best predict exchange rate changes for countries with:
    A) very low rates of inflation and developed capital markets
    B) very low rates of inflation and underdeveloped capital markets
    C) very high rates of inflation and underdeveloped capital markets
    D) very high rates of inflation and developed capital markets

    Answer: C Difficulty: Hard Page: 270

83. Economic theory tells us that _____ rates reflect expectations about likely future inflation rates.
    A) currency
    B) exchange
    C) interest
    D) unemployment

    Answer: C Difficulty: Medium Page: 271

Chapter 8 Foreign Exchange Markets

84. The _____ states that for any two countries, the spot exchange rate should change in an equal amount but in the opposite direction to the difference in the nominal interest rates between the two countries.
    A) Worldwide James Effect
    B) Universal Phillips Effect
    C) International Fisher Effect
    D) Global Miller Effect

    Answer: C Difficulty: Medium Page: 271

85. The International Fisher Effect states that for any two countries, the _____ exchange rate should change in an equal amount but in the opposite direction to the difference in the nominal interest rates between the two countries.
    A) reciprocal
    B) spot
    C) forward
    D) inward

    Answer: B Difficulty: Medium Page: 271

86. According to the Fisher effect, if the real rate of interest in a country is 5 percent and the annual inflation is expected to be 10 percent, the nominal interest rate will be:
    A) 5 percent
    B) 10 percent
    C) 15 percent
    D) 20 percent

    Answer: C Difficulty: Hard Page: 271

87. Empirical evidence suggests that neither PPP theory nor the International Fisher Effect are particularly good at explaining:
    A) long-term movements in exchange rates
    B) interest rates
    C) short-term movements in exchange rates
    D) unemployment rates

    Answer: C Difficulty: Hard Page: 272

88. _____ represent market participants' collective predictions of likely spot exchange rates at specified future dates.
    A) Statutory exchange rates
    B) Speculative exchange rates
    C) Forward exchange rates
    D) Preemptive exchange rates

    Answer: C   Difficulty: Medium   Page: 273

89. The _____ market school argues that forward exchange rates do the best possible job of forecasting future spot exchange rates, so investing in exchange rate forecasting services would be a waste of time.
    A) efficient
    B) closed
    C) inefficient
    D) free

    Answer: A   Difficulty: Medium   Page: 273

90. The _____ market school argues that companies can improve the foreign exchange market's estimate of future exchange rates by investing in forecasting services.
    A) inefficient
    B) free
    C) open
    D) efficient

    Answer: D   Difficulty: Hard   Page: 273

91. A(n) _____ market is one in which prices do not reflect all available information.
    A) efficient
    B) inefficient
    C) free
    D) closed

    Answer: B   Difficulty: Medium   Page: 274

92. In an _____ market, forward exchange rates will not be the best possible predictors of future spot exchange rates.
   A) closed
   B) inefficient
   C) efficient
   D) reciprocal

   Answer: B Difficulty: Hard Page: 274

93. _____ draws on economic theory to construct sophisticated econometric models for predicting exchange rate movements.
   A) Principal investigation
   B) Fundamental analysis
   C) Primary evaluation
   D) Technical analysis

   Answer: B Difficulty: Medium Page: 275

94. _____ uses price and volume data to determine past trends, which are expected to continue into the future.
   A) Principal investigation
   B) Primary evaluation
   C) Fundamental analysis
   D) Technical analysis

   Answer: D Difficulty: Medium Page: 276

95. The type of analysis that predicts exchange rate movements by using price and volume data to determine past trends is called:
   A) fundamental analysis
   B) primary evaluation
   C) technical analysis
   D) principal investigation

   Answer: C Difficulty: Medium Page: 276

96. _____ is based on the premise that analyzable market trends and waves can be used to predict future trends and waves.
    A) Technical analysis
    B) Fundamental analysis
    C) Basic analysis
    D) Central analysis

    Answer: A Difficulty: Medium   Page: 276

97. _____ analysis uses prices and volume data to determine past trends.
    A) Central
    B) Basic
    C) Fundamental
    D) Technical

    Answer: D Difficulty: Hard   Page: 276

98. A country's currency is said to be _____ when the country's government allows both residents and nonresidents to purchase unlimited amounts of foreign currency with it.
    A) technically convertible
    B) freely convertible
    C) externally convertible
    D) nonconvertible

    Answer: B Difficulty: Easy   Page: 276

99. A country's currency is said to be freely convertible when the country's government:
    A) allows residents to purchase unlimited amounts of a foreign currency with it and allows nonresidents to purchase a limited amount of a foreign currency with it
    B) allows both residents and nonresidents to purchase unlimited amounts of foreign currency with it
    C) allows only residents to purchase foreign currency with it
    D) allows both residents, nonresidents, and foreign governments to purchase limited amounts of foreign currency with it

    Answer: B Difficulty: Medium   Page: 276

Chapter 8 Foreign Exchange Markets

100. A currency is said to be _____ when only nonresidents may convert it into a foreign currency without any limitations.
    A) externally convertible
    B) freely convertible
    C) technically convertible
    D) nonconvertible

    Answer: A Difficulty: Medium Page: 276

101. A currency is _____ when neither residents nor nonresidents are allowed to convert it into a foreign currency.
    A) freely convertible
    B) nonconvertible
    C) externally convertible
    D) technically convertible

    Answer: B Difficulty: Medium Page: 276

102. A government restricts the convertibility of its currency to protect the country's _____ and to halt any capital flight.
    A) membership in the World Trade Organization
    B) foreign exchange reserves
    C) political stature
    D) national sovereignty

    Answer: B Difficulty: Hard Page: 277

103. _____ refers to a range of barterlike agreements by which goods and services can be traded for other goods and services.
    A) Separate trade
    B) Reciprocal trade
    C) Countertrade
    D) Alternative trade

    Answer: C Difficulty: Easy Page: 277

Chapter 8 Foreign Exchange Markets

104. If an American grain company exported corn to Russia, and instead of receiving nonconvertible Russian currency in exchange for the corn received Russian crude oil, that would be an example of _____.
    A) countertrade
    B) synergistic trade
    C) separate trade
    D) reciprocal trade

    Answer: A Difficulty: Medium Page: 277

105. According to a study cited in the textbook, _____ of world trade in 1985 involved some form of countertrade agreement.
    A) 5 to 10 percent
    B) 20 to 30 percent
    C) 40 to 50 percent
    D) 70 to 80 percent

    Answer: B Difficulty: Hard Page: 277

Essay Questions

106. What are the functions of the foreign exchange market? Would international commerce be possible without its existence?

    Difficulty: Easy Page: 258

    Answer:
    The foreign exchange market is a market for converting the currency of one country into that of another. For example, an American exporter that gets paid by a German importer in deutsche marks can convert the deutsche marks to dollars on the foreign exchange market. The two main functions of the foreign exchange market are currency conversion and insuring against foreign exchange risk. In terms of currency conversion, the market has four primary functions for international businesses: (1) converting payments a company receives in foreign currencies into the currency of its home country; (2) converting the currency of a company's home country into another currency when they must pay a foreign company for its products and services in their currency; (3) international businesses may use foreign exchange markets when they have spare cash that they wish to invest for short terms in money markets (of another country); and (4) currency speculation. The second function of the foreign exchange market is to provide insurance to protect against the possible adverse consequences of unpredictable changes in exchange rates. This can be accomplished through the use of a forward exchange.

Chapter 8 Foreign Exchange Markets

It is difficult to image how international commerce would work without the existence of the foreign exchange market. Without it, international trade would have to be completed on the basis of barter, rather than currency exchange. As suggested by the author of the textbook, the foreign exchange markets is the lubricant that enables companies based in countries that use different currencies to trade with each other.

107. For a firm that deals in international markets, what does "foreign exchange risk" mean? How could foreign exchange risk affect the profitability of an American agricultural equipment firm exporting tractors to a German buyer?

Difficulty: Medium   Page: 259

Answer:
A foreign exchange risk is a risk that the value of currencies will change in the future. A change in foreign exchange rates could have a dramatic impact on a company engaged in international commerce. For example, if a U.S. agricultural equipment firm had a contract to deliver 100 tractors to a German customer in three months, and the U.S. dollar strengthened against the German deutsche mark (i.e. currency values changed), the U.S. agricultural equipment firm would end up with less dollars (after the deutsche marks it was paid were exchanged for dollars) than originally anticipated.

108. Explain the difference between spot exchange rates and forward exchange rates. Briefly explain how the forward exchange market works.

Difficulty: Medium   Page: 261

Answer:
The spot exchange rate is the rate at which a foreign exchange dealer converts one currency into another currency on a particular day. Thus, when a Japanese tourist in Orlando goes to a bank to convert yen into dollars, the exchange rate is the spot rate for that day. Spot exchange rates change daily, based on the relative supply and demand for different currencies.

Forward exchange rates are rates for currencies quoted for 30, 90, or 180 days into the future (in some cases, it is possible to get forward exchange rates for several years into the future). Forward exchange rates are available because of the volatile and problematic nature of the spot exchange market. Suppose a U.S. importer agreed to paid a Japanese exporter $100 a piece for a large quantity of cameras. The day of the agreement, the exchange rate for dollars and yen was 1:1 (1 dollar for 1 yen). The U.S. importer planed to sell the cameras for $125, guaranteeing himself a profit of $25 per camera. Further suppose that the payment is not due to the Japanese exporter for 30 days, and during the 30 day waiting period, the dollar unexpectedly depreciates against the yen, forcing the exchange rate to one dollar for every .75 yen. Per the original agreement, the U.S. importer still has to pay the Japanese importer 100 yen per camera, but now the exchange rate is not 1 dollar per yen, but is 1 dollar per .75 yen. As a result, the U.S. importer has to pay $1.33 to buy the equivalent of 1 yen. Now, instead of making $25 per camera ($125 selling price - $100 purchase price), the U.S. importer will lose $8 per camera ($125 selling price - $133 purchase price influenced by currency fluctuations). To avoid this potential problem, the U.S. importer could have entered into a 30-day forward exchange transaction with a foreign exchange dealer at, say, 1 dollar for every .95 yen (the forward rate will typically be somewhat lower than the spot rate). By doing this, the importer is guaranteed that he or she will not have to pay more than 1.05 dollars for every 1 yen, which would still guarantee the importer a $20 per profit on the cameras.

109. Where is the foreign exchange market located? What is the nature of the market? Is the market growing or shrinking on a global basis?

Difficulty: Medium   Page: 264

Answer:
The foreign exchange market is not located in any one place. It is a global network of banks, brokers, and foreign exchange dealers connected by electronic communications systems. When companies wish to convert currencies, they typically go through their own banks rather than entering the market directly. The foreign exchange market has been growing at a rapid pace, reflecting a general growth in the volume of cross-border trade and investment.

110. What is the International Fisher Effect? (note: you do not need to provide the mathematical formula provided in the book)

Difficulty: Medium   Page: 271

Answer:
The International Fisher Effect states that for any two countries, the spot exchange rate should change in an equal amount but in the opposite direction to the difference in nominal interest rates between the two countries.

Chapter 8 Foreign Exchange Markets

111. Explain how the psychology of investors and bandwagon effects can have an impact on the movement in exchange rates. Do you believe that bandwagon effects really happen? Explain your answer.

Difficulty: Medium   Page: 272

Answer:
As noted by the author of the textbook, empirical evidence suggests that empirical explanations are not particular good at explaining short-term movements in exchange rates. One reason for this may be the impact of investor psychology on short-run exchange rate movements. Investors, because they are human beings, do not always make decisions based on a rational analysis of the facts. Sometimes investors imitate the actions of someone that is very influential, even if there is no logical reason to do so. Investors also trade based on "hunches" or speculation, which is more psychological in nature than rational. A bandwagon effect in when investors in increasing numbers start following the lead of someone who may be pushing the value of a currency up or down due to psychological reasons. As a bandwagon effect builds up, the expectations of investors become a self-fulfilling prophecy, and the market moves in the way the investors expected.

Ask your students if they believe bandwagon effects actually happen in practice. Most students will say that they do, and have vivid examples to support their conclusions.

112. In the context of forecasting exchange rate movements, describe the difference between fundamental analysis and technical analysis. Which approach is preferred by economists? Why?

Difficulty: Hard   Page: 275

Answer:
Fundamental analysis draws on economic theory to construct sophisticated econometric models for predicting exchange rate movements. The variables contained in these models typically include relative money supply growth rates, inflation rates, and interest rates. In addition, they may include variables related to a countries' balance-of-payments positions. In contrast, technical analysis uses price and volume data to determine past trends, which are expected to continue into the future. This approach does not rely on a consideration of economic fundamentals. Technical analysis is based on the premise that there are analyzable market trends and waves and that previous trends and waves can be used to predict future trends and waves.

Since there is no theoretical rationale for the assumption of predictability that underlies technical analysis, most economists compare technical analysis to fortune-telling, and prefer fundamental analysis. However, despite this skepticism, technical analysis has gained favor in recent years.

Chapter 8 Foreign Exchange Markets

113. Explain the concept of countertrade. When does countertrade make sense? How does countertrade help solve the nonconvertability problem?

Difficulty: Medium Page: 277

Answer:
Countertrade refers to a range of barterlike agreements by which goods and services can be traded for other goods and services. Countertrade makes sense when a country's currency is nonconvertible. For example, the Russian ruble in nonconvertible. What that means it that if a U.S. exporter sold grain to a Russian importer and was paid in rubles, the U.S. exporter could not take the rubles to a bank and have them converted into dollars. The rubles are only of value in Russia. To get around this limitation, the U.S. exporter and the Russian importer might enter into a countertrade agreement, in which the U.S. exporter accepts some type of goods or services in exchange for the grain rather than Russian rubles. For instance, the Russian importer could use rubles to buy Russian crude oil, and exchange the crude oil for the grain. The U.S. exporter could then sell the crude oil for American dollars, and benefit from the transaction.

Chapter 9 The Global Monetary System

True/False Questions

1. The Bretton Woods system called for fixed exchange rates against the U.S. dollar.

   Answer: True   Difficulty: Easy   Page: 287

2. The Bretton Woods system of floating exchange rates collapsed in 1973. Since then the world has operated with a fixed exchange rate system.

   Answer: False   Difficulty: Medium   Page: 287

3. The practice of pegging currencies to gold and guaranteeing convertibility is known as the gold standard.

   Answer: True   Difficulty: Easy   Page: 288

4. The great strength claimed for the gold standard was that it contained a powerful mechanism for simultaneously achieving balance-of-trade equilibrium by all countries.

   Answer: True   Difficulty: Medium   Page: 288

5. The agreement reached at Bretton Woods established two multinational institutions - The World Trade Organization and the World Bank

   Answer: False   Difficulty: Medium   Page: 290

6. As stipulated by the Bretton Woods agreement, the task of the IMF was to maintain order in the international monetary system.

   Answer: True   Difficulty: Medium   Page: 299

7. The Bretton Woods agreement resulted in a commitment not to use devaluation as a weapon of competitive trade policy.

   Answer: True   Difficulty: Hard   Page: 291

8. Although monetary discipline was a central objective, the Bretton Woods agreement recognized that a rigid policy of fixed exchange rates would be too inflexible.

   Answer: True   Difficulty: Medium   Page: 291

9. The system of adjustable parities allows for the devaluation of a country's currency by more than 10% if the IMF agrees that the country's balance of payments is in "fundamental disequilibrium."

   Answer: True   Difficulty: Hard   Page: 292

10. The official name of the World Bank is the International Bank for Reconstruction and Development.

    Answer: True   Difficulty: Medium   Page: 292

11. Most economists trace the breakup of the fixed exchange rate system to the U.S. macroeconomic policy package of 1965-1968.

    Answer: True   Difficulty: Hard   Page: 292

12. The Bretton Woods agreement had an Achilles' heel: the system could not work if its key currency, the British pound, was under speculative attack.

    Answer: False   Difficulty: Medium   Page: 293

13. The purpose of the Jamaica meeting was to revise the IMF's Articles of Agreement to reflect the new reality of floating exchange rates.

    Answer: True   Difficulty: Hard   Page: 294

14. Under a floating exchange rate regime, market forces have produced a volatile dollar exchange.

    Answer: True   Difficulty: Medium   Page: 297

15. The case for fixed exchange rates has two main elements: monetary policy autonomy and automatic trade balance adjustments.

    Answer: False   Difficulty: Medium   Page: 298

16. It is argued that a floating exchange rate regime gives countries monetary policy autonomy.

    Answer: True   Difficulty: Medium   Page: 298

17. Advocates of a floating exchange rate regime argue that removal of the obligation to maintain exchange rate parity restores monetary control to a government.

    Answer: True   Difficulty: Medium   Page: 298

18. Under the Bretton Woods system, if a country developed a permanent deficit in its balance of trade that could not be corrected by domestic policy, the World Bank would agree to a currency devaluation.

    Answer: False   Difficulty: Hard   Page: 299

19. The case for fixed exchange rates rests on arguments about monetary discipline, speculation, uncertainty, and the lack of connection between the trade balance and exchange rates.

    Answer: True   Difficulty: Medium   Page: 299

20. Critics of a floating exchange rate regime argue that speculation causes stability in exchange rates

    Answer: False   Difficulty: Hard   Page: 299

Multiple Choice Questions

21. In 1997, only _____ of the world's viable currencies were freely floating; this includes the currencies of many of the world's larger industrial nations such as the United States, Canada, Japan, and Britain.
    A) 12
    B) 22
    C) 40
    D) 51

    Answer: D   Difficulty: Hard   Page: 287

Chapter 9 The Global Monetary System

22. The Bretton Woods conferences occurred in _____ and established the basic framework for the post-World War II international monetary system.
    A) 1944
    B) 1959
    C) 1968
    D) 1988

    Answer: A Difficulty: Hard Page: 287

23. The Bretton Woods system called for _____ exchange rates against the U.S. dollar.
    A) variable
    B) floating
    C) fixed
    D) fluctuating

    Answer: C Difficulty: Easy Page: 287

24. Under the exchange rate system established by the Bretton Woods agreement, the value of most currencies in terms of _____ was fixed for long periods and was allowed to change only under a specific set of circumstances.
    A) British pound
    B) Japanese yen
    C) U.S. dollars
    D) German deutsche mark

    Answer: C Difficulty: Medium Page: 287

25. The Bretton Woods system of fixed exchange rates:
    A) has continued to be in force since it was adopted
    B) collapsed in 1973
    C) collapsed shortly after it was adopted
    D) collapsed shortly after it was adopted, but has been reinstated and is in effect today

    Answer: B Difficulty: Medium Page: 287

Chapter 9 The Global Monetary System

26. The Bretton Woods conference created two major international institutions. These are:
    A) the International Monetary Fund and the World Bank
    B) the World Trade Organization and the United Nations
    C) the World Currency Exchange and the World Bank
    D) the Bretton Woods Monetary Fund and the World Trade Organization

    Answer: A   Difficulty: Medium   Page: 287

27. The International Monetary Fund and the _____ were created by the Bretton Woods conference.
    A) Bretton Woods Monetary Fund
    B) World Currency Exchange
    C) World Trade Organization
    D) World Bank

    Answer: D   Difficulty: Medium   Page: 287

28. The World Bank and the _____ were created by the Bretton Woods conference.
    A) Bretton Woods Monetary Fund
    B) World Currency Exchange
    C) International Monetary Fund
    D) Global Trade Organization

    Answer: C   Difficulty: Medium   Page: 287

29. As stipulated by the Bretton Woods conference, the goal of the International Monetary Fund was to:
    A) maintain order in the international monetary system
    B) establish a world currency
    C) promote development
    D) set interest rates in members nations

    Answer: A   Difficulty: Medium   Page: 287

30. The acronym IMF stands for:
    A) International Monopoly Function
    B) Interval Monetary Fluctuations
    C) Interagency Monetary Function
    D) International Monetary Fund

    Answer: D   Difficulty: Easy   Page: 287

Chapter 9 The Global Monetary System

31. As stipulated by the Bretton Woods conference, the goal of the World Bank was to:
    A) maintain order in the international monetary system
    B) promote development
    C) set interest rates in member states
    D) establish a world currency

    Answer: B   Difficulty: Medium   Page: 287

32. Under a _____, some currencies are allowed to float freely, but the majority of currencies are either managed in some way by government intervention or pegged to another currency.
    A) random monetary system
    B) regulated standard system
    C) monitored spot market
    D) managed float system

    Answer: D   Difficulty: Easy   Page: 287

33. The Bretton Woods system of fixed exchange rates collapsed in 1973. Since then the world has operated with a:
    A) managed float system
    B) random monetary system
    C) regulated standard system
    D) monitored spot market

    Answer: A   Difficulty: Medium   Page: 287

34. The gold standard has it origin in:
    A) the use of the word "gold" to refer to items of value
    B) the use of gold coins as a medium of exchange
    C) the inherent value placed on gold stones as objects of beauty and value
    D) the use of gold bricks as a medium of exchange between countries

    Answer: B   Difficulty: Medium   Page: 288

35. The practice of pegging currencies to gold and guaranteeing convertibility was referred to as the _____.
    A) premium standard
    B) gold standard
    C) metal standard
    D) federal reserve standard

    Answer: B   Difficulty: Easy   Page: 288

36. By 1880, most of the world's major trading nations, including Great Britain, Germany, Japan, and the United States, had adopted the:
    A) diamond standard
    B) gold standard
    C) federal reserve standard
    D) platinum standard

    Answer: B   Difficulty: Medium   Page: 288

37. The _____ is a monetary standard that pegs currencies to gold and guarantees convertibility to gold.
    A) metal standard
    B) federal reserve standard
    C) premium standard
    D) gold standard

    Answer: D   Difficulty: Easy   Page: 288

38. Under the gold standard, the amount of currency needed to purchase one ounce of gold was referred to as the gold _____ value.
    A) arbitrary
    B) statutory
    C) legal
    D) par

    Answer: D   Difficulty: Medium   Page: 288

39. The great strength claimed for the gold standard was that it contained a powerful mechanism for simultaneously obtained _____ for all countries.
    A) balance-of-trade equilibrium
    B) economic stability
    C) interest rate parity
    D) equal tariff levels

    Answer: A   Difficulty: Medium   Page: 288

40. A country is said to be a balance-of-trade equilibrium when:
    A) the income that its residents earn from the export of manufactured goods equals the income that its residents earn from the export of services
    B) the income that its residents earn from exports is equal to the money that its residents pay for imports
    C) the income that its residents earn from exports in the current fiscal year is equal to the income that its residents earned from exports in the previous fiscal year
    D) the income that its residents earn from the export of raw materials is equal to the income that its residents earn from the export of manufactured goods

    Answer: B Difficulty: Medium Page: 288

41. The gold standard broke down in the _____ as countries engaged in competitive devaluations.
    A) 1910s
    B) 1930s
    C) 1950s
    D) 1970s

    Answer: B Difficulty: Hard Page: 289

42. The gold standard was abandoned in:
    A) 1870
    B) 1889
    C) 1914
    D) 1924

    Answer: C Difficulty: Hard Page: 289

43. In 1944, at the height of World War II, representatives from 44 countries met at _____ to design a new international monetary system.
    A) Richmond, Virginia
    B) San Francisco, California
    C) Bretton Woods, New Hampshire
    D) Morris Plains, New Jersey

    Answer: C Difficulty: Easy Page: 290

Chapter 9 The Global Monetary System

44. In _____, representatives from 44 countries met at Bretton Woods, New Hampshire to design a new international monetary system.
    A) 1922
    B) 1944
    C) 1957
    D) 1981

    Answer: B   Difficulty: Hard   Page: 290

45. The Bretton Woods agreement called for:
    A) variable exchange rates
    B) fixed exchange rates
    C) freely floating exchange rates
    D) a set of "managed" floating exchange rates

    Answer: B   Difficulty: Medium   Page: 290

46. The Bretton Woods system of fixed exchange rates was established in 1944. The central currency of this system was the:
    A) French Franc
    B) German Deutsche Mark
    C) U.S. Dollar
    D) British Pound

    Answer: C   Difficulty: Easy   Page: 290

47. The Bretton Woods agreement called for a system of fixed exchange rates that would be policed by the:
    A) World Bank
    B) United Nations
    C) League of Nations
    D) International Monetary Fund

    Answer: D   Difficulty: Medium   Page: 290

48. Under the Bretton Woods system, which currency served as the base currency?
    A) Japanese yen
    B) British pound
    C) French franc
    D) U.S. dollar

    Answer: D   Difficulty: Medium   Page: 290

Chapter 9 The Global Monetary System

49. The IMF Articles of Agreement were heavily influenced by all of the following except:
    A) the worldwide financial boom
    B) competitive devaluations
    C) trade wars
    D) high unemployment

    Answer: A   Difficulty: Hard   Page: 291

50. A fixed exchange rate regime imposes discipline in two ways: (1) the need to maintain a fixed exchange rate puts a brake on competitive devaluations and brings stability to the world trade environment and (2) a fixed exchange rate regime imposes
    A) social discipline on countries, thereby increasing the standard of living
    B) economic discipline on countries, thereby increasing gross national product
    C) political discipline on countries, thereby curtailing global opportunism
    D) monetary discipline on countries, thereby curtailing price inflation

    Answer: D   Difficulty: Medium   Page: 291

51. An increase in money supply typically leads to an increase in:
    A) employment
    B) price inflation
    C) gross national product
    D) national standard of living

    Answer: B   Difficulty: Medium   Page: 291

52. Fixed exchange rates are seen as a mechanism for achieving the following two objectives:
    A) controlling inflation and economic discipline
    B) controlling unemployment and political discipline
    C) controlling economic stability and increasing gross national product
    D) controlling political stability and economic discipline

    Answer: A   Difficulty: Medium   Page: 291

53. Fixed exchange rates are seen as a mechanism for achieving the following two objectives: (1) controlling inflation and (2)
    A) increasing the standard of living
    B) economic discipline
    C) political stability
    D) increasing gross national product

    Answer: B Difficulty: Medium Page: 291

54. _____ are seen as a mechanism for controlling inflation and imposing economic discipline on countries.
    A) Fixed exchange rates
    B) Floating exchange rates
    C) Global exchange rates
    D) Transnational exchange rates

    Answer: A Difficulty: Medium Page: 291

55. Two major features of the International Monetary Fund (IMF) Articles of Agreement fostered flexibility into the monetary system. These features included (1) IMF facilities and (2):
    A) IMF export assistance
    B) fixed parities
    C) a return to the gold standard
    D) adjustable parities

    Answer: D Difficulty: Hard Page: 292

56. Two major features of the International Monetary Fund (IMF) Articles of Agreement fostered flexibility into the monetary system. These features included (1) adjustable parities and (2):
    A) IMF facilities
    B) IMF export assistance
    C) a return to the gold standard
    D) fixed parities

    Answer: A Difficulty: Medium Page: 292

57. The IMF's system of adjustable parities, under the auspices of the Bretton Woods agreement, allowed for the devaluation of a country's currency by more than _____ if the IMF agreed that the country's balance of payments is in fundamental disequilibrium.
    A) 10%
    B) 20%
    C) 40%
    D) 50%

    Answer: A   Difficulty: Hard   Page: 292

58. The International Bank for Reconstruction and Development (IBRD) is the official name for the:
    A) World Trade Organization
    B) World Bank
    C) International Monetary Fund
    D) Global-Regional Bank

    Answer: B   Difficulty: Easy   Page: 292

59. In the context of the global monetary system, the IBRD stands for the _____.
    A) International Bank for Rents and Deposits
    B) International Bureau for Restraining Devaluations
    C) International Bank for Reconstruction and Development
    D) International Bureau for Research and Development

    Answer: C   Difficulty: Hard   Page: 292

60. The official name of the World Bank is the:
    A) Global Bank for the Financing of Trade and Development
    B) International Bank for Sustained Economic Stability
    C) Global Bank for the Promotion of Trade
    D) International Bank for Reconstruction and Development

    Answer: D   Difficulty: Medium   Page: 292

61. The initial mission of the World Bank was to:
    A) help finance the building of Europe's economy by providing low-interest loans
    B) help small businesses establish export operations
    C) provide letters of credit on behalf of first-time exporters
    D) provide development loans for developing countries in Asia

    Answer: A   Difficulty: Medium   Page: 292

62. Helping finance the building of Europe's economy after World War II by providing low-interest loans was the initial mission of:
    A) The World Trade Organization
    B) The World Bank
    C) The European National Bank
    D) The International Monetary Fund

    Answer: B Difficulty: Medium Page: 292

63. Which of the following statements accurately depicts what happened to the Bretton Woods system of fixed exchange rates?
    A) the system never got off the ground, and collapsed in the late 1940s
    B) the system worked well for about a decade, then collapsed in the mid-1950s
    C) the system began to show signs of strain in the 1960s, and finally collapsed in 1973
    D) the system remained in place until the early 1990s when an international conference was convened in Finland to develop a managed float system

    Answer: C Difficulty: Hard Page: 292

64. The Bretton Woods system of fixed exchange rates collapsed in 1973, and since then we have had a:
    A) stepwise fixed rate exchange system
    B) more rigid and enforceable fixed exchange rate system
    C) managed float system
    D) combination of managed float systems and fixed exchange rate systems

    Answer: C Difficulty: Easy Page: 292

65. Most economists trace the breakup of the fixed exchange rate system to:
    A) the U.S. macroeconomic policy package of 1965-1968
    B) a worldwide recession
    C) Japanese economic policy in the mid 1970s
    D) European economic policy in the 1960s and 1970s

    Answer: A Difficulty: Hard Page: 293

66. In the context of the global money system, in August 1971 President Nixon made the following two announcements: (1) a new 10 percent tax on imports would remain in effect until the trading partners of the U.S. agreed to revalue their currency against the dollar and (2)
    A) the dollar was no longer convertible into gold
    B) the U.S. would no longer support the World Bank
    C) the U.S. planned to devalue its currency by 20 percent
    D) the U.S. planned to called for a second Bretton Woods conference

    Answer: A   Difficulty: Medium   Page: 293

67. The Bretton Woods system had an Achilles' heel: The system could not work if its key currency, the U.S. dollar, was:
    A) overvalued
    B) undervalued
    C) under speculative attack
    D) subject to a high U.S. inflation rate

    Answer: C   Difficulty: Hard   Page: 293

68. The _____ exchange rate regime that followed the collapse of the fixed exchange rate system was formalized in January 1976 when IMF members met in Jamaica and agreed to the rules for the international system that are in place today.
    A) floating
    B) quasi-fixed
    C) open
    D) closed

    Answer: A   Difficulty: Medium   Page: 294

69. The floating exchange rate regime that followed the collapse of the fixed exchange rate system was formalized in January 1976 when IMF members met in _____ and agreed to the rules for the international system that are in place today.
    A) Ireland
    B) Hong Kong
    C) Spain
    D) Jamica

    Answer: D   Difficulty: Medium   Page: 294

70. The three main elements of the Jamaica Agreement were:
    A) the International Monetary Fund was established; gold was abandoned as a reserve asset; and floating rates were declared unacceptable
    B) floating rates were declared acceptable; gold was abandoned as a reserve asset; and total annual IMF quotas were increased to $41 billion
    C) floating rates were declared unacceptable; the International Monetary Fund was abolished; and the World Bank was established
    D) fixed rates were declared acceptable, gold was accepted as a reserve asset; and the total annual IMF quotas were increased to $41 billion

    Answer: B   Difficulty: Medium   Page: 294

71. Which of the following was not one of the main elements of the Jamaica Agreement?
    A) the establishment of the International Monetary Fund
    B) floating rates were declared acceptable
    C) total annual IMF quotas were increased to $41 billion
    D) gold was abandoned as a reserve asset

    Answer: A   Difficulty: Medium   Page: 294

72. The _____ represents the exchange rate of the U.S. dollar against a weighted basket of the currencies of 15 other industrial countries.
    A) Nelson's Assurance Index
    B) Phillips Security Index
    C) Morgan Guaranty Index
    D) Stanley Obligation Index

    Answer: C   Difficulty: Hard   Page: 295

73. The fall in the value of the U.S. dollar between 1985 and 1988 was caused by a combination of:
    A) government intervention and market forces
    B) high inflation and high unemployment
    C) a trade deficit and high consumer debt
    D) worldwide inflation and high unemployment

    Answer: A   Difficulty: Hard   Page: 296

Chapter 9 The Global Monetary System

74. The so called "Group of Five" major industrialized nations includes:
    A) Germany, China, United States, and France
    B) Great Britain, France, Japan, Germany, and the United States
    C) United States, Japan, China, Brazil, and Germany
    D) France, Germany, Japan, China, and the United States

    Answer: B Difficulty: Hard Page: 296

75. Which of the following countries is not included in the "Group of Five" major industrialized countries?
    A) Great Britain
    B) Spain
    C) Japan
    D) Germany
    E) United States

    Answer: B Difficulty: Hard Page: 296

76. The 1995 Plaza Accord, which was sponsored by the financial ministers of the Group of Five major industrial countries, concluded that it would be desirable if:
    A) most major currencies appreciated vis-a-vis the Japanese yen
    B) the World Bank converted to a private organization
    C) the nations of the world returned to the gold standard
    D) most major currencies appreciated vis-a-vis the U.S. dollar

    Answer: D Difficulty: Hard Page: 296

77. Under a floating exchange rate regime, market forces have produced:
    A) a near fixed dollar exchange rate
    B) a predictable dollar exchange rate
    C) a stable dollar exchange rate
    D) a volatile dollar exchange rate

    Answer: D Difficulty: Medium Page: 297

78. The frequency of government intervenes in the foreign exchange markets explains why the current system is often referred to as a managed-float system or a:
    A) functional float system
    B) statutory float system
    C) dirty float system
    D) unwieldy float system

    Answer: C Difficulty: Hard Page: 298

79. The case for floating exchange rates has two main elements. These are:
    A) monetary policy autonomy and automatic trade balance adjustments
    B) sporadic trade balance adjustments and monetary policy autonomy
    C) the impracticality of the gold standard and monetary policy control
    D) monetary policy control and sporadic trade balance adjustments

    Answer: A Difficulty: Medium Page: 298

80. The case for floating exchange rates has two main elements: (1) monetary policy autonomy and (2)
    A) sporadic trade balance adjustments
    B) the impracticality of the gold standard
    C) automatic trade balance adjustments
    D) monetary policy control

    Answer: C Difficulty: Medium Page: 298

81. Automatic trade balance adjustments and _____ are the two main elements in the case for floating exchange rates.
    A) sporadic trade balance adjustments
    B) monetary policy autonomy
    C) a return to the gold standard
    D) monetary policy control

    Answer: B Difficulty: Medium Page: 298

82. It is argued that a _____ exchange rate regime gives countries monetary policy autonomy.
    A) restricted
    B) forward
    C) fixed
    D) floating

    Answer: D Difficulty: Medium Page: 298

83. Under a _____ exchange rate regime, a country's ability to expand or contract its money supply as it sees fit is limited by the need to maintain exchange rate parity.
    A) forward
    B) fixed
    C) narrow
    D) floating

    Answer: B Difficulty: Hard Page: 298

Chapter 9 The Global Monetary System

84. It is argued that under a fixed system, a country's ability to expand or contract its money supply as it sees fit is limited by:
    A) the need to maintain exchange rate parity
    B) the need to restrict price inflation
    C) the need to maintain economic stability
    D) direct oversight by the World Bank

    Answer: A   Difficulty: Hard   Page: 298

85. Advocates of a _____ exchange rate regime argue that removal of the obligation to maintain exchange rate parity restores monetary control to a government.
    A) fixed
    B) floating
    C) narrow
    D) forward

    Answer: B   Difficulty: Hard   Page: 298

86. Floating exchange rates are determined by:
    A) market forces
    B) the IMF
    C) the World Bank
    D) an international commission on exchange rate parity

    Answer: A   Difficulty: Easy   Page: 298

87. Under the Bretton Woods system, if a country developed a permanent deficit in its balance of trade that could not be corrected by domestic policy, the IMF would agree to a:
    A) currency devaluation
    B) increase in employment
    C) increase in output
    D) increase in interest rates

    Answer: A   Difficulty: Medium   Page: 298

Chapter 9 The Global Monetary System

88. The case for fixed exchange rates rests on arguments about monetary discipline, speculation, the lack of connection between the trade balance and exchange rates, and _____.
    A) trade balance adjustments
    B) uncertainty
    C) the impracticality of the gold standard
    D) monetary policy autonomy

    Answer: B Difficulty: Medium Page: 299

89. The case for fixed exchange rates rests on arguments about monetary discipline, uncertainty, the lack of connection between the trade balance and exchange rates, and _____.
    A) speculation
    B) the impracticality of the gold standard
    C) monetary policy autonomy
    D) trade balance adjustments

    Answer: A Difficulty: Medium Page: 299

90. According to our textbook, those in favor of floating exchange rates argue that floating rates:
    A) discourage speculation
    B) help confuse trade imbalances
    C) help adjust trade imbalances
    D) have no effect on trade imbalances

    Answer: C Difficulty: Hard Page: 299

91. "Free float" exchange rates are determined by:
    A) the IMF
    B) market forces
    C) governments
    D) the World Bank

    Answer: B Difficulty: Medium Page: 300

92. Under a pegged exchange rate regime, a country will peg the value of its currency to:
    A) an index of world currencies maintained by the World Bank
    B) that of a major currency
    C) an index of "peer nation" currencies
    D) an index of its historic currency rates

    Answer: B Difficulty: Medium Page: 300

93. Pegged exchange rates are popular among many of the world's:
    A) industrialized nations
    B) largest nations
    C) smaller nations
    D) communist nations

    Answer: C Difficulty: Hard Page: 300

94. There is some evidence that adopting a pegged exchange rate regime:
    A) reduces unemployment in a country
    B) moderates inflationary pressure in a country
    C) increases global GNP
    D) decreases global GNP

    Answer: B Difficulty: Medium Page: 301

95. A recent IMF study concluded that countries with pegged exchange rate regimes had an average annual inflation rate of _____, compared with 14 percent for intermediate regimes and 16 percent for floating regimes.
    A) 4 percent
    B) 18 percent
    C) 14 percent
    D) 8 percent

    Answer: D Difficulty: Hard Page: 301

96. A country that introduces a _____ commits itself to converting its domestic currency on demand into another currency at a fixed exchange rate.
    A) currency board
    B) monetary review commission
    C) exchange rate review commission
    D) certificate board

    Answer: A Difficulty: Medium Page: 301

Chapter 9 The Global Monetary System

97. A _____ is a governing body that manages the value of a currency by holding foreign currency reserves equal to the amount of domestic currency issued at a fixed exchange rate.
    A) exchange rate committee
    B) currency board
    C) certificate board
    D) monetary review commission

    Answer: B Difficulty: Medium Page: 301

98. Over the past 30 years, the activities of the IMF have:
    A) expanded
    B) declined
    C) expanded in developed countries but declined in underdeveloped countries
    D) expanded in underdeveloped countries but declined in developed countries

    Answer: A Difficulty: Medium Page: 302

99. No major industrial country has borrowed funds from the IMF since the:
    A) mid-1950s
    B) mid-1960s
    C) mid-1970s
    D) mid-1980s

    Answer: C Difficulty: Hard Page: 302

100. A _____ occurs when a speculative attack on the exchange value of a currency results in a sharp depreciation in the value of the currency or forces authorities to expend large volumes of international currency reserved and sharply increase interest rates to defend the prevailing exchange rate.
    A) currency crisis
    B) monetary disruption
    C) banking crisis
    D) currency disruption

    Answer: A Difficulty: Medium Page: 303

Chapter 9 The Global Monetary System

101. A _____ refers to a situation in which a loss of confidence in the banking system leads to a run on banks, as individuals and companies withdraw their deposits.
    A) banking crisis
    B) currency crisis
    C) federal reserve crisis
    D) monetary crisis

    Answer: A   Difficulty: Medium   Page: 303

102. A _____ occurs when a country cannot service its foreign debt obligations.
    A) banking crisis
    B) currency crisis
    C) monetary crisis
    D) foreign debt crisis

    Answer: D   Difficulty: Medium   Page: 303

103. Which of the following is not among the four main crises that have been of particular significance for the IMF?
    A) the Third World debt crisis of the 1980s
    B) the U.S. recession of the 1980s
    C) the crisis experienced by Russia as that country moved towards a market-based economic system
    D) the 1995 Mexican currency crisis

    Answer: B   Difficulty: Hard   Page: 303

104. The IMF's involvement in Russia came about as the result of:
    A) a sharp increase in the value of the Russian ruble
    B) a persistent decline in the value of the Russian ruble
    C) high unemployment in Russia
    D) dangerously low inflation in Russia

    Answer: B   Difficulty: Medium   Page: 306

105. The financial crisis that erupted across _____ during the fall of 1997 has emerged as the biggest challenge the IMF has had to deal with.
    A) Eastern Europe
    B) Southeast Asia
    C) Central America
    D) South America

    Answer: B   Difficulty: Hard   Page: 308

Chapter 9 The Global Monetary System

Essay Questions

106. Describe what happened at the 1944 Bretton Woods conference. Are the monetary principles established by the Bretton Woods conference still in effect today?

Difficulty: Easy   Page: 290

Answer:
In 1944, at the height of World War II, representatives from 44 countries met at Bretton Woods, New Hampshire, to design a new international monetary system. The purpose of the conference was to build an economic order that would facilitate postwar economic growth and cooperation. Three primary initiatives resulted from the conference:
a) The establishment of the International Monetary Fund (IMF).
b) The establishment of the World Bank.
c) A call for the establishment of a set of fixed currency exchange rates that would be policed by the IMF.
d) A commitment not to use devaluation as a weapon of competitive trade policy.

The task of the IMF would be to maintain order in the international monetary system, and the World Bank was designed to promote general economic development. In regard to currency exchange rates, all countries were to fix the value of their currency in terms of gold but were not required to exchange their currencies for gold. Only the U.S. dollar remained convertible into gold - at a price of $35 per ounce. Each other country decided what it wanted its exchange rate to be vis-a-vis the dollar and then calculated the gold par value of its currency based on that selected dollar exchange rate. All participating countries agreed to try to maintain the value of their currency within 1 percent of the par value.

Today, the IMF and the World Bank still play a role in the international monetary system. The system of fixed exchange rates established at Bretton Woods worked well until the late 1960s, when it began to show signs of strain. The system finally collapsed in 1973, and since then we have had a managed float system.

107. Describe the role of the World Bank in the international community. How does the World Bank contribute to the overall stability of the global monetary system?

Difficulty: Medium   Page: 292

Answer:
The World Bank was established by the 1944 Bretton Woods agreement. The official name for the World Bank is the International Bank for Reconstruction and Development (IBRD). The bank's initial mission was to help finance the building of Europe's war torn economy by providing low-interest loans. As it turned out, the role of the World Bank in Europe was overshadowed by the Marshall Plan, under which the U.S. lent money directly to European nations to help them rebuild in the aftermath of World War II. As a result, the bank turned its attention to lending money for development in Third World nations.

Although the World Bank does not play a direct role in monetary policy, it contributes to the global money system by providing low interest loans to developing countries. These loans, which are used for such things as public-sector projects (i.e. power stations, roads, bridges, etc.), agricultural development, education, population control, and urban development, are intended to promote economic development and increase the standard of living in developing countries.

As the result of some disappointment in regard to loaning money to countries that do not practice sound economy policy, the World Bank has recently devised a new type of loan. In addition to providing funds to support specific projects, the bank will now also provide loans for the government of a nation to use as it sees fit in return for promises on macroeconomic policy.

108. What is the difference between a free floating exchange rate and a managed or dirty float system?

Difficulty: Medium   Page: 297

Answer:
In a free floating system there is no governmental invention in the market, while in a managed or dirty float system governments intervene to influence the value of their currency.

Chapter 9 The Global Monetary System

109. How do exchange rates affect individual international businesses? Do international businesses like stable rates or volatile rates? Explain your answer.

Difficulty: Medium   Page: 298

Answer:
The volatility of the present system of floating exchange rates is a problem for international businesses. Exchange rates are difficult to predict, and introduce a major source of "uncertainty" in international trade that is unnerving for many businesses. For example, a company like Case Tractor may build a high quality product in the U.S. and make a profit by exporting it to Japan. But if the Japanese yen depreciates against the U.S. dollar, the relative cost of the tractor in Japan will go up. This will either lower the demand for the tractor in Japan or force Case to lower its price (and accept a lower profit).

The majority of international businesses would probably prefer stability in exchange rates. As depicted above, exchange rate fluctuations introduce uncertainty into the international business process, which is uncertain enough to begin with. Imagine how frustrating it must be for the mangers of firms like Case Tractor, who may lose sales in an international market or suffer declines in profitability that has nothing to do with the quality of their products, but hinge solely on currency rate volatility.

110. Describe the difference between fixed and floating exchange rates. Which is better? Explain your answer.

Difficulty: Hard   Page: 298

Answer:
Under a fixed rate system the value of a currency is fixed (usually in terms of U.S. dollars) and is only allowed to change under a specific set of circumstances. The value of a fixed rate system is that it introduces monetary discipline (on a country level), discourages currency speculation, reduces uncertainty (in regard to future currency movements), and, according to the proponents of fixed rates, has little or no effect on trade balance adjustments. In contrast, under a floating rate system, currencies are allowed to float freely (in practice, the majority of floating rate systems are either managed in some way by government intervention or are pegged to another currency). The benefits of a floating rate system is that it gives countries monetary policy autonomy and, according to the proponents, provides a way for countries to correct trade deficits (i.e. an exchange rate depreciation should correct a trade balance by making a country's exports cheaper and its imports more expensive).

Chapter 9 The Global Monetary System

There is no right or wrong answer to this question - we simply don't know which system is better. We do know that a fixed rate system modeled along the lines of the Bretton Woods system will not work. Conversely, advocates of a fixed rate system argue that speculation is a major disadvantage of floating rates. Perhaps a modified fixed rate system will produce the type of economic stability that will contribute to greater growth in international trade and investments.

111. What can international business organizations do to help shape global monetary policy and encourage growth in international trade and investment?

Difficulty: Medium   Page: 298

Answer:
This question is designed to encourage classroom discussion and/or to encourage students to "think" about how international businesses can play a constructive role in shaping monetary policy and increase international trade and investment. Obviously, businesses can lobby their respective governments to encourage steps that minimize currency volatility and maximize international business opportunities. In addition, businesses can act prudently in terms of their individual trade practices, and by doing so, lessen the chance that nations will use their currencies (through devaluation) to protect their local industries. Finally, businesses can help sponsor international forums (like the World Bank) that facilitate the growth in international trade and investment.

112. What is a pegged exchange rate? How does it work? What is the advantage of a pegged exchange rate regime?

Difficulty: Medium   Page: 300

Answer:
Under a pegged exchange rate regime a country will peg the value of its currency to that of a major currency so that, for example, as the United States dollar rises in value, its own currency rises, too. Pegged exchange rates are popular among many of the world's smaller nations. As with a full fixed exchange rate regime, the great virtue claimed for a pegged exchange rate regime is that it imposes monetary discipline on a country and leads to low inflation.

Chapter 10 Global Strategy

True/False Questions

1. There are two basic strategies for improving a firm's profitability - a differentiation strategy and a low cost strategy.

   Answer: True   Difficulty: Easy   Page: 326

2. It is useful to think of the firm as a value chain composed of a series of distinct value creation activities.

   Answer: True   Difficulty: Easy   Page: 326

3. The primary activities in a firm's value chain include human resources, materials management, and manufacturing.

   Answer: False   Difficulty: Medium   Page: 326

4. In the context of the value chain analysis, support activities provide the inputs that allow the primary activities of production and marketing to occur.

   Answer: True   Difficulty: Medium   Page: 326

5. A firm's strategy can be defined as the actions that managers take to attain the goals of the firm.

   Answer: True   Difficulty: Easy   Page: 327

6. The term core competence refers to skills within the firm that competitors can easily match or imitate.

   Answer: False   Difficulty: Easy   Page: 327

7. Firms that operate internationally are typically able to earn a greater return from their distinctive skills, or core competencies.

   Answer: True   Difficulty: Medium   Page: 327

8. Economies that arise from locating overseas operations in countries that expatriate managers find attractive are referred to as location economies.

   Answer: False   Difficulty: Medium   Page: 329

9. The experience curve refers to the systematic reductions in production costs that have been observed to occur over the life of a product.

   Answer: True   Difficulty: Easy   Page: 332

10. Moving down the experience curve causes a firm to increase its cost of creating value.

    Answer: False   Difficulty: Hard   Page: 332

11. The reduction in unit costs achieved by producing a large volume of a product is referred to as economies of scale.

    Answer: True   Difficulty: Easy   Page: 333

12. Firms that compete in the global markets typically face two types of competitive pressure. They face pressures to be globally responsive and pressures for cost reductions.

    Answer: False   Difficulty: Medium   Page: 335

13. According to Theodore Levitt, consumer demands for local customization are on the increase worldwide.

    Answer: False   Difficulty: Hard   Page: 337

14. Pressures for local responsiveness emerge when there are differences in infrastructure and/or traditional practices between countries.

    Answer: True   Difficulty: Medium   Page: 338

15. Firms pursuing a multidomestic strategy orient themselves toward achieving maximum local responsiveness.

    Answer: True   Difficulty: Medium   Page: 340

16. A multidomestic strategy makes most sense when there are low pressures for local responsiveness and high pressures for cost reductions.

    Answer: False   Difficulty: Hard   Page: 340

17. A global strategy makes most sense in those cases where there are strong pressures for cost reductions, and where demands for local responsiveness are minimal.

Answer: True   Difficulty: Hard   Page: 332

18. A transnational strategy is a business strategy that seeks experience-based economies and location economies, transfers distinctive competencies within the firm, and pays attention to pressures for local responsiveness.

Answer: True   Difficulty: Medium   Page: 342

19. A transnational strategy makes sense when a firm faces low pressures for cost reductions and low pressures for local responsiveness.

Answer: False   Difficulty: Hard   Page: 342

20. A transnational strategy is difficult to implement due to organizational problems.

Answer: True   Difficulty: Medium   Page: 342

Multiple Choice Questions

21. There are two basic strategies for improving a firm's profitability. These are:
    A) a differentiation strategy and a low-cost strategy
    B) a premier strategy and a generic strategy
    C) a high-cost strategy and a low-cost strategy
    D) a comparison strategy and a low-cost strategy

    Answer: A   Difficulty: Easy   Page: 326

22. There are two basic strategies for improving a firm's profitability. These are a low-cost strategy and a:
    A) comparison strategy
    B) divergence strategy
    C) generic strategy
    D) differentiation strategy

    Answer: D   Difficulty: Easy   Page: 326

23. According to the textbook, it is useful to think of the firm as a _____ composed of a series of distinct activities, including production, marketing, materials management, R&D, human resources, information systems, and the firm infrastructure.
    A) functional stream
    B) momentum machine
    C) inertia chain
    D) value chain

    Answer: D Difficulty: Easy Page: 326

24. Value chain activities can be categorized as:
    A) primary activities and secondary activities
    B) input activities and throughput activities
    C) profitable activities and unprofitable activities
    D) primary activities and support activities

    Answer: D Difficulty: Medium Page: 326

25. The _____ activities of a firm have to do with creating the product, marketing and delivering the product to buyers, and providing support and after-sales service to the buyers of the product.
    A) support
    B) subordinate
    C) ancillary
    D) primary

    Answer: D Difficulty: Easy Page: 326

26. In the context of value chain analysis, the primary activities of a firm include:
    A) manufacturing, marketing & service, and sales
    B) infrastructure (structure and leadership), human resources, and R&D
    C) R&D, sales, and materials management
    D) manufacturing, human resources, and materials management

    Answer: A Difficulty: Medium Page: 326

Chapter 10 Global Strategy

27. In the context of value chain analysis, the support activities of a firm include:
    A) human resources, management information systems, materials management, and accounting
    B) accounting, infrastructure, R&D, and materials management
    C) manufacturing, marketing and service, R&D, and management information systems
    D) human resources, materials management, infrastructure, and R&D

    Answer: D   Difficulty: Hard   Page: 326

28. In the context of value chain analysis, _____ activities allow the primary activities of production and marketing to occur.
    A) complementary
    B) secondary
    C) support
    D) subsidiary

    Answer: C   Difficulty: Medium   Page: 326

29. In the context of value chain analysis, which of the following is an example of a "primary" activity?
    A) materials management
    B) research and development
    C) manufacturing
    D) human relations

    Answer: C   Difficulty: Medium   Page: 326

30. A firm's _____ can be defined as the actions that managers take to attain the goals of the firm.
    A) systems
    B) value chain
    C) operations
    D) strategy

    Answer: D   Difficulty: Easy   Page: 327

31. Which of the following statements is not an accurate reflection of the impact of global expansion on firm profitability?
    A) a firm can earn a greater return from its core competencies
    B) a firm typically earns less from its distinctive skills
    C) a firm realizes location economies by dispersing particular value creation activities to those locations where they can be performed most efficiently
    D) a firm realizes greater experience curve economies, which reduces the cost of value creation

    Answer: B Difficulty: Medium Page: 327

32. Actions that managers take to attain the firm's goals are referred to as _____.
    A) value chain activities
    B) strategies
    C) systems
    D) operations

    Answer: B Difficulty: Easy Page: 327

33. The term _____ refers to skills within a firm that competitors cannot easily match.
    A) core competencies
    B) indigenous properties
    C) value chain
    D) discriminate attributes

    Answer: A Difficulty: Easy Page: 327

34. According to our textbook, a firm's _____ allow it to reduce the costs of value creation and/or to create value in such a way that premium pricing is possible.
    A) special attributes
    B) discriminate attributes
    C) indigenous properties
    D) core competencies

    Answer: D Difficulty: Medium Page: 327

35. The skills within a firm that competitors cannot easily match or imitate are called:
    A) core competencies
    B) discriminate attributes
    C) value chain
    D) indigenous properties

    Answer: A Difficulty: Easy Page: 327

36. Economies that arise from performing a value creation activity in the optimal location for that activity are called _____.
    A) site expediencies
    B) location economies
    C) site commerce
    D) location synergies

    Answer: B Difficulty: Easy Page: 329

37. Suppose General Motors decided to manufacture brakes in Ireland, because a detailed analysis of country specific advantages indicated that Ireland is the optimal place in the world to produce brakes. In this example, General Motors is capturing _____ by manufacturing brakes in Ireland.
    A) location synergies
    B) site expediencies
    C) site commerce
    D) location economies

    Answer: D Difficulty: Medium Page: 329

38. Locating a value creation activity in the optimal location for that activity can have one or two effects. First, it can lower the costs of value creation and help the firm to achieve a low-cost position, and/or:
    A) it can enable a firm to differentiate its product offering from that of competitors
    B) if can lower the cost of marketing and service
    C) it can expedite the research and development process
    D) it can create political good well

    Answer: A Difficulty: Hard Page: 329

Chapter 10 Global Strategy

39. According to our textbook, a firm creates a _____ by dispersing the stages of its value chain to those locations around the globe where the value added is maximized or where the costs of value creation are minimized.
    A) integrate circle
    B) disperse chain
    C) global web
    D) international mesh

    Answer: C Difficulty: Medium Page: 330

40. In theory, a firm that realizes _____ by dispersing each of its value creation activities to its optimal location should have a competitive advantage vis-à-vis a firm that bases all its value creation activities at a single location.
    A) location economies
    B) site synergies
    C) site commerce
    D) geographical distinctiveness

    Answer: A Difficulty: Medium Page: 331

41. The _____ refers to the systematic reductions in production costs that have been observed to occur over the life of a product.
    A) experience curve
    B) forward advantage
    C) positive-sum result
    D) managed advantage

    Answer: A Difficulty: Easy Page: 332

42. If Goodyear Tire Corporation experienced systematic reductions in the production costs of a particular product over the life of the product, they would be realizing _____ effects.
    A) managed production
    B) forward advantage
    C) experience curve
    D) value chain

    Answer: C Difficulty: Medium Page: 332

43. A number of studies have observed that a product's _____ decline by some characteristic each time accumulated output doubles.
    A) financing costs
    B) production costs
    C) marketing costs
    D) R&D costs

    Answer: B Difficulty: Medium Page: 332

44. _____ refer to cost savings that come from learning by doing.
    A) Learning effects
    B) Exponential effects
    C) Ancillary effects
    D) Indirect effects

    Answer: A Difficulty: Easy Page: 333

45. Learning effects tend to be more significant when a _____ task is repeated because there is more than can be learned about the task.
    A) repetitive manufacturing
    B) standardized manufacturing
    C) technologically complex
    D) standardized service

    Answer: C Difficulty: Medium Page: 333

46. The term _____ refers to the reduction in unit cost achieved by producing a large volume of a product.
    A) volume synergies
    B) captured savings
    C) economies of scale
    D) rent effects

    Answer: C Difficulty: Easy Page: 333

47. If Honda noticed that the unit costs of Honda Accords went down as the number of Accord's produced went up, Honda would be realizing the benefits of _____.
    A) captured savings
    B) volume synergies
    C) economies of scale
    D) rent effects

    Answer: C Difficulty: Medium Page: 333

Chapter 10 Global Strategy

48. The ability to spread fixed costs over a large volume results in a cost-savings phenomenon referred to as:
    A) volume synergies
    B) economies of scale
    C) captured savings
    D) size effects

    Answer: B Difficulty: Medium Page: 333

49. Economies of scale have a number of sources, one of the most important of which seems to be the ability to spread:
    A) fixed costs over a small volume
    B) variable costs over a large volume
    C) fixed costs over a large volume
    D) variable costs over a small volume

    Answer: C Difficulty: Medium Page: 333

50. Firms that compete in the global marketplace typically face two types of competitive pressures. They face pressures for cost reductions and:
    A) pressures for volume increases
    B) pressures to be locally responsive
    C) pressures to be politically savvy
    D) pressures for price reductions

    Answer: B Difficulty: Medium Page: 335

51. Pressures for cost reductions can be particularly intense in industries producing commodity products where meaningful differentiation on nonprice factors is difficult and _____ is the main competitive weapon.
    A) quality
    B) distribution efficiency
    C) sales and service
    D) price

    Answer: D Difficulty: Medium Page: 336

Chapter 10 Global Strategy

52. Among global firms, which of the following is not a factor that is driving pressures for local responsiveness?
    A) differences in distribution channels
    B) differences in infrastructure and traditional practices
    C) similarities in consumer tastes and preferences
    D) host government demands

    Answer: C   Difficulty: Hard   Page: 337

53. Which of the following is not a factor that is driving pressures for local responsiveness among global firms?
    A) similarities in distribution channels
    B) host government demands
    C) differences in infrastructure and traditional practices
    D) differences in consumer tastes and preferences

    Answer: A   Difficulty: Hard   Page: 337

54. Differences in consumer tastes and preferences, differences in infrastructure and traditional practices, differences in distribution channels, and host government demands are factors pressuring firms to be sensitive to _____ in their international strategies.
    A) local responsiveness
    B) global standardization
    C) cost containment
    D) integrating more "commodity" like features

    Answer: A   Difficulty: Medium   Page: 337

55. Harvard Business School Professor Theodore Levitt has argued that consumer demands for local customization are _____ worldwide.
    A) declining
    B) leveling out
    C) increasing
    D) a myth

    Answer: A   Difficulty: Medium   Page: 337

Chapter 10 Global Strategy

56. Firms use four basic strategies to compete in the international environment. These are:
    A) an international strategy, a multidomestic strategy, a global strategy, and a transnational strategy
    B) a cross-cultural strategy, a trade block strategy, a regional strategy, and a world strategy
    C) a domestic-based strategy, an international-focused strategy, a local/regional-based strategy, and a cultural-based strategy
    D) an international strategy, a regional strategy, a global strategy, and a world strategy

    Answer: A Difficulty: Hard Page: 339

57. In the international environment, firms used four basic strategies. These are: an international strategy, a multidomestic strategy, a global strategy, and a _____ strategy.
    A) local/regional
    B) transnational
    C) cross-cultural
    D) trade block

    Answer: B Difficulty: Medium Page: 339

58. Firms use four basic strategies to compete in international markets: an international strategy, a global strategy, a transnational strategy, and a _____ strategy.
    A) multidomestic
    B) cross-cultural
    C) trade block
    D) local/regional

    Answer: A Difficulty: Medium Page: 339

59. The appropriateness of the strategy that a firm uses in an international market varies with the extent of pressures for _____ and _____.
    A) cost reductions; availability of financing.
    B) price concessions; quality improvements
    C) availability of financing; product standardization
    D) cost reductions; local responsiveness

    Answer: D Difficulty: Medium Page: 339

60. The appropriateness of the strategy that a firm uses in an international market varies with the extent of pressures for cost reductions and _____.
    A) local responsiveness
    B) availability of financing
    C) trade block membership
    D) price concessions

    Answer: A   Difficulty: Medium   Page: 339

61. Firms that pursue a _____ strategy try to create value by transferring valuable skills and products to foreign markets where indigenous competitors lack those skills and products.
    A) multidomestic
    B) transnational
    C) global
    D) international

    Answer: D   Difficulty: Medium   Page: 339

62. An _____ strategy makes sense if a firm has a valuable core competence that indigenous competitors in foreign markets lack.
    A) global
    B) international
    C) multidomestic
    D) transnational

    Answer: B   Difficulty: Medium   Page: 339

63. When cost pressures are low and pressures for local responsiveness are low, a(n) _____ strategy is the most appropriate.
    A) multidomestic
    B) transnational
    C) global
    D) international

    Answer: D   Difficulty: Hard   Page: 339

Chapter 10 Global Strategy

64. An _____ strategy makes sense if a firm has valuable core competencies that indigenous competitors in foreign markets lack, and if the firm faces relatively weak pressures for local responsiveness and cost reductions.
    A) international
    B) global
    C) multidomestic
    D) transnational

    Answer: A   Difficulty: Hard   Page: 340

65. A lack of local responsiveness, an inability to realize location economies, and a failure to exploit experience curve effects are disadvantages of a _____ strategy.
    A) international
    B) global
    C) transnational
    D) multidomestic

    Answer: A   Difficulty: Hard   Page: 340

66. When cost pressures are low and the pressures for local responsiveness are high a _____ strategy is the most appropriate.
    A) multidomestic
    B) global
    C) transnational
    D) international

    Answer: A   Difficulty: Hard   Page: 340

67. Firms pursuing a _____ strategy orient themselves towards achieving maximum local responsiveness.
    A) international
    B) global
    C) transnational
    D) multidomestic

    Answer: D   Difficulty: Medium   Page: 340

Chapter 10 Global Strategy

68. Which of the following is not a typical characteristic of multidomestic firms?
    A) extensively customize both their product offerings and their marketing strategy to match different national conditions
    B) try to establish a complete set of value creation activities in each major national market in which they do business
    C) have a low cost structure
    D) do a poor job of leveraging core competencies within the firm

    Answer: C Difficulty: Hard Page: 340

69. The distinguishing feature of multidomestic firms is that they extensively customize both their product offerings and their marketing strategy to match national conditions.
    A) multidomestic
    B) global
    C) transnational
    D) international

    Answer: A Difficulty: Medium Page: 340

70. A weakness of the _____ strategy is that many of the firms that pursue this strategy have developed into decentralized federations in which each national subsidiary functions in a largely autonomous manner.
    A) multidomestic
    B) global
    C) international
    D) transnational

    Answer: A Difficulty: Medium Page: 340

71. Firms that pursue a _____ strategy focus on increasing profitability by reaping the cost reductions that come from experience curve effects and location economies.
    A) multidomestic
    B) transnational
    C) international
    D) global

    Answer: D Difficulty: Medium Page: 342

Chapter 10 Global Strategy

72. The production, marketing, and R&D activities of firms pursuing a _____ strategy are concentrated in a few favorable locations.
    A) international
    B) transnational
    C) global
    D) multidomestic

    Answer: C Difficulty: Medium Page: 342

73. A _____ strategy makes sense when there are strong pressures for cost reductions and where demands for local responsiveness are minimal.
    A) global
    B) multidomestic
    C) transnational
    D) international

    Answer: A Difficulty: Hard Page: 342

74. Pursuing a _____ strategy involves a simultaneous focus on reducing costs, transferring skills and products, and being locally responsive.
    A) global
    B) multidomestic
    C) transnational
    D) international

    Answer: C Difficulty: Medium Page: 342

75. A _____ strategy makes sense when a firm faces high pressures for cost reductions and high pressures for local responsiveness.
    A) transnational
    B) global
    C) international
    D) multidomestic

    Answer: A Difficulty: Hard Page: 342

Chapter 10 Global Strategy

76. According to the textbook, which of the following strategies is difficult to implement due to organizational problems?
    A) transnational
    B) international
    C) global
    D) multidomestic

    Answer: A   Difficulty: Medium   Page: 340

77. According to Christopher Barlett and Sumantra Ghoshal, the flow of skills and product offerings should not be all one way, from home firm to foreign subsidiary. Rather, they argue that the flow should also be from foreign subsidiary to home country, and from foreign subsidiary to foreign subsidiary - a process they call:
    A) global learning
    B) international education
    C) international lore
    D) worldwide effect

    Answer: A   Difficulty: Hard   Page: 342

78. _____ is the flow of skills and product offerings from home firm to foreign subsidiary and from foreign subsidiary to home firm and from foreign subsidiary to foreign subsidiary.
    A) Skills and product offerings transfer
    B) Technical transfer
    C) Knowledge assimilation
    D) Global learning

    Answer: D   Difficulty: Medium   Page: 342

79. According to Barlett and Ghoshal, the _____ strategy is the only viable international strategy.
    A) multidomestic
    B) international
    C) transnational
    D) global

    Answer: C   Difficulty: Medium   Page: 342

Chapter 10 Global Strategy

80. The work of Christopher Barlett and Sumantra Ghoshal is associated with:
    A) global strategy
    B) multidomestic strategy
    C) transnational strategy
    D) international strategy

    Answer: C   Difficulty: Medium   Page: 342

81. Which of the following two international strategies are disadvantaged by a lack of local responsiveness?
    A) global and international
    B) multidomestic and transnational
    C) transnational and global
    D) multidomestic and international

    Answer: A   Difficulty: Medium   Page: 344

82. Which of the following two strategies suffer from a failure to exploit experience curve effects?
    A) international and transnational
    B) multidomestic and international
    C) transnational and global
    D) global and international

    Answer: B   Difficulty: Hard   Page: 344

83. The term _____ refers to cooperative agreements between potential or actual competitors.
    A) tactical union
    B) strategic alliance
    C) political affiliation
    D) economic association

    Answer: B   Difficulty: Easy   Page: 342

84. According to the textbook, the 1980s and 1990s saw:
    A) a rapid decline in the number of strategic alliances
    B) an explosion in the number of strategic alliances
    C) a decline in the number of strategic alliances for international firms and an increase in the number of strategic alliances for multidomestic firms
    D) an increase in the number of strategic alliances for transnational firms and a decline in the number of strategic alliances for global firms

    Answer: B Difficulty: Medium Page: 344

85. Cooperative agreements between potential or actual competitors are called:
    A) economic associations
    B) tactical unions
    C) trade unions
    D) strategic alliances

    Answer: D Difficulty: Easy Page: 344

86. _____ are cooperative agreements between potential or actual competitors.
    A) Strategic alliances
    B) Tactical unions
    C) Economic associations
    D) Trade unions

    Answer: A Difficulty: Easy Page: 344

87. _____ run the range from formal joint ventures to short-term contractual agreements.
    A) Cooperative synergies
    B) Strategic alliances
    C) Franchise organizations
    D) Tactical partnerships

    Answer: B Difficulty: Medium Page: 344

Chapter 10 Global Strategy

88. Which of the following is not an advantage of a strategic alliance?
    A) alliances help facilitate entry into foreign markets
    B) allows a firm to share the fixed costs of developing new product or services with another firm
    C) provides a forum for firms to bring together complementary skills and assets that neither company could easily develop on its own
    D) helps a firm guard its proprietary technology

    Answer: D Difficulty: Medium Page: 343

89. Strategic alliances have three major advantages. These are (1) may facilitate trade into a foreign market, (2) allows firms to share the fixed costs and developing new products or processes, and (3):
    A) an alliance is a way to bring together the complementary skills and assets of the participants
    B) gives competitors a low cost route to new technology
    C) a firm never gives away more than it gains by participating in a strategic alliance
    D) give competitors a low cost route to new markets

    Answer: A Difficulty: Medium Page: 346

90. Robert Reich and Eric Making have argued that _____ between U.S. and Japanese firms are part of an implicit Japanese strategy to keep higher-paying, higher-value added jobs in Japan while gaining the project engineering and production process skills that underlie the competitive success of many U.S. companies.
    A) licensing agreements
    B) strategic alliances
    C) turnkey projects
    D) franchise arrangements

    Answer: B Difficulty: Hard Page: 346

91. One of the principle risks with strategic alliances is:
    A) that they bring together the complementary skills of alliances partners
    B) alliances may facilitate entry into foreign markets
    C) a firm can give away more than it receives
    D) that they allow firms to share fixed costs

    Answer: C Difficulty: Medium Page: 346

Chapter 10 Global Strategy

92. One recent study of 49 international strategic alliances found that _____ ran into serious managerial and financial troubles within two years of their formation.
    A) 1/4
    B) 1/2
    C) 2/3
    D) 3/4

    Answer: C Difficulty: Hard Page: 346

93. Which of the following is not an attribute of a good strategic alliance partner?
    A) is unlikely to opportunistically exploit the alliances for its own ends
    B) shares the firm's vision for the purpose of the alliance
    C) must have capabilities identical to its partner
    D) helps the firm achieve its strategic goals

    Answer: C Difficulty: Hard Page: 346

94. According to the textbook, the success of a strategic alliance is a function of three factors. These are: partner selection, alliance structure, and _____.
    A) similarity in size of the alliance partners
    B) geographic distance between the alliance partners
    C) the manner in which the alliance is managed
    D) government support

    Answer: C Difficulty: Medium Page: 346

95. The success of a strategic alliance is a function of three factors. These are: alliance structure, the manner in which the alliance is managed, and _____.
    A) geographic distance between the alliance partners
    B) similarity in size of the alliance partners
    C) government support
    D) partner selection

    Answer: D Difficulty: Medium Page: 346

96. The success of a strategic alliance is a function of three factors. These are:
    A) alliance governance, level of planning, and the manner in which the alliance is managed
    B) partner selection, alliance structure, and the manner in which the alliance is managed
    C) alliance governance, alliance leadership, and level of planning
    D) partner selection, geographic distance between the alliance partners, and government support

    Answer: B Difficulty: Medium Page: 346

97. The four safeguards against opportunism by alliance partners include:
    A) retaining a CPA to audit the alliance's books, agreeing to share valuable skills and technologies, seeking credible commitments, and shared leadership in alliance activities
    B) walling off critical technology, establishing contractual safeguards, agreeing to swap valuable skills and technologies, and seeking credible commitments
    C) restricting the alliance to activities outside the partner's distinctive competencies, maintaining an atmosphere of secrecy, shared leadership in alliance activities, and seeking credible commitments
    D) establishing contractual safeguards, maintaining an atmosphere of secrecy, retaining a CPA to audit the alliance's books, and shared leadership in alliance activities

    Answer: B Difficulty: Hard Page: 348

98. The four safeguards against opportunism by alliance partners include: walling off critical technology, establishing contractual safeguards, agreeing to swap valuable skills and technologies, and _____.
    A) seeking credible commitments
    B) maintaining an atmosphere of secrecy
    C) retaining a CPA to audit the alliance's books
    D) restricting the life span of the alliance to three years or less

    Answer: A Difficulty: Medium Page: 348

99. Which of the following is not one of the four safeguards against opportunism by alliances partners mentioned in our textbook?
    A) seeking credible commitments
    B) establishing contractual safeguards
    C) avoiding the practice of swapping valuable skills and technologies
    D) walling off critical technologies

    Answer: C Difficulty: Hard Page: 348

100. Walling off critical technology, establishing contractual safeguards, agreeing to swap valuable skills and technologies, and seeking credible commitments are safeguards against _____ by an alliance partner.
    A) expediency
    B) theft
    C) self-interest
    D) opportunism

    Answer: D Difficulty: Medium Page: 348

101. According to the textbook, there are three important antecedents to maximizing the benefits of strategic alliances. These are:
    A) make allowances for cultural differences, building trust, and learning from partners
    B) joint planning, complete disclosure of proprietary technology, limiting the number of alliance partners
    C) restricting the alliance to issues dealing with the core competencies of the alliance partners, complete disclosure of proprietary technology, and learning from partners
    D) joint planning, building trust, and limiting the number of alliance partners

    Answer: A Difficulty: Medium Page: 349

102. There are three important antecedents to maximizing the benefits of strategic alliances. These are making allowances for cultural differences, learning from partners, and _____.
    A) limiting the number of alliance partners
    B) restricting the alliance to issues dealing with the core competencies of the alliance partners
    C) building trust
    D) complete disclosure of proprietary technology

    Answer: C Difficulty: Medium Page: 349

103. According to the textbook, the three most important antecedents to maximizing the benefits of strategic alliances include building trust, learning from partners, and

    _____.
    A) limiting the number of alliance partners
    B) making allowances for cultural differences
    C) complete disclosure of proprietary technology
    D) restricting the alliance to issues dealing with the core competencies of the alliance partners

    Answer: B Difficulty: Medium Page: 349

104. After a five-year study of 15 strategic alliances between major multinationals, Gary Hamel, Yves Doz, and C.K. Prahalad concluded that a major determinant of how much a company gains from an alliance is:
    A) its ability to enhance its reputation
    B) its ability to realize cost savings
    C) its ability to learn from alliance partners
    D) its ability to achieve greater economies of scale

    Answer: C Difficulty: Hard Page: 350

105. _____ is a major determinant of how much a company gains from an alliance, according to a five-year study of 15 strategic alliances between major multinationals completed by Gary Hamel, Yves Doz, and C.K. Prahald.
    A) The ability to learn from alliance partners
    B) The ability to achieve greater economies of scale
    C) The ability to enhance its reputation
    D) The ability to realize cost savings

    Answer: A Difficulty: Hard Page: 350

Chapter 10 Global Strategy

Essay Questions

106. Describe the concept of "core competence." What types of core competencies are the most valuable for penetrating foreign markets?

Difficulty: Easy   Page: 327

Answer:
The term core competence refers to the skills within the firms that competitors cannot easily match or imitate. These skills may exist in any of the firm's value creation activities (i.e. manufacturing, marketing, sales, materials management, etc.). These skills typically enable a firm to produce a product or service that competitors find difficult to duplicate. For instance, Home Depot has a core competence in managing home improvement superstores. Home Depot's competitors have found this core competence difficult to imitate.

Core competencies are the most valuable as a tool for helping firms enter foreign markets when they are unique, when the value placed on them by consumers is great, and when there are very few capable competitors with similar skills and/or products in foreign markets. According to the textbook, firms with unique and valuable skills can often realize enormous returns by applying those skills, and the products they produce, to foreign markets where indigenous competitors lack similar skills and products.

107. What is the experience curve? How can an involvement in overseas markets help a firm capture experience curve advantages more rapidly?

Difficulty: Medium   Page: 332

Answer:
The experience curve refers to the systematic reductions in production costs that have been observed to occur over the life of a product. In general, the experience curve suggests that as a firm produces more of a particular product, the unit price of the product drops. This phenomenon occurs because of learning effects and economies of scale. Learning effects refer to the cost savings that come from learning by doing. Economies of scale refers to the reduction in unit costs achieved by producing a large volume of a product as a result of the ability to spread fixed costs over a larger volume.

Firms can typically move down the experience curve (i.e. realize a reduction in production costs by selling more of a product) faster through involvement in overseas markets. The simple logic is that by going global, a firm expands its customer base and is able to sell a higher volume of its product. By selling a higher volume of its product, a firm can experience learning effects and economies of scale benefits more rapidly.

108. What is the difference between learning effects and economies of scale?

   Difficulty: Medium   Page: 333

   Answer:
   Learning effects refer to cost savings that come from learning by doing. Labor, for example, learns by repetition how to carry out a task, such as assembling airframes, most efficiently. The term economies of scale refers to the reduction in unit cost achieved by producing a large volume of a product. Economies of scale have a number of sources, one of the most important of which seem to be the ability to spread fixed costs over a large volume.

109. Firms that compete in global markets often face pressures for local responsiveness. Describe what is meant by local responsiveness, and identify the underlying reasons that local responsiveness pressures exist.

   Difficulty: Medium   Page: 335

   Answer:
   Many firms enter global markets with the idea of selling essentially the same product in each market that they enter. This approach becomes problematic when the citizens of a particular country ask that the product be customized to fit their particular needs. When the consumer in a country ask that a product be modified to suite their particular tastes, they are in effect asking the international company to be "locally responsive" to their needs. This is where the term local responsiveness comes from.

   Pressures for local responsiveness arise from a number of sources. These sources include: (1) Differences in consumer tastes and preferences across markets; (2) Differences in infrastructure and traditional practices across markets; (3) Differences in distribution channels across markets; and (4) Host government demands.

Chapter 10 Global Strategy

110. Describe the four basic strategies that firms use to compete in international markets. Which strategy is the best?

Difficulty: Medium   Page: 339

Answer:
The four basic strategies that firms use to compete in international markets are: an international strategy, a multidomestic strategy, a global strategy, and a transnational strategy. Each of the strategies is briefly described below.

International Strategy - Firms that pursue an international strategy try to create value by transferring valuable skills and products to foreign markets where indigenous competitors lack those skills and products. These firms tend to centralize product development functions at home, and establish manufacturing and marketing functions in each major country in which they do business. An international strategy makes sense if a firm has a valuable core competence that indigenous competitors in foreign markets lack and if the firm faces relatively weak pressures for local responsiveness and cost reductions. Typically, local responsiveness is fairly modest.

Multidomestic Strategy - Firms pursuing a multidomestic strategy orient themselves toward achieving maximum local responsiveness. These firms tend to transfer skills and products developed at home to foreign markets. Consistent with their strategy of local responsiveness, however, they tend to establish a complete set of value creation activities - including production, marketing, and R&D - in each major market in which they do business. A multidomestic strategy makes sense when there are high pressures for local responsiveness and low pressures for cost reductions. The high cost structure associated with the duplication of production facilities makes this strategy inappropriate in industries where cost pressures are intense.

Global Strategy - Firms that pursue a global strategy focus upon increasing profitability by reaping the cost reductions that come from experience curve effects and location economies. That is, they are pursuing a low cost strategy. The majority of the value chain activities for a global firm are concentrated in a few favorable locations. Global firms are not very locally responsive. Instead, they prefer to market a standardized product worldwide. This strategy makes most sense in those cases where there are strong pressures for cost reductions, and where demands for local responsiveness are minimal.

Chapter 10 Global Strategy

Transnational Strategy - A transnational strategy is an ambitious strategy in which a firm tries to simultaneously exploit experience-base cost economies and location economies, transfer distinctive competencies within the firm, and pay attention to pressures for local responsiveness. This type of strategy makes sense when a firm faces high pressures for cost reductions and high pressures for local responsiveness. Barlett and Ghoshal admit that building an organization that is capable of supporting a transnational strategic posture is complex and difficult. In essence, a transnational strategy requires a firm to simultaneously achieve cost efficiencies, global learning, and local responsiveness. These are contradictory demands which are difficult to achieve at the same time in practice.

Which strategy is the best? There is no compelling answer to this question. The most advantageous strategy is the one that best complements a firm's distinctive competencies and its ultimate goals and objectives.

111. What are strategic alliances? Are strategic alliances on the rise or decline?

Difficulty: Easy   Page: 344

Answer:
Strategic alliances are cooperative agreements between potential or actual competitors. Strategic alliances run the range from formal joint ventures, in which two or more firms have equity stakes, to short-term contractual arrangements, in which two companies agree to cooperate on a particular task. Strategic alliances are definitely on the rise. The 1980s and 1990s have seen an explosion in the number of strategic alliances that have been formed worldwide.

112. Under what circumstances is entering into strategic alliances a risky undertaking?

Difficulty: Medium   Page: 344

Answer:
This question is designed to encourage classroom discussion and/or to encourage students to "think" about the potential hazards of alliance formation. There are many compelling reasons to enter into a strategic alliance with another company. For example, an American firm may find the Japanese market tough to crack without finding a Japanese company to partner with. Similarly, if a company like General Motors decided to speed up its R&D in the area of electric cars, it would be awful tempting to develop an alliance with a foreign producer like Honda or Mazda to share the development expense. The primary disadvantage of entering into strategic alliances is that they often compel firms to share sensitive proprietary information with their alliance partners. This practice can give a potential competitor a low cost route to new technology and markets.

Chapter 11 Entering Foreign Markets

True/False Questions

1. The choice of what foreign markets to enter should be driven by an assessment of relative long-run growth and profit potential.

   Answer: True   Difficulty: Easy   Page: 358

2. The advantages frequently associated with entering a market early are commonly known as preemptive advantages.

   Answer: False   Difficulty: Easy   Page: 361

3. Pioneering costs are costs that an early entrant has to bear that a later entrant can avoid.

   Answer: True   Difficulty: Medium   Page: 361

4. Recent research seems to confirm that the probability that survival decreases if an international business enters a national market after several other foreign firms have already done so.

   Answer: True   Difficulty: Medium   Page: 362

5. A strategic commitment is a decision that is short-term in nature and is fairly easy to reverse.

   Answer: False   Difficulty: Medium   Page: 362

6. In a turnkey project, the contractor agrees to handle every detail of the project for a foreign client, including the training of operating personnel.

   Answer: True   Difficulty: Medium   Page: 365

7. Licensing gives a firm tight control over the manufacturing, marketing, and strategy that is required for realizing experience curve and location economies.

   Answer: False   Difficulty: Medium   Page: 367

8. Whereas licensing is pursued primarily by manufacturing firms, franchising is employed primarily by service firms.

   Answer: True   Difficulty: Medium   Page: 370

Chapter 11 Entering Foreign Markets

9. A primary advantage of franchising is low development costs and risks.

   Answer: True   Difficulty: Medium   Page: 370

10. One of the most significant disadvantages of franchising is quality control.

    Answer: True   Difficulty: Medium   Page: 370

11. A joint venture entails establishment of a firm that is jointly owned by two or more otherwise independent companies.

    Answer: True   Difficulty: Easy   Page: 371

12. Research suggests that joint ventures with local partners face a high risk of being subject to nationalization or other forms of government interference.

    Answer: False   Difficulty: Medium   Page: 371

13. A primary advantage of joint ventures is the sharing of development costs and risks.

    Answer: True   Difficulty: Medium   Page: 371

14. One of the primary advantages of a wholly owned subsidiary is that it gives the firm tight control over operations in different countries that is necessary for engaging in global strategic coordination.

    Answer: True   Difficulty: Medium   Page: 373

15. Establishing a wholly owned subsidiary is generally the most inexpensive method of serving a foreign market.

    Answer: False   Difficulty: Medium   Page: 373

16. If a firm's competitive advantage is based on control over proprietary technological know-how, licensing and joint venture arrangements are preferred methods of foreign market entry.

    Answer: False   Difficulty: Medium   Page: 374

Chapter 11 Entering Foreign Markets

17. Studies have shown that while many large firms tend to be proactive about seeking out opportunities for profitable exporting, many medium-sized and small firms are very reactive.

    Answer: True   Difficulty: Medium   Page: 375

18. A stamp of credit worthiness, which is issued by a bank at the request of an exporter, states the bank will pay a specified sum of money to a beneficiary, normally the exporter, on presentation of particular, specified documents.

    Answer: False   Difficulty: Medium   Page: 381

19. A bill of lading, sometimes referred to as a bill of exchange, is the instrument normally used in international commerce for payment.

    Answer: False   Difficulty: Medium   Page: 382

20. International practice is to use drafts to settle trade transactions.

    Answer: True   Difficulty: Easy   Page: 382

Multiple Choice Questions

21. According to the textbook, the choice of what foreign market to enter should be driven by an assessment of:
    A) relative long-run growth and profit potential
    B) geographic proximity and friendliness of host government
    C) climate and economic stability of host government
    D) friendliness of host government and profit potential

    Answer: A   Difficulty: Medium   Page: 358

22. The advantages frequently associated with entering a market early are commonly known as:
    A) inaugural advantages
    B) first-mover advantages
    C) initial-entrant premiums
    D) proactive-mover benefits

    Answer: B   Difficulty: Easy   Page: 361

Chapter 11 Entering Foreign Markets

23. Which of the following is not a first-mover advantage?
    A) the ability to increase a firm's chances of survival by entering a foreign market before industrial rivals
    B) the ability to build sales volume in a country and ride down the experience curve ahead of rivals
    C) the ability to create switching costs that tie customers to a company's products or services
    D) the ability to preempt rivals and capture demand by establishing a strong brand name

    Answer: A   Difficulty: Hard   Page: 361

24. The disadvantages associated with entering a market early are commonly known as:
    A) first-mover disadvantages
    B) inaugural disadvantages
    C) initial-entrant disadvantages
    D) proactive-mover losses

    Answer: A   Difficulty: Easy   Page: 361

25. _____ are costs that an early entrant has to bear that a later entrant can avoid.
    A) Experimental costs
    B) Untried costs
    C) Introductory costs
    D) Pioneering costs

    Answer: A   Difficulty: Medium   Page: 361

26. _____ costs arise when the business system in a foreign country is so different from that in a firm's home market that the enterprise has to devote considerable effort, time, and expanse to learning the rules of the game.
    A) Pioneering
    B) Early entry
    C) Introductory costs
    D) Inaugural costs

    Answer: A   Difficulty: Medium   Page: 362

Chapter 11 Entering Foreign Markets

27. A _____ is a decision that has a long-term impact and is difficult to reverse.
    A) operational pledge
    B) functional assurance
    C) tactical covenant
    D) strategic commitment

    Answer: D Difficulty: Easy Page: 362

28. The _____ entrant is more likely than the _____ entrant to be able to capture the first-mover advantages associated with demand preemption, scale economies, and switching costs.
    A) small scale, large scale
    B) small scale, moderate scale
    C) large scale, small scale
    D) there is no relationship between scale of entrant and the ability to capture first-mover advantages

    Answer: C Difficulty: Hard Page: 364

29. _____ entry allows a firm to learn about a foreign market while limiting the firm's exposure to that market.
    A) Minimal-commitment
    B) Small-scale
    C) Reduced-commitment
    D) Minimal-scale

    Answer: B Difficulty: Medium Page: 364

30. Most manufacturing firms being their global expansion through _____.
    A) establishing a joint venture with a host country firm
    B) licensing
    C) turnkey projects
    D) exporting

    Answer: D Difficulty: Easy Page: 365

Chapter 11 Entering Foreign Markets

31. Exporting has two distinct advantages. These are:
    A) it avoids the often substantial cost of establishing manufacturing operations in the host country; and it may help a firm achieve experience curve and location economies
    B) access to local partner's knowledge; and politically acceptable
    C) ability to earn returns from process technology skills in countries where FDI is restricted; and politically acceptable
    D) access to a local partner's knowledge and it may help a firm achieve experience curve; and location economies

    Answer: A   Difficulty: Medium   Page: 365

32. Exporting has two distinct advantages: it avoids the often-substantial cost of establishing manufacturing operations in the host country and _____.
    A) it provides a firm the ability to earn returns from process technology skills in countries where FDI is restricted
    B) it is politically acceptable
    C) it may help a firm achieve experience curve and location economies
    D) it provides a firm access to local partner's knowledge

    Answer: C   Difficulty: Medium   Page: 365

33. Exporting has two distinct advantages: it may help a firm achieve experience curve and location economies and _____.
    A) it provides a firm access to a local partner's knowledge
    B) it is politically acceptable
    C) it provides the firm the ability to earn returns from process technology skills in countries where FDI is restricted
    D) it avoids the often substantial cost of establishing manufacturing operations in the host country

    Answer: D   Difficulty: Medium   Page: 365

34. All of the following are disadvantages of exporting except?
    A) it may help a firm achieve experience curve economies
    B) high transportation costs can make exporting uneconomical
    C) tariff barriers can make exporting uneconomical
    D) exporting from a firm's home bases may not be appropriate if there are lower-cost locations for manufacturing the product abroad

    Answer: A   Difficulty: Medium   Page: 365

Chapter 11 Entering Foreign Markets

35. High transport costs, trade barriers, and problems with local marketing agents are disadvantages of _____.
    A) licensing
    B) franchising
    C) exporting
    D) turnkey projects

    Answer: C   Difficulty: Medium   Page: 365

36. Consider the following scenario: Ballard Manufacturing wants to sell its products overseas, but only if it can act on its own and manufacturer its product in a central location. Based on these objectives, the appropriate foreign entry mode for Tucker is:
    A) wholly owned subsidiary
    B) franchising
    C) exporting
    D) licensing

    Answer: C   Difficulty: Medium   Page: 365

37. In a _____ project, the contractor agrees to handle every detail of the project for a foreign client, including the training of operating personnel.
    A) beginning to end
    B) A to Z
    C) front-to-back
    D) turnkey

    Answer: D   Difficulty: Easy   Page: 365

38. A project in which a contractor handles every detail of the project for a foreign client, including training of operating personnel, and then hands the foreign client the key to a plant that is ready for operation is referred to as a:
    A) turnkey project
    B) golden key project
    C) cyclekey project
    D) workkey project

    Answer: A   Difficulty: Easy   Page: 365

Chapter 11 Entering Foreign Markets

39. Creating efficient competitors and lack of long-term market presence are disadvantages of _____.
    A) turnkey projects
    B) licensing
    C) franchising
    D) exporting

    Answer: A   Difficulty: Medium   Page: 366

40. Turnkey projects are a means of exporting _____ to other countries.
    A) commodities
    B) manufacturing goods
    C) process technology
    D) services

    Answer: C   Difficulty: Medium   Page: 366

41. Suppose Exxon, a U.S. company, was contracted by a Saudi Arabian company to build a oil refinery in Saudi Arabia, and the contract specified that Mobil would handle every aspect of the construction of the refinery, including the training of the operating personnel. This type of project is referred to as a:
    A) turnkey project
    B) beginning to end
    C) A to Z
    D) front to back

    Answer: A   Difficulty: Medium   Page: 366

42. Turnkey projects are most common in the following industries:
    A) chemical, pharmaceutical, petroleum refining, and metal refining
    B) textiles, shoes, leather products, and linens
    C) cars, trucks, construction equipment, and farm implements
    D) lumber, furniture, paper, and pulp

    Answer: A   Difficulty: Hard   Page: 366

Chapter 11 Entering Foreign Markets

43. Which foreign market entry strategy has the following disadvantages: lack of long-term market presence, may inadvertently create a competitor, risk selling a firm's competitive advantage?
    A) wholly owned subsidiary
    B) turnkey project
    C) exporting
    D) franchising

    Answer: B Difficulty: Medium Page: 366

44. Which of the following foreign market entry mode takes advantage of a firm's competency in the area of assembling and running technologically complex projects?
    A) licensing
    B) exporting
    C) turnkey project
    D) franchising

    Answer: C Difficulty: Medium Page: 366

45. A _____ agreement is an arrangement whereby a licensor grants the rights to intangible property to another entity for a specified time period in exchange for royalties.
    A) franchising
    B) turnkey
    C) licensing
    D) exporting

    Answer: C Difficulty: Easy Page: 366

46. All of the following are disadvantages of licensing except:
    A) high costs and risks
    B) lack of control over technology
    C) inability to realize location and experience curve economies
    D) inability to engage in global strategic coordination

    Answer: A Difficulty: Medium Page: 367

Chapter 11 Entering Foreign Markets

47. Lack of control over technology, inability to realize location and experience curve economies, and an inability to engage in global strategic coordination are distinct disadvantages of _____.
    A) turnkey projects
    B) exporting
    C) licensing
    D) wholly owned subsidiaries

    Answer: C   Difficulty: Hard   Page: 367

48. Which of the following is not an argument in favor of licensing as a means of foreign market entry?
    A) the firm does not have to have capital to open markets overseas
    B) a firm wants to participate in a foreign market, but is prohibited from doing so by barriers to investment
    C) the firm possesses some intangible property that might have business applications and wants to develop that technology or those applications itself
    D) the firm does not have to bear the development costs and risks associated with opening a foreign market

    Answer: C   Difficulty: Hard   Page: 367

49. Suppose 3M Corporation granted a South Korean company the rights to manufacture "Post-It-Notes" in South Korean in exchange for a royalty fee. This type of arrangement is referred to as a:
    A) franchising agreement
    B) turnkey project
    C) licensing agreement
    D) wholly owned subsidiary

    Answer: C   Difficulty: Medium   Page: 367

50. Patents, inventions, formulas, processes, designs, copyrights, and trademarks are examples of _____ property.
    A) intangible
    B) discernible
    C) tangible
    D) nondescript

    Answer: A   Difficulty: Easy   Page: 367

Chapter 11 Entering Foreign Markets

51. Under a _____ agreement, a firm might license some valuable intangible property to a foreign partner, but in addition to a royalty payment, the firm might also request that the foreign partner license some of its valuable know-how to the firm.
    A) inter-licensing
    B) reciprocal-licensing
    C) cross-licensing
    D) parity-licensing

    Answer: C   Difficulty: Medium   Page: 368

52. An arrangement whereby a company grants the right to intangible property to another firm for a specified time period in exchange for royalties and a license from the foreign partners for some of its technological know-how is referred to as _____.
    A) reciprocal licensing agreement
    B) cross-licensing agreement
    C) parity licensing agreement
    D) inter-licensing agreement

    Answer: B   Difficulty: Medium   Page: 368

53. _____ agreements enable firms to hold each other hostage, which reduces the probability that they will behave opportunistically toward each other.
    A) Cross-licensing
    B) Franchise
    C) Joint venture
    D) Exporting

    Answer: A   Difficulty: Medium   Page: 368

54. Other than licensing, the form of foreign market entry that results in a firm in the host country paying a royalty to the firm that has the rights to a product or service is called _____.
    A) joint venture
    B) exporting
    C) franchising
    D) wholly owned subsidiary

    Answer: C   Difficulty: Medium   Page: 369

Chapter 11 Entering Foreign Markets

55. _____ is basically a specialized form of licensing in which the franchiser not only sells intangible property to the franchisee, but also insists that the franchisee agree to abide by strict rules as to how it does business.
    A) Franchising
    B) Chartering
    C) Exporting
    D) Leasing

    Answer: A Difficulty: Easy Page: 369

56. Low development costs and risks are distinct advantages of:
    A) wholly owned subsidiaries and exporting
    B) exporting and turnkey projects
    C) joint ventures and wholly owned subsidiaries
    D) franchising and licensing

    Answer: D Difficulty: Medium Page: 370

57. Which of the following two modes of foreign market entry typically involves a royalty payment made by the firm in the host country?
    A) licensing and franchising
    B) setting up a wholly owned subsidiary in the host country and exporting
    C) exporting and establishing a joint venture with a host country firm
    D) turnkey projects and establishing a joint venture with a host country firm

    Answer: A Difficulty: Medium Page: 370

58. Lack of control over quality and the inability to engage in global strategic coordination are distinct disadvantages of _____.
    A) franchising
    B) exporting
    C) wholly owned subsidiaries
    D) turnkey projects

    Answer: A Difficulty: Hard Page: 370

Chapter 11 Entering Foreign Markets

59. Whereas primarily _____ firms pursue licensing, primarily _____ firms pursue franchising.
    A) manufacturing, service
    B) agricultural, manufacturing
    C) service, mining
    D) mining, service

    Answer: A Difficulty: Medium Page: 370

60. One of the most significant disadvantages of franchising is _____.
    A) high financial risks
    B) high development costs
    C) quality control
    D) the need for coordination of manufacturing to achieve experience curve and location economies

    Answer: C Difficulty: Medium Page: 370

61. A _____ entails establishment of a firm that is jointly owned by two or more otherwise independent firms.
    A) licensing agreement
    B) wholly owned subsidiary
    C) franchise
    D) joint venture

    Answer: D Difficulty: Easy Page: 371

62. If Exxon and a Russian firm established a jointly owned entity for the purpose of exploring for oil in Northern Siberia, that would be an example of a:
    A) turnkey project
    B) wholly owned subsidiary
    C) joint venture
    D) franchise

    Answer: C Difficulty: Medium Page: 371

Chapter 11 Entering Foreign Markets

63. If Honda and Ford established a jointly owned entity for the purpose of building cars to export to Eastern Europe, that would be an example of a _____ form of foreign market entry.
    A) wholly owned subsidiary
    B) joint venture
    C) turnkey project
    D) franchise

    Answer: B Difficulty: Medium Page: 366

64. Which of the following modes of foreign market entry has the following advantages: firms benefit from a local partner's knowledge of the host country's competitive conditions, a firm shares development costs with a local partner, and in many countries political considerations necessitate this form of entry.
    A) wholly owned subsidiary
    B) franchising
    C) exporting
    D) joint venture

    Answer: D Difficulty: Medium Page: 371

65. The most typical joint venture is:
    A) 80/20, in which there are two partners and one partner holds a substantial majority share
    B) 50/50, in which there are two partners and each partner holds an equal share
    C) 25/25/25/25, in which there are four partners and each partner hold an equal share
    D) 51/49, in which there are two partners and one partner holds a slight majority share

    Answer: B Difficulty: Medium Page: 371

66. In a _____, the firm owns 100 percent of the stock.
    A) joint venture
    B) turnkey operation
    C) wholly owned subsidiary
    D) strategic alliance

    Answer: C Difficulty: Easy Page: 372

Chapter 11 Entering Foreign Markets

67. What is the preferred mode of foreign market entry for a high-tech firms that wants to (1) minimize the risk of losing control over its technological competence; and (2) maintain tight control over its operations?
    A) licensing
    B) franchising
    C) wholly owned subsidiary
    D) turnkey operation

    Answer: C   Difficulty: Medium   Page: 372

68. Suppose Dell Computer decided to build an assembly plant in Poland and, in an effort to maintain maximum control, decided to operate the plant completely on its own. This is an approach to foreign market entry referred to as:
    A) joint venture
    B) turnkey operation
    C) exporting
    D) wholly owned subsidiary

    Answer: D   Difficulty: Medium   Page: 372

69. In a wholly owned subsidiary, the firm owns _____ of the stock.
    A) the majority
    B) 100%
    C) 51%
    D) the minority

    Answer: B   Difficulty: Easy   Page: 372

70. Protection of technology, the ability to engage in global strategic coordination and the ability to realize location and experience economies are distinct advantages of

    _____.
    A) franchising
    B) wholly owned subsidiary
    C) exporting
    D) licensing

    Answer: B   Difficulty: Hard   Page: 373

71. Establishing a wholly owned subsidiary in a foreign country can be done in two ways. These are:
    A) through a turnkey operation or through a licensing agreement
    B) through a joint venture of through acquiring an established firm to promote its products
    C) through setting up a new operation in a foreign country or through acquiring an established firm to promote its products
    D) through licensing agreements or through setting up a new operation in the foreign country

    Answer: C Difficulty: Medium   Page: 373

72. The most costly form of foreign market entry is:
    A) exporting
    B) licensing
    C) franchising
    D) wholly owned subsidiary

    Answer: D Difficulty: Medium   Page: 373

73. If a firm's competitive advantage is based on control over proprietary technological know how, which of the following foreign entry modes should be avoided?
    A) exporting and joint ventures
    B) turnkey projects and franchising
    C) wholly owned subsidiaries and franchising
    D) joint ventures and licensing

    Answer: D Difficulty: Hard   Page: 374

74. If a high-tech firm sets up operations in a foreign country to profit from a core competency in technological know-how, the most advantageous entry mode is:
    A) wholly owned subsidiary
    B) turnkey operation
    C) franchising
    D) licensing

    Answer: A Difficulty: Medium   Page: 374

Chapter 11 Entering Foreign Markets

75. Many service firms favor a combination of franchising and _____ to control the franchises within a particular country or regions.
    A) strategic alliances
    B) subsidiaries
    C) turnkey project partners
    D) licensing agreements

    Answer: B Difficulty: Medium Page: 375

76. The greater the pressures for cost reductions are, the most likely a firm will want to pursue some combination of:
    A) licensing and joint venture
    B) exporting and wholly owned subsidiaries
    C) franchising and exporting
    D) joint ventures and wholly owned subsidiaries

    Answer: B Difficulty: Hard Page: 375

77. In the United States, the most comprehensive source of information for export advice is the:
    A) World Trade Organization
    B) U.S. Department of State
    C) U.S. Department of Commerce
    D) United Nations

    Answer: C Difficulty: Easy Page: 372

78. In the United States, the _____ is the most comprehensive source of information for export advice.
    A) United Nations
    B) U.S. Department of State
    C) U.S. Department of Commerce
    D) World Trade Organization

    Answer: C Difficulty: Easy Page: 376

79. _____ are export specialists that act as the export marketing department or international department for their client firms.
A) Export accounting agencies
B) Export management companies
C) Overseas marketing companies
D) International intermediaries

Answer: B Difficulty: Medium Page: 377

80. Export management companies normally accept two types of export assignments: they start export operations for a firm with the understanding that the firm will take over operations after they are well established, or:
A) they perform start-up with the understanding that the export management company will remain committed for a period of at least ten years
B) they perform start-up with the understanding the export management company will remain committed for a period of at least five years
C) they perform start-up with the understanding that the export management company will have continuing responsibility for selling the firm's products
D) they perform start-up with the understanding the export management company will acquire an equity interest in the exporting firm

Answer: C Difficulty: Hard Page: 377

81. Which of the following was not mentioned in the textbook as a strategy for effective exporting?
A) it is important to hire local personnel to help the firm establish itself in a foreign market
B) particularly for a new exporter, it helps to hire an export management company
C) in many countries it is important to devote a lot of attention to building strong and enduring relationships with local distributors and/or customers
D) it often makes sense to focus on a large number of markets initially

Answer: D Difficulty: Hard Page: 378

82. Three mechanisms for financing exports and imports include:
A) the letter of credit, the draft, and the bill of lading
B) the open note, the bill of cargo, and the stamp of credit worthiness
C) the stamp of credit worthiness, the open note, and the bill of cargo
D) the guaranteed note, the letter of credit, and the bill of shipping

Answer: A Difficulty: Medium Page: 379

83. Three mechanisms for financing exports and imports include the letter of credit, the draft, and the _____.
    A) the open note
    B) the stamp of credit worthiness
    C) bill of lading
    D) the guaranteed note

    Answer: C Difficulty: Medium   Page: 379

84. Three mechanisms for financing exports and imports include the draft, the bill of lading, and the _____.
    A) letter of credit
    B) open note
    C) stamp of credit worthiness
    D) guaranteed note

    Answer: A Difficulty: Medium   Page: 379

85. Three mechanisms for financing exports and imports include the letter of credit, the bill of lading, and the _____.
    A) open note
    B) stamp of credit worthiness
    C) continuous note
    D) draft

    Answer: D Difficulty: Medium   Page: 379

86. In the context of international commerce, the abbreviation L/C stands for:
    A) letter of certification
    B) letter of credit
    C) liability clearance
    D) liberal commerce

    Answer: B Difficulty: Easy   Page: 381

87. Issued by a bank at the request of an importer, a _____ states the bank will pay a specified sum of money to a beneficiary, normally the exporter, on presentation of particular, specified documents
    A) stamp of credit worthiness
    B) letter of credit
    C) bill of lading
    D) draft

    Answer: B   Difficulty: Medium   Page: 381

88. A _____ is a document issued by a bank and states the bank will pay a specified sum of money to a beneficiary, normally an exporter, on presentation of particular, specified documents.
    A) certificate of credit worthiness
    B) bill of lading
    C) letter of credit
    D) draft

    Answer: C   Difficulty: Medium   Page: 381

89. The service fee for a letter of credit is usually between _____ of the value of the letter of credit, depending on the importer's creditworthiness and the size of the transaction.
    A) 0.25 and 1 percent
    B) 0.5 and 2 percent
    C) 1 and 3 percent
    D) 2 and 4 percent

    Answer: B   Difficulty: Hard   Page: 381

90. An importer can guarantee to an exporter that it will get paid through a:
    A) letter of credit
    B) certificate of trust
    C) bill of lading
    D) draft

    Answer: A   Difficulty: Medium   Page: 381

Chapter 11 Entering Foreign Markets

91. A _____, sometimes referred to as a bill of exchange, is the instrument normally used in international commerce for payment.
    A) open note
    B) stamp of credit worthiness
    C) draft
    D) bill of lading

    Answer: C Difficulty: Medium Page: 382

92. The disadvantage of using a letter of credit from the importer's perspective is:
    A) that a service fee must be paid
    B) only importers with questionable credit use letters of credit
    C) a reciprocal letter of credit must be issued by the exporter
    D) that it reveals financial information about the importer to the exporter

    Answer: A Difficulty: Medium Page: 381

93. The instrument normally used in international commerce for payment is referred to as a _____.
    A) draft
    B) stamp of credit worthiness
    C) bill of lading
    D) open note

    Answer: A Difficulty: Medium Page: 382

94. A _____ is simply an order written by an exporter instructing an importer, or an importer's agent, to pay a specified amount of money at a specified time.
    A) letter of credit
    B) draft
    C) stamp of credit worthiness
    D) open note

    Answer: B Difficulty: Medium Page: 382

95. International practice is to use _____ to settle trade transactions.
    A) handshakes
    B) letters of credit
    C) drafts
    D) credit vouchers

    Answer: C Difficulty: Medium Page: 382

Chapter 11 Entering Foreign Markets

96. Drafts fall into two categories. These are:
    A) inspection drafts and duration drafts
    B) sight drafts and time drafts
    C) credit drafts and cash drafts
    D) inspection drafts and cash drafts

    Answer: B Difficulty: Easy   Page: 382

97. Drafts fall into two categories: sight drafts and _____ drafts.
    A) time
    B) credit
    C) duration
    D) inspection

    Answer: A Difficulty: Easy   Page: 382

98. In the context of drafts used in international commerce for payment, a _____ draft allows for a delay in payment - normally 30, 60, 90, or 120 days.
    A) duration
    B) time
    C) sight
    D) inspection

    Answer: B Difficulty: Medium   Page: 382

99. In the context of drafts used in international commerce for payment, a _____ draft is payable on presentation to the drawee.
    A) duration
    B) inspection
    C) time
    D) sight

    Answer: D Difficulty: Medium   Page: 382

100. A _____ draft is presented to the drawee, who signifies acceptance of it by writing or stamping a notice of acceptance of its face.
    A) time
    B) sight
    C) cash
    D) credit

    Answer: A Difficulty: Medium   Page: 382

Chapter 11 Entering Foreign Markets

101. The _____ is issued to the exporter by the common carrier transporting the merchandise.
    A) acceptance certificate
    B) bill of tender
    C) bill of lading
    D) stamp of receipt

    Answer: C   Difficulty: Easy   Page: 379

102. A bill of laden serves three purposes. These are:
    A) it is a certificate of authenticity, proof of insurance, and a contract
    B) it is proof of payment, a certificate of tariff payment, and a contract
    C) it is a receipt, a contract, and a document of title
    D) it is a certificate of authenticity, a letter of credit, and a document of title

    Answer: C   Difficulty: Medium   Page: 379

103. A bill of laden serves three purposes: it is a receipt, a contract, and _____.
    A) a document of title
    B) a letter of credit
    C) it is proof of insurance
    D) it is proof of customs clearance

    Answer: A   Difficulty: Medium   Page: 379

104. A bill of laden serves three purposes: it is a contract, a document of title, and
    _____.
    A) it is proof of customs clearance
    B) a letter of credit
    C) a receipt
    D) it is proof of environmental safety

    Answer: C   Difficulty: Medium   Page: 379

105. A bill of laden serves three purposes: it is a receipt, a document of title, and
    _____.
    A) it is proof of insurance
    B) it is proof of customs clearance
    C) a letter of credit
    D) a contract

    Answer: D   Difficulty: Medium   Page: 379

Chapter 11 Entering Foreign Markets

Essay Questions

106. What is meant by the term, "first-mover advantage?" Describe several first-mover advantages.

    Difficulty: Medium   Page: 361

    Answer:
    The advantages frequently associated with entering a market early are commonly known as first-mover advantages. One first-mover advantage is the ability to preempt rivals and capture demand by establishing a strong brand name. A second advantage is the ability to build sales volume in that country and ride down the experience curve ahead of rivals, giving the early entrant a cost advantage over later entrants. A third advantage is the ability of early entrants to create switching costs that tie customers into their products or services. Such switching costs make it difficult for later entrants to win business.

107. What are pioneering costs? When do these costs arise?

    Difficulty: Medium   Page: 361

    Answer:
    Pioneering costs are costs that an early entrant has to bear that a later entrant can avoid. Pioneering costs arise when the business system in a foreign country is too different from that in a firm's home market that the enterprise has to devote considerable effort, time, and expanse to learning the rules of the game.

108. What are the six different ways for a firm to enter a foreign market? Provide a brief description of each of these foreign market entry strategies.

    Difficulty: Easy   Page: 364

    Answer:
    The six different ways for a firm to enter a foreign market include:

    A. Exporting - involves manufacturing a product in a central location and shipping it to foreign markets for sale.
    B. Turnkey projects - in a turnkey project, a contractor from one country handles every detail of the design, construction, and start-up of a facility in a foreign country, and then hands the foreign client the key to a facility that is ready for operation.

C. Licensing - in a licensing agreement, a company from one country grants the rights to intangible property (such as patents, processes, and trademarks) to a company in another country in exchange for a royalty fee.
D. Franchising - is a specialized form of licensing in which the franchiser sells intangible property (normally processes and trademarks) to a franchisee, but also insists that the franchisee agree to abide by strict rules as to how it does business. The McDonalds Corporation, for example, has been very successful in selling franchises to both domestic and foreign franchisees.
E. Joint Ventures - entails establishing a firm that is jointly owned by two or more otherwise independent firms.
F. Wholly Owned Subsidiary - this form of foreign market entry entails setting up a new operation (or acquiring an existing company) in a foreign country.

109. From the perspective of a domestic firm, what are the advantages and disadvantages of licensing the rights to the company's production process and trademark to a firm in a foreign country? What are some of the ways that a firm can reduce the risk of losing its proprietary know-how to foreign companies through licensing agreements?

Difficulty: Medium   Page: 366

Answer:
The primary advantage of licensing is that the firm does not have to bear the development costs and risks associated with opening a foreign market. As a result, licensing is a very attractive option for firms that lack the capital or risk bearing ability to open overseas markets. Licensing is also an attractive option when a firm is interested in pursuing a foreign market but does not want to commit substantial resources to an unfamiliar or potentially volatile foreign market. Licensing is also used when a firm wishes to participate in a foreign market, but is prohibited from doing so by barriers to investment. Finally, licensing is used when a firm possesses some intangible property (like its trademark) but does not want to pursue a potential application itself. For example, Coca-Cola has licensed its familiar trademark to clothing manufacturers, which have incorporated the design into their clothing.

There are three main drawbacks to licensing. First, if a firm licenses any of its proprietary know-how (such as its production processes) to another company, it risks losing control over this knowledge by permitting access to it by another firm. According to the textbook, many firms have made the mistake of thinking they could maintain control over their know-how within the framework of a licensing agreement. Second, licensing is not an effective way of realizing experience curve and location economies by manufacturing a product in a centralized location. If these attributes are important to a firm, licensing may be a poor choice. Finally, competing in a global market may require a firm to coordinate strategic moves across countries by using profits from one country to support competitive attacks in another. Licensing severely limits a firm's ability to do this. A licensee is unlikely to allow a multinational firm to use its profits (beyond the royalty payments) to support a different licensee operating in another country.

A licensor can reduce the risk of losing proprietary know-how to a foreign partner by entering into a cross-licensing agreement. Under a cross-license agreement, a firm licenses some valuable intangible property (such as a production process) to a foreign partner, but in addition to royalty payments, the firm also requires the foreign partner to license some of its valuable know-how to the firm. Cross-licensing agreements enable firms to hold each other "hostage," thereby reducing the risk they will behave in an opportunistic manner toward each other.

110. What is meant by the term "wholly owned subsidiary?" Under what circumstances is the establishment of a wholly owned subsidiary an appropriate foreign entry strategy?

Difficulty: Medium   Page: 372

Answer:
A wholly owned subsidiary is a company that is completely owned by another company. One choice that a firm has for entering a foreign market is to setup a new operation in that market or purchase an existing firm. In either case, if the original company owns 100% of the new operation, it is "wholly owned subsidiary" of the original firm.

Establishing a wholly owned subsidiary as a entry strategy into a foreign market is appropriate when a firm's competitive advantage is based on technological competence. By establishing a wholly owned subsidiary, a firm reduces the risk of losing control over that competence. This is a particularly important concern for firms that have important proprietary technology. Other forms of foreign market entry, such as licensing and joint venture, do a poorer job of protecting a firm's proprietary technology.

Establishing a wholly owned subsidiary may be appropriate for two additional reasons. First, expanding via the wholly owned subsidiary route gives a firm tight control over its operations in various countries. This strategy maximizes a firm's potential to engage in global strategic coordination (i.e., using profits from one country to support competitive attacks in another). Second, a wholly owned subsidiary strategy may be required if a firm is trying to realize location and experience curve economies.

Chapter 11 Entering Foreign Markets

111. What is an export management company? What should a company do before it hires an export management company to help with its export operations?

Difficulty: Easy   Page: 377

Answer:
An export management company (EMC) is a firm that specializes in helping other firms initiate and manage their export operations. EMCs typically accept two types of assignments. First, they can start exporting operations for a firm with the understanding that the firm will take over operations after they are well established. Second, they can perform start-up export operations for a firm with the understanding that they will maintain an ongoing relationship with the company. EMC are valuable because they specialize in export operations, which often involves a lot of export specific paperwork, knowledge, and networking. By using an EMC, a firm can move much quicker than it could if it had to learn all of the export specific regulations itself, and had to start from scratch in terms of making contacts in foreign countries.

Studies have revealed that there is a wide variation in the quality of EMCs. While some perform their functions very well, others appear to add little value to the exporting companies. Therefore, an exporter should carefully review a number of EMCs, and check references from an EMC's past clients, before deciding on a particular EMC.

Chapter 11 Entering Foreign Markets

112. Describe the mechanisms for financing export and imports. Do you belief that the complexity of export financing deters small firms from becoming involved in exporting? Explain your answer.

Difficulty: Medium   Page: 379

Answer:
There are three principle mechanisms used to finance exports and imports. These are: the letter of credit, the draft (or bill of exchange), and the bill of lading. The following is a description of each one of these items.

Letter of Credit: A letter of credit is issued by a bank at the request of an importer. The letter of credit states the bank will pay a specified sum of money to a beneficiary, normally the exporter, on presentation of particular, specified documents. This process is reflected in the following example. If Goodyear Tire sold 10,000 tires to a company in France, the French company could go to a bank and request a letter of credit to assure Goodyear that it will get paid. If the French company is creditworthy, the bank would issue a letter of credit. The letter of credit would stipulate that upon receipt of the 10,000 tires by the French Company, the bank would pay Goodyear the agreed upon amount. This type of arrangement helps the system of international commerce work. Without some assurance of payment, a company like Goodyear may be reluctant to ship products to a foreign company that it is not very familiar with.

Draft: A draft, sometimes referred to as a bill of exchange, it the instrument normally used in international commerce for payment. A draft is simply an order written by an exporter instructing an importer, or an importer's agency, to pay a specified amount of money at specified time.

Bill of Lading: The third critical document for financing international trade is the bill of lading. The bill of lading is issued to the exporter by the common carrier transporting the merchandise. It serves three purposes: it is a receipt, a contract, and a document of title. As a receipt, the bill of laden indicates the carrier has received the merchandise described on the face of the document. As a contract, it specifies that the carrier is obligated to provide a transportation service in return for a certain charge. As a document of title, it can be used to obtain payment or a written promise of payment before the merchandise is released to the importer. The bill of laden can also function as collateral against which funds may be advanced by the exporter to its local bank before or during shipment and before final payment by the importer.

Does the complexity of this system discourage small businesses from becoming more actively involved in exporting? Probably This question provides a platform for classroom discussion.

Chapter 11 Entering Foreign Markets

113. What is the difference between a sight draft and a time draft?

Difficulty: Medium   Page: 382

Answer:
A sight draft is payable on presentation to the drawee. A time draft allows for a delay in payment - normally 30, 60, 90, or 120 days. It is presented to the drawee, who signifies acceptance of it by writing or stamping a notice of acceptance on its face. Once accepted, the time draft becomes a promise to pay by the accepting party. Time drafts are negotiable instruments; that is, once the draft is stamped with an acceptance, the maker can sell the draft to an investor at the discount from its face value.

Chapter 12 Global Marketing and Product Development

True/False Questions

1. A global marketing strategy, which views the world's consumers as similar in their tastes and preferences, is inconsistent with the mass production of a standardized output.

   Answer: False   Difficulty: Easy   Page: 392

2. Academic research has long maintained that a major factor of success for new-product introductions is the closeness of the relationship between finance and R&D.

   Answer: False   Difficulty: Medium   Page: 393

3. The four elements of a firm's marketing mix include product attributes, distribution strategy, communication strategy, and legal strategy

   Answer: False   Difficulty: Easy   Page: 393

4. According to the textbook, globalization seems to be the exception rather than the rule in many industrial markets.

   Answer: True   Difficulty: Medium   Page: 393

5. The current consensus among academics, in regard to Theodore Levitt's arguments on the globalization of markets, is that Levitt overstates his case.

   Answer: True   Difficulty: Medium   Page: 394

6. Developed countries tend to have less retail concentration than developing countries.

   Answer: False   Difficulty: Medium   Page: 400

7. A country that is characterized by a high percentage of car ownership, a high percentage of households with refrigerators and freezers, and a high percentage of two-income households, will most likely have a low level of retail concentration.

   Answer: False   Difficulty: Hard   Page: 400

8. The most important determinant of channel length is the degree to which the retail system is fragmented.

   Answer: True   Difficulty: Medium   Page: 400

9. Countries with fragmented retail systems also tend to have short channels of distribution.

   Answer: False   Difficulty: Medium   Page: 401

10. Since each intermediary in a channel adds its own markup to the products, there is generally a critical link between channel length and the firm's profit margin.

    Answer: True   Difficulty: Medium   Page: 401

11. International communication occurs whenever a firm uses a marketing message to sell its product in another country.

    Answer: True   Difficulty: Easy   Page: 403

12. A pull strategy emphasized personal selling rather than mass media advertising in the promotional mix.

    Answer: False   Difficulty: Easy   Page: 404

13. A push strategy is generally favored by firms in consumer goods industries that are trying to sell to a large segment of the market.

    Answer: False   Difficulty: Hard   Page: 404

14. Pull strategies tend to be emphasized for industrial products and/or complex new products.

    Answer: False   Difficulty: Medium   Page: 404

15. The shorter the distribution channel, the more intermediaries there are that must be persuaded to carry the product for it to reach the consumer.

    Answer: False   Difficulty: Medium   Page: 404

16. In an international context, predatory pricing exists whenever consumers in different countries are charged different prices for the same product.

    Answer: False   Difficulty: Easy   Page: 408

Chapter 12 Global Marketing and Product Development

17. Arbitrage occurs when an individual or business capitalizes on a price differential between two countries by purchasing the product in the country where prices are low and reselling it in the country where prices are high.

    Answer: True   Difficulty: Medium   Page: 408

18. The elasticity of demand for a product in a given country is determined by a number of factors, of which income level and competitive conditions are perhaps the two most important.

    Answer: True   Difficulty: Medium   Page: 408

19. Dumping occurs whenever a firm sells a product for a price that is less than the cost of producing it.

    Answer: True   Difficulty: Easy   Page: 412

20. Other things being equal, the rate of new-product development seems to be greater in countries where demand is strong, consumers are affluent, and competition is weak.

    Answer: False   Difficulty: Medium   Page: 415

Multiple Choice Questions

21. A _____ marketing strategy that views the world's consumers as similar in their tastes and preferences is consistent with the mass production of a standardized output.
    A) domestic
    B) global
    C) indigenous
    D) national

    Answer: B   Difficulty: Medium   Page: 392

22. A critical aspect of the _____ function is identifying gaps in the market so that new products can be developed to fill those gaps.
    A) materials management
    B) finance
    C) operations
    D) marketing

    Answer: D   Difficulty: Easy   Page: 393

23. Only _____ can tell R&D whether to produce globally standardized or locally customized products.
    A) finance
    B) materials management
    C) marketing
    D) operations

    Answer: C Difficulty: Medium Page: 393

24. Research has long maintained that a major factor of success for new products is the closeness of the relationship between:
    A) finance and marketing
    B) marketing and R&D
    C) finance and materials management
    D) operations and R&D

    Answer: B Difficulty: Hard Page: 393

25. The _____ is the set of choices the firm offers to its targeted market.
    A) production mix
    B) marketing mix
    C) products and services mix
    D) materials mix

    Answer: B Difficulty: Easy Page: 393

26. The marketing mix is the set of choices the firm offers to:
    A) its vendors
    B) its employees
    C) its targeted markets
    D) its external stakeholders

    Answer: C Difficulty: Easy Page: 393

27. The four elements that constitute a firm's marketing mix include:
    A) product attributes, distribution strategy, communication strategy, and pricing strategy
    B) transportation strategy, warehousing strategy, availability of financing, and pricing strategy
    C) promotions strategy, pricing strategy, availability of financing, and distribution strategy
    D) product attributes, promotions strategy, communication strategy, and transportation strategy

    Answer: A   Difficulty: Medium   Page: 393

28. The four elements that constitute a firm's marketing mix include product attributes, distribution strategy, communications strategy, and:
    A) pricing strategy
    B) warehousing strategy
    C) availability of financing
    D) advertising strategy

    Answer: A   Difficulty: Medium   Page: 393

29. A firm's marketing mix includes distribution strategy, communications strategy, pricing strategy, and _____.
    A) advertising strategy
    B) warehousing strategy
    C) availability of financing
    D) product attributes

    Answer: D   Difficulty: Medium   Page: 393

30. Levitt has argued that, due to the advent of modern communications and transport technology, consumer tastes and preferences are becoming _____, which is creating global markets for standardized consumer products.
    A) individualistic
    B) localized
    C) cross-regional
    D) global

    Answer: D   Difficulty: Easy   Page: 394

Chapter 12 Global Marketing and Product Development

31. In his 1983 Harvard Business Review article, Theodore Levitt argued that due to the advent of modern communications and transport technology, consumer tastes and preferences are becoming global, which is creating global markets for standardized consumer products. In regard to these arguments, the current consensus among academics seems to be that Levitt:
    A) was right on
    B) understated his case
    C) was way off
    D) overstated his case

    Answer: D Difficulty: Hard Page: 394

32. _____ refers to the process of identifying distinct groups of consumers whose purchasing behavior differs from others in important ways.
    A) Market segmentation
    B) Consumer differentiation
    C) Demographic profiling
    D) Customer analysis

    Answer: A Difficulty: Medium Page: 396

33. When managers in an international business consider market segmentation in foreign countries, they need to be aware of two main issues. These are:
    A) the differences between countries in the structure of marketing segments, and the existence of segments that transcend national borders
    B) the differences between countries in terms of tariff rates, and the differences between the countries in terms of exchange rates
    C) the differences between countries in terms of barriers to entry, and the differences between countries in terms of economic stability
    D) the differences between countries in terms of culture, and the differences between countries in terms of exchange rates

    Answer: A Difficulty: Hard Page: 396

34. A product can be viewed as a bundle of:
    A) attributes
    B) wants
    C) needs
    D) qualities

    Answer: A Difficulty: Medium Page: 397

35. According to the textbook, the most important aspect of a countries' cultural differences is the impact of:
    A) language
    B) tradition
    C) geographic location
    D) the availability of natural resources

    Answer: B   Difficulty: Hard   Page: 398

36. Across the world, consumer tastes and preferences are becoming more:
    A) ethnocentric
    B) parochial
    C) indigenous
    D) cosmopolitan

    Answer: D   Difficulty: Medium   Page: 398

37. Contrary to Levitt's suggestions, consumers in the most developed countries are often:
    A) willing to sacrifice their preferred attributes for lower prices
    B) willing to accept a global product if it is accepted by consumers in underdeveloped countries
    C) not willing to sacrifice their preferred attributes for lower prices
    D) willing to sacrifice their preferred attributes regardless of the impact on price

    Answer: C   Difficulty: Medium   Page: 398

38. A critical element of a firm's marketing mix is its _____ strategy, which is the means it chooses for delivering the product to the consumer.
    A) materials management
    B) communications
    C) logistics
    D) distribution

    Answer: D   Difficulty: Easy   Page: 399

39. In terms of their distribution strategies, countries differ along three main dimensions. These are:
    A) end-user identification, channel integration, and transportation strategy
    B) customer concentration, channel breadth, and warehousing strategy
    C) wholesale concentration, channel depth, and transportation strategy
    D) retail concentration, channel length, and channel exclusivity

    Answer: D   Difficulty: Medium   Page: 400

Chapter 12 Global Marketing and Product Development

40. The main differences between countries' distribution systems are threefold: retail concentration, channel length, and _____.
    A) transportation strategy
    B) channel exclusivity
    C) channel depth
    D) warehousing strategy

    Answer: B Difficulty: Medium Page: 400

41. The main differences between countries' distribution systems are threefold: channel length, channel exclusivity, and _____.
    A) retail concentration
    B) preferred mode of transportation
    C) warehousing strategy
    D) wholesale concentration

    Answer: A Difficulty: Medium Page: 400

42. The main differences between countries' distribution systems are threefold: channel exclusivity, retail concentration, and:
    A) channel length
    B) wholesale concentration
    C) preferred mode of transportation
    D) warehousing strategy

    Answer: A Difficulty: Medium Page: 400

43. In a _____ retail system, a few retailers supply most of the market.
    A) fragmented
    B) dispersed
    C) focused
    D) concentrated

    Answer: D Difficulty: Easy Page: 400

44. A _____ retail system is once in which there are many retailers, no one of which has a major share of the market.
    A) concentrated
    B) consolidated
    C) focused
    D) fragmented

    Answer: D Difficulty: Medium Page: 400

45. Most of the differences in the retail concentrations of different countries are rooted in:
    A) current events and trade status
    B) economic stature and religious beliefs
    C) history and tradition
    D) geographic location and language

    Answer: C Difficulty: Medium Page: 400

46. In terms of retail concentration, developed countries tend to have a higher degree of concentration than developing countries for all of the following reasons except:
    A) increases in car ownership
    B) a tradition of established local neighborhoods in which people walk to stores
    C) number of households with refrigerators and freezers
    D) number of two-income households that accompany development

    Answer: B Difficulty: Medium Page: 400

47. Channel _____ refers to the number of intermediaries between the product (or manufacturer) and the consumer.
    A) reach
    B) exclusivity
    C) length
    D) distance

    Answer: C Difficulty: Easy Page: 400

48. The number of intermediaries between the product (or manufacturer) and the consumer is referred to as:
    A) channel length
    B) channel distance
    C) channel exclusivity
    D) channel reach

    Answer: A Difficulty: Easy Page: 400

49. If the producer sells directly to the consumer, the channel is _____. If the producer sell through an import agent, a wholesaler, and a retailer, a _____ channel exists.
    A) short, intermediate
    B) long, very short
    C) intermediate, long
    D) short, long

    Answer: D Difficulty: Medium Page: 400

50. Which of the following countries is characterized by fragmented retail systems with long channels of distribution?
    A) Japan
    B) Germany
    C) United States
    D) France

    Answer: A Difficulty: Hard Page: 401

51. _____ is a country that is characterized by fragmented retail systems with long channels of distribution.
    A) Japan
    B) Great Britain
    C) Germany
    D) United States

    Answer: A Difficulty: Hard Page: 401

52. A choice of _____ strategy determines which channel the firm will use to reach potential consumers.
    A) distribution
    B) transportation
    C) communications
    D) operations

    Answer: A Difficulty: Easy Page: 402

Chapter 12 Global Marketing and Product Development

53. Direct selling, sales promotion, direct marketing, and advertising are all apart of a firm's _____ strategy.
    A) communications
    B) distribution
    C) product
    D) operations

    Answer: A Difficulty: Easy Page: 403

54. Direct selling, sales promotion, direct marketing, and _____ are all part of a firm's communications strategy.
    A) pricing
    B) reengineering
    C) warehousing
    D) advertising

    Answer: D Difficulty: Easy Page: 403

55. _____ communications occurs whenever a firm uses a marketing message to sell its products in another country.
    A) Diversified
    B) International
    C) Multi-domestic
    D) Functional

    Answer: B Difficulty: Easy Page: 403

56. The effectiveness of a firm's international communication can be jeopardized by three potentially critical variables. These are:
    A) technological barriers, geographic barriers, and political barriers
    B) economic factors, political-legal barriers, and noise levels
    C) technological factors, source effects, and noise levels
    D) cultural barriers, source effects, and noise levels

    Answer: D Difficulty: Medium Page: 403

57. The effectiveness of a firm's international communication can be jeopardized by three potentially critical variables. These are source effects, noise levels, and _____.
   A) cultural barriers
   B) technological factors
   C) geographic barriers
   D) political barriers

   Answer: A   Difficulty: Medium   Page: 403

58. Three potentially critical variables can jeopardize the effectiveness of a firm's international communications efforts. These are: cultural barriers, noise levels, and:
   A) geographic factors
   B) technological barriers
   C) political barriers
   D) source effects

   Answer: D   Difficulty: Medium   Page: 403

59. The best way for a firm to overcome cultural barriers is to:
   A) hire a large number of local managers
   B) develop cross-cultural literacy
   C) provide training in cultural awareness
   D) operate in markets culturally similar to its home market

   Answer: B   Difficulty: Medium   Page: 403

60. _____ occur when the receiver of the message (i.e. the potential customer) evaluates the message based on the status or image of the sender.
   A) Synergistic effects
   B) Temporal effects
   C) Source effects
   D) Direct effects

   Answer: C   Difficulty: Medium   Page: 403

Chapter 12 Global Marketing and Product Development

61. The types of effects that occurs when the receiver of a message (i.e. the potential customer) evaluates the message based on the status or image of the sender are referred to as:
    A) direct effects
    B) concentric effects
    C) temporal effects
    D) source effects

    Answer: D   Difficulty: Medium   Page: 403

62. In the context to barriers to international communication, _____ refer(s) to the number of other messages competing for a potential consumer's attention.
    A) alternative signals
    B) source effects
    C) noise
    D) channels effects

    Answer: C   Difficulty: Easy   Page: 404

63. In highly developed countries like the United States, noise from firms competing for the attention of target consumers is:
    A) extremely high
    B) extremely low
    C) moderate
    D) not a factor in communication

    Answer: A   Difficulty: Medium   Page: 404

64. The main decision with regard to communications strategy is the choice between a:
    A) external strategy and an internal strategy
    B) aggressive strategy and a conservative strategy
    C) noisy strategy and a quiet strategy
    D) push strategy and a pull strategy

    Answer: D   Difficulty: Medium   Page: 404

65. In regard to communication strategy, a _____ strategy emphasizes personal selling rather than mass media advertising in the promotional mix.
    A) reverse
    B) push
    C) forward
    D) pull

    Answer: B Difficulty: Easy Page: 404

66. In regard to communication strategy, which of the following strategies emphasizes personal selling rather than mass media advertising in the promotional mix?
    A) pull
    B) push
    C) forward
    D) reverse

    Answer: B Difficulty: Easy Page: 404

67. Which of the following communications strategies relies primarily on mass media advertising rather than personal selling?
    A) forward
    B) pull
    C) push
    D) reverse

    Answer: B Difficulty: Easy Page: 405

68. The three main factors that determine the relative attractiveness of push and pull strategies include:
    A) advertising cost, product type relative to consumer sophistication, and channel exclusivity
    B) geographic dispersion of buyers, channel length, and channel exclusivity
    C) product type relative to consumer sophistication, channel length, and media availability
    D) channel exclusivity, advertising cost, and cultural diversity of buyers

    Answer: C Difficulty: Medium Page: 405

Chapter 12 Global Marketing and Product Development

69. The three main factors that determine the relative attractiveness of push and pull strategies include channel length, media availability, and _____.
    A) channel exclusivity
    B) product type relative to consumer sophistication
    C) cultural diversity of buyers
    D) advertising costs

    Answer: B Difficulty: Medium Page: 405

70. According to the textbook, three factors that determine the relative attractiveness of push and pull strategies include product type relative to consumer sophistication, channel length, and _____.
    A) media availability
    B) channel exclusivity
    C) advertising costs
    D) cultural diversity of buyers

    Answer: A Difficulty: Medium Page: 405

71. A _____ strategy is generally favored by firms in consumer goods industries that are trying to sell to a large segment of the market.
    A) pull
    B) conditional
    C) reverse
    D) push

    Answer: A Difficulty: Medium Page: 405

72. A pull strategy is generally favored by:
    A) firms in durable goods industries that are trying to sell to a small segment of the markets
    B) firms in consumer goods industries that are typing to sell to a large segment of the market
    C) firms in commodities industries that are trying to sell to foreign governments
    D) firms in service industries that are typing to sell to a large segment of the market

    Answer: B Difficulty: Medium Page: 405

73. A push strategy is favored by firms that sell:
    A) services
    B) commodities
    C) consumer products or other standardized products
    D) industrial products or other complex products

    Answer: D Difficulty: Medium   Page: 405

74. A _____ strategy is favored by firms that sell industrial products or other complex products.
    A) push
    B) pull
    C) reverse
    D) disperse

    Answer: A Difficulty: Medium   Page: 405

75. In the context of communications strategy, push strategies tend to be emphasized:
    A) for industrial products and/or complex new products, when distribution channels are short, and when few print or electronic media are available
    B) for commodities, when distribution channels are short, and when international markets are attractive for the product
    C) for consumer goods, when distribution channels are long, and when sufficient print and electronic media are available to carry the marketing message
    D) for services, when distribution channels are long, and when international markets are attractive for the product

    Answer: C Difficulty: Medium   Page: 405

76. In the context of communications strategy, pull strategies tend to be emphasized:
    A) for commodities, when distribution channels are short, and when international markets are available for the product
    B) for consumer goods, when distribution channels are long, and when sufficient print and electronic media are available to carry the marketing message
    C) for services, when distribution channels are long, and when international markets are available for the product
    D) for industrial products and/or complex new products, when distribution channels are short, and when few print or electronic media are available

    Answer: B Difficulty: Medium   Page: 405

Chapter 12 Global Marketing and Product Development

77. Push strategies tend to be emphasized for industrial products and/or complex new products, when distribution channels are short, and when _____.
    A) few print or electronic media are available
    B) international markets are available for the product
    C) sufficient print and electronic media are available
    D) distribution channels are difficult to access

    Answer: A   Difficulty: Medium   Page: 405

78. Pull strategies tend to be emphasized for _____.
    A) commodities
    B) consumer goods
    C) industrial goods
    D) services

    Answer: B   Difficulty: Medium   Page: 405

79. Push strategies tend to be emphasized for _____.
    A) services
    B) industrial products and/or complex new products
    C) commodities
    D) consumer goods

    Answer: B   Difficulty: Medium   Page: 405

80. Which of the following is not a justification for global advertising?
    A) it has significant economic advantages
    B) because creative talent is scarce, one large effort to develop a campaign will produce better results than 40 or 50 smaller efforts
    C) many brands are global
    D) cultural differences among nations are such that a message that works in one nation can fail in another

    Answer: D   Difficulty: Easy   Page: 406

Chapter 12 Global Marketing and Product Development

81. There are two main arguments against global advertising. These are:
    A) many brands are global; country differences in advertising regulations may block implementation of global messages
    B) because creative talent is scarce, one large effort to develop a campaign will produce better results than 40 or 50 smaller efforts; it has significant economic advantages
    C) cultural differences among nations are such that a message that works in one nation can fail in another; country differences in advertising regulations may block implementation of global messages
    D) many brands are global; it has significant economic advantages

    Answer: C Difficulty: Medium Page: 406

82. In an international context, _____ exists whenever consumers in different countries are charged different prices for the same product.
    A) price discrimination
    B) global pricing
    C) predatory pricing
    D) standardized pricing

    Answer: A Difficulty: Medium Page: 408

83. If a consumer in Italy paid $45,000 for a BMW and a consumer in Great Britain paid $60,000 for the identical vehicle, that would be an example of:
    A) standardized pricing
    B) price discrimination
    C) global pricing
    D) predatory pricing

    Answer: B Difficulty: Medium Page: 408

84. Two conditions are necessary for profitable price discrimination. These are:
    A) the firm must sell a standardized product; and the firm must be able to keep its national markets separate
    B) the firm must be able to keep its national markets separate; and the existence of different price elasticities of demand in different countries must exist
    C) the firm must rely upon substantial economies of scale; and the firm cannot be a member of a major trade block
    D) the firm must sell highly differentiated products; and the existence of different prices elasticities of demand in different countries must exist

    Answer: B Difficulty: Hard Page: 408

85. Two conditions are necessary for profitable price discrimination: the firm must be able to keep its national markets separate and:
    A) the firm must be able to keep its national markets separate
    B) the firm must rely upon substantial economies of scale
    C) the firm must sell highly differentiated products
    D) the existence of different price elasticities of demand in different countries must exist

    Answer: D   Difficulty: Medium   Page: 408

86. According to the textbook, the elasticity of demand for a product in a given country is determined at least in part by the following two important factors:
    A) geographic location and economic stability
    B) currency rates and interest rates
    C) income level and competitive conditions
    D) tax rates and standard of living

    Answer: C   Difficulty: Hard   Page: 408

87. The use of price as a competitive weapon to drive weaker competitors out of a national market is called:
    A) pillaging pricing
    B) predatory pricing
    C) forward pricing
    D) noncompetitive pricing

    Answer: B   Difficulty: Medium   Page: 411

88. If a manufacturer of specialized medical equipment used price as a competitive weapon to drive competitors out of a national market, that would be an example of:
    A) predatory pricing
    B) pillage pricing
    C) reverse pricing
    D) forward pricing

    Answer: A   Difficulty: Medium   Page: 411

89. _____ pricing is the use of price as a competitive weapon to drive weaker competitors out of a national market.
    A) Synergy
    B) Pillaging
    C) Predatory
    D) Reverse

    Answer: C Difficulty: Medium Page: 411

90. In the context of strategic pricing, _____ occurs whenever a firm sells a product for a price that is less than the cost of producing it.
    A) insourcing
    B) dumping
    C) price reengineering
    D) outsourcing

    Answer: B Difficulty: Easy Page: 412

91. Selling a product for a price that is less than the cost of producing it is called:
    A) outsourcing
    B) reverse pricing
    C) price reengineering
    D) dumping

    Answer: D Difficulty: Easy Page: 412

92. If a Japanese steel manufacture sold steel in the U.S. for a price that was less than the cost of producing the steel, that would be an example of _____.
    A) reverse pricing
    B) dumping
    C) outsourcing
    D) price reengineering

    Answer: B Difficulty: Medium Page: 412

Chapter 12 Global Marketing and Product Development

93. A country is allowed to bring antidumping actions against an importer under Article 6 of GATT as long as two criteria are met. These are:
    A) sales are made at less than fair market value; and when material injury is done to a domestic industry
    B) the importer is not participant in the GATT Agreement; and when no advance notice of the dumping action was provided
    C) when material injury is done to a domestic industry; and the alleged dumping has taken place for more then six months
    D) sales are made at less than fair market value; and the importer is a participant in the GATT Agreement

    Answer: A   Difficulty: Hard   Page: 412

94. Under Article 6 of the GATT Agreement, a country is allowed to bring antidumping actions against an importer as long as two criteria are met: sales are made at less than fair market value and when _____.
    A) the importer is a participant in the GATT Agreement
    B) the alleged dumping has taken place for more than 6 months
    C) material injury is done to a domestic industry
    D) the importer is not a participant in the GATT Agreement

    Answer: C   Difficulty: Medium   Page: 412

95. Under Article 6 of the GATT Agreement, a country is allowed to bring antidumping charges against an importer as long as two criteria are met: material injury is done to a domestic industry and when _____.
    A) the importer is not a participant in the GATT Agreement
    B) the alleged dumping has taken place for more than 60 days
    C) sales are made at less than fair market value
    D) the importer is a participant in the GATT Agreement

    Answer: C   Difficulty: Medium   Page: 412

96. Learning effects and economies of scale underlie the:
    A) experience curve
    B) tactical range
    C) strategic trajectory
    D) operational plane

    Answer: A   Difficulty: Medium   Page: 412

97. Which of the following is not a characteristic of countries where new-product development is strong?
    A) competition is intense
    B) demand is weak
    C) consumers are affluent
    D) more money is spent on basic and applied research and development than in countries where new-product development is weak

    Answer: B   Difficulty: Medium   Page: 415

98. Countries where new-product development is strong have all of the following characteristics except:
    A) competition is weak
    B) more money is spent on basic and applied research and development than in countries where new-product development is weak
    C) consumers are affluent
    D) demand is strong

    Answer: A   Difficulty: Medium   Page: 415

99. Countries where new-product development is strong have all of the following characteristics except:
    A) consumers are poor
    B) competition is intense
    C) demand is strong
    D) more money is spent on basic and applied research and development than in countries where new-product development is weak

    Answer: A   Difficulty: Medium   Page: 415

100. One study cited in the textbook of product development in 16 companies in the chemical, drug, petroleum, and electronics industries suggested that only about _____ of R&D projects ultimately result in commercially successful products or processes.
    A) 10 percent
    B) 20 percent
    C) 30 percent
    D) 40 percent

    Answer: B   Difficulty: Hard   Page: 416

Chapter 12 Global Marketing and Product Development

101. Which of the following is not an objective of tight cross-functional integration between R&D, production, and marketing?
    A) product development projects are driven by internal needs
    B) new products are designed for ease of manufacturer
    C) development costs are kept in check
    D) time to market in minimized

    Answer: A Difficulty: Hard Page: 417

102. Close integration by R&D and _____ is required to ensure that product development projects are driven by the needs of customers.
    A) marketing
    B) human resources management
    C) production
    D) materials management

    Answer: A Difficulty: Medium Page: 417

103. Basic research centers have all of the following characteristics except:
    A) fundamental research is conducted
    B) are typically located in remote locations apart from conventional research talent
    C) are the innovative engines of the firm
    D) attempt to develop the basic technologies that become new products

    Answer: C Difficulty: Medium Page: 419

104. Centers for fundamental research located in regions or cities where valuable scientific knowledge is being created, and where there is a pool of skilled research talent, are referred to as:
    A) applied research centers
    B) commercial research centers
    C) multidisciplinary research centers
    D) basic research centers

    Answer: D Difficulty: Medium Page: 419

105. _____ are the innovation engines of the firm.
    A) Basic research centers
    B) Applied commercialization centers
    C) Strategic development centers
    D) Tactical progress centers

    Answer: A Difficulty: Medium Page: 419

Chapter 12 Global Marketing and Product Development

Essay Questions

106. Describe what is meant by the term "marketing mix." What factors cause a firm to vary its marketing mix across markets?

Difficulty: Easy   Page: 393

Answer:
Marketing mix is a term that describes the set of choices that a firm offers to its customers. The four elements that constitute a firm's marketing mix are product attributes, distribution strategy, communication strategy, and pricing strategy. Many international businesses vary their marketing mix from country to country to take into account local differences. The potential differences between countries cover a wide range of factors, including culture, economic conditions, competitive conditions, product and technical standards, distribution systems, government regulations, and the like. According to the author of the textbook, as a result of the cumulative effects of these differences, it is rare to find a firm operating in an industry where it can adopt the same marketing mix worldwide.

107. What are the factors that influence a firm's ability to sell the same product worldwide? Ideally, is it better for a firm to sell the same product worldwide or would a firm rather customize its products for each individual market?

Difficulty: Medium   Page: 398

Answer:
The three main factors that limit the ability of a firm to sell the same product to all of overseas markets are cultural differences across markets, economic differences across markets, and product and technical standards that differ from country to country.

Cultural Differences Across Markets: In regard to cultural differences across markets, countries vary along a wide range of dimensions. These dimensions include social structure, language, religion, tradition, education, physical stature, and forms of recreation. As a result, consumers in different countries have different tastes and preferences. For example, Japanese people tend to be smaller in stature than Americans. Consequently, American apparel manufacturers must be sensitivity to that when exporting clothing products to Japan. On the other hand, there is some evidence that tastes are converging worldwide, on a number of levels. For instance, Coca-Cola is a near global product, and its taste varies little worldwide. McDonalds Hamburgers are very similar worldwide, as are Levi Jeans and other apparel products. These examples, however, are the exception rather than the rule. In general, cultural differences across markets make it difficult to sell the same product worldwide.

Chapter 12 Global Marketing and Product Development

Economic Differences Across Markets: Just as important as differences in culture are differences in the level of economic development across markets. Firms based in highly developed countries such as the U.S. tend to build a lot of extra performance attributes into their products because their customers want them. Conversely, consumers in developing countries (who have much less buying power) are typically content with much plainer products. This factor makes it difficult to sell the same product worldwide.

Product and Technical Standards Differences Across Markets: Differing product standards mandated by governments can rule out mass production and marketing of a standardized product in many settings. For instance, many appliance that are made for North American consumers cannot be plugged into the wall and run in Europe because of differing voltage requirements. Hundreds of these types of examples exist, which require exporters to customize their products to be suitable for individual foreign markets.

Whether firms prefer product standardization or customization is a difficult question. It is easy to quickly jump to the conclusion that a standardized product would be preferable, because it lends itself to economies of scale across the marketing mix. However, products that must be customized for individual markets have the benefit of representing a "best fit" between the consumer and the product. This may enable a firm to charge a higher price, and recapture some of the economies of scale advantages of a standardized product.

108. How do economic differences between countries affect the important of different product attributes?

Difficulty: Medium   Page: 398

Answer:
As a general rule, consumer behavior is influenced by the level of economic development of a country. Firms based in highly developed countries tend to build a lot of extra performance attributes into their products. Consumers in less developed nations do not usually demand these extra attributes, where the preference is for more stripped down products. In fact, consumers in the most advanced counties often do not want globally standardized products that have been developed with the lowest common denominator in mind. Consumers in these countries are prepared to pay more for products that have added features and whose attributes are customized to their own tastes and preferences.

Chapter 12 Global Marketing and Product Development

109. Explain what is meant by distribution strategy. What are the main differences among countries' distribution systems? Ultimately, how does a firm determine its distribution strategy in individual foreign markets?

Difficulty: Medium   Page: 399

Answer:
A firm's distribution strategy is the way that it gets it product in the hands of consumers. Wholesale, retail, and direct sales are examples of distribution strategies. An international firm's distribution strategy is limited by the nature of the distribution systems that are available in its host countries. The main differences among countries' distribution systems are threefold: retail concentration, channel length, and channel exclusivity. Retail concentration refers to the number of retailers that supply a particular market. In some countries the retail system is very concentrated, and in other countries it is very fragmented. In a concentrated system, a few retailers supply most of the market. In a fragmented system, no one retailer has a major market share. In Germany, for example, four retail chains control 65 percent of the market for food products. This is an example of a very concentrated system. Channel length refers to the number of intermediaries between the producer and the consumer. If the producer sells directly to the consumer, the channel is very short. If the producer sells through several agents and wholesalers, the channel is very long. The most important determinant of channel length is the degree to which the retail system is fragmented. Fragmented retail systems tend to promote the growth of wholesales to serve retailers, which lengthens channels. Finally, channel exclusivity refers to how difficult the channel is to penetrate. For example, it is often difficult for a new firm to get access to shelf space in U.S. grocery stores because retailers tend to prefer to carry the products of long-established manufacturers like Procter & Gamble and General Mills. Channel exclusivity is very high in Japan, which makes the Japanese market so difficult to penetrate effectively. In Japan, relationships between manufacturers, wholesalers, and retailers often go back decades. Many of these relationships are based on the understanding that distributors will not carry the products of competing firms.

Ultimately, a firm's choice of distribution strategy in its international markets is influenced by which channels are available (i.e. channel exclusivity may eliminate some choices) and by the relative costs and benefits of each remaining alternative. The relative costs of each remaining alternative are affected by the three factors discussed above. For instance, if a food products company entered a foreign market that has very long, exclusive channels (which is often the case when the market if fragmented), selling to wholesalers might make the most economic sense. It would be difficult (if not impossible) for the importer to obtain shelf space in local supermarkets without the help of local wholesalers. Conversely, if the channels were short (which is often the case in highly concentrated markets), the importer may be able to sell directly to the retailer.

Chapter 12 Global Marketing and Product Development

110. Describe the concept of channel length? How does a firm determine its channel length?

Difficulty: Medium   Page: 400

Answer:
Channel length refers to the number of intermediaries between the producer (or manufacturer) and the consumer. If the producer sells directly to the consumer, the channel is very short. If the producer sells through an import agent, a wholesaler, and a retailer, the channel is long. The choice of a short or long channel is primarily a strategic decision for the producing firm. However, some countries have longer distribution channels than others. The most important determinant of channel length is the degree to which the retail system is fragmented. Fragmented retail systems tend to promote the growth of wholesalers to serve retailers, which lengthens channels.

111. In regard to communication strategy, what is the difference between a push versus a pull strategy? Provide an example of an appropriate application of a push strategy and an example of an appropriate application of a pull strategy.

Difficulty: Medium   Page: 404

Answer:
The main decision with regard to communications strategy is the choice between a push and a pull strategy. A push strategy emphasizes personal selling rather than mass media advertising in the promotional mix. A pull strategy depends more on mass media advertising to communicate the marketing message to potential customers.

A push strategy is favored by firms that sell industrial products or other complex products. One of the strengths of direct selling is that it allows the firm to educate potential customers about the features of the product. Push strategies also tend to be emphasized (somewhat by default) when distribution channels are short and when few print or electronic media are available. An example of when a push strategy would be appropriate is a machine tool company that is selling a new manufacturing robotics product. The direct selling nature of the push strategy would provide the firm a forum to educate their potential customers relative to the merits of the new product.

A pull strategy is generally favored by firms in consumer goods industries that are trying to sell to a large segment of the market. For such firms, mass communication has cost advantages, and direct selling is rarely used. Pull strategies are also used when distribution channels are long. In most cases, using direct selling to push a product through many layers of a distribution channel would be impractical. As a result, a pull strategy, which makes use of print or electronic media to get its message across, is much more practical. An example of when a pull strategy would be appropriate is a soft drink company marketing its product in a new country that has fairly long distribution channels but sufficient media available.

112. In the context of international communication, describe the concept of "noise." Is the noise level higher in developed or developing countries? Why?

Difficulty: Medium   Page: 404

Answer:
Noise tends to reduce the probability of effective communication. Noise refers to the amount of other messages competing for a potential consumer's attention, and this too varies across countries. In highly developed countries such as the U.S., noise is extremely high. Fewer firms vie for the attention of prospective customers in developing countries, and the noise level is lower.

113. Discuss the concept of predatory pricing. Is predatory pricing ethical? What, if anything, should governments do to limit the influence predatory pricing by importers on domestic industries? Explain your answer.

Difficulty: Medium   Page: 411

Answer:
This question is designed to stimulate classroom discussion and/or encourage students to "think" about the ethics of predatory pricing. Predatory pricing is the use of price as a competitive weapon to drive weaker competitors out of a national market. Once the competitors have left the market, the firm can raise prices and enjoy high profits. For such a pricing strategy to work, the firm must normally have a profitable position in another national market, which it can use to subsidize aggressive pricing in the market it is trying to monopolize. Many Japanese firms have been accused of pursuing this strategy, along with firms from other countries.

Predatory pricing can run afoul of antidumping regulations. Technically, dumping occurs when a firm sells a product for a price that is less than the cost of producing it. Dumping can result in retaliatory tariffs. For instance, in 1988 the Busch administration placed a 25 percent duty on the imports of Japanese light trucks into the U.S. Should other measures be used to protect domestic industries from predatory pricing by foreign importers. This question may provide an interesting forum for classroom discussion.

Chapter 13 Global Operations Management

True/False Questions

1. Materials management is the activity that controls the transmission of physical materials through the value chain, from procurement through production and into distribution.

   Answer: True   Difficulty: Easy   Page: 429

2. Two important objectives shared by manufacturing and materials management are to lower costs and to simultaneously increase product quality.

   Answer: True   Difficulty: Medium   Page: 429

3. The main management technique that companies are using to boost their product quality is called reengineering.

   Answer: False   Difficulty: Medium   Page: 429

4. A standard designed to assure the quality of products and processes is referred to as ISO 9000.

   Answer: True   Difficulty: Easy   Page: 430

5. ISO 9000 is an Asian quality certification process.

   Answer: False   Difficulty: Medium   Page: 430

6. Political economy, culture, and relative factors costs are similar across the countries of the world.

   Answer: False   Difficulty: Easy   Page: 431

7. The concept of economies of scale tells us that as plant output expands, unit costs increase.

   Answer: False   Difficulty: Easy   Page: 432

8. Flexible manufacturing technologies allow a company to produce a wider variety of end products at a unit cost that at one time could be achieved only through the mass production of a standardized output.

   Answer: True   Difficulty: Medium   Page: 432

9. Flexible manufacturing technologies are unique in their ability to help companies produce highly standardized products for a global clientele.

   Answer: False   Difficulty: Medium   Page: 432

10. A product with a high value-to-weight ratio is expensive and does not weigh very much.

    Answer: True   Difficulty: Easy   Page: 434

11. The arguments for concentrating production at a few choice locations are strong when fixed costs are substantial, the minimum efficient scale of production is high, and flexible manufacturing technologies are not available.

    Answer: False   Difficulty: Hard   Page: 435

12. The arguments for concentrating production at one or a few locations are not as compelling when fix costs are low, the minimum efficient scale of production is low, and flexible manufacturing technologies are not available.

    Answer: True   Difficulty: Hard   Page: 435

13. Needs that are the same all over the world are called global needs.

    Answer: False   Difficulty: Easy   Page: 435

14. Concentrating a firm's manufacturing facilities in an optimal location and serving the world market from that single location makes sense when trade barriers are low.

    Answer: True   Difficulty: Medium   Page: 435

15. Decentralizing a firm's manufacturing facilities in various regional or national markets that are close to major markets makes sense when the product's value-to-weight ratio is high.

    Answer: False   Difficulty: Medium   Page: 435

16. The decision about whether a firm should make or buy the component parts that go into the final product is referred to as a sourcing decision.

    Answer: True   Difficulty: Easy   Page: 440

17. A piece of equipment that can be used for only one purpose is referred to as a universal asset.

    Answer: False   Difficulty: Easy   Page: 442

18. Proprietary product technology is technology unique to a firm.

    Answer: True   Difficulty: Easy   Page: 442

19. The greatest advantage of buying component parts from independent suppliers is that the firm can maintain its flexibility.

    Answer: True   Difficulty: Medium   Page: 443

20. The benefits of manufacturing components in-house seem to be greatest when highly specialized assets are involved, when vertical integration is necessary for protecting proprietary technology, or when the firm is simply more efficient than external suppliers at performing a particular activity.

    Answer: True   Difficulty: Hard   Page: 444

Multiple Choice Questions

21. The process of creating a product is called _____.
    A) bureaucracy
    B) materials management
    C) production
    D) administration

    Answer: C   Difficulty: Easy   Page: 429

22. _____ is the activity that controls the transportation of physical materials through the value chain, from procurement through production and into distribution.
    A) Operations
    B) Production
    C) Materials management
    D) Bureaucracy

    Answer: C   Difficulty: Easy   Page: 429

Chapter 13 Global Operations Management

23. The activity that controls the transportation of physical materials through the value chain, from procurement through production and into distribution is called:
    A) bureaucratic management
    B) transportation management
    C) materials management
    D) conveyance management

    Answer: C   Difficulty: Easy   Page: 429

24. Materials management includes _____, which refers to the procurement and physical transmission of material through the supply chain, from suppliers to consumers.
    A) interchange
    B) logistics
    C) reciprocation
    D) conveyance

    Answer: B   Difficulty: Easy   Page: 429

25. The procurement and physical transmission of material through the supply chain, from suppliers to customers, is referred to as:
    A) logistics
    B) conveyance
    C) interchange
    D) reciprocation

    Answer: A   Difficulty: Easy   Page: 429

26. Two important objectives shared by both manufacturing and materials management are to simultaneously:
    A) increase quality and increase revenues
    B) increase product awareness and lower costs
    C) lower costs and increase quality
    D) increase revenues and decrease customer complaints

    Answer: C   Difficulty: Medium   Page: 429

27. Two important objectives shared by both manufacturing and materials management are to simultaneously lower costs and:
    A) decrease customer complaints
    B) increase product awareness
    C) increase revenues
    D) increase quality

    Answer: D Difficulty: Medium Page: 429

28. Which of the following is not a result of improved quality control?
    A) greater product quality means lower warranty costs
    B) increased product quality means lower scrap costs
    C) increased product quality means higher rework
    D) productivity increases because time is not wasted manufacturing poor-quality products that cannot be sold

    Answer: C Difficulty: Medium Page: 429

29. The main management technique that companies are utilizing to boost their product quality is:
    A) total qualify management
    B) materials management
    C) reengineering
    D) logistics

    Answer: A Difficulty: Easy Page: 429

30. _____ is the main management technique that companies are utilizing to boost their product quality.
    A) Total feature management
    B) Logistics
    C) Total quality management
    D) Materials management

    Answer: C Difficulty: Easy Page: 429

Chapter 13 Global Operations Management

31. Saving time by not producing poor quality products that cannot be sold, lowering rework costs, lowering scrap costs, and lowering warranty costs are the intended results of:
    A) total feature management
    B) reengineering
    C) logistics
    D) total quality management

    Answer: D   Difficulty: Medium   Page: 429

32. The TQM concept was developed by a number of American consultants such as:
    A) Martin Wolf, R.B. Weber, and Raymond Vernon
    B) W. Edwards Deming, Joseph Juran, and A.V. Feigenbaum
    C) J.H. Dunning, M. McQueen, and Michael Porter
    D) Paul Krugman, Raymond Vernon, and Michael Porter

    Answer: B   Difficulty: Easy   Page: 429

33. In Europe, the European Union requires that the quality of a firm's manufacturing processes and products be certified under a quality standard known as _____ before the firm is allowed access to the European marketplace.
    A) total quality management
    B) reengineering
    C) BT 12000
    D) ISO 9000

    Answer: D   Difficulty: Easy   Page: 430

34. ISO 9000 is a standard designed to assure the quality of products and products entering the:
    A) North American Free Trade Agreement marketplace
    B) Andean Group marketplace
    C) European Union marketplace
    D) MERCOSUR marketplace

    Answer: C   Difficulty: Medium   Page: 430

35. The key decision factors that pertain to where an international firm locates its manufacturing facilities can be grouped under three broad headings. These are:
    A) political factors, economic factors, and legal factors
    B) country factors, technological factors, and product factors
    C) product factors, service factors, and labor factors
    D) language factors, cultural factors, and transportation factors

    Answer: B Difficulty: Medium Page: 431

36. The key decision factors that pertain to where an international firm locates its manufacturing facilities can be grouped under three broad headings. These are country factors, technological factors, and _____ factors.
    A) labor
    B) product
    C) economic
    D) political

    Answer: B Difficulty: Medium Page: 431

37. Country factors, product factors, and _____ factors are the broad headings that contain the key decision factors that pertain to where an international firm locates its manufacturing facilities.
    A) labor
    B) economic
    C) technological
    D) political

    Answer: C Difficulty: Medium Page: 431

38. Technological factors, product factors, and _____ factors are the broad headings that contain the key decision factors that pertain to where an international firm locates its manufacturing facilities.
    A) political
    B) country
    C) economic
    D) legal

    Answer: B Difficulty: Medium Page: 431

39. Three characteristics of a manufacturing technology that are particularly interesting to international firms when making manufacturing location decisions are: (1) the level of its fixed costs, (2) its minimum efficient scale, and (3)
    A) its flexibility
    B) its variable costs
    C) the technological sophistication of the manufacturing process
    D) the cost of moving manufacturing executives overseas

    Answer: A Difficulty: Medium Page: 431

40. Three characteristics of a manufacturing technology that are particularly interesting to international firms when making manufacturing location decisions are: (1) the level of its fixed costs, (2) its flexibility, and (3)
    A) the cost of moving manufacturing executives overseas
    B) its minimum efficient scale
    C) its variable costs
    D) the technological sophistication of the manufacturing process

    Answer: B Difficulty: Medium Page: 431

41. In some cases the _____ costs of setting up a manufacturing plant are so high that a firm must serve the world market from a single location or from a very few locations.
    A) changeable
    B) reoccurring
    C) fixed
    D) variable

    Answer: C Difficulty: Easy Page: 431

42. The concept of economies of scale tells us that as plant output expands unit costs _____.
    A) increase
    B) decrease
    C) remain the same
    D) expand exponentially

    Answer: B Difficulty: Easy Page: 432

43. The concept of _____ tells us that as plant output expands unit costs decrease.
    A) economies of production
    B) cost relativity
    C) cost economies
    D) economies of scale

    Answer: D Difficulty: Medium Page: 432

44. The _____ declines with output until a certain output level is reached; at which point further increases in output realize little reduction in unit costs.
    A) component expense curve
    B) unit expense line
    C) unit cost curve
    D) component cost slope

    Answer: C Difficulty: Hard Page: 432

45. Manufacturing technologies designed to reduce setup times, increase use of individual machines through better scheduling, and improve quality control at all stages of manufacturing is called:
    A) multifaceted production
    B) lean production
    C) lateral production
    D) temporal production

    Answer: B Difficulty: Medium Page: 432

46. _____ is a manufacturing technology designed to reduce setup times, increase use of individual machines through better scheduling, and improve quality control at all stages of manufacturing.
    A) Lean production
    B) Lateral production
    C) Temporal production
    D) Multifaceted production

    Answer: A Difficulty: Easy Page: 432

47. According to the textbook, _____ manufacturing technologies provide a company the ability to produce a wider variety of end products at a unit cost that at one time could be achieved only through the mass production of a standardized output.
    A) multifaceted
    B) lateral
    C) side by side
    D) flexible

    Answer: D   Difficulty: Medium   Page: 432

48. Recent research suggests that the adoption of _____ manufacturing technologies may actually increase efficiency and lower unit costs relative to what can be achieved by the mass production of a standardized output.
    A) lateral
    B) flexible
    C) multifaceted
    D) side by side

    Answer: B   Difficulty: Medium   Page: 432

49. All of the following are advantages of flexible manufacturing except:
    A) improved efficiency
    B) flexible manufacturing technologies allow companies to customize products to suite the unique demands of small consumer groups
    C) increase customer responsiveness
    D) flexible manufacturing technologies help firms standardize products for different national markets

    Answer: D   Difficulty: Medium   Page: 432

50. Which of the following is not one of the objectives of flexible manufacturing technology, or lean production?
    A) reduce setup times for complex equipment
    B) bring a factory into compliance with ISO 9000
    C) improve quality control at all stages of the manufacturing process
    D) increase utilization of individual machines through scheduling

    Answer: B   Difficulty: Medium   Page: 432

51. The term _____ refers to the ability to produce a wider variety of end products at a unit cost that at one time could be achieved only through the mass production of a standardized output.
    A) assembly-line like customization
    B) standardized customization
    C) mass customization
    D) economies of customization

    Answer: C Difficulty: Medium Page: 432

52. _____ implies that a firm may be able to customize its product range to suit the needs of different customer groups without bearing a cost penalty.
    A) Assembly-like customization
    B) Standardized customization
    C) Economic customization
    D) Mass customization

    Answer: D Difficulty: Hard Page: 432

53. Research suggests that the adoption of _____ manufacturing technologies may increase efficiency and lower unit costs relative to what can be achieved by the mass production of standardized output.
    A) flexible
    B) elastic
    C) rigid
    D) malleable

    Answer: A Difficulty: Medium Page: 432

54. A _____ is a grouping of various types of machinery, a common materials handler, and a centralized cell controller.
    A) malleable manufacturing unit
    B) elastic manufacturing station
    C) rigid machine unit
    D) flexible machine cell

    Answer: D Difficulty: Medium Page: 433

Chapter 13 Global Operations Management

55. In terms of making a location decision, when fixed costs are substantial, the minimum efficient scale of production is high, and flexible manufacturing technologies are available, it makes sense to:
   A) manufacture the product in every country in which it is sold
   B) concentrate production at a few choice locations
   C) spread production over as many locations as possible
   D) outsource production to a third party

   Answer: B Difficulty: Medium Page: 434

56. In terms of making a manufacturing decision, when fixed costs are low, the minimum efficient scale of production is low, and flexible manufacturing technologies are not available, it makes sense to:
   A) concentrate production at a few choice locations
   B) outsource production to a third party
   C) manufacture in each major market in which the firm is active
   D) manufacture the product in every country in which it is sold

   Answer: C Difficulty: Medium Page: 434

57. The arguments for concentrating production at one or a few locations are not compelling when:
   A) fixed costs are low, the minimum efficient scale of production is low, and flexible manufacturing technologies are not available
   B) fixed costs are high, the minimum efficient scale of production is high, and flexible manufacturing technologies are available
   C) fixed costs are low, the minimum efficient scale of production is high, and flexible manufacturing technologies are not available
   D) fixed costs are moderate, the minimum efficient scale of production is high, and flexible manufacturing technologies are available

   Answer: A Difficulty: Hard Page: 434

58. Two product factors impact location decisions. These are:
   A) the product's value-to-weight ratio and whether the product serves universal needs
   B) the product's shape and the product's weight
   C) the product's content and the product's point-of-origin
   D) the product's technological sophistication and the product's shape

   Answer: A Difficulty: Medium Page: 434

Chapter 13 Global Operations Management

59. Two product factors impact location decisions. These are (1) the product's value-to-weight ratio and (2)
    A) the product's technological sophistication
    B) whether the product serves universal needs
    C) the product's weight
    D) the product's shape

    Answer: B Difficulty: Medium   Page: 434

60. Two product factors impact location decisions. These are (1) whether the product serves universal needs and (2)
    A) the product's shape
    B) the product's point-of-origin
    C) the product's weight
    D) the product's value-to-weight ratio

    Answer: D Difficulty: Medium   Page: 434

61. Needs that are the same all over the world are referred to as _____ needs.
    A) specific
    B) domestic
    C) universal
    D) individualistic

    Answer: C Difficulty: Easy   Page: 435

62. _____ needs are the same all over the world.
    A) Precise
    B) Individualistic
    C) Domestic
    D) Universal

    Answer: D Difficulty: Easy   Page: 435

Chapter 13 Global Operations Management

63. Which of the following two factors correctly depict the manufacturing attributes of a product that has universal needs?
    A) since there are few national differences in consumer taste and preferences for such products, the need for local responsiveness is reduced, manufacturing should be concentrated at an optimal location
    B) since there are many national differences in consumer taste and preferences for such products, the need for local responsiveness is reduced, manufacturing should be concentrated at an optimal location
    C) since there are few national differences in consumer taste and preferences for such products, the need for local responsiveness is increased, manufacturing should take place in each major market in which the firm is active
    D) since there are many national differences in consumer taste and preferences for such products, the need for local responsiveness is increased, manufacturing should take place in each major market in which the firm is active

    Answer: A   Difficulty: Hard   Page: 435

64. The most attractive manufacturing strategy for producing universal needs is to:
    A) manufacture the product in each major market in which the firm is active
    B) manufacture the product in at least one location on each continent in which the product is sold
    C) concentrate manufacturing at an optimal location
    D) concentrate manufacturing in a market that is part of a major trade block

    Answer: C   Difficulty: Medium   Page: 435

65. There are two basic strategies for locating manufacturing facilities. These are:
    A) concentrating them in the optimal location and serve the world market from there and, concentrate them in markets that are parts of major trade blocks
    B) locate at least one manufacturing facility in each continent in which the firm is active and, concentrate manufacturing at an optimal location
    C) concentrate them in the optimal location and serve the world market from there and, decentralizing them in various regional or national locations that are close to major markets
    D) concentrate them in markets that are part of major trade blocks and, centralizing them at a single location

    Answer: C   Difficulty: Medium   Page: 435

66. There are two basic strategies for locating manufacturing facilities. These are: (1) concentrating them in the optimal location and serving the world from there, and (2)
    A) concentrate them in markets that are part of major trade blocks
    B) decentralizing them in various regional or national locations that are close to major markets
    C) centralizing them to a single location
    D) locate at least one manufacturing facility in each continent in which the firm is active

    Answer: B Difficulty: Medium Page: 435

67. Concentration of manufacturing makes sense when:
    A) trade barriers are high
    B) the product's value-to-weight ratio is high
    C) the product's value-to-weight ratio is low
    D) the product does not serve universal needs

    Answer: B Difficulty: Hard Page: 435

68. Placing manufacturing facilities in one concentrated location makes sense for all of the following reasons except:
    A) trade barriers are high
    B) the product serves universal needs
    C) important exchange rates are expected to remain relatively stable
    D) the production technology has high fixed costs or a high minimum efficient scale or a flexible manufacturing technology exists.

    Answer: A Difficulty: Hard Page: 435

69. Placing manufacturing facilities in one concentrated location makes sense for all of the following reasons except:
    A) the product serves universal needs
    B) trade barriers are low
    C) important exchange rates are expected to be volatile
    D) differences in factor costs, political economy, and culture have a substantial impact on the costs of manufacturing in various countries

    Answer: C Difficulty: Hard Page: 435

70. Decentralization of the location of a firm's manufacturing locations makes sense for all of the following reasons except:
    A) trade barriers are low
    B) volatility in important exchange rates is expected
    C) the production technology has low fixed costs, low minimum efficient scale or a flexible manufacturing technology exists
    D) the product does not serve universal needs

    Answer: A   Difficulty: Hard   Page: 435

71. Decentralization of a firm's manufacturing locations makes sense for all of the following reasons except:
    A) trade barriers are high
    B) the product's value-to-weight ratio is high
    C) the production technology has low fixed costs
    D) the product serves universal needs

    Answer: B   Difficulty: Hard   Page: 435

72. Decentralization of manufacturing is appropriate when:
    A) the product serves universal needs
    B) important exchange rates are expected to remain relatively stable
    C) the product's value-to-weight ratio is high
    D) trade barriers are high

    Answer: D   Difficulty: Hard   Page: 435

73. Initially, many foreign factories are established where:
    A) labor costs are high
    B) labor costs are low
    C) labor costs are on par with the manufacturer's typical costs
    D) labor intensive manufacturing is the exception rather than the norm

    Answer: B   Difficulty: Easy   Page: 438

74. The strategic role of foreign factories is typically to:
    A) produce labor-intensive products at as low a cost as possible
    B) appease foreign governments by producing jobs in their countries
    C) increase product quality
    D) provide domestically managers foreign experience

    Answer: A   Difficulty: Medium   Page: 438

75. Decisions about whether a firm should make or buy the component parts that go into the final product are called _____ decisions.
    A) end-user
    B) synergistic
    C) sourcing
    D) feedforward

    Answer: C Difficulty: Easy Page: 440

76. International businesses frequently face _____ decisions, which are decisions about whether they should make or buy the component parts that go into their finished products.
    A) inception
    B) conception
    C) originating
    D) sourcing

    Answer: D Difficulty: Easy Page: 440

77. The arguments that support making component parts in-house (i.e. vertical integration) are fourfold:
    A) lower costs, facilitates investments in highly specialized assets, protects proprietary product technology and, facilitates the scheduling of adjacent processes
    B) greater flexibility, helps a firm capture orders from international customers, facilitates investments in highly standardized assets and, facilitates the scheduling of adjacent processes
    C) helps a firm capture orders from international customers, lower costs, facilitates investments in highly standardized assets and, facilitates the scheduling of adjacent processes
    D) lower costs, greater flexibility, facilitates the scheduling of adjacent customers and, facilitates investments in highly specialized assets

    Answer: A Difficulty: Hard Page: 440

78. The arguments that support vertical integration include: lower costs, facilitates investments in highly specialized assets, protects proprietary technology and:
    A) helps the firm capture orders from international customers
    B) facilitates the scheduling of adjacent processes
    C) greater flexibility
    D) facilitates investment in highly standardized assets

    Answer: B Difficulty: Medium Page: 440

Chapter 13 Global Operations Management

79. The arguments that support vertical integration include: facilitates investments in highly specialized assets, protects proprietary product technology, facilitates the scheduling of adjacent processes, and:
    A) lowers costs
    B) helps the firm capture orders from international customers
    C) greater flexibility
    D) simpler tax accounting

    Answer: A Difficulty: Medium Page: 440

80. In general, when substantial investments in specialized assets are required to manufacture a component, a firm will:
    A) prefer to make the component internally rather than contract it out to a supplier
    B) find a alternative method of manufacturing the component
    C) contract out the production of the component rather than make it internally
    D) discontinue making the product that the component goes into

    Answer: A Difficulty: Medium Page: 441

81. Proprietary product technology is technology that is:
    A) widely shared among firms
    B) unique to a country
    C) unique to the firm
    D) unique to a particular industry

    Answer: C Difficulty: Medium Page: 442

82. The advantages of buying component parts from independent suppliers are that it gives the firm the following advantages:
    A) it may help the firm to capture orders from international customers, facilitates the scheduling of adjacent processes and, greater flexibility
    B) greater flexibility, facilitates the scheduling of adjacent processes and, protects proprietary production technology
    C) facilitates investments in highly specialized assets, protects proprietary product technology and, facilitates the scheduling of adjacent processes
    D) greater flexibility, it can help drive down the firm's cost structure and, it may help the firm to capture orders from international customers

    Answer: D Difficulty: Hard Page: 443

83. The advantages of buying component parts from independent suppliers includes: (1) it gives the firm greater flexibility, (2) it can help drive down the firm's cost structure, and (3)
   A) it may help the firm to capture orders from international customers
   B) it facilitates the scheduling of adjacent processes
   C) if facilitates investments in highly specialized assets
   D) it protects proprietary production technology

   Answer: A Difficulty: Medium Page: 443

84. The advantages of buying component parts from independent suppliers includes: (1) it can help drive down the firm's cost structure, (2) it may help the firm to capture orders from international customers, and (3)
   A) it protects proprietary production technology
   B) it leads to greater flexibility
   C) it facilitates investments in highly specialized assets
   D) it facilitates the scheduling of adjacent processes

   Answer: B Difficulty: Medium Page: 443

85. The advantages of buying component parts from independent suppliers includes: (1) it gives the firm greater flexibility, (2) it may help the firm to capture orders from international customers, and (3)
   A) it protects proprietary production technology
   B) it facilitates the scheduling of adjacent processes
   C) it facilitates investments in highly specialized assets
   D) it can drive down the firm's cost structure

   Answer: D Difficulty: Medium Page: 443

86. According to the textbook, the benefits of manufacturing components in-house seem to be greatest when all of the following factors are involved except:
   A) when highly specialized assets are involved
   B) when the firm is simply more efficient than external suppliers at performing a particular activity
   C) when maximum flexibility is necessary
   D) when vertical integration is necessary for protecting proprietary technology

   Answer: C Difficulty: Hard Page: 443

87. The benefits of _____ seem to be greatest when highly specialized assets are involved, when vertical integration is necessary for protecting proprietary technology, or when the firm is simply more efficient than external suppliers at performing a particular activity.
    A) buying component parts from independent suppliers
    B) manufacturing components in-house
    C) buying components from a merchandise mart
    D) buying components at a trade show

    Answer: B Difficulty: Medium   Page: 443

88. The greatest advantage of buying component parts from independent suppliers is:
    A) lower costs
    B) offsets
    C) supports TQM
    D) strategic flexibility

    Answer: D Difficulty: Medium   Page: 443

89. The term _____ refers to the practice of outsourcing the production of some component parts to a foreign country in hopes that it may help the firm capture more orders from that country.
    A) reciprocal trade tactic
    B) neutralize trade
    C) countertrade
    D) offset

    Answer: D Difficulty: Medium   Page: 444

90. Many Japanese automakers have cooperative relationships with their suppliers that go back for decades. These types of relationships are referred to as:
    A) operating arrangements
    B) firm-to-firm cooperative arrangements
    C) integral forms of integration
    D) strategic alliances

    Answer: D Difficulty: Medium   Page: 444

Chapter 13 Global Operations Management

91. Strategic alliances with suppliers was pioneered in:
    A) America by large chemical producers like Dow
    B) Japan by large auto companies such as Toyota
    C) Europe by large electronics firms like Philips
    D) Germany by telecommunications companies like Deutsche Telekom

    Answer: B Difficulty: Medium Page: 445

92. In general, the trends toward just-in-time systems (JIT), computer-aided design (CAD), and computer-aided manufacturing (CAM) seem to have increased pressures for firms to establish _____ relationships with their suppliers.
    A) strictly arms-length
    B) intermediate term
    C) long-term
    D) short-term

    Answer: C Difficulty: Medium Page: 445

93. _____, which encompasses logistics, embraces the activities necessary to get materials to a manufacturing facility, through the manufacturing process, and out through a distribution system to the end user.
    A) Materials management
    B) Bureaucracy
    C) Production
    D) Wares operations

    Answer: A Difficulty: Easy Page: 445

94. The potential for reducing costs through more efficient materials management is:
    A) enormous
    B) moderate
    C) minor
    D) insignificant

    Answer: A Difficulty: Easy Page: 44

Chapter 13 Global Operations Management

95. According to the textbook, for the typical manufacturing firm, material costs account for between _____ percent of revenues depending on the industry.
    A) 15-25
    B) 30-40
    C) 50-70
    D) 80-90

    Answer: C Difficulty: Hard Page: 445

96. Pioneered by _____ firms during the 1950s and 1960s, just-in-time inventory systems now play a major role in most manufacturing firms.
    A) German
    B) American
    C) Japanese
    D) British

    Answer: C Difficulty: Medium Page: 445

97. The basic philosophy behind _____ systems is to economize on inventory holding costs by having materials arrive at a manufacturing plant "just in time" to enter the production process.
    A) management by objectives
    B) reengineering
    C) just-in-time
    D) total quality management

    Answer: C Difficulty: Easy Page: 446

98. The basic philosophy behind just-in-time systems (JIT) is to:
    A) economize on costs by paying suppliers just-in-time to avoid late charges
    B) economize on training costs by providing training to employees just-in-time for them to implement new strategies
    C) economize on personnel costs by hiring the right number of people just-in-time to meet organizational needs
    D) economize on inventory holding costs by having materials arrive at a manufacturing plant just-in-time to enter the production process.

    Answer: D Difficulty: Medium Page: 446

Chapter 13 Global Operations Management

99. In the context of materials management, the acronym JIT stands for:
   A) Jobber-In-Training
   B) Job-In-Transit
   C) Joint-In-Transpiration
   D) Just-In-Time

   Answer: D Difficulty: Easy   Page: 446

100. A drawback of a _____ system is that it leaves a firm without a buffer stock of inventory.
   A) total-quality management
   B) just-in-time
   C) management by objectives
   D) reengineering system

   Answer: B Difficulty: Medium   Page: 446

101. Under a _____ system, parts enter the manufacturing process immediately; they are not warehoused.
   A) just-in-time
   B) reengineering
   C) soft manufacturing
   D) maximum fluency

   Answer: A Difficulty: Hard   Page: 446

102. In the context of materials management, the acronym EDI stands for:
   A) Electronic Data Intelligence
   B) Eliminate Distribution Intermediaries
   C) Eastern Distribution Interchange
   D) Electronic Data Interchange

   Answer: D Difficulty: Easy   Page: 448

103. According to the textbook, _____ systems require Internet-based computer links between a firm, its suppliers, and its shippers.
   A) electronic data interchange
   B) electronic data intelligence
   C) elastic data interchange
   D) elastic demographic interchange

   Answer: A Difficulty: Medium   Page: 448

104. Suppliers typically use a _____ link to send invoices to purchasers.
    A) elastic demographic interchange
    B) elastic data interchange
    C) electronic data intelligence
    D) electronic data interchange

    Answer: D Difficulty: Medium Page: 448

105. A _____ system allows suppliers, shippers, and the purchasing firm to communicate with each other in "real time," which vastly increases the flexibility and responsiveness of the supply system.
    A) elastic logistics interchange
    B) electronic data interchange
    C) electronic data intelligence
    D) elastic data interchange

    Answer: B Difficulty: Medium Page: 448

Essay Questions

106. Define the term "materials management." Discuss the relationship between materials management and logistics.

    Difficulty: Easy Page: 429

    Answer:
    Materials management can be defined as "the activity that controls the transmission of physical materials through the value chain, from procurement through production and into distribution." Materials management includes logistics, which refers to the procurement and physical transmission of material through the supply chain, from suppliers to customers.

Chapter 13 Global Operations Management

107. Discuss the overall objectives of international firms in terms of manufacturing and materials management.

Difficulty: Medium   Page: 429

Answer:
International firms have four principle objectives in the area of manufacturing and materials management. The first two objectives are to lower costs and increase quality. In this respect, international firms are no different than their strictly domestic counterparts. Cost reductions can be realized through improved efficiency and through eliminating defective products from both the supply chain and the manufacturing process. Implementing Just-In-Time manufacturing is an important step in achieving these objectives. Quality improvement can be realized through a number of initiatives, including total quality management (TQM) and ISO 9000 certification.

The second two objectives that are shared by the majority of international firms in this area relate directly to their international efforts. First, a firm's manufacturing and materials management functions must be able to accommodate demands for local responsiveness. For instance, an American exporter may have to vary the design of a product that is manufactured and sold in the U.S. to meet European standards. Second, a firm's manufacturing and materials management function must be able to respond quickly to shifts in consumer demand. For instance, if a trend developed in Asia towards a preference for lower-fat foods, the importers of food products to Asia that respond to this trend the most rapidly would have a substantial advantage.

108. Define the term "total quality management (TQM)." What is the relationship between TQM and manufacturing?

Difficulty: Medium   Page: 429

Answer:
TQM is a management philosophy that takes as its central focus the need to improve the quality of a company's products and services. TQM is the main management technique that is utilized to improve the quality of the products that emerge from manufacturing processes.

Chapter 13 Global Operations Management

109. How does an international firm decide where to locate its manufacturing activities? Include in your answer a discussion of country factors, technological factors, and product factors.

Difficulty: Hard   Page: 431

Answer:
The key factors involved in making location decisions, which entail the dual considerations of minimizing costs and increasing quality, can be grouped under three broad headings: country factors, technological factors, and product factors.

Country Factors: This is a large area of consideration, which encompasses a lot of factors. As described throughout the textbook, the advantage of producing in one country opposed to another varies along a number of dimensions. In Chapter 4, for example, we saw that due to differences in factor costs, certain countries have a comparative advantage for producing certain products. In Chapters 2 and 3 we saw how differences in political economy and national culture influence the desirability of location decisions. In this regard, all other things being equal, a firm should locate its manufacturing activities in countries that have hospitable political, economy, and factor cost environments.

Other country specific factors play a role in location decisions. These factors include formal and informal trade barriers and rules and regulations regarding foreign direct investment. Another country factor is expected movements in currency exchange rates. Adverse changes in exchange rates can quickly alter a country's attractiveness as a manufacturing site. Firms should consider the potential living conditions of their expatriate managers when making locations decision, and also the quality of the local labor pool.

Technological Factors: The three primary factors that drive location decisions in terms of technology are a manufacturing activity's level of fixed costs, its minimum efficient scale, and its flexibility. In terms of fixed costs, when the fixed costs of setting up a manufacturing operation are high, a firm must serve the world market from a single location or from a few locations. This is the case with aircraft manufacturing, for example. On the other hand, when fixed costs are low, a firm can scatter its manufacturing activities throughout the world to better accommodate local markets. In terms of minimum efficient scale, the larger the minimum efficient scale of a plant, the greater is the argument for centralized production at a single location. This factor motivates companies like Caterpillar Tractor, which makes heavy construction equipment in huge plants, to locate in a single location. Finally, in regard to flexibility, when flexible manufacturing technologies are available, a firm can manufacture products customized to various national markets at a single factory at the optimal location.

Product Factors: Two product features impact location decisions. The first is the product's value-to-weight ratio because of its influence on transportation costs. If a product has a high value-to-weight ratio, like semiconductors, it can be shipped around the world, and the shipping cost would represent only a small portion of the total cost of the product. Conversely, a product with a low value-to-weight ratio, like soft drinks, almost have to be mixed and bottled in the location in which they are sold, because the cost of shipping a 50 cent can of Coke from one country to another would represent a significant part of the value of the product. The second product consideration pertains to whether the product serves universal needs. If so, the need for local responsiveness is reduced, and the product can be produced at its ideal location.

As this discussion indicates, location decisions are complex for international firms. A consideration and weighing of all of the issues involved will result in the best overall decision.

110. Describe the terms flexible manufacturing and mass customization.

Difficulty: Medium   Page: 432

Answer:
The term flexible manufacturing - or lean production as it is often called - covers a range of manufacturing that are designed to (a) reduce setup times for complex equipment, (b) increase utilization of individual machines through better scheduling, and (c) improve quality control at all stages of the manufacturing process. Flexible manufacturing technologies allow a company to produce a wider variety of end products at a unit costs that at one time could be achieved only through the mass production of a standardized output. The term mass customization has been coined to describe this ability. Mass customization implies that a firm may be able to customize its product range to suit the needs of different customer groups without bearing a cost penalty. Research suggests that the adoption of flexible manufacturing technologies may increase efficiency and lower unit costs relative to what can be achieved by the mass production of a standardized output.

Chapter 13 Global Operations Management

111. What are Make-or-Buy Decisions? What are the advantages of make versus buy and visa-versa? Are these decisions harder for international opposed to strictly domestic firms? Explain your answer.

Difficulty: Medium   Page: 440

Answer:
A make-or-buy decision pertains to whether a business should make or buy the component parts that go into its final product. In other words, should a firm vertically integrate to manufacture its own component parts or should it purchase the parts from outside suppliers? For many firms, the make-or-buy decision is a difficult one, because there are good arguments to support either position.

The Advantages of Make: The arguments that support making component parts in-house (i.e. vertical integration) include: lower costs, facilitating specialized investments, proprietary product technology protection, and improved scheduling. In terms of lower costs, it may pay a firm to manufacture its own component parts, if no cheaper source (assuming quality remains consistent) is available. In terms of facilitating specialized investments, when a firm needs a component part that is highly customized and specialized, it is often best for the firm to manufacturer the part itself. Having a supplier manufacture the part would be awkward, because the supplier would rely strictly on one buyer to purchase the part and the buyer would typically have only the one supplier to furnish the part. In terms of protecting proprietary product technology, the more involvement that a firm has with suppliers, the more likely it is that proprietary information will be lost. As a result, a firm that has highly sensitive proprietary technology may be ahead to produce its own component products. Finally, improved scheduling can result from producing in-house rather than relying upon suppliers. The author of the textbook indicates that this is the weakest argument for vertical integration.

The Advantages of Buy: The advantages of buying component parts from independent suppliers is that it gives the firm greater flexibility, it can help drive down the firm's cost structure, and it may help the firm to capture orders from international customers. In regard to flexibility, by outsourcing the manufacture of its component parts, a firm can switch suppliers as circumstances dictate. This could provide a firm a substantial advantage in a rapidly changing environment. In terms of costs, using suppliers to manufacture component parts allows a firm to narrow its scope, and the resulting administrative overhead costs may be smaller. Finally, an advantage of buying rather than making component parts is that the relationships that are established through buying parts may lead to sales of the firm's final product. For example, if an American firm negotiated the purchase of component parts from several Brazilian firms, that would put the American firm in a position to develop a network of contacts in Brazil that might ultimately result in sales of its finished product.

The make-buy decision is harder for international firms than domestic firms because their decision set is simply more complex. For instance, it may appear desirable to purchase parts from a foreign supplier, but what about political stability in the supplier's country, foreign exchange risk, and the host of other questions that must be answered in international trade?

112. Discuss the advantages of entering into strategic alliances with suppliers? In general, is alliance formation a good idea for international firms?

Answer:
This question is designed to elicit classroom discussion. It is also a good "thought" question for an exam. The number of strategic alliances between firms from different countries is growing and is becoming an increasingly important option for international firms. For example, in recent years we have seen an alliance between Kodak and Canon, under which Canon builds photocopiers to be sold by Kodak.

There are a number of advantages and disadvantages of alliances that may be pointed out by students. The advantages include a sharing of production costs and risks, along with joint marketing and R&D. Also, the long-term relationship that develops between the alliance partners may engender trust and be beneficial for both firms. On the other hand, many of the disadvantages of using suppliers rather than producing products in-house apply to strategic alliances. For instance, proprietary technology may be lost to an alliance partner. This represents a compelling disadvantage of strategic alliances, particularly if the alliance partners are in the same industry.

There is no right or wrong answer to the question of whether alliances are good or bad for international businesses. This topic, however, provides an excellent forum for classroom discussion.

Difficulty: Medium   Page: 444

113. Describe the concept of "Just-In-Time" manufacturing. What are the advantages and disadvantages of the Just-In-Time system?

Answer:
The basic philosophy behind just-in-time (JIT) manufacturing is to economize on inventory holding costs by having materials arrive at a manufacturing plant "just in time" to enter the product process. This results in potential cost savings and quality improvements. The cost savings come from speeding up inventory turnover, thus reducing inventory holding costs, as well as warehousing and storage costs. In addition, JIT systems can lead to quality improvements. Under a JIT system, parts enter the manufacturing process immediately. This allows defective inputs to be spotted right away. The problem can then be traced to the supply source and fixed before more defective parts are produced. The disadvantage of a JIT system is that it leaves a firm without a buffer stock of inventory. As a result, a labor dispute at a supplier's plant or a disruption in the transportation system (such as the UPS strike) could leave a manufacturer without adequate component parts.

Difficulty: Easy   Page: 446

Chapter 14 Global Human Resource Management

True/False Questions

1. Human resource management refers to the activities an organization carries out to utilize its human resources effectively.

    Answer: True   Difficulty: Easy   Page: 456

2. The role of HRM has a similar level of complexity for a domestic and an international firm.

    Answer: False   Difficulty: Easy   Page: 456

3. An expatriate manager is a citizen of one country who is working abroad in one of the firm's subsidiaries.

    Answer: True   Difficulty: Medium   Page: 457

4. Compensation policy is concerned with the selection of employees for particular jobs.

    Answer: False   Difficulty: Easy   Page: 449

5. Staffing policy can be a tool for developing and promoting corporate culture.

    Answer: True   Difficulty: Medium   Page: 457

6. Research has identified three types of staffing policies in international businesses: the ethnocentric approach, the polycentric approach, and the geocentric approach.

    Answer: True   Difficulty: Medium   Page: 457

7. An geocentric staffing policy is one in which all key management positions are filled by parent country nationals.

    Answer: False   Difficulty: Medium   Page: 457

8. A polycentric staffing policy is one in which parent-country nationals fill all key management positions.

    Answer: False   Difficulty: Medium   Page: 458

9. According to a study conducted by R.L. Tung, European-based multinationals experience a much higher expatriate failure rate than either Japanese or United States multinationals.

   Answer: False   Difficulty: Hard   Page: 461

10. According to a study by R.L. Tung, the number one reason for expatriate failure among U.S. multinationals is the inability of the expatriate manager's spouse to adjust.

    Answer: True   Difficulty: Medium   Page: 462

11. Mendenhall and Oddou identified four dimensions that seem to predict success in foreign postings: self-orientation, others-orientation, perceptual ability, and cultural toughness.

    Answer: True   Difficulty: Medium   Page: 464

12. A recent survey by Windam International, a HRM management consulting firm, found that spouses were included in preselection interviews for foreign postings nearly 90 percent of the time.

    Answer: False   Difficulty: Hard   Page: 465

13. Historically, most international businesses have been more concerned with management development than with training.

    Answer: False   Difficulty: Medium   Page: 466

14. Cultural training seeks to foster an appreciation for the host country's culture.

    Answer: True   Difficulty: Easy   Page: 466

15. French is the language of world business.

    Answer: False   Difficulty: Medium   Page: 466

16. According to the textbook, almost all expatriates believe that a position in a foreign country is beneficial to their careers.

    Answer: False   Difficulty: Medium   Page: 469

17. Substantial differences exist in the compensation of executives at the same level in various countries.

    Answer: True   Difficulty: Easy   Page: 470

18. According to the textbook, an expatriate's total compensation package may amount to three times what he or she would cost the firm in a home country posting.

    Answer: True   Difficulty: Medium   Page: 472

19. The components of the typical expatriate compensation package are a base salary, a foreign service premium, allowances of various types, tax differentials, and benefits.

    Answer: True   Difficulty: Medium   Page: 472

20. Unless a host country has a reciprocal tax treaty with the expatriate's home country, the expatriate may have to pay income tax to both the home and the host country governments.

    Answer: True   Difficulty: Easy   Page: 473

Multiple Choice Questions

21. Human resource management refers to the activities an organization carries out to utilize its _____ effectively.
    A) customers
    B) external stakeholders
    C) human resources
    D) suppliers

    Answer: C   Difficulty: Easy   Page: 456

22. _____ management refers to the activities an organization carries out to utilize its human resources effectively.
    A) Human resource
    B) External stakeholder
    C) Positive-sum
    D) Personnel psychology

    Answer: A   Difficulty: Easy   Page: 456

23. The activities an organization carries out to utilize its human resources effectively is referred to as:
    A) positive-sum management
    B) human resource management
    C) stakeholder management
    D) personnel psychology management

    Answer: B Difficulty: Easy Page: 456

24. The activities which include determining the firm's human resource strategy, staffing, performance evaluation, management development, compensation, and labor relations are referred to as:
    A) personnel psychology management
    B) stakeholder management
    C) human resource management
    D) positive-sum management

    Answer: C Difficulty: Medium Page: 456

25. A(n) _____ manager is a citizen of one country who is working abroad in one of his or her firm's subsidiaries.
    A) expatriate
    B) cross-divisional
    C) cross-cultural
    D) ethnocentric

    Answer: A Difficulty: Easy Page: 457

26. A citizen of one country who is working abroad in one of his or her firm's subsidiaries is called an:
    A) ethnocentric manager
    B) cross-cultural manager
    C) expatriate manager
    D) cross-divisional manager

    Answer: C Difficulty: Easy Page: 457

27. Kenneth Johnson works for Dell Computer (a U.S. based firm) but is assigned to Dell's sales office in Germany. Under these circumstances, Mr. Johnson would be called an _____ manager.
    A) ethnocentric
    B) cross-cultural
    C) expatriate
    D) cross-divisional

    Answer: C Difficulty: Medium Page: 457

28. _____ is concerned with the selection of employees for particular jobs.
    A) Compensation policy
    B) Staffing policy
    C) Performance appraisal policy
    D) Training policy

    Answer: B Difficulty: Easy Page: 457

29. The policy concerned with the selection of employees for particular jobs is referred to as:
    A) compensation policy
    B) organization policy
    C) staffing policy
    D) internal stakeholder policy

    Answer: C Difficulty: Easy Page: 457

30. The term corporate culture refers to an organization's _____.
    A) compensation systems
    B) norms and value systems
    C) standing among its peer firms
    D) policies, rules, and regulations

    Answer: B Difficulty: Medium Page: 457

31. An individual whose behavioral style, beliefs, and value system are consistent with that of the company that she works for is said to be compatible with her company's:
    A) corporate culture
    B) corporate structure
    C) corporate resources
    D) corporate bureaucracy

    Answer: A Difficulty: Hard Page: 457

32. Research has identified three types of staffing policies in international businesses: (1) the ethnocentric approach, (2) the polycentric approach, and (3) the
    A) networkcentric approach
    B) intercentric approach
    C) globalcentric approach
    D) geocentric approach

    Answer: D Difficulty: Medium Page: 457

33. The three types of staffing policies in international business are:
    A) the ethnocentric approach, the polycentric approach, and the geocentric approach
    B) the globalcentric approach, the networkcentric approach, and the geocentric approach
    C) the geocentric approach, the networkcentric approach, and the polycentric approach
    D) the intercentric approach, the polycentric approach, and the networkcentric approach

    Answer: A Difficulty: Medium Page: 457

34. The three types of staffing policies in international business are the polycentric approach, the geocentric approach, and the _____ approach.
    A) networkcentric
    B) globalcentric
    C) intercentric
    D) ethnocentric

    Answer: D Difficulty: Medium Page: 457

35. An _____ staffing policy is one in which all key management positions are filled by parent company nationals.
    A) ethnocentric
    B) intercentric
    C) polycentric
    D) geocentric

    Answer: A Difficulty: Medium Page: 457

36. An ethnocentric staffing policy is one in which all key management positions are filled by:
    A) host company nationals
    B) the best people available, regardless of whether they are parent company nationals or host company nationals
    C) parent company nationals
    D) contract employees typically obtained from a consulting firm

    Answer: C Difficulty: Medium Page: 457

37. Which of the following is not a reason for pursuing an ethnocentric staffing policy?
    A) if a firm is trying to create value by transferring core competencies to a foreign operation, it may believe that the best way to do this is to transfer parent country nationals who have knowledge of that competency to the foreign operation
    B) the firm may believe there is a lack of qualified individuals in its own parent company to fill senior management positions
    C) the firm may see an ethnocentric staffing policy as the best way to maintain a unified corporate culture
    D) the firm may believe there is a lack of qualified individuals in the host country to fill senior management positions

    Answer: B Difficulty: Hard Page: 458

38. There are two reasons that the ethnocentric staffing policy is on the wane in most international businesses. These are:
    A) an ethnocentric staffing policy limits advancement opportunities for host country nationals and an ethnocentric policy can lead to "cultural myopia"
    B) an ethnocentric staffing policy is the most expensive of the alternatives and an ethnocentric policy limits advancement opportunities for parent country personnel
    C) an ethnocentric staffing policy limits the cultural awareness of parent company personnel and an ethnocentric policy can lead to "cultural myopia"
    D) an ethnocentric staffing policy is the most expensive of the alternatives and an ethnocentric policy limits the cultural awareness of parent company personnel

    Answer: A Difficulty: Medium Page: 458

Chapter 14 Global Human Resource Management

39. A _____ staffing policy requires host country nationals to be recruited to manage subsidiaries, while parent company nationals occupy key positions at corporate headquarters.
    A) polycentric
    B) geocentric
    C) ethnocentric
    D) intercentric

    Answer: A   Difficulty: Medium   Page: 459

40. A polycentric staffing policy requires _____ to be recruited to manage subsidiaries, while _____ occupy key positions at corporate headquarters.
    A) host country nationals, parent country nationals
    B) parent country nationals, contract employees from an international employment firm
    C) parent country nationals, host country nationals
    D) contract employees from an international employment firm, host country nationals

    Answer: A   Difficulty: Hard   Page: 459

41. According to the textbook, one advantage of a _____ staffing policy is that firms are less likely to suffer from cultural mypoia.
    A) geocentric
    B) intercentric
    C) polycentric
    D) ethnocentric

    Answer: C   Difficulty: Medium   Page: 459

42. A _____ staffing policy seeks the best people for key jobs throughout the organization.
    A) intercentric
    B) ethnocentric
    C) geocentric
    D) polycentric

    Answer: C   Difficulty: Medium   Page: 459

43. Which of the following is not an advantage of a geocentric approach to staffing for international businesses?
    A) uses human resources efficiently
    B) helps build a strong culture
    C) inexpensive to implement
    D) helps build a strong informal management network

    Answer: C   Difficulty: Medium   Page: 459

44. Which of the following international strategies is most compatible with an ethnocentric staffing policy?
    A) transnational strategy
    B) global strategy
    C) multidomestic strategy
    D) international strategy

    Answer: D   Difficulty: Medium   Page: 460

45. Which of the following international strategies is most compatible with a polycentric staffing policy?
    A) international strategy
    B) global strategy
    C) multidomestic strategy
    D) transnational strategy

    Answer: C   Difficulty: Medium   Page: 460

46. Which of the following two international strategies are most compatible with an geocentric staffing policy?
    A) global and transnational
    B) multidomestic and transnational
    C) international and multidomestic
    D) global and multidomestic

    Answer: A   Difficulty: Medium   Page: 460

Chapter 14 Global Human Resource Management

47. Two of the three common international staffing policies rely on extensive use expatriate managers. These are:
    A) ethnocentric, geocentric
    B) polycentric, intercentric
    C) ethnocentric, intercentric
    D) polycentric, geocentric

    Answer: A   Difficulty: Hard   Page: 460

48. An _____ approach to staffing has the following advantages: (1) overcomes lack of qualified managers in host nation, (2) unified culture, and (3) helps transfer core competencies.
    A) polycentric
    B) geocentric
    C) ethnocentric
    D) intercentric

    Answer: C   Difficulty: Hard   Page: 460

49. An _____ approach to staffing has the following advantages: (1) alleviates cultural myopia, (2) inexpensive to implement.
    A) polycentric
    B) intercentric
    C) geocentric
    D) ethnocentric

    Answer: A   Difficulty: Hard   Page: 460

50. An _____ approach to staffing has the following advantages: (1) uses human resources effectively, (2) helps build strong culture and informal management network.
    A) ethnocentric
    B) geocentric
    C) intercentric
    D) polycentric

    Answer: B   Difficulty: Hard   Page: 460

Chapter 14 Global Human Resource Management

51. An _____ approach to staffing has the following disadvantages: (1) produces resentment in host country, (2) can lead to cultural myopia.
    A) polycentric
    B) intercentric
    C) ethnocentric
    D) geocentric

    Answer: C Difficulty: Hard Page: 460

52. An _____ approach to staffing has the following disadvantages: (1) limits career mobility, (2) isolates headquarters from foreign subsidiaries.
    A) polycentric
    B) intercentric
    C) geocentric
    D) ethnocentric

    Answer: A Difficulty: Hard Page: 460

53. The premature return of an expatriate manager to his of her home country is referred to as:
    A) expatriate relief
    B) expatriate failure
    C) expatriate rotation
    D) expatriate timing

    Answer: B Difficulty: Easy Page: 461

54. _____ is the premature return of an expatriate manager to his or her home country.
    A) Expatriate rotation
    B) Expatriate timing
    C) Expatriate relief
    D) Expatriate failure

    Answer: D Difficulty: Easy Page: 461

55. One estimate of the costs of expatriate failure is that the average cost per failure to the parent company can be as high as _____ time the expatriate's annual domestic salary plus the cost of relocation.
   A) 1.5
   B) 3
   C) 5
   D) 7

   Answer: B Difficulty: Hard Page: 461

56. Research suggests that between _____ of all American employees sent abroad to developed nations return from their assignments early.
   A) 4 and 12 percent
   B) 8 and 22 percent
   C) 16 and 40 percent
   D) 26 and 56 percent

   Answer: C Difficulty: Hard Page: 461

57. According to a study conducted by R.L. Tung, _____ of U.S. multinationals experience expatriate failure rates of 10 percent or more.
   A) 91%
   B) 76%
   C) 44%
   D) 17%

   Answer: B Difficulty: Hard Page: 462

58. Which of the following was not identified by R.L. Tung as a reason for expatriate failure among U.S. expatriate managers?
   A) poor pay
   B) difficulties with new environment
   C) inability of spouse to adjust
   D) personal or emotional problems

   Answer: A Difficulty: Medium Page: 462

59. All of the following were identified by R.L. Tung as a reason for expatriate failure among U.S. expatriate managers except:
    A) manager's personal or emotional maturity
    B) inability to cope with larger overseas responsibility
    C) inability of spouse to adjust
    D) poor working conditions overseas

    Answer: D Difficulty: Medium Page: 462

60. The results of a study by R.L. Tung Indicated that the most consistent reason cited by European expatriates for expatriate failure among their group was:
    A) personal or emotional problems
    B) inability to cope with larger overseas responsibilities
    C) poor pay
    D) the inability of the manager's spouse to adjust to a new environment

    Answer: D Difficulty: Hard Page: 462

61. According to a study by R.L. Tung, the number one reason that both American and European expatriate managers fail is:
    A) inability of their spouses to adjust
    B) inability of the managers themselves to adjust
    C) lack of technical competence on the part of the managers
    D) lack of managerial competence of the part of the managers

    Answer: A Difficulty: Medium Page: 462

62. According to the results of a study of R.L. Tung, the number one reason that Japanese expatriate managers fail is:
    A) inability of spouse to adjust
    B) lack of technical competence
    C) personal or emotional problems
    D) inability to cope with larger overseas responsibilities

    Answer: D Difficulty: Medium Page: 462

Chapter 14 Global Human Resource Management

63. A recent study by International Orientation Resources, an HRM consulting firm, found that 60% of expatriate failures occur because of three reasons. These reasons are:
    A) the inability to cope with larger overseas responsibility, the lack of technical competence, and the manager's personal or emotional maturity.
    B) the inability of a spouse to adjust, the inability of the manager to adjust, and other family problems
    C) poor pay, the inability of a spouse to adjust, and the lack of technical competence
    D) the inability to cope with larger overseas responsibilities, the inability of the manager to adjust, and other family problems

    Answer: B Difficulty: Hard Page: 462

64. A recent study by International Orientation Resources, an HRM consulting firm, found that 60% of expatriate failures occur because of three reasons. These reasons are (1) the inability of a spouse to adjust, (2) the inability of the manager to adjust, and (3):
    A) inadequate compensation
    B) the inability to cope with larger overseas responsibilities
    C) other family problems
    D) the lack of technical competence

    Answer: C Difficulty: Medium Page: 462

65. A recent study by International Orientation Resources, an HRM consulting firm, found that 60% of expatriate failures occur because of three reasons. These reasons are the (1) inability of a spouse to adjust, (2) other family problems, and (3):
    A) the inability of the manager to adjust
    B) inadequate compensation
    C) the lack of technical competence
    D) the inability to cope with larger overseas responsibilities

    Answer: A Difficulty: Medium Page: 462

66. Mendenhall and Oddou identified four dimensions that seem to predict success in expatriate selection. These are:
    A) self-orientation, others-orientation, perceptual ability, and cultural toughness
    B) cognitive ability, subjective ability, positive affect, and cultural awareness
    C) self-orientation, cognitive ability, subjective ability, and cultural toughness
    D) subjective ability, others-orientation, perceptual ability, and cultural awareness

    Answer: A Difficulty: Medium Page: 464

67. Mendenhall and Oddou identified four dimensions that seem to predict success in expatriate selection: (1) self-orientation, (2) others-orientation, (3) perceptual ability, and _____.
A) cultural toughness
B) global-orientation
C) cognitive ability
D) subjective ability

Answer: A   Difficulty: Medium   Page: 464

68. Mendenhall and Oddou identified four dimensions that seem to predict success in expatriate selection: (1) others-orientation, (2) perceptual ability, (3) cultural toughness, and (4) _____.
A) global-orientation
B) cognitive ability
C) self-orientation
D) subjective ability

Answer: C   Difficulty: Medium   Page: 464

69. If you were transferred abroad and didn't like the local cuisine, this might mean that you lacked attributes of Mendenhall and Oddou's _____ dimension.
A) self-orientation
B) others-orientation
C) perceptual ability
D) cultural toughness

Answer: B   Difficulty: Medium   Page: 464

70. According to Mendenhall and Oddou, the attribute of _____ strengthens an expatriate's self-esteem, self-confidence, and mental well-being.
A) cultural toughness
B) perceptual ability
C) others-orientation
D) self-orientation

Answer: D   Difficulty: Medium   Page: 464

Chapter 14 Global Human Resource Management

71. According to Mendenhall and Oddou, the attribute of _____ enhances the expatriate's ability to interact effectively with host country nationals.
    A) others-orientation
    B) self-orientation
    C) cultural toughness
    D) perceptual ability

    Answer: A   Difficulty: Medium   Page: 464

72. The two factors that are particularly important in developing a health degree of _____, are relationship development and willingness to communication.
    A) cultural toughness
    B) perceptual ability
    C) others-orientation
    D) self-orientation

    Answer: C   Difficulty: Medium   Page: 464

73. According to Mendenhall and Oddou, expatriate managers who lack _____ tend to treat foreign nationals as if they were home country nationals.
    A) cultural toughness
    B) self-orientation
    C) others-orientation
    D) perceptual ability

    Answer: D   Difficulty: Medium   Page: 464

74. According to Mendenhall and Oddou, the attribute of _____ provides an expatriate the ability to understand why people of other countries behave the way they do, that is, the ability to empathize with them.
    A) cultural toughness
    B) perceptual ability
    C) self orientation
    D) others-orientation

    Answer: B   Difficulty: Medium   Page: 464

75. According to Mendenhall and Oddou, _____ refers to the fact that how well an expatriate adjusts to a particular posting tends to be related to the country of assignment.
    A) cultural toughness
    B) expatriate stamina
    C) country-specific durability
    D) expatriate persistence

    Answer: A   Difficulty: Medium   Page: 464

76. Only _____ of the firms in the study conducted by R.L. Tung used formal procedures and psychological tests to assess the personality traits and relational abilities of potential expatriates.
    A) 5%
    B) 15%
    C) 30%
    D) 45%

    Answer: A   Difficulty: Hard   Page: 465

77. The type of training that seeks to foster an appreciation for the host country's culture is called:
    A) cultural training
    B) technical training
    C) language training
    D) practical training

    Answer: A   Difficulty: Easy   Page: 466

78. The type of training that is aimed at helping an expatriate managers and his or her family ease themselves into day-to-day life in the host country is called:
    A) cognitive training
    B) practical training
    C) technical training
    D) cultural training

    Answer: B   Difficulty: Easy   Page: 467

79. According to one study of repatriated employees, _____ didn't know what their position would be when they returned home.
   A) 10-20 %
   B) 25-35 %
   C) 45-55 %
   D) 60-70 %

   Answer: D   Difficulty: Hard   Page: 467

80. _____ programs are designed to increase the overall skill levels of managers through a mix on ongoing management education and rotations of managers through a number of jobs within the firm to give them varied experiences.
   A) Organizational development
   B) Technical development
   C) Management development
   D) Personnel development

   Answer: C   Difficulty: Medium   Page: 467

81. A _____ program is intended to develop a manager's skills over his or her career with a firm.
   A) organizational development
   B) personnel development
   C) management development
   D) technical development

   Answer: C   Difficulty: Medium   Page: 465

82. The most common approach to expatriate pay is the _____.
   A) merit approach
   B) correspondence approach
   C) balance sheet approach
   D) parity approach

   Answer: C   Difficulty: Medium   Page: 470

83. In regard to expatriate pay, the _____ equalizes purchasing power across countries so employees can enjoy the same living standard in their foreign posting that they enjoyed at home.
    A) balance sheet approach
    B) standard of living approach
    C) merit approach
    D) correspondence approach

    Answer: A Difficulty: Medium Page: 470

84. In regard to expatriate pay, the balance sheet approach accomplishes two objectives. These are:
    A) equalizes purchasing power across countries so employees can enjoy the same living standard in their foreign posting that they enjoyed at home, and provides financial incentives to offset qualitative differences between assignment locations
    B) relieves an employee of the burden of paying taxes on income earned overseas, and provides an employee a standard 25% increase in pay for taking an overseas assignment
    C) equalizes purchasing power across countries so employees can enjoy the same living standard in their foreign posting that they enjoyed at home, and relieves an employee of the burden of paying taxes on income earned overseas
    D) provides financial incentives to offset qualitative differences between assignment locations, and provides an employee a standard 25% increase in pay for taking an overseas assignment

    Answer: A Difficulty: Medium Page: 471

85. The _____ attempts to provide expatriates with the same standard of living in their host countries as they enjoy at home plus a financial inducement for accepting an overseas assignment.
    A) merit approach
    B) correspondence approach
    C) parity approach
    D) balance sheet approach

    Answer: D Difficulty: Easy Page: 471

86. A _____ is extra pay the expatriate receives for working outside his or her country of origin.
    A) parity adjustment
    B) expatriate special circumstance
    C) foreign service premium
    D) allowance

    Answer: C Difficulty: Medium Page: 472

87. The extra pay an expatriate receives for working outside his or her country of origin is referred to as a:
    A) foreign service premium
    B) allowance
    C) expatriate special circumstance
    D) parity adjustment

    Answer: A Difficulty: Medium Page: 472

88. The form of compensation that compensates an expatriate for having to live in an unfamiliar country isolated from family and friends is referred to as a:
    A) expatriate special circumstance
    B) allowance
    C) parity adjustment
    D) foreign service premium

    Answer: D Difficulty: Medium Page: 472

89. Four types of allowance are often included in an expatriate's compensation package. These are:
    A) travel allowances, emergency allowances, training allowances, relocation allowances
    B) hardship allowances, housing allowances, cost-of-living allowances, and education allowances
    C) emergency allowances, hardship allowances, training allowances, cost-of-living allowances
    D) housing allowances, travel allowances, cost-of-living allowances, and relocation allowances

    Answer: B Difficulty: Medium Page: 472

90. Four types of allowances are often included in an expatriate's compensation package: a hardship allowance, a housing allowance, a cost-of-living allowance, and a _____ allowance.
   A) training
   B) relocation
   C) travel
   D) education

   Answer: D Difficulty: Medium Page: 472

91. Four types of allowances are often included in an expatriate's compensation package: a housing allowance, a cost-of-living allowance, an education allowance, and a _____ allowance.
   A) training
   B) relocation
   C) hardship
   D) travel

   Answer: C Difficulty: Medium Page: 472

92. In regard to the types of allowances often included in an expatriate's compensation package, a _____ allowance is paid when the expatriate is being sent to a difficult location.
   A) education
   B) housing
   C) hardship
   D) cost-of-living

   Answer: C Difficulty: Medium Page: 473

93. In regard to the types of allowances often included in an expatriates compensation package, a _____ allowance is often paid to ensure that the expatriate will enjoy the same standard of living in the foreign posting as at home.
   A) housing
   B) education
   C) hardship
   D) cost-of-living

   Answer: D Difficulty: Medium Page: 473

94. Unless a host country has _____ with the expatriate's home country, the expatriate may have to pay income tax to both the home and host country governments.
    A) diplomatic relations
    B) a trade treaty
    C) a positive balance of trade
    D) a reciprocal tax treaty

    Answer: D Difficulty: Medium Page: 473

95. When a reciprocal tax treaty is not in force, the firm typically:
    A) pays one-third of the expatriate's income tax in the host country
    B) pays one-half of the expatriate's income tax in the host country
    C) pays the expatriate's income tax in the host country
    D) requires the expatriate to pay his or her own income tax in the host country

    Answer: C Difficulty: Medium Page: 473

96. The _____ function of an international business is typically responsible for international labor relations.
    A) international business
    B) human resource management
    C) finance and accounting
    D) legal

    Answer: B Difficulty: Medium Page: 473

97. From a strategic perspective, the key issue in international labor relations is:
    A) the degree to which organized labor can limit the choices of an international business
    B) the degree to which organized labor increases the costs of conducting international business
    C) the degree to which organized labor discourages participation in international business
    D) the degree to which organized labor resists the transfer of domestic employees to overseas operations

    Answer: A Difficulty: Medium Page: 473

98. _____ unions generally try to get better pay, greater job security, and better working conditions for their members through collective bargaining with management.
    A) Management
    B) Labor
    C) Statutory
    D) Volunteer

    Answer: B Difficulty: Easy Page: 474

99. A principle concern of domestic unions about multinational firms it that the multinational can counter their bargaining power with:
    A) work schedules tied to global rather than domestic standards
    B) wage rates tied to global rather than domestic standards
    C) the power to import labor from abroad
    D) the power to move production to another country

    Answer: D Difficulty: Medium Page: 474

100. Organized labor has responded to the increased bargaining power of multinational corporations by taking three actions:
    A) trying to impose regulations on multinationals through organizations such as GATT, trying to establish international labor organizations, applying pressure on the governments of major industrial nations to impose stricter regulations on multinationals
    B) trying to establish regional labor organizations, trying to establish international organizations to act as advocates for the employees of multinationals, and lobbying for national legislation to restrict multinationals
    C) trying to establish international labor organizations, lobbying for national legislation to restrict multinationals, and trying to achieve international regulations on multinationals through such organizations as the U.N.
    D) trying to impose regulations on multinationals through organizations such as the International Monetary Fund, applying pressure on the governments of major industrial nations to impose stricter regulations on multinationals, trying to establish regional labor organizations

    Answer: C Difficulty: Hard Page: 474

Chapter 14 Global Human Resource Management

101. Organized labor has responded to the increased bargaining power of multinational corporations by taking three actions. These are: trying to establish international labor organizations, lobbying for national legislation to restrict multinationals, and:
   A) applying pressure on the governments of major industrial nations to impose stricter regulations on multinationals
   B) trying to achieve international regulations on multinationals through such organizations as the United Nations
   C) trying to establish regional labor boards
   D) trying to lobby multinational corporations to restrict their global reach to three or fewer foreign countries

   Answer: B Difficulty: Medium Page: 474

102. In the context of international labor relations, the acronym ITS stands for:
   A) International Trade Secrets
   B) International Trade Statistics
   C) International Trade Secretariats
   D) International Trade Sanctions

   Answer: C Difficulty: Medium Page: 474

103. In the 1960s organized labor began to establish a number of _____ to provide worldwide links for national unions.
   A) International Trade Secretariats
   B) International Trade Boards
   C) International Trade Commissions
   D) International Trade Federations

   Answer: A Difficulty: Medium Page: 474

104. According to the textbook, in practice, the International Trade Secretariats have had:
   A) resounding success
   B) virtually no success
   C) moderate success
   D) good success in industrialized nations, but less success elsewhere

   Answer: B Difficulty: Medium Page: 475

105. The main difference between international businesses in terms of their approaches to international labor relations is:
    A) the degree to which labor relations activities are centralized or decentralized
    B) the degree to which labor relations are formal or informal
    C) the degree to which labor relations are given a high priority or a low priority
    D) the degree to which labor relations are internally or externally managed

    Answer: A   Difficulty: Hard   Page: 475

Essay Questions

106. Describe the concept of human resources management. What extra challenges confront an international business in this area?

    Difficulty: Easy   Page: 456

    Answer:
    Human resource management (HRM) refers to the activities an organization carries out to utilize its human resources effectively. These activities include staffing, training and management development, performance appraisal, compensation, labor relations, and determining the firm's human resources strategy. To maximize human resources effectiveness, all of these activities should be performed with the firm's overall strategy, goals, and objectives in mind.

    International businesses are faced with a number of extra challenges in this area. These extra challenge result primarily from the fact that countries differ in terms of their cultures, customs, philosophies of management, compensation systems, etc. As a result, a firm must adjust its HRM program (to varying degrees) to be compatible with each country that it does business in. In addition, selecting expatriate managers it is a challenge. A expatriate manager must have the technical skills necessary to do the job, along with a personal disposition and a family situation that is conductive to living in a foreign country for an extended period of time. The relatively high expatriate failure rate experience by U.S. multinationals attests to the difficulty of this challenge. Finally, international businesses must decided how to structure their overseas operations, which involves determining the appropriate roles of parent country and host country management personnel.

Chapter 14 Global Human Resource Management

107. Discuss the differences between an ethnocentric approach, a polycentric approach, and a geocentric approach to staffing for international businesses. What is the rationale behind each of these approaches? How does a firm's staffing policy relate to the strategy that it is pursuing in a foreign country?

Difficulty: Hard   Page: 457

Answer:
Ethnocentric Approach: An ethnocentric staffing policy is one in which all key management positions are filled by parent country nationals. Firms pursue an ethnocentric staffing policy for three reasons. First, the firm may believe there is a lack of qualified individuals in the host country to fill senior management positions. Second, the firm may see an ethnocentric staffing policy as the best way to maintain a unified corporate culture. For instance, many Japanese firms prefer that their foreign operations be headed up by Japanese managers, because these managers will be intimately familiar with the firm's culture and values. Third, if the firm is trying to create value by transferring core competencies to a foreign operation, it may feel that the best way to do this is to transfer parent country nationals who have knowledge of that competency to the foreign operation.

Polycentric Approach: A polycentric staffing policy requires host country nationals to be recruited to manage foreign operations, while parent country nationals occupy key positions at corporate headquarters. The principle advantage of adopting a polycentric approach is that the firm is less likely to suffer from cultural myopic. Host country managers are unlikely to make the mistakes arising from cultural misunderstandings that expatriate managers are subject to. Another advantage of the polycentric approach is that it is less expensive than other approaches to implement. By hiring host country personnel to fill management positions, the firm will not incur a significant amount of expatriate expense.

Geocentric Approach: A geocentric staffing policy tries to identify the best people available for management jobs, regardless of nationality. There are several advantages to this approach. First, it enables the firm to make the best personnel selections possible, without regard to nationality. In other words, a firm is not handcuffed in regard to who it can hire because of a candidate's nationality. Second, a geocentric policy enables the firm to build a cadre of international executives who feel at home working in a number of different cultures. This is a critical consideration if the firm has future international business expansion in mind. The multicultural composition of the management team that results from geocentric staffing tends to reduce cultural myopic and enhances local responsiveness.

A firm's staffing policy does related to the overall global strategy it is trying to pursue (global strategy was covered in Chapter 10). Overall, an ethnocentric approach is compatible with an international strategy, a polycentric approach is compatible with a multidomestic strategy, and a geocentric approach is compatible with both global and transnational strategies. Large international businesses may pursue a combination of these strategies to achieve the optimal staffing policy/international strategy mix.

108. What is an expatriate manager? What are some of the steps that an international business can take to enhance the success of their expatriate manager program?

Difficulty: Medium   Page: 457

Answer:
An expatriate manager is a citizen of one country who is working abroad in one of his or her firm's subsidiaries. For example, if a manager for Disney (an American company) was moved from Orlando, Florida to Paris, France to work at Euro Disney, he or she would be an expatriate manager.

Selecting expatriate managers is a challenge because an individual who takes an assignment in a foreign country must have both the technical skills necessary to do the job and the personality disposition and family situation conductive to living and working overseas. The success of an expatriate program begins with the proper "selection" of expatriate personnel. Mehdenhall and Oddou have identified four dimensions that seem to predict success in foreign postings: self-orientation, others-orientation, perceptual ability, and cultural toughness. These factors should be considered in expatriate selection. Expatriate selection should be followed by expatriate training and management development. The training should include cultural training, language training, and practical training focused on living in a foreign country. Expatriates should also be prepared for repatriation. Upon returning home, a former expatriate manager can find himself or herself without a clear job or career path if repatriation is not an ongoing consideration during the expatriate period.

Other HRM issues should be carefully designed to accommodate the complex issues involved in employing expatriate managers. These issues include performance appraisal and compensation. Firms should work hard to reduce bias in performance appraisals, by both parent company and host country supervisors. Compensation programs should be thoughtfully prepared to adequately compensate expatriate managers for overseas assignments.

109. What are management development programs? How can international businesses use management development programs as a strategic tool?

Difficulty: Medium   Page: 465

Answer:
Management development programs are designed to increase the overall potential of employees by providing them training and a variety of experiences. For instance, a management development program might involve regularly scheduled educational programs, training, workshops covering a wide range of issues, and a program of rotating employees through foreign assignments to provide them international experience.

As a strategic tool, management development programs can play an important role in international businesses. These program can help a firm build a corporate culture that is sensitive to international business issues. In addition, in house company training programs, workshops, and off-site training can foster a sense of unity among the employees as well as the development of technical skills. In addition, the introduction of company songs, uniforms, T-shirts, and other firm specific initiatives can help build a manager's identification with the company and company spirit.

All of these initiatives can help build unity among the employees and the units of a firm, which may be particularly important for international businesses that have a number of disperse locations.

Management development programs are designed to increase the overall skill levels of managers through a mix of ongoing management education and rotations of managers through a number of jobs within the firm to give them varied experiences.

110. What is the purpose of cultural training for an expatriate? How can "culture shock" be avoided?

Difficulty: Medium   Page: 466

Answer:
Cultural training seeks to foster an appreciation for the host country's culture. The belief is that understanding a host country's culture will help the manager empathize with the culture, which will enhance his or her effectiveness in dealing with host-country nationals. It has been suggested that expatriates should receive training in the host country's culture, history, politics, economy, and so on. If possible, it is also advisable to arrange for a familiarization trip to the host country before the formal transfer, as this seems to ease culture shock. Given the problems related to spouse adaptation, it is important that the spouse, and perhaps the whole family, be included in cultural training programs.

Chapter 14 Global Human Resource Management

111. Discuss the issue of expatriate compensation. Suppose you worked for a firm that transferred you from the United States to a developing country in Asia or South America. How do you think you should be compensated relative to your peers in similar jobs at home?

Difficulty: Medium   Page: 470

Answer:
This question is designed to encourage classroom discussion and/or to encourage students to "think" about how expatriate managers should be compensated. The issue of expatriate compensation is a difficult one. Substantial differences exist in the compensation of executives at the same level in various countries. These differences raise the question: should a firm pay its expatriate managers the prevailing wage rate in the country that they are working in, or should a firm pay all of its expatriate managers at the same level of responsibility a similar amount of pay? There is no standard answer to this question. The most common approach to expatriate pay is the balance sheet approach. This approach equalizes purchasing power across countries so employees can enjoy the same standard of living in their foreign postings that they enjoyed at home. In addition, this approach provides financial incentives to offset qualitative differences between assignment locations.

Consistent with this approach, the components of the typical expatriate compensation package are a base salary, a foreign service premium, allowances of various types, tax differentials, and benefits. In some cases, expatriates receive extra "hardship" allowances for living is a particularly difficult location. All together, an expatriate's compensation package may amount to three times what he or she would receive at home. Bear in mind, however, that the expatriate may be living and working in a difficult overseas assignment.

Ask your students to comment on this issue. It provides an interesting forum for classroom discussion.

Chapter 14 Global Human Resource Management

112.   What is the principle role of labor unions? What concerns does labor have about multinational firms?

Difficulty: Medium   Page: 473

Answer:
The principle role of labor unions is to try to get better pay, greater job security, and better working conditions for the members through collective bargaining with management. Unions' bargaining power is derived largely from their ability to threaten to disrupt production, either by strike or some other form of work protest. This threat is credible, however, only insofar as management has no alternative but to employ union labor.

With this in mind, a principle concern of domestic unions about multinational firms is that a company can counter their bargaining power with the power to move production to another country. Another concern is that international businesses will keep highly skilled tasks in its home country and farm out only low skilled tasks to foreign plants. A final concern arises when international businesses attempt to import employment practices and contractual agreements from its home country. When these practices are alien to the host country, organized labor fears the change will reduce its influence and power.